Preparing for the Multistate Bar Examination

Multiple-Choice Strategies and Multiple-Choice Questions, Answers, and Explanations on Every MBE Topic and Subtopic

Volume I: All Subjects

Nelson P. Miller and Tonya Krause-Phelan

Preparing for the Multistate Bar Examination: multiple-choice strategies and multiple-choice questions, answers, and explanations on every MBE topic and subtopic. Volume I: all subjects.

Miller, Nelson P., and Tonya Krause-Phelan

Published by:

Crown Management LLC – January 2017

1527 Pineridge Drive
Grand Haven, MI 49417
USA

ISBN: 978-0-9980601-3-2

All Rights Reserved
© 2017 Nelson P. Miller
c/o 111 Commerce Avenue S.W.
Grand Rapids, MI 49503
(616) 301-6800 ext. 6963

Table of Contents

PART I: The Multistate Bar Examination 1
    A. Overview 1
    B. Time 1
    C. Tracking Time 2
    D. Finishing Early 3
    E. Scoring 3
    F. Scaling 4
    G. Subjects 4
        1. Civil Procedure 5
        2. Constitutional Law 6
        3. Contracts 7
        4. Criminal Law and Procedure 7
        5. Evidence 8
        6. Real Property 9
        7. Torts 10

PART II: Multiple-Choice Strategies 12
    A. Multiple Choice Matters 12
    B. Design 12
    C. Signals and Triggers 13
    D. Question Calls 13
    E. Options 14
    F. Qualifiers 14
    G. Distractors 15
    H. Procedural Context 16
    I. Approach 16
    J. IRAC 17
    K. Wrong Options 18
    L. Errors 18
    M. Guessing 19

PART III: Multiple-Choice Questions 21
    A. First MBE Practice Exam 22
        1. Part I—First 100 Questions 23
        2. Part II—Second 100 Questions 51
    B. Second MBE Practice Exam 83
        1. Part I—Third 100 Questions 83
        2. Part II—Fourth 100 Questions 116

PART IV: Multiple-Choice Answers & Explanations 155
    A. First MBE Practice Exam 155
        1. Part I—First 100 Questions 155
        2. Part II—Second 100 Questions 173
    B. Second MBE Practice Exam 198
        1. Part I—Third 100 Questions 198
        2. Part II—Fourth 100 Questions 223

PART V: Tables and Indices 249
    A. MBE Subjects Keyed to Multiple-Choice Questions 249
    B. MBE Topics Table Keyed to Multiple-Choice Questions 250
    C. Answer Sheets 261

Conclusion 302
    A. Perspectives 302
    B. Growth 302
    C. Outcomes 303
    D. Alternatives 303
Acknowledgments 305
About the Authors 306

Part I: The Multistate Bar Examination

A. Overview

The Multistate Bar Examination is a six-hour, 200-question multiple-choice test scoring 175 of the 200 questions. The examiners use the other 25 unscored questions as pre-test questions. The Multistate Bar Examination appears on the bar exams of all states other than Louisiana and U.S. territories other than Puerto Rico. The District of Columbia's bar exam also includes the Multistate Bar Examination. The Multistate Bar Examination is the same in every state.

The Multistate Bar Examination is a one-day, all-day examination, given on the same day in every location. Examinees take 100 questions in a morning three-hour block and, after a two-hour lunch break, the second 100 questions in an afternoon three-hour block. State bar exams also include an essay portion (often the Multistate Essay Examination) and may include a performance portion (often the Multistate Performance Test). Examiners administer other bar-exam components on a second, and in some cases a third, day.

You are very likely to have to do well on the Multistate Bar Examination in order to pass a bar exam and receive a law license. States typically weight the Multistate Bar Examination at up to fifty percent of the exam's total score. Indeed, the Uniform Bar Examination used in half of the states weights the Multistate Bar Examination at fifty percent of the exam's total score.

The Multistate Bar Examination tests the seven subjects of civil procedure, constitutional law, contracts, criminal law and procedure, evidence, real property, and torts. Plan early to do well on these subjects. Take these courses in law school whether or not your curriculum requires that you do so. Learning a subject in a short bar-review course just before the bar exam is not ideal. Refreshing yourself on a subject that you have already learned in a law school course is far better than learning the subject for the first time in your bar-review course.

The National Conference of Bar Examiners drafts the Multistate Bar Examination. Its website provides a five-page outline showing the tested topics and sub-topics in each of the seven subject areas. The five-page outline also indicates the proportion of questions asked on various topics. Examining the outline should convince you of the need to study these topics while also serving as a focus, reminder, and guide during your studies.

B. Time

The Multistate Bar Examination gives you 1.8 minutes for each of its 200 multiple-choice questions, in two three-hour sessions of 100 multiple-choice questions each. That time of just less than two minutes means that you must complete 33 to 34 questions every hour to keep on pace to finish all multiple-choice questions.

Time may be the single most-important condition with which you must deal effectively to do well on the Multistate Bar Examination. When you are practicing multiple-choice questions, you should know the amount of time that you have to answer each question and should gage how you are doing. Develop the skill to answer within the time that the Multistate Bar Examination allows. You do yourself little good to confirm the comprehensive knowledge base and analytical skill that multiple-choice questions require unless you can apply the knowledge and exercise the skill quickly enough to finish the Multistate Bar Examination.

Time management is thus a critical success strategy for the Multistate Bar Examination. You must learn to use your time strategically. If you rush through leaving too much extra time at the end for review, then you will have compromised your ability to answer correctly the first time through. If on the other hand you drag through failing to finish timely, then you will get zero credit for unanswered questions and only random credit for answers that you guess when you have no time to read the question.

Falling behind and rushing through final questions is also not a sensible option because of the errors that rushing creates. Time stress reduces concentration, resulting in reduced performance. Practice under the allotted time constraint until you no longer feel rushed. Accustom yourself thoroughly to the time constraint until the clock no longer affects your concentration. Habituation to exam conditions is an important practice to ensure maximal performance.

As you navigate the exam's time pressure, remain fully in the moment. You cannot answer all questions at once. Looking ahead to answering 100 questions in three hours may unnerve you. Don't look ahead. Answer one question at a time while periodically checking your progress.

As soon as you finish one question, forget it, and move on to the next question. Ruminating over a prior answer while you attempt to answer the next question will not improve the prior answer but will instead delay you in completing the next answer. Don't let tough questions sap your confidence. Instead, let easy questions boost your confidence.

C. Tracking Time

Given that the Multistate Bar Examination requires that you answer 200 questions total in two three-hour sessions of 100 questions each, working out to 1.8 minutes per question or 33 to 34 questions every hour, how do you track that time?

A simple and accurate way of tracking time is to figure that you must complete a little more than one question every two minutes. At 30 minutes, you should have completed about 17 questions, while at one hour you should have completed about 34 questions. Halfway through at the hour-and-a-half mark, you should have completed 50 questions. Two hours into the exam, you should have completed about 67 questions. At two-and-a-half hours, you should have completed 84 questions, to complete 100 questions by the end of the third hour. The sequence for every half hour is thus 17, 34, 50, 67, 84, and 100 questions. Note these numbers when the exam begins, and use them to track your time.

With effective bar-exam preparation, you should find yourself quickly ahead of time, enough so that you can pace yourself. If you can build a small cushion of time, getting five minutes ahead early, then that cushion can relieve time pressure, which should make you even more efficient at reading, reflecting, and answering.

Do *not* stick on questions. If you don't know the answer to one question, then mark whatever answer seems best, moving promptly on because the next question and each question after it will have just as much value. Remember that twenty-five questions are pre-test questions that the National Conference of Bar Examiners will not even count against your score. The question that you could not answer may be a defective pre-test question. Otherwise, every question has equal weight. Keep moving.

D. Finishing Early

Following the above approaches, and with effective study and substantial practice, you may well finish each of the two three-hour Multistate Bar Examination multiple-choice sessions with ten or twenty minutes or more to spare. If in your practice sessions you find yourself finishing way too early, then slow down your approach.

Finishing ahead of time can nonetheless provide good benefit in that you have time to go back to check and confirm or change answers. Don't hesitate to do so. Make good use of extra time to confirm or correct answers.

You may recall the frustration of getting an answer correct the first time but changing it to a wrong answer when re-reading the question and second-guessing your analysis. Research shows that examinees typically *benefit* from changing answers. The reason that second-guessing can seem hazardous is that examinees find it hard to forget the times when changing answers led to a wrong answer. We remember our losses and regrets much more than our successes.

Avoid reading too much into a question. Examiners expect you to figure out the answer from a single reading. However, if upon review a different answer seems like the better choice, then odds favor that changing to the new choice will improve your score. If you finish early, then by all means, reread your answers and change wrong answers.

E. Scoring

Learn how your state's bar examiners will score your bar exam. Scoring practices including the weight given to each section and minimum passing scores vary from state to state, particularly within states that do not follow Uniform Bar Examination format. The National Conference of Bar Examiners maintains individual state scoring information on its website, which would also be available directly from the state's bar examiners.

While you expect to perform at your best no matter how the examiners score your effort, scoring can matter in how you allocate your preparation time and effort. The bar exam tends to reward comprehensive rather than peculiar performance. You should not generally plan to overcome poor performance on one section of the bar exam with stellar performance on another. Instead, plan to perform with at least minimal competence on all parts of the exam, even if your state bar weighs all parts of the exam equally.

You may feel that the strength of your skill in one area will offset weakness in another, but you may instead find that remediating the weakness with a little more bar preparation pays greater scoring dividends than honing your strength. After all, low scores leave more room for improvement than do high scores. Olympic performers can only achieve tiny gains no matter how hard or long they struggle because they are already near optimal athletic performance.

In the same way, given that you have only limited time, you don't want to invest all your efforts into achieving a tiny gain in one area that will have an inconsequential effect on your overall performance. For the same investment of time and energy, you may have a huge leap in overall ability if you focus on your weak spots. You always want to find the areas that offer you the greatest potential for improving performance. The incremental gain that your studies achieve may be greater in your poorer performance areas than in your better areas.

Moreover, a few state bars require that you reach a minimum score in one or more parts of the bar exam no matter how high the rest of your bar-exam score is. If you do decide to ignore a difficult area of the law that you just cannot seem to master after at least some diligent study, then be sure that it is a *small subtopic* that you are ignoring, one unlikely to be on the exam or if on the exam likely to be only a very small part of it.

F. Scaling

Do not worry unduly about your bar exam being especially difficult compared to prior exams. The National Conference of Bar Examiners *scales* Multistate Bar Examination scores. The examiners add a certain number of points, usually in the range of 10 to 15 points, to your raw score in order to equate the exam's difficulty to the difficulty of prior exams. If your exam turned out to be more difficult than prior exams, then you will receive additional scaled points to ensure that the exam's difficulty does not affect your results.

If your raw scores on practice exams are just below your state's required passing score, then scaling may help you pass. Scaling improves your Multistate Bar Examination raw score, although you will not know until after the exam by how much. Read more about scaling on the National Conference of Bar Examiners website. While the National Conference of Bar Examiners scales the Multistate Bar Examination, state bars may or may not scale scores on their state-specific essay or performance tests. Investigate your state bar examiners' scaling and scoring practices until you know approximately what score you must obtain for your practice and assessment purposes, and are confident that the examiners will treat you fairly.

G. Subjects

Knowing the content of your bar exam, meaning the law that the exam actually tests, is critical to your preparation. Law is vast. Fortunately, the bar exam tests only a slice of that vast amount of law. Even more fortunately, bar examiners disclose in advance the subject areas that they will test. Not only do they disclose the law fields that will be on the exam, but for certain tests, in particular the Multistate Bar Examination, they also disclose the testable topics and subtopics within those fields. Only a fool or glutton for punishment would disregard these disclosures and attempt to study all fields and all topics within those fields.

Beyond the advantage of disclosure of fields, topics, and subtopics, you may also locate resources, particularly but not exclusively commercial bar-preparation-course resources, that summarize topic-testing patterns. For instance, to teach a free state-specific bar-preparation essay workshop at the authors' law school, one of the authors studies and summarizes the testing pattern of the subject for the past ten-plus years.

You can thus see how knowing the fields and their topics and subtopics, and then adding to it some sense of the most-frequently tested topics within fields, can give you both confidence and a genuine advantage. Research field, topic, and subtopic coverage as you prepare for the bar exam.

Every examinee understands that to perform well on the bar exam, you need a certain minimum level of knowledge. What you might not appreciate is that some evidence suggests that reaching a much higher level of knowledge than the minimum that the bar exam requires does not necessarily give you an advantage. Bar examiners possess a requisite level of knowledge. They also expect examinees, most of whom are very recent law school graduates, to possess a certain level of knowledge, certainly one that demonstrate competence but not necessarily one that demonstrates deep subject mastery. The questions are, after all, fairly rudimentary in their nature simply because of the bar exam's limited time and restrictive format.

Examiners can't do too much with a multiple-choice question, given the time and format limitations, not to mention the limitations imposed by relatively objective evaluation and scoring. Given these time-and-format limitations and the examiners' tempered expectations, you may find yourself doing better on practice questions in areas where your level of knowledge is good but not necessarily outstanding, masterful, or excellent.

You may, in other words, not be doing yourself any favors by applying the superior knowledge that you have in one or more topics or subtopics, gained for instance through a research paper, teaching-assistant role, or clerkship. Sometimes you need to fly at 1,000 feet rather than 100 feet, meaning that sometimes you need to think at a simpler level than at the most-complex level of which you are capable. Some things you need to simplify and clarify, even while you hope to demonstrate your overall mastery of any subject. You can know too much, just as you can know too little. Next consider some special problems that the Multistate Bar Examination subjects present.

1. Civil Procedure

Procedure questions present two distinct challenges when compared to substantive-law (doctrinal) questions. First, examiners often interweave procedural questions with substantive law, making issue spotting more complex. After all, procedural issues arise out of substantive-law claims.

For example, the process for entering a judgment requires that a certain party, perhaps a creditor, have a certain kind of claim, perhaps an unpaid debt, on which to enter the judgment. Your challenge is to see the procedural question rather than allow the substantive law to distract you. Don't, for instance, turn a plain question on the procedure for entry of judgment into a complex question over the validity of an obligation or of creditor or debtor rights.

Second, the procedural issues may be harder to identify. With substantive-law questions, rights, obligations, charges, claims, and defenses are the core issues. For substantive-law questions, you must be sure that you know the law, meaning the concepts, rules, elements, conditions, and definitions. Thus, substantive-law subjects like torts, crimes, and contracts often lend themselves well to orderly outlines where one law construct bears clear relationship to other law constructs, so that your law knowledge builds from one concept to another. If you can recall a little, you can often recall a lot.

By contrast, civil-procedure questions tend to present problems in the context of the adversary system, where the parties and court are required to react to strategies as they unfold. Civil procedure's content structure involves process knowledge—actions, reactions, and decision standards—rather than a hierarchical outline of descending claims. You must recall rules, procedures, and standards associated with interests, objectives, actions, options, responses, and decisions. You must also be sure that you understand the parties' competing strategic interests.

The three major civil-procedure topics of *personal jurisdiction, subject-matter jurisdiction*, and *venue* are examples. While you must know the rules, standards, and definitions associated with each of those topics, the jurisdiction and venue issues will arise when a party with one set of interests and objectives strategically sues another party in a certain court and location, to which the second party must respond, perhaps requiring a court's ruling. Whatever procedural rules you apply, perhaps involving pleading, joinder, discovery, summary judgment, trial, post-trial proceedings, or appeal, you must do so cognizant of the parties' strategic interests and options, and the standards the law requires the court to apply.

In some questions, particularly where summary judgment is involved, you may have to deploy this process knowledge in the context of substantive claims. You may have to know a little about the law's substance in order to make a right judgment about the available procedures. For example, evaluating a summary-judgment motion that tests the sufficiency of the evidence of proof of breach in a negligence action requires that you know at least a little about the tort law of negligence and its element breach. Don't get lost in the substantive law. Know the civil procedure. But build and trust your knowledge of the substantive law so that you have a firm foundation for applying the procedure. See the Multistate Bar Examination topic and subtopic outline for more detail.

2. Constitutional Law

Constitutional law has a unique content structure that requires an exam approach unlike other subjects. Constitutional-law questions are uniformly *whether a certain action is constitutional*. Making that analysis often requires two steps, first to determine whether the government had the power to take the questioned action and second whether the Constitution limits that power.

So for example, acts of Congress must fall within Congress's enumerated powers, while acts of the President must fall within the President's enumerated powers or powers appropriately delegated by Congress. You must know those federal enumerations and delegations of limited power to answer constitutional-law questions correctly, while recognizing that states retain expansive police powers.

Yet you must also know the limits on those enumerated, delegated, and retained powers. Limits on power include the many individual rights guaranteed in the Bill of Rights, some rights that the Constitution does not enumerate, and more generally what due process or equal protection require. Be especially on the lookout for due-process limitations.

Constitutional-law questions also often require that you also recognize and address an underlying federalism or separation of powers issue, which likewise limits government's authority. While these constructs depend on clauses within the Constitution and its amendments, you must very often recall and apply the Supreme Court's standard or multi-part test for that constitutional construct.

Recognizing the specific constitutional issue, recalling the specific provision and associated Supreme Court test, and analyzing any associated due process or equal protection issues do not quite complete your challenge, though. The actors and actions themselves vary widely. A constitutional-law fact pattern may involve the President exercising war, appointment, or veto powers, Congress authorizing federal regulation of commerce, a federal agency promulgating those regulations, a state legislature enacting legislation affecting interstate commerce, a state agency regulating speech or association, or a private person or entity acting in violation of law, rule, or regulation.

You must have not only clear knowledge of the basic constitutional-law constructs but also fluency in their application, a process that one scholar likens to peeling an onion very quickly so as to avoid painful eyes and tears running down your cheeks. Prepare earnestly to develop that fluency and facility. See the Multistate Bar Examination topic and subtopic outline for more detail.

3. Contracts

Contract-law questions tend to have lots of facts, such as a series of written or oral communications, dates, quantities, terms, and conditions. While contract-formation law (offer, acceptance, and consideration) is relatively straightforward, examiners often have to give you extra facts in order to reach and test that law. Fact patterns grow even longer and more complex when they involve employees or agents acting for a corporate party or the interests of third-party beneficiaries, often the case for contract-law questions.

Complex fact patterns require more time and effort. You have to get the facts straight. Complex facts invite error in assembling the facts into a meaningful scenario. Reading the question's call before reading the full fact pattern can help you extract and organize relevant facts. Quickly outlining the facts or drawing a picture of them can be another helpful tactic.

Contracts questions can also lend themselves readily to multiple sub-parts or to a final twist or turn as to the outcome. This characteristic means that you can be forming ideas as you read the question, only to find by the end of the question that the examiner wants you to think about something else altogether. This feature is another reason that reading the call of the question first can be a good idea. Know the law, but be sure to read and understand the facts, just as much in contracts questions as elsewhere.

As to the law itself, contract law has its own overarching order to it. That order first involves which law applies, the U.C.C. or common law. You may then have to consider first whether the parties formed a contract, then whether a party breached the contract, whether that party has defenses, or whether the non-breaching party should have certain breach remedies.

The sub-question of contract formation also has an overarching order to it involving offer, acceptance, consideration, and terms.

These larger frameworks remain important even if your sharply analytic mind wants to seize upon one of contract law's many minor rules and address only that rule. Be cautious of falling into the trap of deciding or addressing a question on a subsidiary contracts rule when following the larger frameworks may show you other more-important issues. See the Multistate Bar Examination topic and subtopic outline for more detail.

4. Criminal Law and Procedure

Criminal-law questions can be different in that they may quote or paraphrase portions of a statute that you must apply to determine whether the suspect has committed a crime. In that respect, criminal-law questions can involve relatively routine and straight-forward application of black-letter law to clear and often compelling facts.

In applying a given criminal-code statute, though, you may have to recall and apply key common-law or criminal-code definitions for traditional terms of art. Recalling and applying unstated definitions adds a manageable challenge. You need only have studied those definitions to the point of achieving fluency in spotting their factual triggers, recalling the actual definition, and applying it swiftly and surely in your analysis.

Defenses to specific crimes are also popular but manageable test subjects. Once again, you need only have studied those defenses to the point of achieving fluency in spotting their factual triggers, recalling the defense's conditions, and applying those conditions swiftly and surely in your analysis.

The special challenge that criminal-law questions often present has to do with the suspect's state of mind. You must often read the presented statute or summary very carefully to discern the wrongdoer's state of mind to see if that state of mind satisfies what the statute requires for conviction. You must read and construe scant facts very carefully for state-of-mind evidence. Do not miss that evidence.

While state of mind presents its own peculiar examination issue, the examiner may use other elements of the charge, such as entry or possession, to test your treatment of a close-call issue. Multiple-choice questions are too short to test much more than one element. Indeed, the Multistate Bar Examination designs fact patterns and question calls to isolate and test one rule of law rather than several rules or elements. Focus your reading of criminal-law questions to identify the tested element of the charge.

In contrast to criminal-law questions, focusing on discrete elements of the charge, criminal-procedure questions usually test narrow constitutional-law constructs. For example, the constitutional construct may in the context of a criminal search be *reasonable expectation of privacy*, or in the arrest context *probable cause*, or in the Miranda context *custodial interrogation*. Focus your reading of criminal-procedure questions to identify the tested constitutional-law construct.

You must often know and recall the Supreme Court's latest iteration of these and other constitutional-law constructs. The Supreme Court articulates those constructs in the precarious balance between effective police investigation versus the individual rights of the criminally charged. Pay particular attention to recent Supreme Court decisions and hot topics relating to criminal procedure. See the Multistate Bar Examination topic and subtopic outline for more detail.

5. Evidence

Among all bar-tested subjects, evidence questions may be the most discrete and peculiar, qualities that can surprise and mislead you. You may feel that evidence relates closely to civil procedure and criminal procedure, and even to criminal law, torts, contracts, property, and any other subject frequently involving litigation. Yet while other subjects may often implicate the existence or sufficiency of evidence, with the exception of criminal procedure they do not typically address the *admissibility* of that evidence, which is the core evidence subject. The rules of evidence are a world unto themselves.

For example, criminal procedure considers the admissibility of evidence in the peculiar context of constitutional rights and protections. Criminal-procedure questions address evidence admissibility under the confrontation clause, privilege against self-incrimination, and exclusionary rule for evidence obtained in violation of Fourth Amendment rights, all special criminal-procedure rules rather than ordinary rules of evidence.

Similarly, civil-procedure questions can involve summary-judgment rules as to the sufficiency of evidence and the form, by affidavits or otherwise, in which a party presents evidence. Summary-judgment questions involve civil-procedure rules, not evidence rules. Evidence questions have their own complex set of rules. Distinguish evidence questions from procedure questions and questions having to do with the substance of contracts, torts, and property claims.

The fact patterns in evidence questions are often short. Your challenge is not so much in reconstructing the parties' strategic interests, which are instead often obvious. The party offering the evidence wants it in, while the objecting party wants it out. You can usually quickly discern why one party wants the evidence in and the other party wants it out. Be sure to do so.

Your bigger challenge with evidence questions is instead to recognize that parties may offer evidence for two or more different purposes, some of which the rules countenance and others of which the rules do not. For example, a party may offer certain evidence either to prove character consistent with conduct, on the one hand, or to attack credibility, on the other hand. Different rules determine the admissibility of each form of evidence, either character evidence or credibility evidence. To answer an evidence question correctly, you often have to distinguish for which of two or more purposes the proponent offers the evidence.

As this point suggests, your major challenge then is in knowing the evidence rules. If you must analyze quickly and clearly several layered issues to see which evidence rule answers the specific question, then you must be fluent in the evidence rules.

Relevance and undue prejudice, requiring discerning probative value versus prejudicial effect, are frequent issues in evidence questions. But do not let relevance and prejudice issues distract you when the fact pattern and question call proceed promptly to hearsay or privilege issues. Similarly, while a fact pattern may implicate hearsay or privilege, ignore those issues of the question call directs you to witness foundation, document authentication, or the best-evidence rule. In other words, be ready to relinquish your first thought as soon as the fact pattern and question call direct you to another evidence issue.

These features of evidence questions make skill at issue spotting, accuracy of rule recall, facility in rule application, and fluency in written analysis all key evidence-question skills. Most of all, you need precise knowledge of the rules. Examiners often test not the major rule but its minor exception or peculiar balancing test.

To simplify the considerable issue-spotting challenges, consider focusing first on *what* the proponent offers, meaning whether testimony, tangible evidence (an exhibit to authenticate), or demonstrative evidence. If the proponent offers testimony, then consider whether the testimony describes what the witness *saw* (foundation issues around personal knowledge), *heard* (hearsay issues), *happened in the past* (character evidence), or *reviewed* (expert testimony). See the Multistate Bar Examination topic and subtopic outline for more detail.

6. Real Property

Property-law questions can challenge you with complex fact patterns involving multiple parties, transactions, events, and dates. Be sure to take the extra bit of time to note and even diagram those facts to get them straight. You may know and like the technical clarity of property law. Yet if you consistently get the facts wrong, you will answer property-law questions incorrectly.

While property-law facts are often complex, property law itself is complex. Property law is just foreign and unfamiliar enough for many examinees, to present significant recall and fluency challenges. The various joint, present, and future interests of property owners, the rights of others arising by covenant, use, or zoning, peculiar concerns over conveying real property, mortgaging real property, and ways in which property law treats title transfer and recording, are all technical issues with which examinees may have no practical or clinical experience. Preparing exhaustively will meet those challenges. You may, in other words, be relying here solely on classroom instruction. Take that instruction in earnest.

Property law also has specific doctrines that can give examinees special difficulty. The Rule Against Perpetuities is the bane of many examinees, as can also be the related treatment of future interests. You are not alone if you find these rules a special challenge. Indeed, these subjects can be so difficult as to cause some examinees to question whether mastery of the subjects is worth the time and effort.

If you choose to spend less time on especially difficult rules, then be sure to spend adequate time on the rest of the property-law subject. Do not dismiss property law as unmanageable. Practice property-law questions. You may love property law, or you may not, but in either case, you can master enough of the subject to achieve the score that you need. See the Multistate Bar Examination topic and subtopic outline for more detail.

7. Torts

The subject of torts has a straight-forward content structure often making it a favorite of examinees. You must generally recall and name the tort claim. You must then recall the claim's elements or, if it doesn't have elements, its definition, conditions, or factors. You must then apply that law to the facts.

Tort law can present a moderate challenge in recalling the many claims and their elements. Invasion of privacy, for example, may come in any one of the four different forms of intrusion, appropriation, public disclosure, and false light, depending on the jurisdiction. The numerous elements of misrepresentation (a false material representation made knowingly to induce reliance causing loss) and, separately, defamation (false words published of and concerning the plaintiff that together with extrinsic facts lower the plaintiff's reputation causing special damages other than in the case of an exception to special damages) are each subtle. Elements of a claim may also overlap, making them read more like meandering definitions.

One event may also give rise simultaneously to multiple different tort claims. While as you read a fact pattern you should promptly note any claims that may apply, resist jumping to conclusions as to which of several tort claims the question addresses, until you have read the question call. Be ready to consider a tort other than the one that first occurred to you, when the question call sends you in that new direction.

Many examinees feel that they know tort law's claims well enough to recall their elements, definitions, and conditions. Tort law's challenge is often instead in the breadth of its application. Torts can arise anywhere persons act creating foreseeable risks of harm. Law recall may not be your torts challenge. Applying tort law in the widest variety of factual contexts may instead be your challenge.

You may get tort questions in contexts that you know, such as driving motor vehicles. Or you may get tort questions in contexts that you don't know, such as engineering a building, marketing a drug, or manufacturing a product. Don't let unfamiliar context disarm you. Trust that the examiners will give you the facts that you need to know. Apply the law rigorously, even when you don't fully get the facts in an unfamiliar context.

Beyond knowing tort claims and being able to apply them in unfamiliar settings, you also need to know tort defenses. One tort claim such as negligence may implicate several defenses such as a limitations period, immunity of one form or another, contributory or comparative negligence, or assumption of the risk. Maintain a familiar mental checklist of defenses.

While recalling claims and elements, and recalling and applying defenses, present straightforward challenges, a greater challenge can be in the examiner's decision to test any number of special torts rules. Those rules can include subtopics like: the First Amendment's effect on defamation of public officials and figures adding an actual-malice element; the expert-witness requirement to establish the professional's standard of care in malpractice cases other than for obvious malpractice; and the three forms of design, manufacturing, and warning defect in products-liability cases, including the seven factors of the Second Restatement's risk-utility test to determine when a product is in a defective condition unreasonably dangerous.

While considering torts a straightforward and manageable subject, do not underestimate its subtlety and complexity. See the Multistate Bar Examination topic and subtopic outline for more detail.

Part II: Multiple-Choice Strategies

A. Multiple Choice Matters

Your performance on the Multistate Bar Examination's multiple-choice questions is as important an ingredient to your success as any other thing that you can do to pass the bar exam. You have no way around it: you must do reasonably well on the bar exam's multiple-choice questions.

You may feel, as many examinees do, that you are better at essays or perhaps will be better at a performance test if your bar exam has one. You may believe that as a strong writer, you will do well enough on the essay section of the test to bring up your multiple-choice score to an overall passing level. You may even feel that you have just *never been good* at multiple-choice questions, as if being good at multiple-choice questions is an attribute with which one is born or not born.

If these statements sound like you, then put aside all such thinking now. You can and will improve your multiple-choice skills and scores with appropriate resources and concerted, believing, and discerning effort. Multiple-choice questions require certain skills that you can and must learn, hone, and practice. Make your goal to do well enough on multiple-choice questions not to have to have your other work carry you through. Commit to making multiple-choice questions your strong suit, not weak suit.

B. Design

As any law graduate knows perfectly well, multiple-choice questions begin with a fact pattern that examiners call the *root* or *stimulus*. Questions then provide enough procedural context to support the call of the question that examiners call the *stem*. Questions in the Multistate Bar Examination style then offer four answer choices that examiners call the *options*.

The National Conference of Bar Examiners gives other helpful clues to how examiners design Multistate Bar Examination questions. First, examiners design questions so that you should be able to answer *without reading the options*. Of course, you should read *every* option because you must choose the best one. One option should supply you with a definitively correct answer. But depending on how effective your bar preparation has been, you should nonetheless have a good sense of what the correct answer is even before reading the options.

That design means that you should be reading the options primarily to *confirm* an answer you have already discerned. Answer options do not, for instance, supply additional facts for you to process to choose the best answer. This benefit of developing an answer before finding one among the options is another reason why it was important to practice your fluency in law concepts. You want to force yourself into confirming a choice before looking at the possibilities.

Second, examiners design questions to test only one rule. Answer options may present several alternative rationales, each reflecting a different rule, but the fact pattern and question should require knowledge of only the one rule that the correct answer reflects.

Third, fact patterns have the minimum number of actors necessary to support the question. You won't find extra figures whose roles and actions have no bearing on the question.

Fourth, fact patterns use roles (baker, plumber, employer, etc.) rather than proper nouns (Bill, Mary, Gerry, etc.). You shouldn't be confusing actors and actions.

Trust that the National Conference of Bar Examiners drafts sound and fair questions. If you see practice multiple-choice questions that do not follow these conventions, then you are looking at old, not newer, released questions, or questions that someone other than the National Conference of Bar Examiners drafted.

C. Signals and Triggers

Because of the large number of questions and thus necessarily small number of facts in each question, and because the examiners are testing subtle rules, every word of the facts can be consequential. Even more so than in the case of essay questions, examiners use words and short phrases as signposts and signals.

Certain words like *contractor* and *subcontractor* or *lender* and *borrower* will construct and highlight the parties' relationship. Watch for words that define the critical relationship.

Other words usually having some law content, like *owner, title, claim,* or *charge*, must trigger your recognition of the tested law issue. Watch for words that highlight the law issue.

Other words, often adverbs like *carefully* or *unintentionally,* or prepositional phrases like *without knowledge*, must rule out other possible issues so that you focus only on the tested issue. Don't miss these rule-out markers.

In its few remaining words, the fact pattern must also give you the data, such as dates or perhaps clues to an actor's state of mind, to answer the question. Recognize that relevant data. Practicing many multiple-choice questions, where you promptly review answers and explanations, has the effect of honing your skill at recognizing and relying on signals, signposts, and triggers.

D. Question Call

For strong multiple-choice performance, you must pay particular attention to the call of the question or *stem*. Obviously, if you read and construe the question call incorrectly, then you are very likely to choose the wrong option. Your law recall and analytic skill may be perfect, but you will have answered the wrong question.

The calls of Multistate Bar Examination questions are usually sound in their construction. For example, the committees drafting and approving the questions, and the psychometric expert guiding the drafters, generally eschew the too-easy-to-confuse negative question calls such as, "Which of the four defendants would *not* be liable?" or "Which of the following outcomes is *least* likely?" If you see a rare negative question call, be especially careful to follow it closely rather than mistakenly read its negative request in the positive.

The question calls can, though, have awkwardly formal, cautious constructions, as in "Which of the following would be the most likely basis for the court's ruling granting the motion?" or "On what rationale would the court most likely award judgment against the homeowner?" Read awkward question calls in their more-direct and shorter meaning, such as, "Why grant the motion?" or "Why would the homeowner lose?" Your mind will naturally want to do so. Encourage it, indeed train it.

When necessary or helpful, quickly translate the question call into something firmer and more obvious to guide your selection of the one right option. When you see questions that include phrases like "the most likely basis," "most likely rule," or "most likely award," the examiners are acknowledging that more than one option may be plausible, which will not generally aid in your analysis because you are still looking for the one correct answer. Simply ask *why*, expecting that one answer will be clearly correct even if other answers appear possible or even plausible. Make your best effort to recall the rule that clearly justifies the one correct option.

E. Options

One of the distinct features that examinees observe in multiple-choice answer options is that they often pair a conclusion such as *yes* or *no*, or *granted* or *denied*, with a justification. Often, the justification begins with *because* before reciting a law, rule, or principle, as in *yes because summary judgment is appropriate in the absence of a genuine issue of material fact* paired with other options like *no because summary judgment is inappropriate when the evidence raises a genuine issue of material fact*. Indeed, two options are often *yes because* or *granted because* while the other two options are *no because* or *denied because*.

The construct of two options beginning with the same conclusion *yes, yes*, and then *no, no*, or *granted, granted,* and then *denied, denied*, require you to both reach the correct conclusion and also know the justifying rationale or dispositive rule. It is often not enough, in other words, to reach the correct conclusion without also knowing the supporting law, rule, or rationale. In many questions, examiners balance the conclusions equally in pairs of two as just shown, in which case the examinee must know the rationale (or be able to rule out a false rationale) no matter which conclusion the examinee draws.

In other questions, examiners supply three options each of which draws one conclusion, but with different rationales, and only one option with the opposite conclusion. Do not prefer either conclusion simply because one conclusion has more or fewer options among which to choose. In other words, a single *no* option may be correct even if the other three options are all *yes*. Strategies of that type mislead. Use your law knowledge, not game strategy.

F. Qualifiers

As just indicated, *because* is a common unconditional qualifier to distinguish among options that draw the same conclusion. *Because* is not the only qualifier. Examiners also use *if*, *unless*, *provided that* or *as long as*, and other conditional qualifiers when the fact pattern has a latent ambiguity. Conditional qualifiers test your logic skills, the kind of skills that should be fully familiar to you insofar as they enabled you to get a qualifying LSAT score to get into law school.

Most obviously, the law, rule, principle, or statement following the unconditional qualifier *because* implies a straightforward logical justification connecting the fact pattern to the conclusion, as in *this option answers the question because the following rule logically compels that answer.* Examiners may occasionally substitute the modifiers *since* and *as* for *because*, each meaning the same thing that the rationale compels the conclusion.

By contrast, conditional qualifiers *if, unless,* and *provided* serve a slightly different function. The law, rule, or principle that follows a conditional qualifier like *if* may clarify which law the undisclosed and imaginary jurisdiction follows, for instance a majority or minority rule. Multistate questions can often involve non-uniform law in which the examinee may know the law subject but have legitimate question over which of two or more rules apply in the imaginary jurisdiction. Conditional qualifiers like *if, unless,* and *provided* will often confirm for the examinee that the question expects the examinee to apply a specific rule among several possible options, as in the following examples:

- *Yes, if following the traditional premises-liability classifications.*
- *No, provided that the modern foreseeability test applies.*
- *Granted, unless in a contributory-negligence jurisdiction.*
- *Denied, as long as the rules permit pleading amendment.*

Conditional qualifiers like *if, unless,* and *provided,* can also clarify or confirm different reasonable interpretations of the facts. The short fact patterns of a multiple-choice question cannot possibly resolve every possible interpretation into one. The fact pattern may leave you leaning toward one interpretation but uncertain that you have inferred as the examiners expected. The justification following conditional qualifiers can confirm that you are drawing the intended inference, as in the following examples:

- *Yes, if the man's status is that of a trespasser.*
- *No, provided that the explosion was reasonably foreseeable.*
- *Granted, unless the owner's actions constituted consent.*
- *Denied, as long as the conspiracy evidence is plausible.*

G. Distractors

Another feature of Multistate Bar Examination questions is that all three incorrect answers will be credibly attractive options. Conventional wisdom suggests that one or two options will be obvious throwaways, while the other options will present deliberately close calls as to which answer is the best option. Conventional wisdom is wrong. The National Conference of Bar Examiners intends that the correct answer be clearly correct and clearly the best answer but also that *all three remaining options* be credible distractors. You certainly won't find any humorously wrong options intended to entertain you along the way.

Credible distractors are often correct but irrelevant statements of law that simply do not apply to resolve the call of the question and support that answer option. Distractors can also be incorrect but plausible-sounding rule statements including such things as a minority rule where a majority rule applies, a rule where an exception to the rule applies, or an exception where the rule applies. Distractors can also be incomplete statements that do not go far enough to resolve the question. Distractors can also misrepresent or misconstrue the facts that the fact pattern just gave you. They can also deliberately but subtly swap roles, for instance perpetrator for victim, movant for non-movant, or proponent of the proffered evidence for opponent of the evidence.

Because all three incorrect options will be credible distractors, you should make more effort to answer the question as you read it *before reading the options*. Reading the options before you make any effort to discern the answer may mislead you to seize upon and incorrectly rationalize an attractive distractor. Also, because all four options will be credible but only one option correct, and the three wrong options credibly attractive distractors, you should train yourself to read all four options even when you are confident that you know and have located the correct answer. You may instead have chosen an attractively credible distractor.

H. Procedural Context

Question design, though, is not quite as simple as facts (root), question call (stem), and answers (options). After or in the midst of the fact pattern, questions must also supply the *procedural or practice context*, meaning the judge-lawyer-client-and-opposing-party part that creates the strategic tension.

Examiners deliberately vary the procedural and practice contexts for the calls of the questions. Each call of the question is not as simple as a straightforward evaluation like "Does plaintiff have a claim?" or "Do the parties have a contract?" Rather, examiners include many different procedural and practice contexts. Those practice contexts may involve client intake and interview, factual investigation, pleading, discovery, pretrial motions, alternative dispute resolution, trial events, post-judgment proceedings, appeals, office practice, meetings, and transactions. Here are a few of many possible examples:

- "How should the trial judge rule on the objection?"
- "Which would be the best method of discovery?"
- "Would an appeal be available to the employer?"
- "What is the effect of the officer's testimony?"
- "Which is the best advice regarding the claim?"
- "How would the creditor best enforce the judgment?"

Getting the context right is its own skill, requiring special concentration. You may know the law and understand the facts but misread and misunderstand your particular procedural stance or practice role. Don't rush through the procedural and practice context.

I. Approach

While the approach may seem unnatural and forced, practice reading the call of the question first before going back and reading the full question. You may also find it helpful to scan the answer options quickly before reading the fact pattern.

Here is why you should consider first reading the call of the question and scanning the answer options *before* reading the fact pattern. The examiner designs the fact pattern of a multiple-choice question to trigger your law recall. Read any fact pattern, and you should notice legal issues that spur law recall. When you read the call of the question first, you learn the procedural context and, along with it, confirm the law subject area, especially if you also scan the answer options and those options confirm the subject area.

When you then return to the top to read the full facts, those facts should be triggering relevant rather than irrelevant law recall. By reading the call of the question first and scanning the options so that you already know the law subject, the facts will trigger relevant law, while you ignore false triggers of irrelevant law. For example, you can read a criminal-procedure fact pattern more quickly and confidently knowing in advance that the question is on criminal procedure than you would if you mistakenly guessed that it was a fact pattern and question having to do with evidence, property law, or some other subject area.

Once you have quickly read the call of the question and maybe scanned the options to get a sense of the law subject, and then read the full fact pattern carefully, recognizing the issue and recalling and applying the law as you do so, you should be able to answer the call of the question without even looking at the options. Allow and indeed encourage yourself to do so. Preserve and amplify in the back of your mind, rather than squelch and silence, those tenuous hypotheses that your mind generates as you read the fact pattern. Then formulate an answer as you finish reading the call of the question and before reading the options. The best option should then jump out at you, free of the attractive but incorrect distractors.

Also, read and answer every multiple-choice question in order. Unlike some multiple-choice exams, with the Multistate Bar Examination *you face no penalty for wrong answers.* Thus, *answer every question in order, even if you must guess.*

Some examinees adopt a practice of skipping hard questions, expecting to return to them after completing the rest of the exam. Skipping questions introduces the stress and hazards of not having time to return, losing track of which questions the examinee did not answer, and starting to answer questions out of order so that the examinee records multiple wrong, unintended answers.

Rather than skip a hard question, choose the best answer but mark the question to return to it later if you have the time. While you may mark as many as a dozen or even two dozen questions, many examinees finish with thirty minutes or more of extra time, giving them time to return to every one of those questions marked as difficult.

J. IRAC

The IRAC method of reasoning is not only for essay questions but has its own application to multiple-choice questions. The above sections of this chapter should already have shown you how important the skills of spotting the issue, recalling and applying the law, and concluding are to answering multiple-choice questions. Multiple-choice questions are not some peculiar matching game divorced from legal reasoning. They are instead routine and highly structured tests of exactly what lawyers do day to day in analyzing law questions. Recognizing that you are using IRAC skills to answer multiple-choice questions can go a long way toward reinforcing the same skills that you will need for both essay and multiple-choice questions.

IRAC analysis is also a primary way in which you can diagnose and improve your multiple-choice performance. When you miss a multiple-choice question, take yourself back through your thoughts on that question, asking first whether you spotted the issue, then recalled the rule, then applied the rule correctly, and finally drew the correct conclusion. Use the answer explanation in conjunction with the IRAC method to discern whether you are missing answers because you failed to spot the issue, failed to recall the rule, failed to apply the rule, or drew illogical conclusions.

Using IRAC to diagnose your performance issues can help you strengthen the weaker aspects of your performance. You may need to practice issue spotting, or learn more law, or sharpen your analytic skill, or simply be more logical about your conclusions. IRAC is king here as elsewhere.

K. Wrong Options

Obviously, you will not immediately know the answer to every question. Many questions will involve choosing between two or three options that each appear to you to be plausible. In those situations where two answers both look correct, your challenge is not so much to choose the correct option as to reject the *incorrect* option. Multistate Bar Examination success has much to do with rejecting subtly incorrect options in favor of choosing wholly correct options. Indeed, even when you know that you have identified the correct option, you should confirm that the other options are incorrect.

To identify an incorrect option, first recognize that to be a correct answer an option must be *entirely correct*, not just correct in part. Usually, in these close-call questions, you are not looking for an option that is *entirely* incorrect but only *partly* incorrect.

So how are Multistate Bar Examination options incorrect? Some options misrepresent the facts just given. When the facts in the question's root say one thing and an option says anything different about the facts, rule out that option. An option cannot correctly contradict the facts. Nor can a correct option over-extend the facts or decide a fact issue that the root leaves open. Examiners deliberately write incorrect options that go too far with the facts including in resolving factual disputes.

Next, rule out options that state incorrect law. Examiners will write incorrect options using outdated law, overruled law, law overstating or understating actual requirements, and simply nonsensical statements that sound like law.

Then, rule out options the conclusion of which or rationale for which sounds incorrect. Options are sometimes wrong because they have the correct conclusion along with a correct rule but the rule does not compel the conclusion. These options present non-sequiturs, often attempting to use, say, a tort rule to justify a contract conclusion. The rule is right but the application wrong. The option's rule must match the rule that decides the issue. Don't choose a negligence-concept option when the fact pattern and question call raise an intentional-tort issue. Match option rule to fact-pattern rule.

Options are also sometimes wrong because their rationale is overbroad, especially when they include absolutes like *never* and *always*. Options are also sometimes wrong because another option is somewhat more clear and precise in the way that the rationale compels the conclusion. Choose the more-precise option over the one that leaves ambiguity.

L. Errors

Examinee errors on multiple-choice questions fall into familiar patterns. As you practice multiple-choice questions, diagnose your error pattern for missing answers. Correct common mistakes that you discover in your practice answers.

For example, some examinees fail to assemble in their minds the fact scenario as the examiner wrote it. Sometimes this error is the result of the examinee knowing too much about similar fact patterns, for instance from having worked in that non-law field or having had a similar event happen. If the fact pattern seems familiar to you, then don't let your experience mislead you to add facts that are not present or change facts that are present. Go with what the facts tell you, not with what you think would or should have happened.

Other examinees fail to construct the procedural and practice context, and construe the call of the question, as the examiner wrote it. For instance they may frequently swap roles, mistakenly assuming that the *employer* filed the motion when instead the *employee* filed the motion, or misreading *sustain* to mean *overrule* in the context of an evidentiary offer. Read procedural and practice context, and the question call, very carefully.

Other examinees just don't know the law well enough to avoid attractive correct-but-inapplicable law distractors. Be sure to bring your full substantive law knowledge to bear on multiple-choice questions. Law practice is for lawyers who know law. Learn the details, not simply the broad concepts.

Other examinees fail to reason logically and analytically. They do not spot the issue, recall the rule, and apply law to facts to decide whether the scenario satisfies elements, factors, and conditions. Don't forget your analytic skill on multiple-choice questions. Work carefully through multiple-choice questions as you would essay questions.

M. Guessing

When you don't know the law and thus do not know the answer, no simple strategy like always choosing option C, or always choosing the longest option, shortest option, or only option deciding the question the other way, will save you. The National Conference of Bar Examiners uses psychometric experts to ensure that examinees cannot game the Multistate Bar Examination.

Yet even when you do not know the one single correct option, you may know just enough to influence positively your probability of choosing more rather than fewer correct options. Out of a 200-question exam, you are likely to be unsure of a good number of answers, enough answers that making better choices on uncertain answers will improve your score, even if only slightly. Slight improvement may be all that you need to pass the bar exam.

If you must guess because you cannot recall the applicable law and no answer clearly appears to be the correct answer, then choose an option strategically. Your strongest strategy then is to rule out incorrect options in the manner that a paragraph above describes.

Do not grow too frustrated at only being able to narrow the number of attractive options. Narrowing your guess to just two options substantially increases your chance of a correct answer. Increased probabilities matter. Use every bit of your knowledge, even when and indeed especially when your knowledge is incomplete. Your knowledge will also be incomplete at times in practice. Following reasoned hunches can be a helpful exam strategy, even if in practice you would instead do the research.

When all else fails, and you have nothing to distinguish two or more options, then avoid options that simply repeat results without supporting logic or rationale, such as a conclusion that a homeowner should prevail because he owns the home, or a contractor should prevail because he had a contract. The Multistate Bar Examination tests applying law to facts. Choose options that do so.

Then move on to the next question with a fresh attitude. Whether the prior question was hard or easy has nothing to do with how you should answer the next question. The Multistate Bar Examination makes every question independent of every other question. If you miss one question, then you will not necessarily miss the next question or a later question. Every new question is a new opportunity for success or error.

Part III: Multiple-Choice Questions

Instructions on Use

Because the Multistate Bar Examination requires that you answer 100 questions in three hours before a lunch break plus another 100 questions after a lunch break, this book organizes its 400 practice questions into four separate 100-question banks.

While you may find it convenient to circle the answer on the question's page, doing so will prevent you from practicing the same question again without seeing your prior answer. Instead, consider using the answer sheets at the end of the book's Part V.

To simulate Multistate Bar Examination conditions, you should take exactly three hours for each 100-question bank. To simulate one full all-day 200-question Multistate Bar Examination, you should complete one 100-question bank in three hours, take a two-hour break, and then complete another 100-question bank in three more hours. The book's four 100-question banks thus enable you to practice an entire six-hour, 200-question Multistate Bar Examination not just once but twice.

The value of practicing these questions, though, is largely in confirming or correcting your answers using the answers and explanations in the book's Part IV. So while you should practice these questions in earnest, devoting committed time to answering one question after another, you should also devote time to confirming or correcting your answers using the book's next part in conjunction with the questions in this part. The next part's answers and explanations help confirm the law for you and also teach you law that you don't yet know.

Of course, you don't have to complete all 100 questions of one of the four banks in a single sitting, or two 100-question banks in consecutive sittings, as the Multistate Bar Examination requires. You should instead practice multiple-choice questions frequently whenever you have twenty minutes, thirty minutes, an hour, or other amounts of time. You would then take the time to refer to the answers and explanations to confirm or correct your knowledge.

You can also use the subjects table in the book's Part V to test yourself on any one or more of the Multistate Bar Examination's seven subjects. For example, if you want to test yourself only on torts questions, then refer to Part V's subjects table for the numbers of the torts questions, and answer only those questions.

Yet to build stamina, habituate yourself to test conditions, and learn to gage time, you should also practice the 100-question banks in a single three-hour block. Use liberally, often, and flexibly the questions in this part and the answers and explanations in the next part.

A. First MBE Practice Exam

1. Part I—First 100 Questions (Questions 1-100)

1. A shopper purchased an electric fryer from a local retailer. A defect in the fryer caused it to catch fire on its first use, damaging the shopper's home. The shopper sued the retailer, who confirmed that a national manufacturer of kitchen equipment had made and distributed the fryer to the retailer under an agreement that provided for the manufacturer to provide the retailer with defense and indemnity. How should the retailer enforce its indemnity rights against the manufacturer?

A. The retailer should demand dismissal of the shopper's case unless the shopper adds the manufacturer as a defendant.
B. The retailer should implead the manufacturer as a third-party defendant in the shopper's case when the retailer answers.
C. The retailer should settle the shopper's claim for whatever the shopper demands and then sue the manufacturer for that amount.
D. The retailer should counterclaim against the shopper requiring the shopper to bring the manufacturer in as a defendant.

2. Automotive supplier and assembler signed an agreement for supplier to provide assembler with 100 panels for $50 per panel. Assembler claimed that two days later, supplier agreed to furnish an additional 40 panels for $40 per panel. Supplier denies it and claims that the parol evidence rule excludes any testimony regarding the alleged oral agreement. How should the court rule?

A. Excluded because it conflicts with the written agreement.
B. Excluded because the written agreement is fully integrated.
C. Not excluded because it occurred after the contract was signed.
D. Not excluded because the written agreement is not integrated.

3. An officer arrested a young man for illegal drug possession and placed him in the back of the patrol car. On the way to the jail, the officer asked the young man his name to which he replied, "None of your business." The officer said, "You are in big trouble. I might be able to help you if you tell me who your supplier is before we get to the jail. Once we arrive at the jail, you are out of my hands and I cannot help you." Scared, the young man told the officer the name of his supplier and admitted to selling drugs. The prosecutor charged the young man with drug possession. What is the best argument to suppress the young man's admission?

A. Questions and comments in the patrol car created an unduly coercive atmosphere.
B. The officer should have known questions and comments would cause the young man to confess.
C. The questions constituted custodial interrogation without first reading *Miranda* warnings.
D. The young man invoked his *Miranda* rights when he refused to tell the officer his name.

4. A city lawfully changed the zoning on one side of a street from mixed residential-and-business use to solely residential, attempting to preserve the primarily residential character of the neighborhood consistent with the master plan. The other side of the street remained mixed residential-and-business use consistent with the master plan for further business and commercial development in that area. A resident whose home was then in the residential-only district sought city approval to operate a business from her home. What action should the resident pursue?

A. Claim a non-conforming use.
B. Claim a change in circumstances.
C. Rely on the doctrine of amortization.
D. Seek a variance.

5. A concert producer told an equipment consultant that he wanted the best speakers available on the market. The consultant sold the producer speakers that the consultant bragged were indeed the best available. Musicians nevertheless complained worse than ever about the new speakers. When the producer saw a musicians' survey showing that the speakers were actually fairly unpopular, the producer demanded a refund. The consultant refused despite admitting that he had known of the survey. The producer consulted counsel about a fraud claim against the consultant. What is the best evaluation of that claim?

A. There is an actionable claim for fraud because the consultant knew the statement was false.
B. There is an actionable claim for fraud because the producer relied on the consultant.
C. There is no actionable claim for fraud because the producer had sophisticated musicians.
D. There is no actionable claim for fraud because the consultant's bragging was not verifiably false.

6. A county clerk refused to issue a marriage license to a county resident based on the state's new law prohibiting marriage licenses to issue to residents who owed more than $1,000 in arrears on a child-support order. The resident filed a federal action challenging the state law as a violation of due-process rights. What standard should the federal court apply to determine the statute's constitutionality?

A. Whether the statute is necessary to serve a compelling state interest.
B. Whether the statute relates substantially to an important government interest.
C. Whether the resident can show that the law has no important public purpose.
D. Whether the resident can show that the law has no rational basis.

7. Prosecutors charged a motorcyclist with operating his motorcycle under the influence of narcotics. The motorcyclist vehemently denied the allegations. At trial, the prosecutor called a witness who testified that she was driving her car in the lane next to the motorcyclist's lane when the witness saw the motorcycle moving erratically and at a high rate of speed. The witness further testified that her car was going 55 miles per hour, from which she estimated that the motorcycle was going at least 75 miles per hour. Is the witness's testimony admissible?

A. Yes because lay witnesses may testify to facts but must not draw conclusions.
B. Yes because the witness's testimony is a present sense impression.
C. Yes if the witness shows that she is testifying from experience and knowledge.
D. No because speed estimates involve expert opinions based on special knowledge.

8. A homeowner paid premiums for home insurance. A fire loss caused the homeowner to submit a claim under the insurance. The insurer's claim denial led the homeowner to file a class action on behalf of all similarly situated homeowners who paid premiums to the insurer for the same insurance. The class action alleged fraud and consumer-protection-act violations. The court certified the class action. After extensive discovery and briefing, the court dismissed the class action, ruling that the insurer had done nothing wrong in selling the policy to the homeowner or in denying the homeowner's claim. Which of the following best describes the rights of the class members?

A. The dismissal does not bind the class members, who may each sue on their own behalf.
B. The dismissal binds the class members, who now have no remaining right of action.
C. The class members' rights depend on whether they joined the action as class representatives.
D. The class members' rights depend on whether they also opted to retain the lawyer.

9. A distributor of kitchen equipment agreed to provide a home-appliance retailer with 100 commercial-grade mixers at a specific price and by a specific date, for the retailer to hold a special sale. On that date, the distributor delivered to the retailer only 98 of the specified mixers rather than 100 mixers as the agreement required. What are the retailer's options with respect to the agreement?

A. The retailer may accept all mixers or reject all mixers but claim contract breach either way.
B. The retailer must accept all mixers but may claim contract breach for the remaining mixers.
C. The retailer must reject all mixers if wishing to pursue a contract-breach claim.
D. The retailer must accept all mixers with no breach claim, due to substantial performance.

10. While performing a routine traffic stop for speeding, a police officer noticed that the driver became nervous and kept looking at the glove box. The police officer suspected the driver was transporting narcotics. The officer called for a canine unit to be sent to the scene and, while waiting for the canine unit, placed the driver in the back of the patrol car and handed him his speeding ticket. When the driver asked to leave, the police officer told the driver he had to wait until the canine unit sniffed his car. A half hour later, the canine unit arrived, and the dog responded positively for drugs. A search of the car discovered a brick of cocaine in the glove box. If before trial the driver's defense lawyer moves to suppress the cocaine and the trial court grants the motion, then what will be the most likely reason?

A. The officer's refusal to let the driver leave and unnecessary delay after issuing the traffic ticket amounted to an unreasonable seizure without probable cause.

B. The canine sniff amounted to an unreasonable search because the dog trespassed on the driver's property.
C. A search based on the automobile exception may not be based on a drug detection dog's positive alert.
D. Law enforcement has not established a drug detection dog's positive alert to be accurate enough to serve as a basis for probable cause.

11. An elderly man inherited an ornate heirloom fireplace mantel following the death of his parents. The elderly man still owed money on a business loan security for which he had granted to a bank, on all present and after-acquired personal property. The elderly man found that he could easily place the heirloom mantel over the existing fireplace mantel at his suburban home without damaging the permanent mantel. In doing so, the elderly man told his adult daughter that he wanted her to have the heirloom mantel for her own at his passing. The elderly man soon passed away, by will conveying everything to his adult daughter except deeding the home to a suburban charity. The estate had plenty of cash assets to pay off the business loan. Who gets the heirloom mantel?

A. The daughter.
B. The bank.
C. The charity.
D. The charity, but it must pay the daughter its value.

12. A local prosecutor charged a prominent business owner with criminal conversion of product inventory. The local newspaper accurately published that the prosecutor had criminally charged the business owner with wrongdoing. The prosecutor subsequently dismissed the charge when realizing that the matter involved nothing more than a civil dispute with a supplier over the amount and terms of payment. The owner's business reputation nonetheless plummeted as a consequence of the newspaper report, notwithstanding that the newspaper promptly reported the charge's voluntary dismissal. The business owner demanded that the newspaper retract its publication of the criminal charges, or the owner would sue for defamation. What is the best advice to the newspaper regarding retraction?

A. The newspaper should immediately retract because it will have otherwise defamed the owner.
B. The newspaper should retract as prudent business even though it did not defame the owner.
C. The newspaper should not retract because to do so will establish actionable defamation.
D. The newspaper has no obligation to retract because it published nothing other than the truth.

13. A member of Congress assigned a lawyer staff member to prepare talking points on legislation that the member planned to propose. The legislation would prohibit owners of any residential property held out for lease anywhere within the United States from discriminating against any prospective tenant based on the tenant's choice of gender identity. What is the strongest constitutional authority that Congress could have for enacting the legislation?

A. The Fourteenth Amendment's enforcement clause.
B. Article IV's privileges and immunities clause.

C. Article I, Section 8's interstate commerce clause.
D. Article I, Section 8's general welfare clause.

14. Prosecutors charged a homemaker with presenting an insufficient-funds check (bouncing the check). Testifying at trial, the homemaker denied that the writing and signature on the check were hers. The prosecution called the homemaker's longtime former roommate to testify that based on her personal knowledge of the homemaker's handwriting, she believed the handwriting on the check to be the homemaker's. If defense counsel objects on grounds that the roommate was not an expert in handwriting analysis, then is the roommate's testimony admissible?

A. Yes because the roommate had personal knowledge.
B. Yes because under the business-records exception.
C. No because the roommate is not a qualified handwriting expert.
D. No because the court did not certify the roommate as a handwriting expert.

15. Two adjacent business owners engaged in a bitter dispute over several issues. The dispute began when one hosted a charitable event that interfered with the other's business. The other business retaliated, and further retaliation and escalation ensued. When one of the owners sued the other owner over the retaliatory actions, the other owner counterclaimed. At a scheduling conference, it appeared to the trial judge that the owners' litigation would be bitter, burdensome, distracting, expensive, and unproductive. What procedure would most-likely help resolve the dispute?

A. Dismiss the case due to its inappropriateness for court resolution, requiring the parties to seek private relief.
B. Order specific terms summarily before discovery and hearing as the trial judge determines to be reasonable.
C. Order the parties to private arbitration before a retired judge to relieve the burden on the court's docket.
D. Order the parties to mediation before a skilled professional to help them fashion compromise alternative relief.

16. A roofer was under contract to shingle an owner's mansion with moss-green shingles while the owner was away. Halfway through the job, the roofer ran out of moss-green shingles and so finished the job with harvest-gold shingles. When the owner returned, the roofer demanded the contract price of $20,000. How should the court rule on the roofer's contract-breach claim and owner's counterclaim?

A. Judgment for $20,000 minus an amount for non-matching shingles due to substantial performance.
B. Judgment for $20,000 with no reduction due to satisfactory and substantial performance.
C. No recovery because the roofer did not complete perfect tender as the agreement required.
D. No recovery and the roofer liable for any costs over $20,000 for replacing the wrong shingles.

17. A man dressed in black and wearing a skeleton mask robbed a local bank. A witness getting a good look at the robber described him as a large and tall male with long dark hair. The witness also told police in which direction the robber had run when

he left the bank. Within several minutes and a few blocks from the bank, police officers saw a man who fit the robber's description. The officers detained the man, handcuffed him, put him in the police cruiser, and took him to the bank. The police officers told the witness they captured the robber and asked the witness to identify the robber. The officers took the witness outside to the police cruiser so she could look at the man in their car. The witness identified the man as the robber. Prosecutors charged the man with bank robbery. How should the trial court rule if the man's lawyer moves to suppress the identification procedure?

A. Grant the motion because to be a valid showup, police must tell witnesses that the suspect may or may not be the perpetrator.
B. Grant the motion because the man was entitled to a lawyer once the police narrowed the field of suspects down to one person.
C. Deny the motion because the man was not entitled to a lawyer under these circumstances.
D. Deny the motion because the man did not request a lawyer's presence during the identification procedure.

18. A season-ticket holder to an outdoor summer commercial concert series brought intoxicating drinks and marijuana into the venue for the first several events. Each time, when other patrons called the season-ticket holder's rowdy behavior to security's attention, the event producer confiscated the drinks and marijuana, and warned the season-ticket holder not to do so again because it violated well-publicized event rules. If the conduct occurred yet again, may the producer revoke the holder's season tickets?

A. Yes, because the producer has an obligation to comply with law.
B. Yes, because the season-ticket holder had only a license.
C. No, because the season-ticket holder had a contract right to attend.
D. No, because the season-ticket holder would still have a right to comply.

19. A negligently constructed and maintained store product display fell onto a retail consultant, knocking her over. The fall fractured the consultant's hip, putting her in the hospital for several weeks and causing her to miss months of work. The incident also broke the consultant's notebook computer on which she performed consulting work. The consultant met with a lawyer regarding the potential damages value of a negligence claim. What economic loss supports the consultant's damages element of her negligence claim?

A. The consultant's damaged or destroyed computer meant that she would lose the value of the earnings she could have made with it.
B. The consultant's inability to work from the broken hip meant that she would lose clients and profits from her consulting business.
C. The consultant's medical treatment for the broken hip meant that she had mounting medical expense and loss of earnings.
D. The consultant's medical treatment for the broken hip meant that she had pain, suffering, disability, and lost enjoyment of life.

20. A new state law prohibited any public official from providing welfare benefits to residents who did not have the documented status to remain lawfully in the

United States. Before the state legislature adopted the new statute, a local official had previously granted food assistance and other public-welfare relief to several residents whom the official knew did not have documentation for lawful status. In an action prosecuting the official for the new statute's violation, which constitutional provision would most help the official's defense?

A. The Fourteenth Amendment's due-process clause.
B. The Fourteenth Amendment's equal-protection clause.
C. The Fourteenth Amendment's privileges-and-immunities clause.
D. Article I, Section 10's ex-post-facto clause.

21. A factory worker injured her arm in a stamping machine. The worker sued the manufacturer, claiming that the machine's design flaw caused her injury. At trial, the worker called as a witness a man who was operating the stamping machine next to her machine. The man testified to seeing the worker passed out on the floor with her arm mangled and bleeding profusely. The man further testified that in his opinion the machine's internal timing switch must have short-circuited, causing the servo motor that raised and lowered the stamping action to operate when it should not have operated, causing her injury. On cross-examination, the man admitted that based on his experience observing persons smoking or ingesting marijuana, the worker had appeared to be under the influence of and high on marijuana just before her injury. Assuming timely objections, which of the man's statements are admissible?

A. All the testimony is admissible.
B. None of the testimony is admissible.
C. Only testimony of the worker's injury and being under the influence is admissible.
D. Only testimony about what caused the machine to malfunction is admissible.

22. A drain backed up resulting in water destroying a business's equipment and tools. Cleanup crews traced the backup to the malfunction of a one-way valve in the drain line. The business owner delivered the faulty valve to its manufacturer with a demand that the manufacturer confirm the valve's defect and pay for the water damage. When the manufacturer denied any defect in the valve, the business owner demanded the valve's return for an independent expert's inspection. The manufacturer indicated that the valve was no longer available, having been destroyed during inspection and testing. Which of the following describes the most-likely effect of the valve's unavailability?

A. A court hearing the business owner's case will sanction the manufacturer for failing to reasonably preserve evidence.
B. A court hearing the business owner's case will dismiss the case for the business owner's failure to preserve evidence.
C. No reasonable lawyer would file a products-liability case without having available the offending product to inspect.
D. The valve's unavailability will have no effect on the business owner or manufacturer because cleanup crews traced the backup.

23. A sportsman agreed to sell a charter captain his fishing boat by meeting him at the marina at a specific hour on a certain date to exchange the boat's title for $50,000. Neither the sportsman nor the charter captain appeared at the specified time and

date or took any other action relating to the agreement. What are the contract rights of the parties?

A. The sportsman may sue the captain for not bringing the money.
B. The captain may sue the sportsman for not conveying the boat title.
C. Either party may sue because both parties had a duty to perform.
D. Neither party may sue because performances were conditions precedent.

24. Police suspected a man was growing marijuana in his home. In an effort to gather evidence to establish probable cause for a search warrant, the narcotics detective drove to the man's house, parked across the street, and watched the man's house. Seeing no suspicious activity after three hours, the detective requested a drug canine unit. The dog did not positively signal for the presence of drugs when taken around the outside of the man's home, so the dog handler took the dog onto the front porch and knocked on the front door. When no one answered, the dog handler allowed the dog to sniff first the porch and then the front door, at which point the dog positively signaled for the presence of drugs. Based on that information, police obtained a search warrant to search the man's home, discovering 100 marijuana plants inside the man's home. If the man's lawyer moves to suppress the evidence in a charge of manufacturing marijuana, what is the prosecutor's best argument for admission?

A. The narcotics dog never entered the home and so no search occurred.
B. Police activity is not a search when officers are merely trying a knock and talk.
C. The man did not have an expectation of privacy on his front porch.
D. Police may use narcotics dogs in any reasonable manner to look for evidence of drugs.

25. A property owner leased an artist's studio to a sculptor for three years at $1,000 per month rent. The lease permitted sublease or assignment. After one year of paying the property owner rent, the sculptor subleased the studio to a painter for one year at the same rent. However, the painter moved out after six months without having paid any rent. When the sublease expired, the sculptor moved back in for the final year of the three-year lease but paid no rent. Who owes the property owner how much in rent?

A. The sculptor owes $12,000 and the painter owes $12,000.
B. The sculptor owes $18,000 and the painter owes $6,000.
C. The sculptor owes the property owner $24,000 in rent.
D. The sculptor owes the property owner $12,000 in rent.

26. A defective piece of industrial equipment seriously injured its operator. The operator sued the equipment's designer, manufacturer, and installer, each of whom was negligent in a way that contributed to the operator's injury. Near trial, the operator's lawyer conducted settlement negotiations with the designer whom the lawyer regarded as least culpable. The operator had been demanding $200,000 in total from all defendants but accepted the designer's offer of $20,000, expecting that later settlements from or judgments against the manufacturer and installer would make up the difference. What document should the operator's lawyer prepare or approve for

the operator's signature to effectuate the settlement?

A. A release of the liability of all persons and entities, and their insurers, agents, and employees, in consideration of the designer's settlement.
B. A release of the liability of the designer and its insurers, agents, and employees, reserving rights against other persons and entities.
C. A release of liability for negligent equipment design, reserving rights as to all other negligence actions under which any party may be liable.
D. A release of liability for $20,000, reserving rights to recover more than that amount from any party other than the settling designer.

27. A state legislature enacted a statute that provided for the indefinite incarceration and confiscation of the assets of all members of a certain terrorist cell connected with a local bombing. Law enforcement subsequently arrested a suspected member of the cell, following which a local prosecutor charged the suspected member with the statute's violation. Which of the following constitutional rights should the suspected member rely on in defense of the prosecution?

A. The statute is an unconstitutional bill of attainder.
B. The statute is void for vagueness.
C. The statute regulates an exclusively federal concern.
D. The statute abridges First and Fourteenth Amendment rights.

28. A wife was married to a husband whom authorities alleged was a member of an organized crime enterprise involving construction-contract kickbacks. After her husband's death, authorities called the wife to testify in a criminal-racketeering case against several other alleged members of the racketeering enterprise. Authorities reasonably believed that if the wife testified truthfully, she would acknowledge that her husband had told her privately and frequently during their marriage that he considered the racketeering necessary business. What result if the authorities question the wife to elicit that testimony but wife's counsel objects?

A. Held inadmissible under the marital-communications privilege.
B. Held admissible because all privilege ended when the husband died.
C. Held admissible as a co-conspirator's admission.
D. Held admissible as an excited utterance.

29. A lender sued a borrower in federal court under diversity jurisdiction to foreclose on inventory. The borrower denied the allegations of default while alleging as defenses misrepresentation in the terms of the loan and non-compliance with statutory notice requirements for foreclosure. Following discovery, the lender moved for summary judgment. The lender's motion asserted that there was no genuine issue of material fact that the borrower had failed to meet the express payment terms and that the lender had supplied the statutory notice for foreclosure. How must the borrower respond to avoid summary judgment?

A. Articulate in a brief filed in court precisely what legal authority on which the borrower relies to claim misrepresentation and inadequate notice.

B. Assert and support by affidavit, deposition, or exhibit specific facts showing the lender's misrepresentation and statutorily inadequate notice.
C. Serve discovery requests for information reasonably calculated to lead to admissible evidence of misrepresentation and statutorily inadequate notice.
D. Request an extension of time within which to respond while seeking the lender's stipulation to an order for facilitative mediation to settle the case.

30. A retiree hired a tradesman to remodel her home, knowing the tradesman was not licensed and hoping to save money. The retiree paid the tradesman a deposit. The tradesman performed, but the retiree did not pay the contract balance because of a dispute over the quality of the tradesman's work. The licensing statute's purpose is to protect consumers from unqualified builders. What are the relative rights of the parties with respect to the deposit, disputed work, and balance non-payment?

A. The retiree may recover her deposit because the tradesman was unlicensed.
B. Neither party may recover because they were *in pari delicto*.
C. The tradesman may recover if he proves his work was contract compliant.
D. The tradesman may recover only in quantum meruit.

31. A young woman hired a lawyer to represent her regarding an embezzlement investigation. The lawyer contacted the investigating detective who confirmed he had obtained a warrant for the young woman's arrest. The detective agreed that the young woman could appear the following morning for booking and arraignment. The young woman left the lawyer's office and went home. Within minutes of arriving home, the detective knocked on the young woman's door and said he was there to arrest her. The young woman protested that she was supposed to go for booking and arraignment the following morning. The detective said he changed his mind and refused to let the young woman call her lawyer. Once at the jail, the young woman asked the detective if she could call her lawyer. The detective pretended to call the lawyer on his cell phone and told the young woman that her lawyer had left her office and could not be reached until the next day. Feeling abandoned, the young woman said she might as well talk. The young woman confessed and told the detective where she hid the money. Meanwhile, the lawyer arrived at the jail. When she asked to see her client, the detective told the lawyer the young woman no longer wanted the lawyer to represent her. Further, the detective refused to let the lawyer talk to the young woman. The young woman's lawyer filed a motion to suppress her statements. How should the court rule?

A. Grant the motion because the lawyer invoked the young woman's rights.
B. Grant the motion because the detective's deception was so egregious that it denied the young woman's due-process rights.
C. Deny the motion because the young woman knowingly, intelligently, and voluntarily waived her rights.
D. Deny the motion because the young woman did not properly invoke her rights.

32. A landowner granted a valid written driveway easement to a neighbor who in exchange agreed to pay for paving both adjacent parcels' driveways. The neighbor neglected to record the easement but did

31

complete and regularly use the paved driveway on the landowner's land, sometimes even parking vehicles on the landowner's land. The landowner then granted a bank a deed of trust for a construction loan to build a house on the land. The bank promptly recorded the deed of trust. When the landowner failed to complete the house, the bank foreclosed on the trust deed and sought to sell the land free and clear of the neighbor's driveway easement. What right does the neighbor have, assuming that the jurisdiction has a conveyance statute that requires either recording or constructive notice?

A. The neighbor retains the easement right because the bank received its trust deed later.
B. The neighbor retains the easement right because of the bank's constructive notice.
C. The neighbor loses the easement right for having failed to record the writing.
D. The neighbor loses the easement right because trust deeds precede easements.

33. Two competing dry cleaners struggled to survive an economic downturn. They each adopted several means to drive the other out of business. They undercut one another's prices. They hired away one another's help. They bad-mouthed one another's cleaning quality to customers. They reported one another to the local prosecutor. They advocated with the local bank to refuse one another further credit and to foreclose on loans. They even sued one another over spurious allegations. The court ordered their civil lawsuit to mediation. What is their relative liability to one another?

A. The dry cleaners may have liability to one another for fraudulent, negligent, and innocent misrepresentation.
B. The dry cleaners may have liability to one another for commercial disparagement and interference with business relations.
C. The dry cleaners may have liability to one another for competing to drive one another out of business without interest.
D. The dry cleaners have no liability to one another given the common law's policy to protect economic interests and liberty.

34. An activist entered a state energy department office building where the activist spilled black oil sludge on the floor and set it on fire in protest of state energy policies. Firefighters quickly doused the flames without substantial harm to person or property. Officials charged the activist with violating a state statute that prohibits starting fires in public buildings. The activist sought dismissal of the criminal charge claiming that prosecution was unconstitutional. How should the trial court rule?

A. Dismiss the charge as violating the activist's First Amendment free-speech rights.
B. Dismiss the charge because the activist damaged no property other than his own.
C. Allow the charge because the activist engaged in conduct rather than speech.
D. Allow the charge as narrowly drawn to further substantial government interest.

35. Prosecutors charged a racetrack owner with arson, alleging that he burned down a barn on the horse racetrack he owned with a partner. At the trial, the owner's defense counsel called the partner who testified that he was with the defendant

owner at the barn when the owner accidentally threw a smoldering cigarette butt into a hay pile. Defense counsel also elicited the partner's testimony that the partner was of good character. On cross-examination, the prosecutor asked the partner if he was also charged with arson for the burning of the same barn. What is the correct ruling if the defense lawyer objects to the prosecutor's question?

A. Overruled because the prosecutor is using extrinsic evidence of specific acts to impeach.
B. Overruled because the prosecutor is seeking to show the witness's bias.
C. Sustained because the witness has not yet been convicted of the crime.
D. Sustained because on the witness's Fifth Amendment right against self-incrimination

36. A passenger died in a motor-vehicle crash after the vehicle's defective airbag suddenly exploded without warning. The passenger's estate sued the airbag manufacturer for products liability and made the appropriate jury demand. The manufacturer's defense counsel recommended removing the case to federal court based on diversity jurisdiction. Before approving removal, the manufacturer wanted to know how it would affect the estate's jury demand, meaning whether a jury would still decide the case if tried in federal court. Which of the following best describes how the federal court would resolve the question of whether either party has a right to jury trial?

A. The choice of the plaintiff estate already made in state court before removal.
B. The choice of the defendant manufacturer to be made in federal court after removal.
C. The current practice of the state court from which the defendant removes the case.
D. The historical practice at common law at the time of the 7th Amendment's adoption.

37. An amateur prospector sold a collector a shiny blue rock for $20. Neither party knew what the rock was other than to recognize that it was attractive but may or may not be valuable. The rock turned out to be an extraordinarily large uncut sapphire valued at $2.3 million. If the prospector sued the collector to rescind the contract, then what would be the result?

A. The prospector would win because of mutual mistake of fact.
B. The prospector would win because of misunderstanding.
C. The prospector would lose under the conscious-ignorance doctrine.
D. The prospector would lose because her mistake was unilateral.

38. Police arrested a young man for burglary and placed him in an interrogation room. When the detective arrived, she read the young man his *Miranda* warnings. The young man said he did not feel like talking. The detective handed the young man her business card and said, "That's too bad. I can only help you if you talk to me. If you change your mind, give me a call." The detective then left the room. Once the young man was placed in a cell, other jail inmates told the young man he was foolish for not talking to the detective. The young man asked a jail guard to call the detective back to the jail. When the detective came back to the jail, she read the *Miranda* warnings to the defendant again. The young man signed a waiver card and confessed to the burglary. How should the trial court rule

if the young man's lawyer files a motion to suppress his confession?

A. Grant the motion because the detective continued to interrogate the young man after he had initiated his right to silence.
B. Grant the motion because the detective was prohibited from placing the young man in a cell where other inmates could try to convince him to talk to the detective.
C. Deny the motion because the young man reinitiated communication with the detective.
D. Deny the motion because the detective needed the young man to confess to protect the public.

39. A property developer rented a rehabbed house to a young couple who could not qualify for a housing loan. After one year, the young couple decided to accept the developer's oral offer to sell the house to the couple for twenty percent over the amount of the developer's outstanding loan on the house. Although neither side put anything in writing, the couple paid the twenty percent and also took over the loan payments, real estate taxes, and home insurance. Two years later, after the young couple accepted an offer to sell the home to a buyer for a substantial profit, the developer refused to convey title. What are the relative rights of the developer and young couple?

A. The developer has no enforceable obligation to convey title because of the statute of frauds.
B. The developer must convey title, the young couple having partially performed.
C. The developer need not convey title but must reimburse the young couple if not.
D. The developer and young couple will split the sale profits equally in quantum meruit.

40. A young woman told her boyfriend several secrets in confidence. The secrets included incidents of childhood sexual abuse and the challenges the incidents created with intimate relationship. In time, the dating relationship ended. The former boyfriend then told several of the young woman's friends about the young woman's secrets. The young woman was shocked, embarrassed, and humiliated by her former boyfriend's disclosures, each of which was true but the disclosure of which would have deeply offended the reasonable person. What potential tort claim does the young woman have against her former boyfriend?

A. Appropriation of likeness.
B. Intrusion on seclusion of persona.
C. Public disclosure of private facts.
D. False light.

41. A religious college terminated one of its professors for posting a blog on a popular website. Contrary to the college's mission, the professor's blog argued that religion is a dangerous and divisive force in the world today without which society would be much better. The professor retained counsel to sue the college for reinstatement and damages. Counsel's investigation showed that the state's education department accredited the college and that the college received approximately one third of its annual operating budget from state funds. Did the college violate the professor's free-speech rights under the U.S. Constitution?

A. No because the college has its own First Amendment and Fourteenth

Amendment rights to employ only those who embrace its mission.
B. No because the college's actions were not state actions against which the First Amendment and Fourteenth Amendment protect.
C. Yes because the college's state accreditation and funding make the college's actions state actions under the First Amendment and Fourteenth Amendment.
D. Yes because the First Amendment and Fourteenth Amendment prohibit private employers from interfering with protected free speech.

42. Authorities arrested a machinist, charging him with the battery of a co-worker. At trial, the machinist testified that he struck the co-worker only in self-defense because the co-worker had threatened to kill him. In rebuttal, the prosecutor called a former roommate of the machinist to testify that the machinist had hit him two years ago at home but then claimed self-defense. The former roommate's testimony is:

A. Admissible as a state-of-mind exception for hearsay purposes.
B. Admissible because it contradicts the machinist's assertion.
C. Inadmissible because it is extrinsic evidence of a specific act.
D. Inadmissible as violating the privilege against self-incrimination.

43. An inventor sued the invention's licensee in a two-count complaint. The first count alleged damages from breach of the license agreement. The second count alleged specific performance of that agreement. The licensee moved for summary judgment based on claim preclusion. The trial judge filed a court paper titled "Opinion and Order" that granted the licensee's motion as to the damages count because there was no genuine issue that a prior final judgment on the merits precluded this new case. The Opinion and Order then dismissed the count for specific performance as moot given that the order had already dismissed the damages count. Is the Opinion and Order a final judgment from which an appeal lies?

A. Yes, the Opinion and Order is a final judgment because it disposes of all claims in the case.
B. Yes, the Opinion and Order is a final judgment because it contains language of judgment.
C. No, the Opinion and Order is not a final judgment because it is not titled "Judgment."
D. No, the order is not a final judgment because it does not expressly grant a right to appeal.

44. When renting a car, a tourist initialed the box indicating that she agreed to pay $50 per gallon for gas if she failed to return the car with a full tank. When she returned the car empty, the agency charged her $750 for gas that would have cost $50 retail. What result if the tourist challenged the charge in court?

A. The tourist will lose because of only substantive and not procedural unconscionability.
B. The tourist will lose because of only procedural and not substantive unconscionability.
C. The tourist will win because of substantive unconscionability.
D. The tourist will win because of procedural unconscionability.

45. Police arrested a woman for murdering her husband. Once placed in an interrogation room, a detective *Mirandized* the woman as follows: "You have the right to remain silent. Your statement will be used against you at trial. At some point in the process, the court will give you a lawyer." After hearing the warnings, the woman signed a waiver card. She then confessed to killing her husband. How should the trial court rule when the woman's lawyer files a motion to suppress the confession?

A. Grant the motion because the detective did not accurately advise the woman of her *Miranda* rights.
B. Grant the motion because the detective did not ask the woman if she understood her rights before she signed the waiver card.
C. Deny the motion based on the homicide exception to the *Miranda* rule.
D. Deny the motion because the detective effectively advised the woman regarding her right against self-incrimination and her right to a lawyer.

46. A developer divided 200 acres of land into two parcels of 100 acres each. The developer then platted the first 100-acre parcel for residential subdivision of 50 lots and the second 100-acre parcel for office development, consistent with all land-use and zoning restrictions. The developer then sold all 50 residential lots under deeds with reciprocal residential-use restrictions as to grantees, heirs, and assigns. An investor bought the 100-acre office-development parcel. If the investor bought 10 of the adjacent residential lots from lot owners who didn't want to live next to an office development, may the investor develop those 10 lots for office use when developing the 100-acre office development?

A. No, because of the reciprocal residential-use restrictions.
B. No, because of the land-use and zoning restrictions.
C. Yes, because the lot owners who sold didn't want to build residential.
D. Yes, because of the unity of residential and office-development title.

47. A mother who was engaged in a child-custody dispute with a father falsely reported to police that the father had sexually abused their child. The prosecutor filed criminal charges against the father as a result of the mother's false police report. By retaining criminal defense counsel, the father was able to show the prosecutor that the charges were false, after which the prosecutor abandoned and dismissed the charges. What must the father prove to establish a civil tort claim against the mother for malicious prosecution?

A. The family court awarded the mother temporary custody of the child as a result of her false police report.
B. The mother had made other false police reports like this one, so that the prosecutor should not have believed the mother.
C. The mother had no probable cause to make the false police report and instead acted with ulterior motive such as custody.
D. The prosecutor had no probable cause to bring the charges and instead acted with malice against the father.

48. A public-interest organization with standing challenged in state court a new state law that restricted late-term abortions. The organization's challenge relied on due-process provisions of both the U.S. Constitution and the state's constitution. The state's highest court eventually ruled

that the new state law violated both the due-process provision of the U.S. Constitution and the similar due-process provision of the state's constitution. If the state's attorney general petitioned the U.S. Supreme Court for review, then would the Supreme Court have jurisdiction to decide the case?

A. No because of the state high court's adequate and independent state grounds.
B. No because the state high court did not decide the constitutionality of federal law.
C. Yes because the state high court applied due process under the U.S. Constitution.
D. Yes because abortion is a fundamental privacy right under the U.S. Constitution.

49. A customer fell suffering injury on the sidewalk in front of a proprietor's ice-cream store. The customer's counsel intended to call a declarant who would testify that a witness now lives in Europe told the declarant that when the witness saw the proprietor attempting to fix a flaw in the sidewalk a week before the customer's fall and injury. Counsel intended to use the declarant's testimony to prove the proprietor's control over the sidewalk. Is the declarant's testimony admissible?
A. Yes because the witness is unavailable to testify.
B. Yes for the limited purpose of proving control.
C. No because as to a subsequent remedial measure.
D. No because hearsay and outside of any exception.

50. A shareholder sued a public corporation alleging misrepresentations in the corporation's securities filings. After modest discovery, the trial court dismissed the case on the public corporation's motion for summary judgment for lack of a genuine issue of material fact, after the unrepresented shareholder was unable to articulate the specific misrepresentations on which the shareholder's vague claims relied. Within days of the trial court's dismissal, the shareholder had sued the public corporation again, alleging similarly vague but arguably slightly different misrepresentations in the corporation's same securities filings. Which of the following describes the best grounds on which the public corporation can move for summary judgment?

A. Public corporations owe no duties to their shareholders cognizable in private action.
B. Corporate immunity of a public corporation against civil actions by private individuals.
C. Issue preclusion barring the shareholder from re-litigating the same or similar issues.
D. Claim preclusion barring the shareholder from re-litigating the same or similar claims.

51. An alumnus learned that her old sorority sister had fallen on hard times and so promised to gift her $100,000, in front of witnesses. That same day of the promise, the alumnus suffered a heart attack and died without having conveyed the $100,000 gift. The executor of the alumnus's estate declined to perform the promise. May the sorority sister enforce the alumnus's promise?

A. Yes, because it was made before witnesses who can prove it.
B. Yes, because the promise vested at the time made.

C. No, because it was gratuitous and exceeds statutory amounts.
D. No, because death terminates gratuitous assignments.

52. While on routine patrol, an officer noticed a woman driving erratically. When the officer activated his cruiser's overhead lights, the car sped up. The officer followed the car as the woman turned several corners quickly, drove through a store parking lot, and finally stopped at the end of a dead-end street. The officer arrested the woman for careless driving and disobeying a police signal. The officer handcuffed the woman and placed her in the back of his cruiser. The officer then searched the woman's car. During the search, the officer found marijuana and a pistol. How should the trial court rule when the woman's lawyer files a motion to suppress the marijuana and handgun?

A. Deny the motion because the officer had probable cause to believe the car contained crime evidence.
B. Deny the motion because the woman was a fleeing suspect.
C. Deny the motion because the officer could take inventory of the car's contents.
D. Grant the motion because the woman no longer posed a danger to the police officer.

53. In exchange for a few calves, a farmer executed a writing sufficient to convey an undescribed easement for a driveway for ingress and egress by a neighboring dairy herder and successors and assigns. The drive that the herder began using substantially improved the herder's access to the herder's own barns and lands even though not strictly necessary for access. The herder thereafter used the drive more and more consistently, even making small improvements such as lightly grading and filling the drive. In time, much longer than the jurisdiction's period for adverse possession, both the farmer and the herder conveyed their lands to adult children between whom a dispute arose as to the continued use of the undescribed drive. What are their respective rights?

A. The farmer's children have the right to exclude the herder's children from any drive.
B. The farmer's children must allow some drive but may designate a different drive.
C. The herder's children still have the right to use the same drive.
D. The herder's children have only the right to compensation for the lost drive.

54. An exterminator recruited a key employee away from a competitor. The exterminator induced the key employee to disclose the competitor's customer list and other trade secrets to the exterminator in breach of the key employee's confidentiality and non-compete agreement with the competitor. The exterminator then used the confidential customer list and other trade secrets to target the competitor's customers with a successful marketing campaign. What tort liability does the exterminator have to the competitor?

A. No liability because the exterminator was merely competing for business.
B. Liability for injurious falsehood in the disparagement-of-trade form.
C. Liability for injurious falsehood in the disparagement-of-title form.
D. Liability for tortious interference with business relations.

55. A U.S. senator with a special interest and expertise in foreign relations proposed that Congress adopt legislation permitting the Senate Foreign Relations Committee to publish to the president a list of U.S. ambassador candidates. The proposed legislation would then require the president to select and nominate ambassador candidates only from the committee's list. In deference to the president's power, the proposed legislation would then provide for automatic appointment of the president's nomination chosen from the committee's list, without Senate action if the Senate did not act within forty days. Would the legislation be constitutional if adopted?

A. No because the legislation would violate the Constitution's appointments clause.
B. No because the legislation would interfere with the president's plenary foreign power.
C. Yes because the legislation recognizes presidential appointment of ambassadors.
D. Yes because the legislation furthers Congress's regulation-of-foreign-commerce power.

56. At a local chamber-of-commerce luncheon, a citizen introduced the mayor by saying that the mayor set a good example for flexibility by changing his mind for the right price. The mayor sued the citizen for slander. The citizen defended the action arguing that the statement was true. The citizen offered testimony that the mayor had a reputation for dishonesty, a bribery conviction three years earlier, and voted to approve a developer's rezoning application after the developer paid for the mayor to take a cruise. Which testimony is admissible?

A. Reputation for dishonesty and bribery conviction.
B. Bribery conviction and rezoning vote after paid-for cruise.
C. Reputation for dishonesty and rezoning vote after paid-for cruise.
D. Reputation for dishonesty, bribery conviction, and rezoning vote after paid-for cruise.

57. A plaintiff creditor's attorney hired a process server to serve summons and complaint on the defendant debtor in a federal lawsuit. The process server knocked at the door of the defendant debtor's home. A sixteen-year-old boy answered saying that he was the defendant debtor's son residing in the home with the defendant debtor. After a short conversation, the process server left the summons and complaint with the son. Did this action effect proper service?

A. No, because due process requires tag-style service in these circumstances.
B. No, because the boy was not of legal age as the service rules require.
C. Yes, because the boy resides in the home and is of suitable age and discretion.
D. Yes, because the defendant debtor was dodging service.

58. Buyer and seller are both merchants. Buyer sends seller a Purchase Order for one hundred 9" clamps. Seller responds with its standard-form Acknowledgment, stating that it will fill buyer's order with one hundred 9" clamps and further stating that it disclaimed all implied warranties. Seller ships the clamps. Buyer accepts them but finds that many of the clamps are defective. Buyer returns the unused clamps and sues seller for breach of contract. Which of the following is the most likely result?

A. Buyer will prevail since seller's Acknowledgment could not become part of the contract.
B. Buyer will prevail because seller's Acknowledgment materially altered the contract.
C. Seller will prevail because buyer accepted the Acknowledgment's terms by accepting the goods.
D. Seller will prevail because the Acknowledgment's terms automatically became part of the contract.

59. Customs agents found several hidden containers of illegal methamphetamine among hunting gear each of two men were wearing while attempting to enter the country from Canada. The agents separated the two men for questioning, during the course of which the younger man said that he had told the older man that they should have entered another way because of the entry point's high level of enforcement. Is this evidence sufficient to charge the younger man with conspiracy to import illegal substances?

A. Yes, because the younger man's statement shows agreement to import.
B. Yes, because the agents found illegal substance on both men.
C. No, because the agents have no evidence of an agreement to import.
D. No, because the younger man was cooperating with the agents.

60. A landowner conveyed his lands to his friend for life, then to a farmer and rancher as joint tenants with the right of survivorship. The rancher, farmer, and friend were subsequently in a single motor-vehicle accident in which all three died within the hour. Hospital records confirmed that they died in that order, first the rancher, then the farmer, and then the friend. The jurisdiction does not have a simultaneous-death act in place. Who takes the farm?

A. The friend's heirs.
B. The farmer's heirs.
C. The rancher's heirs.
D. The landowner or his heirs.

61. A rancher determined to reduce the size of his open-range cattle herd. The rancher rounded up cattle to cull and sell 100 cattle that he reasonably believed were his own cattle. The rancher later learned that 20 of the culled and sold cattle belonged to his former ranch manager. The manager consulted a lawyer over what claim the manager would have regarding the rancher culling cattle that the rancher reasonably but mistakenly believed to be his own property. What is the correct advice?

A. No intentional-tort claim because mistake, whether or not reasonable, negates intent.
B. No intentional-tort claim because mistake, as long as reasonable, negates intent.
C. Intentional-tort claim because mistake, even if reasonable, does not negate intent.
D. Intentional-tort claim only if the rancher's mistake was unreasonable.

62. A pharmaceutical company advertised and marketed a drug as safe for the elderly, consistent with then-current studies. Widespread sales and use of the drug soon proved the drug unsafe for and hazardous to the elderly. A law firm brought a class action against the company on behalf of hundreds of allegedly injured elderly users of the drug. The class action

pled claims under the state's law for strict liability for harm suffered as a result of factually false advertising. The company moved to dismiss the false-advertising claim, asserting as grounds its First Amendment rights. How should the court rule on the motion?

A. Grant the motion because the company made the statements without actual malice.
B. Grant the motion because the company's claims were protected commercial speech.
C. Deny the motion because the Constitution does not protect false commercial speech.
D. Deny the motion because the states regulate drugs as a matter of health and safety.

63. Prosecutors charged an attorney's client with money laundering. The prosecutor served a trial subpoena on the attorney to produce her client's private bank records that the client had delivered to the attorney. The attorney moved for a protective order against the prosecutor's subpoena, claiming various privileges. Opposing the motion, the prosecutor requested that the court compel compliance with the subpoena. How should the court rule?

A. Order the records protected as within the attorney-client privilege.
B. Order the records protected as within the attorney-work-product privilege.
C. Order the records protected as within the privilege against self-incrimination.
D. Compel production as outside of any applicable privilege.

A. Compel production as outside of any applicable privilege.

B. Compel production because Attorney has no duty of confidentiality to Defendant.
C. Grant protective order because it would violate Defendant's privilege against self-incrimination.
D. Not compel production because it would violate the attorney client privilege.

64. A motorist struck and seriously injured a pedestrian in the City of New York. The pedestrian, a citizen of Tunisia, had permanent residence status in the United States and was domiciled in New York at the time of the accident. The pedestrian wishes to sue the motorist, a citizen of Canada, in the Southern District of New York on state law claims for the pedestrian's injury. The pedestrian's claim approximates $120,000 in value. Does the pedestrian have the federal forum she seeks?

A. Yes, because the federal diversity statute deems her a citizen of New York.
B. Yes, because state-law claims against foreign nationals embed federal issues.
C. No, because her claim has too low of a value for a federal forum.
D. No, because she has no constitutional nor statutory basis for subject-matter jurisdiction.

65. Retailer wrote to manufacturer to "ship 175 Model X Hearing Aids at catalog price." Manufacturer instead shipped 175 Model Y Hearing Aids. Model Y was superficially similar to Model X but had different working parts. Model Y was an obsolete model with no market demand. On tender of delivery, retailer discovered the discrepancy and demanded that manufacturer deliver Model X instead. Manufacturer refused. If retailer sues for breach of contract, then what result?

41

A. Manufacturer wins, because the parties reached no meeting of the minds.
B. Manufacturer wins, because shipment was a counteroffer that retailer rejected.
C. Retailer wins, because Model Y was obsolete with no market demand.
D. Retailer wins, because manufacturer's shipment was acceptance of retailer's offer.

66. A collector owned classic vehicles that he employed a mechanic to tend and clean. The mechanic clumsily dropped one of the vehicles from a lift one day, destroying the vehicle while the collector watched in horror. In reaction, the collector picked up a heavy wrench from an adjacent workbench and struck the mechanic hard over the head with it, fracturing his skull and causing his death. Which is the most serious common-law crime of which prosecutors could convict the collector?

A. Battery.
B. Involuntary manslaughter.
C. Voluntary manslaughter.
D. Murder.

67. A grandfather conveyed a parcel of land "to my granddaughter and her heirs, but should my granddaughter or her heirs use the property for illegal purposes, then to my grandson and his heirs." In a jurisdiction that applies the common-law rule against perpetuities, what is the grandson's interest in the property?

A. An executory interest.
B. A contingent remainder.
C. A vested remainder.
D. Right of entry.

68. A demented and occasionally violent nursing-home resident died suddenly. Autopsy and investigation confirmed an aide's purposeful poisoning as the cause of the resident's death. Authorities convicted the aide of a homicide for the resident's death. The resident's family consulted a lawyer regarding civil claims regarding the poisoning. What tort did the aide commit?

A. Assault.
B. Battery.
C. Intentional infliction of emotional distress.
D. Negligence.

69. A state leased public lands for a local energy company to develop natural-gas fields. While an out-of-state company had bid higher for the lease, the state chose the local company because of its promise to pass savings along to in-state natural-gas customers. The out-of-state company challenged the state's action alleging that it unconstitutionally discriminated in favor of local and against out-of-state interests in ways that burdened interstate commerce. Which of the following best evaluates the out-of-state company's constitutional argument?

A. The out-of-state company should lose because reduced local gas costs constitute a compelling state interest.
B. The out-of-state company should lose because as a market participant rather than regulator the state may prefer local interests.
C. The out-of-state company should prevail because the state was irrational in rejecting its higher bid in favor of a lower bidder.

D. The out-of-state company should prevail because the state unconstitutionally burdened interstate commerce.

70. Prosecutors charged a man with the murder of a woman who had not been seen for a decade but whose body no one had found. The prosecution presented substantial circumstantial evidence both that the man had murdered the woman and that the woman was in fact dead. The prosecution nonetheless requested that the trial judge instruct the jury with a presumption that the jurisdiction had long recognized that the jurors must presume dead a person who has been missing for more than seven years. Would the court properly give the prosecution's requested instruction?

A. Yes because the instruction is extraordinarily reasonable.
B. Yes because the defendant may rebut the presumption.
C. No because absence for seven years does not necessarily mean death.
D. No because it would be a mandatory presumption on an element of a criminal charge.

71. A patient sued a physician in a medical-malpractice action filed in an Indiana state court. The plaintiff patient's process server served summons and complaint on the defendant physician personally at the physician's office on July 5, 2015. The plaintiff patient, an Ohio citizen, sought $80,000. The defendant physician, an Indiana citizen, took the complaint to his attorney's office on July 31, 2015, seeking options. May the defendant physician's attorney remove the action to federal court?

A. Yes, because of complete diversity and an amount meeting the jurisdictional minimum.
B. Yes, because tort claims for medical malpractice raise federal questions.
C. No, because defendant is a citizen of Indiana, where plaintiff filed the action.
D. No, because the 21-day period for removing the action has expired.

72. Seller and buyer agreed by telephone that seller would sell buyer 450 headsets at $1 each for delivery within one month. One week later, seller learned that a labor strike had increased the price to seller. Seller telephoned buyer demanding $1.25 per headset for the contract. Buyer agreed to pay the increased price. Seller delivered, and buyer accepted delivery. Seller invoiced buyer at the new price, but buyer sent a check for the $450 original contract price with a note that buyer had agreed only because he had to have the headsets. If seller sued buyer for the difference, then what would be the result?

A. Seller would prevail because it was commercially reasonable for seller to increase profit.
B. Seller would prevail because of a good faith, commercially reasonable purpose for the increase.
C. Buyer would prevail because buyer received no consideration for the increased price.
D. Buyer would prevail because buyer signed no writing recording the contract modification.

73. A man wandered through an urban neighborhood in the middle of the night in a psychotic state because of a drug imbalance. A woman with a drawn gun approached the man demanding that he stop and turn over

all his money or she would shoot him in the gut. The man instead pointed at the gun and laughed saying that her dog needed a haircut. Rattled by the man's response, the woman walked off. The man realized only later what had happened. If prosecutors charge the woman with the following crimes, each more serious than the prior one, then which is the most serious of which a jury may convict?

A. No crime.
B. Attempted larceny.
C. Attempted battery.
D. Attempted robbery.

74. A landowner entered into a future-advance mortgage with a bank, secured by a mortgage on land. The landowner subsequently drew $30,000 against the mortgage. The bank, though, mistakenly delayed in recording the mortgage. At the time of delayed recording, the bank discovered the landowner's recorded conveyance of the land to a buyer after the mortgage date but before the mortgage's recording. The buyer had no knowledge of the mortgage before paying the landowner $150,000 for the land and recording the conveyance after diligent title search. The jurisdiction, which follows the lien theory of mortgages, has a statute stating that "any conveyance of an interest in land is not valid against any subsequent purchaser for value without notice who first records." Will the bank prevail in an action to seeking declaration that the buyer owns the land subject to the $30,000 mortgage?

A. Yes, because the bank acquired its interest for value before the buyer recorded.
B. Yes, because the mortgage was merely security for a loan rather than for purchase.
C. No, because the buyer purchased for value and recorded first without notice.
D. No, because the jurisdiction follows the lien theory of mortgages.

75. A mason was laying block with the help of an assistant. The mason decided to play a prank on the assistant. The mason sent the assistant into a storage trailer to look for a tool but then locked the assistant in the trailer for several minutes while the mason and others on the job laughed at the trapped assistant's shouting and banging. The assistant suffered an attack of claustrophobia and injured himself attempting to knock open the door. Which tort claim or claims do these facts support for the assistant against the mason?

A. Assault, battery, and intentional infliction of emotional distress.
B. Assault and battery.
C. Battery and false imprisonment.
D. False imprisonment.

76. Consistent with a proposed treaty that the president refused to sign, Congress enacted legislation creating an executive agency to designate special-use wilderness areas out of federal lands. Authorized special uses included energy development, forestry projects, resort and recreational development, and biodiversity protections, among others. The legislation required the agency to submit designations back to a Senate committee for review and approval or rejection on committee majority. On which of the following grounds would a public-interest organization with standing to challenge the legislation best make that challenge?

A. As an unconstitutional delegation of legislative authority to the executive agency.

B. As unconstitutional interference with the president's authority in foreign affairs.
C. As an unconstitutional requirement for an executive agency to report to Congress.
D. As an unconstitutional legislative-committee restriction on executive-agency authority.

77. Securities regulators charged several executives of a multinational corporation with securities fraud. The regulators granted immunity to a corporate secretary on the agreement that she would authenticate notes that she had written after a meeting at which the executives had discussed the alleged fraud. The secretary would testify that she prepared her notes on her own initiative so that she would remember what the executives had discussed at the meeting. The regulators offered the notes as proof of what the executives had discussed at the meeting. How should the court rule?

A. Bar the notes because the secretary's immunity makes her testimony unreliable.
B. Bar the notes as hearsay outside of any exception to the hearsay rule.
C. Admit the notes as within the business-records exception to the hearsay rule.
D. Admit the notes as within the past-recollections-recorded exception to the hearsay rule.

78. The national manager of an Oregon resort determined to pursue a valid claim against a corporate supplier of goods and services to the resort. Seeking a favorable forum, the manager filed suit against the supplier in a Nevada state court. The defendant supplier was incorporated in Delaware with its principal place of business in California. The manager's counsel personally served summons and complaint on the defendant supplier's chief executive officer while he vacationed in Las Vegas, Nevada. How should the court rule if the defendant supplier timely files a motion challenging the state court's personal jurisdiction over the supplier?

A. Grant the motion, dismissing the case without prejudice.
B. Deny the motion because the supplier is subject to specific jurisdiction.
C. Deny the motion because the supplier is subject to general jurisdiction.
D. Deny the motion because the supplier is subject to transient jurisdiction.

79. On December 20, a coffee shop entered into a written contract with a baker under which the coffee shop agreed to purchase from the baker all baked-good requirements for the next calendar year. The contract provided that the coffee shop had no obligation to accept any specific quantity other than all daily baked-goods requirements. The contract further provided that the baker agreed to supply the shop's requirements at a fixed price specified in the contract, cash on delivery. After three months of contract performance, a rise in costs induced the baker to decide that he could no longer afford to supply the shop's requirements at the agreement's stated price. If the coffee shop sues to enforce the agreement, will the coffee shop prevail?

A. No, because the contract lacked mutuality of obligation as to both parties.
B. No, because the contract lacked a specific quantity making the contract illusory.
C. Yes, because requirements contracts do not need consideration to be enforceable.

D. Yes, because requirements are sufficiently specific and valuable as consideration.

80. A man whose girlfriend left him for a musician went to the club at which the musician was about to perform. Determining to get even by causing the musician public embarrassment, the man slipped two sleeping pills into the musician's drink just before the performance. While the pills would not have endangered a person of normal health, the musician was secretly already under the influence of various substances that reacted so severely with the sleeping pills as to cause the musician to lapse into a coma and then die. Is the man guilty of first-degree murder in a common-law jurisdiction defining first-degree murder as premeditated or committed by poison?

A. Yes, but only because the murder was premeditated.
B. Yes, but only because the murder was by poison.
C. No, because the man lacked the requisite intent.
D. Yes, because the murder was both premeditated and by poison.

81. A matriarch devised her parcel of land to her daughter and her daughter's heirs "so long as the property is used for residential purposes, then to my niece and her heirs." The rest of the matriarch's property passed through the residuary clause of her will to her grandson. The daughter lived on the land until her death, when ownership passed to her husband who resided on the land only a short time before vacating and leasing to a developer to build a shopping center. The matriarch's grandson and the niece both filed quiet title and ejectment actions. Applying common law, how should the court rule as to ownership of the land?

A. For the daughter's husband.
B. For the niece.
C. For the developer.
D. For the grandson.

82. A landowner who was an animal lover and animal-rights advocate maintained her lands for the beneficial use and protection of wild animals natural to the area. The landowner objected to a hunter's lawful hunting on adjacent public lands. To spite the landowner, the hunter lawfully shot and killed one each of several different wild animals on the public lands, stringing the dead carcasses up on the public lands in a location highly visible to the landowner's residence and leaving a highly distressing message on the landowner's telephone to look out her window. What tort may the hunter have committed?

A. The public-disclosure form of invasion of privacy.
B. The intrusion form of invasion of privacy.
C. The false-light form of invasion of privacy.
D. Outrage, also known as intentional infliction of emotional distress.

83. City commissioners grew concerned with the economic impact of pickets and protests on local businesses dependent on tourism. The commission thus enacted an ordinance prohibiting picketing on any issue other than issues relating to city zoning and land uses at the picket's location. Protesters wishing to challenge proposed state legislation on labor issues sued the city to overturn the anti-picketing ordinance on

First Amendment grounds. Which of the following options best states the probable outcome?

A. The city prevails because the ordinance was a content-neutral regulation.
B. The city prevails because the ordinance regulated conduct rather than speech.
C. The protesters prevail because the ordinance discriminates among protests.
D. The protesters prevail because the ordinance regulates speech based on content.

84. A bicyclist sued a motorist alleging that the motorist ran a stop sign, struck the bicyclist hard with the motorist's vehicle, and seriously injured the bicyclist due to negligence. At trial, the motorist called a witness who testified that the bicyclist had later admitted that the vehicle barely grazed the bicyclist. On cross-examination, the bicyclist's counsel asked the witness whether the motorist's insurer employed the witness as an insurance adjuster on the bicyclist's claim. The motorist's counsel objected to the question. Should the court require the witness to answer?

A. Yes for both impeachment purposes and to prove the motorist's coverage.
B. Yes but for impeachment purposes only with a limiting instruction.
C. No because the rules prohibit evidence of liability insurance.
D. No because the existence or non-existence of insurance is irrelevant.

85. A homeowner suffered loss due to break-in and theft despite having paid a security company for an alert system and protection. The homeowner's claims against the security company accrued on the January 1, 2013 date of the break-in. The homeowner filed her breach-of-contract complaint against the security company on December 19, 2014, shortly before the two-year limitations period would have expired. On January 12, 2015, the homeowner amended her complaint to add her negligence claim against the security company. Assuming the negligence claim also has a two-year limitations period, then how should the court rule on the security company's motion to dismiss the negligence claim as time barred?

A. Deny the motion as premature until the homeowner has discovery from the security company.
B. Deny the motion because the negligence claim arose out of the same transaction or occurrence.
C. Grant the motion as time barred because the limitations period expired on January 1, 2015.
D. Grant the motion only if both claims arose out of the same transaction or occurrence.

86. A high school graduate was about to take a job at a factory. The graduate's grandfather told the graduate that if the graduate went to college instead, the grandfather would reimburse the graduate for tuition at the end of each completed term and, if he earned all A grades in any term, then buy the graduate a new car. The graduate enrolled in college, completed his first term earning a B average, and demanded the tuition and car. The grandfather replied that he only intended to show the graduate that he could get good grades and an education. Does the graduate have breach-of-contract claims against his grandfather for the tuition and car?

A. Yes for the tuition payment but no for the car.

B. Yes for the car but no for the tuition payment.
C. No claim for either tuition or car because no consideration.
D. No claim for either tuition or car because no written promise.

87. Two delivery persons sharing a van stopped at a convenience store for snacks. While the clerk was showing one where a beverage was located, the other reached into the cash drawer stealing cash. The theft startled the other who noticed but said nothing to the clerk. Instead, he simply paid the clerk for the beverage and left the store disgustedly shaking his head. The one who stole the cash offered to pay for the beverage, but the other declined. If the clerk discovered and reported the theft, but the thief fled, would the above evidence support an accomplice conviction for the one who bought the beverage?

A. Yes, because his actions facilitated a known theft.
B. Yes, because he failed to act reasonably to prevent theft.
C. No, because he did not intend to promote the theft.
D. No, unless the principal, the real thief, was also charged.

88. A grower owned a large parcel of land. The western half was undeveloped, and the eastern half contained a grove of apple trees. The grower gave to a buyer a deed conveying "the western half of the parcel from the western boundary to the grove of apple trees, comprising 220 acres." Survey later determined that the land conveyed to the buyer was 229 acres. Which of the following accurately describes the deeded interest?

A. The deed is invalid because of mutual mistake.
B. The deed is invalid because parole evidence cannot determine intent.
C. The deed is valid, and the buyer owns 220 acres.
D. The deed is valid, and the buyer owns 229 acres.

89. A gymnast asked her coach to help her stretch out before a competition according to custom. The coach did so in the usual contact fashion with the gymnast cooperative and not complaining. The gymnast later complained that the coach had injured the gymnast's back and inappropriately touched the gymnast during the stretching. What tort, if any, has the coach committed?

A. Battery for the back injury only.
B. Battery for inappropriate touching only.
C. Battery for both the hamstring injury and inappropriate touching.
D. No intentional-tort claims.

90. A caucus in Congress opposed a series of Supreme Court decisions granting greater procedural protections to individuals convicted in state court of violent crimes defined under state law. The caucus determined to advocate with its party leadership for legislation that would eliminate Supreme Court jurisdiction to hear appeals seeking direct rather than merely habeas review of criminal cases that state high courts had decided. Which of the following options best states the grounds on which Congress could adopt such legislation?

A. Congress has express power to limit Supreme Court appellate jurisdiction.

B. State law alone traditionally determines the definition and treatment of crimes.
C. Separate habeas actions are the only proper means for federal review of state cases.
D. The Supreme Court has no original jurisdiction for review of state-court judgments.

91. State officials charged the bookkeeper of a construction contractor with defrauding the state of construction funds in the contractor's billings. At trial, the bookkeeper called as a witness the contractor's president who testified that the bookkeeper had a longstanding reputation for scrupulous honesty in the bookkeeper's work. The bookkeeper's counsel then sought over the other side's objection to elicit the president's testimony that the contractor had entrusted hundreds of thousands of dollars to the bookkeeper on several specific occasions. How should the court rule on the testimony's admissibility?

A. Inadmissible because specific instances of conduct as to good character.
B. Inadmissible because extrinsic evidence on a collateral matter.
C. Admissible because probative of the bookkeeper's honesty.
D. Admissible because an accused's evidence of a relevant character trait.

92. Plaintiff investor timely filed her federal-court complaint on July 1st, serving it by mail on August 1st on the defendant investment advisor located in another state. The defendant advisor answered the complaint on August 21st without filing a Rule 12 motion. The advisor's answer denied many allegations while raising affirmative defenses only of waiver and accord and satisfaction. On September 3rd, and without moving for leave to amend, the defendant advisor filed an amended answer raising for the first time the defense of lack of personal jurisdiction. Has the defendant investment advisor waived the defense of lack of personal jurisdiction?

A. Yes, because the investment advisor did not raise the defense in a pre-answer Rule 12 motion.
B. Yes, because the investment advisor did not raise the defense in the original answer.
C. Yes, because the investment advisor failed to move for leave before filing the amended answer.
D. No, because an amended pleading once as a matter of course within 21 days preserves the defense.

93. A vehicle owner put a note in his neighbor's mailbox saying that he had finally decided to sell the classic vehicle that his neighbor had long coveted, at $5,000 anytime within the next two weeks. A week later, and without hearing from his neighbor, the vehicle owner put another note in his neighbor's mailbox canceling the offer because his other vehicle had broken down and he needed to drive the classic vehicle. As soon as the neighbor received the second note later that same day, the neighbor went to the owner's house with $5,000 demanding the vehicle, but the owner refused. Does the neighbor have a breach-of-contract action for the vehicle?

A. No, because the owner revoked his offer for good reason once his other vehicle broke down.
B. No, because the neighbor gave no consideration for keeping the offer open for two weeks.

C. Yes, because the owner's note to keep the offer open two weeks was a binding option contract.
D. Yes, because the owner's offer was a firm offer not subject to revocation.

94. An informant wearing a recording device told a well-known illegal-drug distributor that he needed to refresh his drug supply. The informant said that he would meet the distributor in 24 hours at an arranged spot with $10,000 to pay for the drugs. The distributor replied that he would need the 24 hours to retrieve the drugs but would meet as arranged. Two hours later, police arrested the distributor. In a common-law jurisdiction, has the distributor committed attempted distribution?

A. Yes, because he had reached an agreement to distribute.
B. Yes, because he had expressed the intent to distribute.
C. No, because he was only dealing with an informant.
D. No, because he had not committed acts in furtherance.

95. A decedent had executed a will devising a parcel of land "to my sister for life, then to my brother for life, and then to my nieces and nephews." The sister and brother contracted to sell the land to a buyer for $225,000. At the closing, the sister and brother tendered a quitclaim deed to the buyer, who refused to complete the sale. The sister and brother brought suit against the buyer for specific performance. Will the court award specific performance in a jurisdiction that does not follow the Doctrine of Worthier Title?

A. Yes, because the quitclaim deed conveyed the sellers' entire interest.
B. Yes, because the sellers' interest is freely alienable.
C. No, because the jurisdiction does not follow the Doctrine of Worthier Title.
D. No, because the title is unmarketable.

96. A seven-year-old boy watched his father polish the family vehicle using an electric buffing gun that rotated the buffing head at a high rate of speed. When the father had finished and left, the boy decided to buff the neighbor's adjacent vehicle using the same high-speed gun. The boy badly damaged the vehicle's finish and body with the gun. The neighbor demanded that the father's homeowner's insurer whose liability policy covered the boy pay for the vehicle damage. The insurer consulted a lawyer about whether to pay the demand. Which of the following is the best recommendation based on the standard of care applicable to the boy?

A. Deny the claim because children with good intentions make sympathetic defendants.
B. Deny the claim because children that age have no negligence liability.
C. Pay the claim because a child engaged in that activity has an adult's liability.
D. Pay the claim because a neighbor should not have to worry about vehicle damage.

97. An integrated state bar from which a lawyer must receive a license in order to practice law in the state adopted a rule prohibiting licensure for any person who had been a member of a terrorist organization. The bar's application form required applicants to disclose whether they had ever belonged to such an organization. An

applicant who was otherwise qualified for a license applied but refused to answer the question about past terrorist-organization membership. The bar accordingly denied the application. What result if the applicant challenged the denial based on the applicant's federal right to freedom of association?

A. Applicant loses because terrorist-organization membership endorses terrorism.
B. Applicant loses because the U.S. Constitution does not protect as to licenses.
C. Applicant wins because freedom of association protects organization membership.
D. Applicant wins because past membership doesn't show intent to further illegal aims.

98. A bar owner hired a well-known derelict to set fire to the bar on Christmas Eve so that the bar owner could defraud an insurance company into paying for renovations. The derelict burned himself badly when setting the fire, resulting in his hospitalization and then death. An arson investigator learned from the derelict's friend that the derelict had admitted to the friend just before the derelict's death that the bar owner had hired the derelict to set the fire. In a trial of bar owner's claim against the insurer, which the insurer denied based on suspected arson, how should the court rule if the insurance company calls the friend as a witness to the derelict's statement?

A. Admissible because a statement against interest.
B. Admissible because a statement by a co-conspirator.
C. Inadmissible because hearsay outside any exception.
D. Inadmissible because the conspiracy had already ended.

99. On March 1st, defense counsel in a federal case called the plaintiff's lawyer in the same case and made several professionally inappropriate threats. Defense counsel's threats included misstatements of law and misrepresentations of fact. The next day, the plaintiff's lawyer served on defense counsel a proposed Rule 11 motion threatening sanctions unless defense counsel withdrew the threats, misstatements, and misrepresentations. Defense counsel's only response was to leave a phone message repeating the same things. On March 24th, the plaintiff's lawyer filed the Rule 11 motion with the federal court. What is the likely outcome of the motion?

A. The court will grant the motion because defense counsel made threats, misstatements, and misrepresentations.
B. The court will grant the motion only if hearing establishes that sanctions are necessary to deter defense counsel.
C. The court will deny the motion because the plaintiff's lawyer did not wait the required safe-harbor period before filing.
D. The court will deny the motion because defense counsel did not make the statements in a writing presented to the court.

100. A driver and his passenger were involved in an automobile accident. The passenger made a demand on the driver for $100,000, alleging that the driver was negligent in running a red light. The driver believed instead that he had the green light. Other eyewitnesses also disagreed over the light's color. Before the passenger filed suit, the driver offered the passenger

$50,000 to settle all claims arising from the accident and forgo suit. The passenger accepted the offer. Before payment of the $50,000, the driver repudiated his promise to pay the passenger $50,000. The passenger sued, asking for the $50,000 settlement amount. What is the result?

A. The passenger wins because the agreement was an enforceable compromise of a disputed claim.

B. The passenger wins because the driver's promise was enforceable without consideration.

C. The driver wins because his indefinite promise did not specify when payment was to be made.

D. The driver wins because public policy voids a promise made against belief of responsibility.

2. Part II—Second 100 Questions (Questions 101-200)

101. A gang leader demanded that a new member drive him to a liquor store so that the leader could rob it. After the leader got out of the vehicle and entered the store, the new member saw a police vehicle, got scared, and drove off without waiting for the gang leader to rob the store and return to the vehicle. Inside the store, the gang leader pulled a handgun on the merchant, who in turn pulled a shotgun from under the counter, tossed a quarter on the counter, and told the leader to get lost. The leader took the quarter and left. Police arrested the new member moments later when the merchant described the vehicle. Was the new member an accomplice to robbery?

A. No, because the new member withdrew before the crime.
B. No, because the merchant did not fear the gang leader.
C. No, because the police deterred the new member.
D. Yes, because the new member furthered the crime before withdrawing.

102. The respective deeds of a farm and a ranch established the boundary between them as "a line drawn along the middle of the river." Over time, the river changed course so that 10 acres of land that was formerly on the farmer's side of the river moved to the rancher's side. Who owns the 10 acres, assuming that the declaratory-judgment action took place in a riparian state?

A. The owner of the ranch, because accretion belongs to the riparian owner.
B. The owner of the ranch, if the requirements for adverse possession are satisfied.
C. The owner of the farm, because accretion does not change property rights.
D. The owner of the farm, because avulsion does not change property rights.

103. A worker cleaning up fallen tree limbs seriously injured his eye when a chipper a co-worker was operating shot out wood chunks. The worker retained a lawyer to investigate whether the worker had a cause of action against the chipper manufacturer for negligent design. Investigation showed that the worker's supervisor had failed to train the worker to stay back from the chipper, an industry standard required chipper makers to guard against thrown chunks, the co-worker was unaware of the worker's presence, and an OSHA citation against the employer for failing to provide workers with eye protection. Which of these discoveries would most aid the worker's negligent-design cause of action?

A. The supervisor's failure to train the worker.
B. The industry standard to guard against chunks.
C. The co-worker was unaware of the worker's presence.
D. The OSHA citation for failure to provide eye protection.

104. A young city resident known for having developed substantial skill as a military gamer went on a shooting rampage that left several other city residents dead or seriously injured. In response, the city council adopted an ordinance prohibiting retailers from publicly displaying or selling to any person any material that may harm

minors because of its violent or sexually explicit graphic content. Local officials then prosecuted the owner of a gaming store that the young gamer had frequented and that continued to display and sell gaming materials within the scope of the new ordinance. Which of the following options represents the best constitutional argument in the store owner's defense?

A. The ordinance is excessively vague and overbroad under the First and Fourteenth Amendments.
B. The ordinance violates free speech and expression unless the materials are utterly without redeeming value.
C. The ordinance violates equal protection because it treats graphic content different from printed materials.
D. The ordinance violates equal protection because it treats minors different from how it treats adults.

105. A prosecutor charged a high-school basketball coach with unlawful distribution of controlled drugs. At trial, the coach testified in his own defense that he often gave public talks against the use of drugs, hated drugs, did not use drugs, and never distributed drugs. In rebuttal, the prosecutor called an undercover police officer who would testify that the coach had indeed distributed drugs to the undercover officer on a prior occasion two years earlier. Should the court admit the undercover officer's testimony?

A. Yes for contradicting the coach's testimony and impeaching the coach as a witness.
B. Yes because the coach's prior bad act shows disrespect for law and public health.
C. No because one prior distribution of drugs does not establish character for lying.
D. No because the testimony would contradict on a collateral rather than material matter.

106. A negligent car driver who was an Oregon citizen was injured in a collision with a negligent trucker who was a Maryland citizen. The driver had $100,000 in damages. The car driver's passenger, also an Oregon citizen, suffered injuries valued at $35,000 in damages. May the passenger join in the car driver's federal-court action to sue both the driver and trucker?

A. No, because his claim is less than the jurisdictional minimum.
B. No, because adding him would destroy diversity jurisdiction.
C. Yes, because federal-question jurisdiction exists for the claims.
D. Yes, because his claim arises out of the same transaction or occurrence.

107. A sportsman loaned $1,000 to his best friend. Although the loan soon fell due, neither spoke of the loan again. The sportsman died after the statute of limitations on enforcing the loan had expired. The executor of the sportsman's estate found the loan note among the sportsman's papers and wrote a letter demanding payment. The friend replied in a signed writing saying that he would pay the entire loan and interest within six months. When the executor demanded payment on the due date, the friend replied that he had since then learned that the statute of limitations had run and would not pay because the sportsman had never asked him. What is the most likely result, if the executor pursues the loan claim?

A. The executor will prevail because he is not bound by the statute of limitations.

B. The executor will prevail because the friend acknowledged his debt in the letter.
C. The executor will not prevail because the estate gave no new consideration for the promise.
D. The executor will not prevail because the limitations period expired before the sportsman died.

108. A young woman took several clothing items into a retailer's changing room, where she stuffed one item into the large pocket of her overcoat intending to walk out of the store and steal it. Leaving the other items in the changing room, the young woman moved down the aisles toward the door until she noticed a loss-control officer standing at the store exit. To avoid getting caught, the young woman removed the item from her overcoat pocket, placing it on the nearest rack. She then attempted to leave the store without any items, but the loss-control officer stopped her, explaining that they had it all on video. What crime if any did the young woman commit?

A. Larceny, because she intended theft and hid and moved the item.
B. Attempted larceny, because she never left the store with the item.
C. No crime, because she might just have decided to buy the item.
D. No crime, because she never left the store with the item.

109. A collector purchased an expensive painting to hang in his home. The collector then gave the painting to his son with a letter saying, "If and when you don't hang this painting, I want it back." Later, the son moved into a studio apartment and had no place to hang the painting. Instead of giving it back to the collector, the son consigned it to an art dealer for sale. A thief then stole the painting from the dealer. The thief then sold the painting to a buyer who knew nothing of the stealing or the title history of the painting. To whom should the court award the painting in a lawsuit over its possession?

A. The buyer, because he purchased in good faith for value.
B. The collector, because of the condition subsequent he put on the gift to the son.
C. The son, because the collector's condition subsequent was invalid.
D. The art dealer, because the son consigned the painting for sale.

110. A domestic terrorist constructed and detonated a small bomb, maiming several innocent victims. Investigation revealed that the terrorist had stolen the items to make the bomb from a hardware store the managers of which should have detected and deterred the theft. The victims consulted a lawyer over whether to sue the hardware store in negligence. What is the best evaluation?

A. Strong on breach, strong on cause in fact, strong on proximate cause.
B. Strong on breach, strong on cause in fact, weak on proximate cause.
C. Weak on breach, weak on cause in fact, strong on proximate cause.
D. Weak on breach, weak on cause in fact, weak on proximate cause.

111. A committee of the U.S. House of Representatives drafted federal legislation purporting 1to authorize both marriages and divorces as a matter of federal law. The committee then sought counsel on the best means to ensure that the legislation, if

passed by Congress and signed by the president, would survive constitutional challenge. Which of the following options would be the best means of ensuring the legislation's survival?

A. Limit the legislation to marriages and divorces in which at least one party is a military servicemember.
B. Limit the legislation to marriages that federal judges perform and divorces that federal courts decide.
C. Limit the legislation to marriages and divorces performed only in the District of Columbia.
D. Construe the legislation as implementing an executive agreement defining basic human rights.

112. A motorist struck and injured a pedestrian as the pedestrian was crossing in the crosswalk at an intersection. The motorist maintained that the traffic light had been green for the motorist when the pedestrian stepped into the crosswalk, while the pedestrian said the opposite that the light was red. At trial, the motorist called as a witness a motorcyclist who had been approaching the same intersection from the same direction at the moment of the incident, and who testified that the light was indeed green. On cross-examination by the pedestrian's counsel, counsel asked the motorcyclist if he was under the influence of illegal drugs at the moment of his observation. Must the motorcyclist answer the question?

A. No because counsel cannot impeach the motorcyclist without a conviction.
B. No because the motorcyclist has a privilege against self-incrimination.
C. Yes because the motorcyclist by testifying has waived any privilege.

D. Yes because the influence of drugs could affect the reliability of the observation.

113. A trespasser, a citizen of Pennsylvania, was injured while walking home down train tracks when the unsecured door of a freight train struck him. The railway's corporate citizenship is New York. The trespasser filed suit in federal court in New York, alleging negligence. Pennsylvania common law ascribes to the railway only a duty to avoid willful and wanton misconduct. Federal common law prescribes a duty of ordinary care. Which law as to the duty the railway owed must the federal court follow?

A. Federal common law because the law is procedural in nature.
B. Federal common law because the law is substantive in nature.
C. State law because the law is procedural in nature.
D. State law because the law is substantive in nature.

114. A gardener owned a tractor for cultivating vegetables in his backyard. A neighbor who wanted to plant his own garden sent the gardener a note offering to buy the tractor for $500. The gardener responded in a letter stating he would sell the tractor for $600 and hold the offer open for one month. Within the month, the neighbor learned from a farmer that the farmer had bought the gardener's tractor for $600. So the neighbor went to the gardener with $600 in cash to accept the gardener's offer. The gardener refused the money, explaining that he had already sold the tractor. Does the neighbor have a breach-of-contract claim against the gardener?

A. Yes, because the gardener's offer was irrevocable for one month.
B. Yes, because the gardener did not notify the neighbor of revocation.
C. No, because the neighbor learning of the tractor's sale was notice of revocation.
D. No, because the gardener's offer to sell at $600 reject the neighbor's $500 offer.

115. A tired traveler briefly left his laptop computer at his airport-terminal seat while getting a drink of water from a nearby fountain. When the traveler turned back, he saw a burly man closing up and preparing to carry away an identical laptop computer that the tired traveler mistook as his own but instead belonged to that man. The tired traveler accosted the burly man and, when the man rightly refused to turn over the computer, the traveler slugged the man, grabbed the man's laptop still mistakenly thinking that it was the traveler's own, and ran with it through the terminal toward his gate. If police stop the traveler after an alert from the man who owned the laptop, will they have grounds to charge the traveler with robbery?

A. Yes, because the traveler's mistake is no defense and may have been unreasonable.
B. Yes, because the traveler slugged the man and used force to take the computer.
C. No, because the traveler only used his fist rather than a weapon to take the computer.
D. No, because the traveler did not have the required intent but was only mistaken.

116. After two years of dating, a gambler bought a wedding ring, proposed marriage to his sweetheart, and when she accepted placed the ring on her finger. Six months later, the gambler's sweetheart broke off the engagement when she learned how serious his gambling problem was. The gambler brought a replevin action for the return of the engagement ring. What is the result in the gambler's lawsuit to recover the ring?

A. She keeps the ring as a valid inter vivos gift.
B. He gets the ring back because he bought and owned it, and can do as he pleases.
C. He gets the ring back because his gift was conditional until marriage completed it.
D. The court will order the ring's sale and equal division of the proceeds.

117. A patient scheduled a surgery on the patient's right knee. The surgeon mistakenly operated on the patient's left knee rather than the patient's right knee. The patient continued to have right knee pain after the mistaken surgery on the left knee, and so the surgeon later operated on the right knee successfully. In a trial of the patient's malpractice case against the surgeon, the patient presented these proofs without expert testimony as to the customary practice to ensure operation on the correct limb. The surgeon's lawyer moved for judgment as a matter of law. What is the correct ruling?

A. Motion denied because jurors determine reasonableness under all circumstances.
B. Motion denied because no expert testimony is required for obvious breaches.
C. Motion granted because expert testimony is required to establish the custom.
D. Motion granted because the surgeon performed a successful second surgery.

118. A homebuilder bought abandoned farmlands at the edge of a developing suburban area, planning to develop the abandoned lands for residential use consistent with the current zoning. Alarmed at a study showing the dwindling open areas in the county due to suburban development, county commissioners adopted regulations that prohibited any construction on certain open lands including those lands that the homebuilder had purchased. The homebuilder was unable to build the planned housing, use the lands for any other purpose, or sell the lands to any other purchaser. What result if the homebuilder sues the county claiming a regulatory taking?

A. County wins because the homebuilder retained title to the abandoned lands.
B. County wins because the regulation did not cause any physical intrusion.
C. Homebuilder wins because the county's preservation objective was not compelling.
D. Homebuilder wins because the regulation prevented all beneficial use of the lands.

119. A homeowner purchased and installed a new oven to complete a kitchen renovation. Heat from the oven's sides set the homeowner's new kitchen cabinetry on fire, causing extensive property damage. The homeowner sued the oven's manufacturer in products liability. At trial, the homeowner's counsel introduced as evidence three letters that the manufacturer had received before selling the oven to the homeowner. Each letter complained of similar oven fires from the same overheating cause as that which the homeowner alleged. How should the court rule if the manufacturer's counsel objects that the letters are hearsay?

A. Admit the letters as evidence both of the defect itself and the manufacturer's notice.
B. Admit the letters but instruct the jury that they are evidence only of notice, not defect.
C. Deny admission of the letters but allow counsel to read them into evidence.
D. Deny admission of the letters because they are hearsay and not within any exception.

120. While a traveler whose domiciliary was in Alabama was abroad, a creditor sued him in Michigan court. The creditor served the traveler by publication in an Alabama newspaper before obtaining a default judgment. The traveler had no claim-related contact with Michigan. Upon the traveler's return to Alabama, the creditor sought to enforce the Michigan judgment against the traveler in an Alabama court. Should the Alabama court enforce the Michigan judgment?

A. No, because without due process it is not entitled to full faith and credit.
B. No, if the Alabama court determines that the traveler had no notice of the action.
C. Yes, because of the full faith and credit clause of the U.S. Constitution.
D. Yes, because any action by the traveler to resist is an improper collateral attack.

121. In response to an advertisement, a homeowner asked a contractor to estimate the cost of providing and installing new window screens. After measuring, the contractor prepared and delivered a written $350 estimate. The homeowner wrote across the estimate and mailed it that he would pay only $300, to which the

contractor wrote on the estimate and mailed it back that he would do the work for $325. One week later, having received no response, the contractor wrote the homeowner another note conceding that the homeowner had won, that the contractor would do the work for $300, and that the contractor would be there in two weeks. The homeowner received the contractor's final note within the two weeks but did not respond. On the appointed date, the contractor went to the home while the homeowner was at work and installed the screens. What is the parties' contract status?

A. A contract based on the homeowner's failure to respond within a reasonable time.
B. An express contract based on the contractor's installation of the screens.
C. An implied-in-fact contract based on the contractor's installation of the screens.
D. No contractual relationship.

122. Members of rival hunting clubs argued over who had interfered with whose hunting rights. The leader of one club pulled out a handgun, aimed it directly at the leader of the other club, and said that he was going to end the argument right then once and for all. In response, the leader of the other club pulled out his own handgun and fired on the other leader first, the bullet hitting him in the gut and dropping him face down on the ground, defenseless. The shooting leader nonetheless stepped forward, stood over the fallen leader, and fired a second shot that pierced the fallen leader's heart, killing him. Of which crime could authorities convict the shooter?

A. Murder only.
B. Manslaughter only.
C. Murder or manslaughter.
D. No crime, because of self-defense.

123. A statesman owned a country estate in a jurisdiction with a 20-year statute of limitations for ejectment actions. An avid hunter who wanted to make the estate her own moved onto it so as to take it by adverse possession. After 10 years, the hunter left the estate for distant parts. Hearing that the hunter had moved, a naturalist moved onto the estate so as to take it by adverse possession, remaining for the next 15 years. The statesman then sued the naturalist in ejectment, claiming that naturalist was a trespasser. What is the most likely result in the statesman's suit for ejectment?

A. Naturalist wins by tacking the hunter's 10 years onto her 15 years.
B. Statesman wins, because hunter and naturalist were not in privity.
C. Naturalist wins, because statesman should have sued the hunter, too.
D. Statesman wins, because neither hunter nor naturalist entered under color of title.

124. A supplier stopped by a retail-store customer to deliver a load of new product. While unloading the new product in a rear cargo bay for deliveries, the supplier suffered serious injury when the cargo bay's overhead door closed suddenly on the supplier's neck and back. Investigation revealed poor maintenance of the door and prior similar malfunctions. How should the supplier's lawyer plead the supplier's negligence action against the retail-store customer in a jurisdiction following the traditional premises-liability classifications?

A. The store breached its duty, owed an invitee, of reasonable care.

B. The store breached its duty, owed a licensee, to cure hidden defects.
C. The store breached its duty, owed a licensee, to warn of hidden defects.
D. The store breached its duty, owed anyone, to warn of known hidden danger.

125. Congress enacted legislation prohibiting commodities traders from taking undue advantage of anyone entering the commodities markets. The legislation provided for criminal charge and conviction, with incarceration for long terms and substantial financial penalties, for any trader violating the prohibition. Because the legislation did not further define *undue advantage* and may have interfered with the commodities market's efficient operation, an association of business professors sued in federal court claiming that the legislation was unconstitutional and seeking an injunction against its enforcement. Does the association have standing to maintain the litigation?

A. Yes because the lawsuit challenged the constitutionality of a federal statute.
B. Yes because the association seeks conclusive relief in the form of injunction.
C. No because the association's injury is inadequate to ensure a real controversy.
D. No because no one has yet suffered conviction under the challenged criminal statute.

126. A serious back injury from a motor-vehicle accident caused by a negligent driver disabled a carpenter from continuing his trade. The driver maintained that the carpenter's spotty work record before the accident suggested that the carpenter already had a back problem before the accident. Medical imaging after the accident suggested some evidence of chronic conditions predating the accident but also evidence of new trauma-induced back conditions consistent with a motor-vehicle accident. At trial, the carpenter's counsel asked the carpenter on direct examination whether he had ever felt any back problems before the accident. Assuming that the carpenter's truthful answer would be no such problems, would the testimony be admissible?

A. Yes because probative of the carpenter's motor-vehicle-accident injury.
B. Yes because the carpenter may give a lay opinion based on his own observation.
C. No because the carpenter has no qualification to give an expert medical opinion.
D. No because the post-accident pain could have been from a chronic condition.

127. A grower sued a dairy farmer for failing to pay for hay that the grower had supplied to feed the dairy farmer's cows. The dairy farmer was upset at the grower's suit because the grower had always carried the dairy farmer through hard times, and the dairy farmer had always eventually paid. The dairy farmer had long ignored that the grower had for years trespassed on the dairy farmer's lands when operating and storing equipment. The dairy farmer consulted a lawyer about the best way to raise the dairy farmer's trespass claim against the grower. What would be the lawyer's best advice?

A. File a separate lawsuit alleging the dairy farmer's unrelated trespass claim.
B. File a trespass counterclaim in the grower's pending unpaid-hay lawsuit.
C. File an affirmative defense claiming set-off for the trespass damages.
D. Do not file any trespass claim because the grower has only sued in contract.

128. A retailer wrote a painter promising to pay the painter $10,000 if the painter repainted the retailer's shop while the retailer was closed and away on vacation. The retailer's letter supplied the painter with the retailer's cell phone to reach her while she was away. The painter bought supplies and started painting on the retailer's first day away on vacation. One day later, the retailer called the painter to revoke her offer because she had decided that she could not afford the $10,000 cost. Would the painter prevail in a breach-of-contract action against the retailer?

A. No, because the retailer offered a unilateral contract, which the painter had not yet completed.
B. No, because the painter knew the retailer was away but made no effort to notify of acceptance.
C. Yes, because the retailer's offer gave the option of accepting by promise or performance.
D. Yes, because the painter had begun to perform under a unilateral contract.

129. Police officers developed probable cause that the defendant was a drug dealer and that he kept large amounts of heroin in his home. After obtaining a valid search warrant, police officers went to the defendant's home to execute the warrant. Before using a battering ram to break down the defendant's door, the police did not knock and announce their presence and purpose. After searching the defendant's home, police officers found packets of heroin and several guns. The prosecutor charged the defendant with drug and weapons possession. The defendant filed a motion to suppress the evidence, alleging a violation of the Fourth Amendment. How should the trial court rule?

A. Grant the motion because the exclusionary rule is a constitutional requirement.
B. Grant the motion because by not knocking and announcing, the police created an unnecessary risk of harm.
C. Deny the motion because the police officers acted in good-faith reliance on the search warrant.
D. Deny the motion because the exclusionary rule is not the proper remedy for not knocking and announcing.

130. An investor bought an interest in his poor aunt's home. They deeded their interests as tenants in common. Shortly after the purchase, the investor leased the home's lightly used lower level to a rent-paying tenant so that the investor would realize a prompt return on his investment. The aunt objected to sharing her home with a tenant, but the investor ignored her demands. What result if the aunt sues to evict the tenant?

A. The court will void the lease and evict the tenant.
B. The court will grant the tenant the lower level's exclusive use.
C. The court will grant the tenant shared use with the aunt.
D. The court will dismiss the suit, leaving the parties to work it out.

131. The owner of a seaplane carelessly left open the drain valves of the seaplane's pontoons after a morning flight. A pilot borrowing the seaplane later that morning carelessly neglected to check and close the drain valves according to routine post-flight inspection. As a result of the carelessness of

both the owner and the pilot, the seaplane's pontoons flooded, and the seaplane sank, destroying its value. In a comparative-negligence jurisdiction, which of the following best evaluates the seaplane owner's negligence claim against the pilot who borrowed the seaplane?

A. The owner has a claim against the pilot, the value of which will be reduced by the percentage of the owner's own negligence.
B. The owner has a claim against the pilot, the value of which will be reduced by the percentage of the pilot's negligence.
C. The owner has no claim against the pilot because the owner's comparative negligence will bar his claim.
D. The owner has no claim against the pilot because the pilot's negligence depended on the owner's negligence.

132. In order to raise revenue to cover projected budget deficits, Congress imposed a substantial tax on every batch of a certain synthetic compound that forestry researchers had developed to spray over forests to prevent the spread of a devastating fungus. Only one manufacturer produces the compound in only one state. Without the periodic spraying of federal and private lands, the fungus would have devastated hardwood stocks significantly adversely affecting the lumber industry. The tax will likely reduce the amount of spraying that foresters can afford, likely causing a significant loss within the lumber industry. What result if lumber-industry representatives with standing file suit challenging the tax's constitutionality?

A. Lumber industry wins because the tax falls on only one state and is insufficiently uniform.
B. Lumber industry wins because the tax will significantly adversely affect interstate commerce.
C. Congress wins because the tax is a necessary and proper means of exercising authority over federal lands.
D. Congress wins because of its plenary power to tax, and this tax has no constitutionally prohibited purposes.

133. An operator got his sleeve caught in an unguarded part of the machine he was operating. The machine very badly mangled his arm and nearly pulled him into the machine. A co-worker took cellphone video of the operator trapped in the machine, covered in blood, and screaming for help. The co-worker uploaded the video to social media but then lost all but a dramatic still screenshot. When the operator sued the machine manufacturer in products liability, the manufacturer denied the severity of the event and injury, and objected to the operator's use as evidence of the co-worker's remaining screenshot. Should the court admit the screenshot as evidence?

A. Yes because a court cannot exclude an image that shows actual injury.
B. Yes because the image is probative of a disputed material fact issue.
C. No as to the still image, only the original video or if lost then a reliable duplicate.
D. No because the operator has not shown that a duplicate is unavailable.

134. A branding consultant sued a client in federal court for the contract price of a branding program that the client had requested and put in place but for which the

client had not paid. The client lost the consultant's suit, resulting in a judgment that the client must pay the unpaid contract price. The client then filed suit in federal court against the consultant alleging that the branding program, although still in place, was unfit for the client's use. If the consultant moves to dismiss the client's claim for not having pled it as a counterclaim in the consultant's prior lawsuit, how should the court rule?

A. Deny the motion because a counterclaim in a prior suit has no effect on making that same claim subsequently.
B. Deny the motion because the counterclaim would not have had an immediate connection to the original claim.
C. Grant the motion because the counterclaim was available and would have been between the same two parties.
D. Grant the motion because the counterclaim would have borne a logical relationship to the original claim.

135. A landscaper wrote to an arborist offering to purchase 500 juniper saplings from the arborist at a price of $10 per sapling, provided that the arborist deliver the saplings within two weeks and bear the cost of transporting. The arborist received the order, loaded the saplings, and delivered the saplings within one week, well before the two weeks expired. The landscaper refused delivery of the saplings. Does the arborist have a breach-of-contract claim against the landscaper?

A. No, because the arborist never notified of acceptance.
B. No, because a party may revoke a unilateral contract any time before acceptance.
C. Yes, because the arborist accepted by tendering the requested performance.
D. Yes, because the landscaper made an irrevocable firm offer.

136. While on routine late-night patrol in a downtown business district, a police officer saw a young man walking down the street with his hands in his pocket. When the young man noticed the police car, he ran away, but the officer cornered the young man, got out of his car, approached the young man, and asked him why he ran. The young man mumbled a response that the officer could not understand. Thinking the young man might be involved in drug activity and that he might be armed, the officer patted the outside of the young man's clothing. Although he did not feel any weapons, the officer felt something that, upon squeezing it further, he thought might be a prescription medication bottle that his training and experience suggested might contain illegal drugs. The officer seized a pill bottle from the young man's pocket that contained crack cocaine. What is the young man's best argument to suppress the evidence?

A. Because the officer did not possess a reasonable and articulable suspicion that criminal activity was afoot, the officer was not allowed to seize anything he found during the patdown.
B. Because the officer was not performing a lawful patdown, the officer was not authorized to fully search the defendant.
C. Because the officer did not feel a weapon during the patdown, he was required to allow the defendant to go on his way.
D. Because the officer manipulated the item he felt during the patdown to determine what it was, the seizure of the pill bottle was not justified.

137. The owner of a lake-view lot bought the adjacent vacant parcel closer to the lake to ensure that no one would build on it and obstruct the owner's lake view. The lake-view owner then substantially improved the home with the lake view. The lake-view owner later sold the vacant parcel to a family for picnicking and boating but with a deed restriction against building on it. The family recorded the deed with the building restriction. Years later, after both the lake-view owner and family members had died, an heir of the family members began constructing a cottage on the vacant parcel that would obstruct the adjacent home's lake view. What result if the heir to the lake-view owner sued to enjoin the construction?

A. The court will enjoin because of common-law rights of lake view.
B. The court will enjoin, enforcing the recorded building restriction.
C. The court will not enjoin because a servitude does not survive the grantee's death.
D. The court will not enjoin because a servitude does not survive the grantor's death.

138. A chainsaw injured a woodsman when its chain suddenly sheared and struck the woodsman. The woodsman had been using the chainsaw for the work that he had described to the salesperson who sold him the chainsaw. He had been using it in the manner depicted in its advertising on its box and in its instructions. Inspection suggested a defect in the manufacture of the chain and design of its assembly. The woodsman retained a lawyer to pursue injury claims. The lawyer determined to plead all potential theories of products liability. What claims should the lawyer plead?

A. Breach of express and implied warranty, negligence, and strict products liability for design, manufacturing, and warning defects.
B. Lack of merchantability, product unfitness for its particular purpose, and unreasonably dangerous marketing of a design.
C. Breach of industry standards, unfitness as to stated warranties, and abnormally dangerous product characteristics.
D. Consumer-protection act violations, consumer-product-safety act violations, and failure to give timely product notice and recall.

139. Individuals of certain nationalities perpetrated terrorist attacks on commercial airliners. If Congress enacted legislation imposing rigorous airport screening for only those individuals of the same nationality as the terrorist attackers, which of the following options states the best grounds on which to challenge that legislation?

A. Article I, Section 8's commerce clause.
B. The Fifth Amendment's due-process clause.
C. Article IV's privileges-and-immunities clause.
D. The Fourteenth Amendment's privileges-and-immunities clause.

140. A truck driver for a freight company fell asleep while driving long-haul in the early morning, crashing into the rear of a car and seriously injuring a child occupant. Remorseful at his carelessness, the driver visited the hospital days later where he apologized to the parents and child. Counsel for the child later offered the driver's apology as evidence of the driver's

negligence in a lawsuit against the freight company after counsel for the freight company had called the driver as a witness to deny negligence. If the court admits the apology as negligence evidence, then what would be the strongest grounds?

A. Statement of then-existing state of mind.
B. Statement by a party opponent's agent.
C. Declarant admission against interest.
D. Prior inconsistent statement.

141. A small-business owner filed a complaint against a national retailer seeking to enjoin the national retailer from marketing a product by the same name as, but half the cost of, a product sold locally by the small-business owner. At the hearing on the small-business owner's motion for preliminary injunction, the small-business owner presented substantial evidence that the national corporation's sales would destroy the small business, ruin the reputation of its owner, and put several local individuals out of work. The legal basis for the small-business owner's claim was unclear. Which of the following conditions for preliminary injunction should defense counsel challenge to defeat the motion for preliminary injunction?

A. Likelihood of success on the merits.
B. Irreparable harm if no injunction.
C. Inadequacy of money damages.
D. The balance of greater harm.

142. A homeowner planned to sell her home without repairing roof leaks that were causing major water damage inside the home. The homeowner painted over evidence of the interior water damage to ensure that prospective buyers did not discover the damage or its roof-leak cause. The homeowner then showed the home to a buyer who contracted on the spot to purchase the home for $300,000. The homeowner did not disclose the water damage or roof leaks, which the buyer only discovered shortly before the purchase closed. The buyer refused to close because of the $30,000 repair cost for the water damage and roof leaks. What result if the homeowner sues the buyer for breach of contract?

A. Buyer prevails because the buyer did not agree to the contract's essential terms.
B. Buyer prevails because the homeowner fraudulently concealed material conditions.
C. Homeowner prevails because the homeowner made no affirmative misrepresentations.
D. Homeowner prevails because the buyer failed to employ an inspector as due diligence.

143. A boyfriend and girlfriend broke up, the boyfriend telling the girlfriend to leave his home and never come back. The girlfriend left but on learning that the boyfriend was going to be away that night returned for her clothing and other personal items. She forced a window open for entry because the boyfriend had locked the door. While gathering her things, she also took the boyfriend's compact-disc music recordings to quickly make copies and discretely return later that night. Back at home, though, she decided to keep the recordings rather than copy them, to get back at the boyfriend. What crime or crimes has the girlfriend committed?

A. Neither larceny nor burglary.
B. Larceny but not burglary.
C. Burglary but not larceny.

D. Both burglary and larceny.

144. A landlord agreed in writing to lease an apartment to a tenant for one year beginning on an upcoming date. When the date arrived, though, the tenant found a prior tenant still in the apartment and refusing to leave. The tenant notified the landlord who confirmed that the prior tenant's lease had expired just before the new tenant's occupancy date. What legal action would properly provide the new tenant with actual possession?

A. Only an eviction action by the landlord to remove the prior tenant.
B. An eviction action by either the landlord or new tenant to remove the prior tenant.
C. Only an eviction action by the new tenant to remove the prior tenant.
D. Nothing other than the new tenant's self-help because the prior tenant is a holdover.

145. A landowner was clearing small trees from his land using an axe. A government forester entered the land to inspect the landowner's work. When the forester approached the landowner interrupting the work, the landowner told the forester to get off the land. The forester just began to recite the government authority on which the forester was acting, when the landowner suddenly raised the axe and swung it down toward the feet of the forester. The forester jumped back at the landowner's swing with the axe and fainted, even as the landowner laughed. Which is the best evaluation of the forester's assault claim?

A. The landowner has probably not committed an assault on the forester because the forester should not have fainted under circumstances where the landowner only had cause to laugh.
B. The landowner has probably not committed an assault on the forester because the forester should not have jumped back and instead should have stood his ground on the government authority on which he acted.
C. The landowner has likely committed an assault on the forester because the landowner intentionally created the forester's imminent apprehension of a harmful contact while having the apparent present ability to carry it out.
D. The landowner has likely committed an assault on the forester because the landowner intended or knew to a substantial certainty that the forester would faint, coming into contact with the land.

146. Following reports of the pending sale of prime real estate to foreign ownership, a state legislature enacted legislation prohibiting aliens, whether resident or non-resident, from owning real property in the state having a value greater than ten million dollars. A non-resident alien subsequently signed a purchase agreement to buy an office tower in the state having a value several times the legislative limit. The non-resident alien simultaneously filed a federal-court action seeking an injunction against the legislation's enforcement. May the federal court hear the action?

A. No because aliens may not sue states in federal court.
B. No because only states may define who may own state land.
C. Yes because international law forbids alien discrimination.
D. Yes because the court has federal-question jurisdiction.

147. Prosecutors called a jewelry-store clerk to testify at the criminal trial of a robbery suspect. The clerk was present in the store when the robbery occurred. The clerk's trial testimony revealed that, nervous about testifying, she had refreshed her memory of the event by reading an investigating police officer's report of the crime. The officer prepared the report promptly after the crime after having been on scene immediately after the crime. How should the court treat defense counsel's request to examine the report?

A. Prohibit examination because the clerk did not read and approve the report when events were still fresh in mind.
B. Prohibit examination if the clerk read the report before trial, unless the clerk also refreshed her memory on the stand.
C. Permit examination only of those parts of the report that record the clerk's own statement to the investigator.
D. Permit examination if the clerk used the report while testifying, but exercise discretion if only read before trial.

148. A business partner learned by tip from the partnership's bookkeeper that the other partner was planning to exhaust the partnership's line of credit at a local bank and transfer the funds to an account in a foreign country where the other partner resided. The business partner retained counsel to prevent the other partner's actions, believing that the other partner intended to abscond with the funds. Which of the following describes the best action counsel could take to prevent loss of the funds?

A. Serve in person on the other partner a cease and desist letter on counsel's stationery.
B. Serve by regular mail to the local bank a notice and demand letter on counsel's stationery.
C. File an action seeking an ex parte temporary restraining order to serve on the local bank.
D. File an action and serve in person on the other partner a motion for preliminary injunction.

149. An architect formed a contract with a construction lender to conduct continuous on-site inspections at the construction site for an office building, for purposes of documenting the completion of work and authorizing construction-loan draws. Immediately after entering the contract, the architect suffered a disabling injury as a passenger in a motor-vehicle accident. Unable any longer to move about the construction site, the architect offered the lender instead to review construction documents. What result if the lender sues the architect for damages relating to the architect's failure to perform the inspections contract?

A. Architect wins for having offered a reasonable substitute obligation.
B. Architect wins because the contract assumed his ability to perform.
C. Lender wins because the architect failed to fulfill contract expectations.
D. Lender wins because the architect's duty to perform was personal.

150. A ship's captain and first mate were passing through customs after docking their ship at a U.S. port after returning from a Central American destination. Searching their backpacks, customs officials found dozens of packets of cocaine sewn into the backpack linings. The officials promptly moved the captain and first mate into

separate rooms for questioning where after intense questioning the first mate broke down sobbing "I told him that we'd get caught here instead of the other port." The captain said nothing in questioning. Authorities indicted both for conspiracy to import cocaine. The prosecutor introduced only the above evidence at the first mate's separate trial. When the prosecution rested its case, defense counsel promptly moved for a verdict of acquittal for insufficient evidence of the crime. How should the court rule?

A. Grant the motion because the first mate withdrew from the conspiracy by voluntarily giving a statement against his co-conspirator.
B. Grant the motion because the prosecution's evidence at most established only that the captain and first mate committed separate crimes.
C. Deny the motion because the prosecution's evidence shows that both the captain and first mate possessed the cocaine.
D. Deny the motion because the prosecution's evidence shows that both the captain and first mate agreed to import cocaine.

151. An investor signed an agreement with a farmer to purchase development lands, with the closing and conveyance within two months. The investor promptly located a big-box retailer to purchase the development lands from the investor for a new store. The investor and retailer entered into a signed purchase agreement with closing to take place two weeks after the investor would receive the farmer's title to the lands. A delay occurred in the farmer's closing with the investor, requiring the investor to notify the retailer that the investor could not close in time. If the farmer did convey title to the investor a month later than promised, but the investor refused to convey to the retailer because another buyer was willing to pay more, then may the retailer compel specific performance of the investor's sale to the retailer?

A. No because the farmer never signed an agreement to convey to the retailer.
B. No because the investor unreasonably delayed after notice of the closing's delay.
C. Yes because the investor still acted within a reasonable time after the scheduled close.
D. Yes because the retailer's contract merged into the investor's deed from the farmer.

152. A homeowner constructed a wood deck attached to his home along the boundary between his property and the neighbor's property. Later, the neighbor notified the homeowner that much of the deck was on the neighbor's property and that it should be removed. When the homeowner protested, the neighbor commissioned a survey that confirmed that the homeowner had constructed a substantial part of his deck on the neighbor's land. The neighbor repeated his demand that the deck be removed. The homeowner, who could not believe the survey results, consulted a lawyer. What evaluation should the lawyer make of the homeowner's conduct?

A. The homeowner's construction of the deck does not constitute a trespass to the neighbor's land because it was innocently constructed by the homeowner.
B. The homeowner's construction of the deck constitutes a trespass to the neighbor's land because the homeowner's mistaken

understanding is of no consequence to the fact of the entry.
C. The homeowner's construction of the deck constitutes a trespass to the neighbor's land because the homeowner should have known he was building on the neighbor's land.
D. The homeowner's construction of the deck may constitute a trespass to the neighbor's land but is not so substantial that the homeowner should worry.

153. The high priest of a cult of devil worshippers sacrificed a feral dog at a recognized ceremony within the cult's regular religious practices. The sacrifice involved the dog's live torture before slow and exceedingly painful death. The local animal-protection society complained to animal-protection officials who arrested the priest for criminal charge of animal cruelty under state law. If the priest appeals his conviction, asserting constitutional grounds in defense, then what result?

A. Conviction sustained because devil worship falls outside any protection.
B. Conviction sustained because religious belief does not warrant animal cruelty.
C. Conviction overturned because of the priest's freedom to practice religion.
D. Conviction overturned because of the reasonableness of cult members' beliefs.

154. A hospital patient fell and fractured her hip while moving, alone and dizzy, from the hospital bed to the in-room bathroom. The patient sued the attending physician on the theory that the physician should have ordered nurses to keep the bedrails up so that the patient could not get out of the bed without nursing assistance. At trial, the patient's counsel offered the hospital records to show the absence of any physician order for keeping the bedrails up. If properly authenticated by a recordskeeper, then are the hospital records admissible for that purpose?

A. Yes because within the business-records exception to the hearsay rule.
B. Yes because a statement against the physician's interests by an agent.
C. No because the nurses should testify as the best evidence of an absent order.
D. No because the records are hearsay and not within any recognized exception.

155. A motor vehicle ran through a red light, killing a pedestrian in the crosswalk. Police determined that the vehicle driver was drunk. The pedestrian's estate sued the vehicle owner under a statute that made the owner liable for the driver's permissive use of the vehicle. The vehicle owner defended on the basis that the driver, who had no memory of the accident, must have suffered a sudden and unanticipated epileptic seizure. The estate's counsel determined to discover the driver's medical condition before and after the accident relating to any seizure disorder and the likelihood of seizure. The driver is not a party. Which of the following describes the best way to discover that evidence?

A. Retain a private investigator to interview the driver and make a written report.
B. Request that the driver submit to an independent neurological examination.
C. Subpoena the driver to deposition with an accompanying document request.
D. Serve interrogatories on the driver for the driver to answer under oath.

156. A commodities broker contracted to harvest a landowner's soybean crop as soon as the crop dried. The landowner, concerned that winter rain and snow would destroy the crop, subsequently alerted the broker that the crop had dried making it ready for harvest. However, several other similar jobs distracted the broker until heavy rains had indeed destroyed the landowner's crop. What result if the landowner sues the broker for the crop loss?

A. Broker wins because the contract supplied no time for performance.
B. Broker wins because the landowner did not warn of heavy rains.
C. Landowner wins because the broker had reason to foresee the loss.
D. Landowner wins because the loss occurred during the contract term.

157. A hunter and his friend were discussing the merits and demerits of certain hunting equipment and methods late at night around the campfire. Upset at the hunter's opinion regarding the merits of a certain handgun that the hunter favored for finishing the kill, the friend tossed the handgun into the campfire. Furious at his friend's action, the hunter picked up one of the good-size stones ringing the campfire and struck his friend on the head with it. The friend died shortly later from intracranial bleeding. Which of the following is the most serious crime of which a jury could convict the hunter in a common-law jurisdiction?

A. Murder.
B. Voluntary manslaughter.
C. Involuntary manslaughter.
D. Assault.

158. A real-estate mogul died leaving an office-building property to his only child and a stepchild as joint tenants with right of survivorship. The child and stepchild agreed that the stepchild, who had worked in the mogul's business, would manage the office building. Several years later, the stepchild incurred a $100,000 personal debt on which the creditor recorded a judgment lien against the office building as a state statute permitted. The stepchild died before paying any part of the judgment and before the creditor had attempted to enforce the judgment lien against the office-building property. May the creditor enforce the judgment lien against the office-building property now that the stepchild debtor has died?

A. Yes because the stepchild debtor had not paid any part of the judgment.
B. Yes because the devise could only create a tenancy in common, not joint tenancy.
C. No because the creditor's recording of the judgment lien severed the child's interest.
D. No because the child became the sole owner of the building at the stepchild's death.

159. A resident lived in a posh development with the houses crowded closely together. A neighbor with teenage children moved in next door. The neighbor's teenagers frequently played amplified guitars, drums, and other rock-band instruments late into the night in the neighbor's garage. The resident called the police over the noise, who confirmed that the noise probably violated local ordinance but who also indicated that nothing would be done about it. The resident was fed up calling the police over the neighboring garage band's noise-ordinance violations. Wondering whether there was anything else he could do to put a stop to the sleep-

shattering racket, the resident consulted an attorney. What would be proper legal advice?

A. The resident may be able to pursue a nuisance action to stop the ordinance violations.
B. The resident may be able to pursue a trespass action to stop the ordinance violations.
C. The resident may be able to pursue invasion of privacy claims to stop the teenagers.
D. The resident has no tort remedy and can only hope the city enforces the ordinance.

160. A female employee made a federal claim of sexual harassment against her employer. The employment contract required that the parties arbitrate the claim. When presented with the list of qualified arbitrators, the employer's counsel struck all of the women arbitrators from the list giving as a reason that women arbitrators might favor the female employee. The parties thus arbitrated the case before a panel of three male arbitrators who found in the employer's favor. The female employee then challenged the entry of a federal-court judgment on the arbitration award. What result if the female employee argues that the employer's striking all women arbitrators was unconstitutional?

A. Award stricken because gender discrimination does not survive intermediate scrutiny.
B. Award stricken because gender discrimination denied a jury of the employee's peers.
C. Award entered because gender discrimination here meets the strict-scrutiny test.
D. Award entered because gender discrimination here satisfies the rational-basis test.

161. A motor vehicle struck a pedestrian in the crosswalk at a stop sign. The motorist contended that the pedestrian had stepped out in front of the moving vehicle already entering the intersection after having stopped. The pedestrian contended that the motorist had suddenly pulled out after the pedestrian was already in the crosswalk. A witness testified at trial that a bystander eyewitness had said at the moment of the accident to look at the crazy motorist who was running into a pedestrian. The motorist then offered the testimony of another witness who would testify that the same bystander said a day later that the pedestrian had stepped out in front of the moving vehicle. Is the latter testimony admissible?

A. Yes both to impeach the bystander's credibility and to prove the pedestrian's own fault.
B. Yes but only to impeach the bystander's credibility and not as to any party's fault.
C. No because the bystander is not testifying, making the statement inadmissible hearsay.
D. No unless the bystander has an opportunity to explain the apparent contradiction.

162. A metropolitan hospital system sued a regional health insurer for anti-competitive practices relating to the insurer's refusal to accept the system's hospital and medical care providers as part of the insurer's in-plan coverage. The system's counsel requested to inspect and copy the insurer's electronically stored information relating to the criteria on which the insurer determined

whether to include or exclude medical care providers and facilities from its in-plan coverage. The insurer estimated at $450,000 the cost of responding to the system's request because of the difficulty of locating and identifying the electronically stored information, while preserving privileged information. Which of the following best describes measures that the court may approve to reduce and balance the burden of complying with the system's request?

A. Sampling, cost-shifting, quick-peek, and claw-back provisions.
B. Contempt including monetary sanctions, and dismissal of claims.
C. Severance of claims and parties, and bifurcation of issues for trial.
D. Facilitative mediation, early neutral evaluation, and arbitration.

163. A nephew worked in his uncle's farming business for many years. The uncle, who planned to retire, had the farming business appraised at $300,000. The uncle then offered to sell the business to his nephew for $175,000 because of the nephew's devoted years of service to the uncle. The nephew accepted his uncle's offer if the landowners whose lands the business farmed agreed to assign the leases to the nephew. The uncle got the landowners to consent to the assignment of the leases to the nephew, telling the nephew that he would then have a lawyer document their agreement. Consultation with the lawyer convinced the uncle to change his mind and to sell the business instead on the open market for full value. Would the nephew prevail in an action against his uncle to enforce the business's sale to the nephew?

A. No because the nephew's consideration was substantially less than market value.
B. No because the lawyer had not yet documented the parties' agreement.
C. Yes because the lawyer's drafting was merely to document an agreement already made.
D. Yes because neither party controlled the landowners' consent to assignment.

164. A competitive weightlifter used steroids to recover from an injury and increase performance. The weightlifter knew that loss of mood control including raging was a potential side effect of the steroids. Prosecutors charged the weightlifter with common-law battery relating to an incident at the gym. At trial, defense counsel requested a jury instruction that if the steroids had so influenced the weightlifter that he would not have committed the crime without the steroids, then the jury should acquit. In support of the instruction, defense counsel pointed to conflicting evidence that the weightlifter was either badly addicted to the drug, took it from his coach believing it to be only vitamins, or struck the victim responding to taunts about drug abuse. Defense counsel also presented expert testimony that the drug can induce uncontrollable raging in a reasonable person. Which evidence most supports the requested instruction?

A. The weightlifter's addiction.
B. The weightlifter's mistake relying on the coach.
C. The weightlifter's responding to the victim's taunts.
D. The expert testimony of uncontrollable raging.

165. A speculator mortgaged land that the speculator owned in order to borrow $150,000 to invest in other ventures. The lender recorded the mortgage. The

speculator then sold the mortgaged land to a hunter who hoped to build a hunting cabin on the land. In completing the conveyance, the speculator signed a deed that clearly identified the mortgage and mortgage amount. The deed further recited that the hunter took the land subject to the mortgage and that the hunter expressly assumed and promised to pay the mortgage obligation. The deed did not require the hunter to also sign, but the hunter accepted the conveyance, recorded the deed, took possession of the property, and began paying the mortgage. Years later, the hunter grew tired of hunting, abandoned plans to build a cabin, and defaulted on the loan obligation. If the lender duly forecloses and sells the land leaving a $50,000 deficiency, then who has the primary liability on the deficiency?

A. The speculator who made the note and granted the mortgage, the hunter only a guarantor.
B. The speculator because the hunter did not sign the deed, the property having been sold.
C. The hunter for having made payments to the lender, thus being estopped from denial.
D. The hunter for having accepted the deed and thus its conditions and obligations.

166. A college student located a schoolroom in which to study. There was a laptop computer in a backpack belonging to a staff member, on a table in the room. With no one in sight, the student removed the computer, opened it, altered the background and screensaver, and randomly deleted some files. The student snuck the laptop computer back into the backpack, having thoroughly enjoyed messing with the computer's background, screensaver, and files. The staff member entered the room and saw the student just as the student was setting down the backpack. Does the staff member have a tort claim against the student?

A. Yes so long as the student's actions interfered with the staff member's use of the computer.
B. Yes even if the student's actions did not interfere with the staff member's use of the computer.
C. No even if the student's actions interfered with the staff member's use of the computer.
D. No unless the student's actions deprived the staff member of the computer's use.

167. A state legislature enacted legislation to encourage local technology manufacturing. The legislation taxed the gross sales of companies that assembled computers, smartphones, and other electronic equipment in the state but granted credits against the tax for every component purchase that the assembler made within the state. Some assemblers continued to purchase all components from outside the state, paying the full tax. Other assemblers on-shored or re-shored their component purchases to within the state, successfully reducing or even eliminating the tax. What result if the fully taxed assemblers challenge the constitutionality of the tax in a court having jurisdiction to hear the challenge?

A. Tax constitutional because it treats all in-state assemblers equally.
B. Tax constitutional because it duly fosters in-state manufacturing.
C. Tax unconstitutional because gross-revenue taxes reduce commerce.
D. Tax unconstitutional because it favors in-state over out-of-state products.

168. Detectives investigated a suspicious fire at a manufacturing plant, concluding that the fire was arson. The detectives interviewed and obtained a signed statement from a worker at the scene who from a photo lineup identified a suspect whom the worker thought he had seen carrying a gas can in the area just before the fire. Detectives took a video statement from another worker who also identified the same suspect. When timecards at the suspect's workplace showed that the suspect had left work an hour before the fire and returned an hour after it, prosecutors charged the suspect with arson. The two workers who identified the suspect disappeared before trial. What evidence may the court admit over the suspect's confrontation-clause objection if the evidence is properly authenticated?

A. The worker's statement identifying the suspect from a photo lineup.
B. The detectives' testimony that a photo lineup led to the suspect's identification.
C. The other worker's video statement identifying the same suspect.
D. The timecards from the suspect's workplace.

169. A Hollywood star sued a New York tabloid in federal court, invoking its diversity jurisdiction to maintain a defamation claim. The federal court issued an order to attend a Rule 16 conference 45 days from the date of the order. The star's lawyer directed a law clerk to prepare initial disclosures due 21 days before the Rule 16 conference. Which of the following best describes the information that the law clerk should prepare to make the initial disclosures?

A. Experts, witnesses, supporting documentation, damages computations, and insurance.
B. Disputed facts, disputed legal issues, evidence issues likely to arise, and motions in limine.
C. Privileges asserted, discovery objections, discovery cost issues, and order of discovery.
D. Settlement demand, required settlement terms, settlement options, and settlement goal.

170. A performance artist recruited an agent to book shows for the artist. Because the artist had a new and unconventional act, the artist and agent signed a one-year contract that paid the agent 20% of the artist's earnings rather than the 15% entertainment-industry standard. The agent did so well for the artist in the first year that the artist gave the agent 25% rather than the 20% contract amount. They then agreed to continue the contract into a second year, copying the original contract, updating the date, and signing the updated contract. What result if after another successful year, the artist and agent disputed what amount the artist owed the agent?

A. Award 25% representing the course of dealing.
B. Award 20% representing the express contract term.
C. Award 15% representing the industry standard.
D. Award quantum meruit damages for value received.

171. A plant manager refused to move a night-shift worker to the day shift. In retaliation, the night-shift worker secretly put a double dose of an over-the-counter laxative in the manager's coffee, bragging to

his fellow night-shift workers that the boss was going to be experiencing a little discomfort. A double dose of laxative would not have done more to a person of normal health. However, unknown to the worker, the manager was on other medications that, mixed with the laxative, caused the manager to suffer seizures and die. Prosecutors charged the worker with first-degree murder. What result on the charge, assuming that the jurisdiction defines first-degree murder to include premeditated murder or poisoning?

A. Charge fails.
B. Charge stands based on the worker's premeditation and poisoning.
C. Charge stands only because the worker acted with premeditation.
D. Charge stands only because the worker used poisoning.

172. An accountant, a psychologist, and a therapist purchased a small office building, taking a deed as tenants in common. The three professionals each took an office suite within the building, while they shared the building's restroom, kitchen, supply room, and lavatory. After four years, the therapist decided to take a year off to travel and so rented out her office suite and access to the restroom, kitchen, supply room, and lavatory, to a masseuse tenant for that one year. Neither the accountant nor psychologist consented to the lease. Both didn't want to share an office building with a masseuse. What result if they sue to evict?

A. Masseuse evicted because a tenant in common cannot lease without consent.
B. Masseuse remains in the therapist's office suite while evicted from the other rooms.
C. Masseuse retains the lease but shares all possession with the accountant and psychologist.
D. Masseuse retains exclusive possession of the office suite and shares the other rooms.

173. A bank manager was closing a bank branch office for the evening. Just as the manager walked to the front door to lock it, a man approached the door from the outside, took hold of the door handle, and pulled it open. The bank manager stopped the man, saying that the branch was closed for the evening. The man stood in the open door, arguing with the bank manager. The bank manager would not relent, insisting that the branch was closed. The man then pulled a knife from his pocket and brandished it at the bank manager. The bank manager shoved out the door the man who was brandishing the knife at him, and locked the door. The man fell heavily backward, severely cutting the back of his head. The man's lawyer made a demand for compensation from the bank manager for the man's injury. Which is the best response?

A. To request proof of damages because the bank manager is liable.
B. To request an explanation of the man's motive for brandishing the knife.
C. To deny the demand because the bank manager is not liable.
D. To apologize for the man's injury and hope that he does not sue.

174. Local craft-beer brewers nationwide have increased their national and international market share relative to the share of long-standing major brewers. However, state regulation of craft-beer brewers differs from state to state. To further promote domestic craft-beer

breweries, Congress enacted legislation requiring a federal food-and-drug agency to promulgate uniform nationwide rules for craft-beer brewing. Before the designated agency promulgated any rules or even held any hearings to consider rulemaking, an agency official spoke publicly in favor of rules that would require brewers to pasteurize (heat) their brews for public safety. What result if a group of brewers who opposed pasteurization sued in federal court to prohibit the agency from adopting any rules require pasteurization?

A. Hold hearings and refuse an injunction on an agency showing that pasteurization is safer.
B. Hold hearings and grant an injunction on a brewer showing of other safe processes.
C. Stay the action until the agency proposes regulations and then hold hearings.
D. Dismiss the action because it does not yet present a justiciable case or controversy.

175. An undercover police officer overheard and secretly recorded a conversation between two men whom authorities later charged as co-conspirators in the illegal transport of undocumented aliens across the border. Although the recording was partly inaudible, the conversation confirmed that the two men had accepted substantial sums of money to conceal and move the aliens through customs inspections at the border. Prosecutors then called the officer at trial to testify to the conversation. If defense counsel objected to the testimony, then how should the court rule?

A. Testimony admissible because the audio recording was partly inaudible.
B. Testimony admissible because the best-evidence rule does not require the recording.
C. Testimony inadmissible because the best-evidence rule requires use of the recording.
D. Testimony inadmissible because hearsay outside of any recognized exception.

176. A minority shareholder sued a privately held corporation for shareholder oppression. The shareholder's lawyer served the summons and complaint on the corporation. Corporation counsel determined to appear for and defend the corporation despite that corporation counsel was only an infrequent litigator. Corporation counsel served an answer and affirmative defenses. The trial court then issued a scheduling order setting dates for pleading amendment, discovery cut-off, witness and exhibit lists, and dispositive motions, followed by a final pretrial conference. Corporation counsel neglected the other dates but appeared for the final pretrial conference. Which of the following best describes the consequences of corporation counsel's neglect?

A. The trial court may bar the minority shareholder from calling witnesses and offering exhibits at trial, particularly if counsel's neglect prejudiced the corporation.
B. The trial court may bar the corporation from calling witnesses and offering exhibits at trial, particularly if counsel's neglect prejudiced the minority shareholder.
C. The trial court may dismiss the lawsuit for failure of the parties to conduct discovery and notify the trial court of witnesses and exhibits in advance of trial.
D. The trial court may not impose any sanction on either the minority shareholder or privately held corporation because

scheduling orders are for parties' convenience.

177. A custodial service contracted with a health clinic to clean the clinic every night to hospital standards. A patient of the clinic contracted a serious infection that investigators traced to an examination room that the custodial service had failed to clean to hospital standards. The patient sued not only the clinic for malpractice and breach of contract but also the custodial service for breach of contract. How should the court rule on the custodial service's motion to dismiss?

A. Deny the motion on public policy because the custodial service violated hospital standards.
B. Deny the motion because the clinic intended the custodial service's promise to benefit the clinic's patients.
C. Grant the motion because the patient was only an incidental beneficiary of the custodial service's promise.
D. Grant the motion because the cleaning contract did not name the patient as a party to the contract.

178. An adult brother and sister had a close relationship in which, though they lived in separate cities, they visited one another often. Authorities arrested the brother, charging him with armed robbery of a jewelry store in which the hooded perpetrator threatened the sales clerk with a gun before taking $500 in cash and $1,000 in jewelry from the store. At trial, prosecutors called the clerk and other witnesses in efforts to identify the hooded perpetrator as the brother. In the brother's case, defense counsel called only the sister to testify to the alibi that the brother was with the sister in a distant city at the moment of the crime. The court instructed the jury that the prosecution must prove each element of the crime beyond a reasonable doubt. What if any additional instruction should the court give on the brother's alibi defense?

A. The jury must acquit if the brother's alibi evidence raises reasonable doubt.
B. The jury must acquit if it has reasonable doubt that the brother was at the store.
C. The brother must only produce sufficient evidence to establish alibi.
D. The brother need only prove alibi by preponderance of the evidence.

179. A woman determined to honor and favor her sweet adult daughter over the woman's rebel son. The woman instructed her lawyer to prepare a deed to the woman's home in her daughter's favor. The woman then executed the deed and left it with her lawyer with the oral instruction that the lawyer return the deed to the woman undelivered if the woman ever asked but otherwise to convey the deed to her daughter when the woman died. Learning of the escrowed deed from the lawyer, the daughter secretly conveyed the home to a glamorous boyfriend. The daughter died a few years later in a motor-vehicle accident, leaving her entire estate to her new husband. The woman died of grief a short while later without having further instructed the lawyer as to the return or delivery of the deed. The woman's rebel son would have received the woman's entire estate if she had died intestate, but she instead willed her entire estate to a charity. Who gets the woman's home?

A. The glamorous boyfriend through the daughter's conveyance.

B. The daughter's husband through the daughter's estate.
C. The rebel son as if the woman had died intestate.
D. The charity through the woman's will and estate.

180. A store owner suffered losses due to looting during local power outages over the course of one summer. The outages occurred during predictable peak demand times associated with hot weather and air-conditioner usage. The store owner was fed up with the looting. That winter, he purchased a gun with which to defend his store when the hot weather and power outages returned. But when he heard a warning from his trade association about store-owner liability, he decided to get a legal opinion. What would be the most appropriate counsel to the store owner about his civil liability for use of the gun to defend his store and its goods during looting?

A. To shoot in defense of the store and its goods whenever it appeared reasonable, even if mistaken.
B. To shoot in defense of the store and its goods only when genuinely necessary, understanding that there would be no excuse for mistakes whether reasonable or not.
C. Not to shoot in defense of the store and its goods unless the looters looked as if they could shoot back in their own defense.
D. Not to shoot in defense of the store and its goods.

181. Congress makes annual appropriations of federal aid to schools at all levels, through comprehensive education programs. One part of that federal aid goes to grants for public and private colleges and universities to construct new school buildings. Congress also makes those building grants available to private religious colleges and universities provided that any such grant recipient not use any part of the federal grant funds to construct any building used for instruction in religious subject matters. If a taxpayer group having standing challenged the religious-institution building grants on constitutional grounds, then what result?

A. Grants permitted because aid for secular purposes does not promote sectarian purposes.
B. Grants permitted because building construction alone does not unduly establish religion.
C. Grants not permitted because financial aid to a religious institution promotes religion.
D. Grants not permitted because building aid excessively entangles government in religion.

182. A lawyer representing an employee client in a wrongful-termination case against the employer interviewed several of the client's co-workers. One of the co-workers told the lawyer that the client-employee's supervisor had said that the employer was firing the employee because of age rather than for any misconduct or non-performance. Yet when the lawyer called the same co-worker to testify to the same information at trial, the co-worker surprised the lawyer by saying that the employer fired the employee for doing poor work. The lawyer, though, had made a secret audio recording of the co-worker's interview. Should the court admit the recording if the lawyer offers it?

A. No because the secret recording violates the co-worker's confrontation-clause rights.
B. No because the audio recording is inadmissible hearsay outside of any exception.
C. Yes but only to impeach the co-worker's credibility and not as substantive evidence.
D. Yes to impeach the co-worker's credibility and as substantive evidence of motive.

183. A grower sued a produce distributor in federal court under diversity jurisdiction for breach of contract to purchase citrus fruits. The grower's complaint alleged an amount in controversy in excess of $75,000. The distributor's answer denied liability but admitted that the grower had alleged a controversy in excess of $75,000. The federal court scheduled a Rule 16 conference at which it required representatives for both parties to attend with full authority to settle. The order setting the Rule 16 conference also indicated that the court would review jurisdiction, venue, indispensable parties, and other preliminary matters, and dismiss any claims for which there was no basis in federal court. At the Rule 16 conference, the judge learned from the parties' representatives that the amount in controversy was $50,000. Which of the following best describes the action that FRCP 16 authorizes the court to take at the Rule 16 conference to end the case?

A. Dismiss the action for lack of subject-matter jurisdiction.
B. Enter judgment for grower against distributor for $50,000.
C. Enter judgment for grower against distributor for $75,000.

D. Appoint a magistrate judge to hear dispositive motions.

184. A builder sold a new rural home to a family based on the knowing false representation that a state park surrounded the home in a manner that would leave the adjacent lands forever undeveloped. The family purchased the home out of the specific desire to live in the undeveloped wilds. Within a few months, a developer purchased adjacent lands where the developer began to bulldoze the wilds for a golf course. The golf-course development substantially increased the value of the family's new home. What result if the family promptly sues to void the contract?

A. Builder wins because a few months is too late to avoid the contract.
B. Builder wins because the family suffered no loss in monetary value.
C. Family wins because the contract was void ab initio (from its outset).
D. Family wins because the contract was voidable at the family election.

185. A driver moved without providing a forwarding address for mail. For that reason, the driver did not receive notice that his driver's license had lapsed, nor did he notice the lapse from the license itself. The driver was driving at a safe and lawful speed through a neighborhood when a child darted out from between cars and in front of the driver's vehicle. The vehicle struck and killed the child because the driver had no ability to see and avoid the child. Prosecutors charged the driver with the misdemeanor of driving without a valid license, to which the driver pled guilty. What result if prosecutors also charge the driver with misdemeanor manslaughter?

A. Not guilty because the driver lacked criminal intent.
B. Not guilty because the misdemeanor did not cause the death.
C. Guilty because not renewing the license was negligence.
D. Guilty because licenses are to ensure safe drivers.

186. An executive owned two lots overlooking the ocean, one slightly higher and behind the other. The executive built a retirement home on the higher back lot. To fund the construction, he agreed orally to sell the lower ocean-side lot to a friend who wanted beach access provided that the friend never build on the lot so as to preserve the executive's view. The executive's deed to the friend, which only the executive signed, included the grantee's covenant that neither the grantee nor successors, heirs, or assigns would build on the lot, specifically to preserve the ocean view for the higher back lot's owner and successors, heirs, and assigns. The friend accepted and recorded the deed. Years later, the executive decided to retire somewhere else and so sold the back lot and its home to a sports agent. The friend then promptly sold the vacant lot to a developer who began construction of a fabulous ocean-front home. What result if the sports agent sues to enjoin the developer's construction?

A. Developer wins because the grantee friend never signed the executive's deed.
B. Developer wins because equitable servitudes do not survive promisor conveyance.
C. Sports agent wins because equitable servitudes run with the land binding on notice.
D. Sports agent wins because the executive built before the developer bought and began.

187. A rancher maintained a large herd of cattle. Under federal regulations, the cattle were periodically tested for a rare disease. If uncontrolled, the disease could affect the beef supply in a way that would cripple the entire ranching industry. Three of the rancher's prize cows tested positive for the disease. Federal officials condemned the rancher's herd on the basis of the positive tests. The rancher was desolate that his entire herd would be lost simply because three of the cows had tested positive. He consulted a lawyer about legal rights and remedies for the condemnation of his herd. What is the most appropriate evaluation?

A. The rancher has a tort claim for conversion of the entire herd.
B. The rancher has a tort claim for conversion of the herd except the three infected cows.
C. The rancher has no tort claim because of public necessity.
D. The rancher has no tort claim because of private necessity.

188. Both chambers of a state legislature voted unanimously in favor of a bill to place a Christmas display including a nativity scene in the capitol rotunda. The scene would be on temporary public display from Thanksgiving through New Year's Day each year, alongside permanent displays of state tourism sites, state resources, and state industries. Private citizens would donate the display, which the state would then own and maintain. What result if as soon as the governor signed the Christmas-display legislation, a public-interest organization with standing filed suit in a court with jurisdiction, challenging the display's constitutionality?

A. Display held unconstitutional because the state cannot own religious displays.
B. Display held unconstitutional because not primarily celebrating a secular holiday.
C. Display held constitutional because donated by private citizens from private funds.
D. Display held constitutional because shown alongside permanent secular displays.

189. Authorities charged a financier with criminal fraud for using a get-rich-quick scheme to bilk an investor out of thousands of dollars. The scheme allegedly involved fraudulent financing of fake film ventures to reach state tax credits. At trial, in addition to presenting evidence on the specific scheme supporting the financier's charge, the prosecutor also offered evidence that the financier had once written a substantial bad check and once tried to sell a risky investment in a poorly planned time-share program. If defense counsel objects, then how should the court rule?

A. Admissible as evidence of motive, preparation, or plan.
B. Admissible as evidence of propensity for violence.
C. Inadmissible as improper character evidence.
D. Inadmissible as a subject only for cross-examination.

190. A software company licensed a program to a publisher for use at the publisher's headquarters location. When the publisher opened two additional offices in other regions, the publisher's technology manager copied the program onto computers at those new locations. When the software company discovered the copying, it sued the publisher in federal court under diversity jurisdiction. The software company claimed damages for breach of contract, conversion, and violation of federal copyright laws. The software company included a jury demand. Before the Rule 16 conference, the trial judge asked the law clerk to confirm with research which of the software company's claims the court must try to a jury and which the judge must decide. Which of the following best describes the jury and judge claims?

A. The judge should try the contract, conversion, and copyright claims, not the jury.
B. A jury should try the contract, conversion, and copyright claims, not the judge.
C. The judge should try the conversion claim but a jury the contract and copyright claims.
D. A jury should try the copyright claim but the judge the contract and conversion claims.

191. An investor formed a contract to purchase a commercial property from its owner, contingent on the investor obtaining bank financing for the purchase. The investor did not seek and therefore did not secure bank financing, when bank financing might have been available. The investor then refused to close on the purchase, citing the financing contingency. What result if the property's owner sues?

A. Investor prevails because the investor did not obtain financing.
B. Investor prevails because the contract did not require financing application.
C. Owner prevails because the law will excuse the condition to avoid forfeiture.

D. Owner prevails because the law will imply reasonable efforts to obtain financing.

192. The defendants pled mistake as to each of the following charges. On presentation of false identification, one defendant sold beer to an underage seventeen-year-old minor in violation of a state statute prohibiting that sale. Unaware that the person attempting to restrain him was an undercover federal agent trying to arrest for drug smuggling, another defendant struck and injured the agent resulting in an assault charge. Another defendant had sex with a fifteen-year-old minor who told the defendant that she was eighteen years old, resulting in a felony charge of statutory rape for sex with an underage minor. Relying on bad advice from counsel that abandonment for more than a year nullified a marriage, another defendant married a second wife before divorcing a first wife, resulting in a charge of bigamy for multiple marriages at once. As to which of these charges is mistake most likely to constitute a defense?

A. The charge of selling alcohol to an underage minor.
B. The charge of assaulting an undercover agent.
C. The charge of statutory rape for sex with an underage minor.
D. The charge of bigamy for marriage to more than one spouse at a time.

193. A developer befriended an heiress who by inheritance owned a thousand-acre parcel of prime residential-development lands with a river bisecting it. On a helicopter flight over the parcel on their way to a lavish meal, the heiress agreed to sell the developer 200 contiguous acres out of the 1,000 acres, at a price of $5,000 per acre. At the meal, the developer wrote out that agreement, which the heiress promptly signed. The agreement did not further specify the location of the 200 acres other than that the creek must cross the parcel. The heiress and developer visited the lands several more times but were unable to agree on and stake out the parcel's final location. What result if the developer sues the heiress for specific performance?

A. Developer wins because the court's equitable powers enable it to fashion relief.
B. Developer wins because the agreement required good faith in executing its terms.
C. Heiress wins because the agreement did not adequately state the purchase price.
D. Heiress wins because the agreement did not adequately describe the lands.

194. A company operated a fleet of fishing boats using practices hazardous to its fishing crews. The company's practices earned the crews substantial wages beyond those ordinarily earned by others in the same fishing industry. The crews, including those members who were injured by the practices, understood and accepted the risks. But competitor fleets and members of the local fishing community objected to the company's hazardous practices. They retained a lawyer who filed negligence claims on their behalf to stop the company's hazardous practices injuring the company's crew members. The company's lawyer filed a motion to dismiss the lawsuit. How should the court rule?

A. Deny the motion to dismiss.
B. Adjourn pending evidence of the public effect of the crews' injuries.
C. Under advisement pending research on competitive effects.
D. Grant the motion to dismiss.

195. Federal narcotics agents arrested a hairdresser for suspicion of selling illegal drugs out of the hairdresser's salon. The assistant U.S. attorney responsible for prosecuting the charge instead dismissed the charge and granted the hairdresser immunity in exchange for cooperation in an ongoing narcotics investigation. The state licensing board nonetheless notified the hairdresser to appear for a cosmetology-license revocation hearing, relying on a state licensing statute that prohibited salon use for illegal purposes. At the hearing revoking the hairdresser's license, the state's only evidence of illegal activity was a redacted affidavit from an informant whose name the state refused to disclose. What is the hairdresser's strongest constitutional argument to have the license revocation set aside and her license restored?

A. The inability to confront and cross-examine the lone witness violated due process.
B. The license-revocation proceeding denied full faith and credit to the prior dismissal.
C. Only courts, not administrative tribunals, have power to revoke employment licenses.
D. Federal regulation of narcotics preempts state proceedings based on the same conduct.

196. A client sent a confidential email to the client's lawyer instructing the lawyer to prepare a deed conveying the client's real property to the client's adult child. The client's letter further instructed the lawyer to backdate the deed to make the deed appear to have been executed before the date that a substantial new tax on property transfers took effect. The lawyer refused to backdate the deed, and so the client did so on the client's own. Tax authorities later charged the client with tax evasion for the transaction and then demanded that the lawyer produce the letter as evidence of the client's wrong. How should the court rule on the production demand?

A. Order production because the client, not the lawyer, has the privilege.
B. Order production because the client's letter attempted to further crime or fraud.
C. Deny production because of the client's privilege against self-incrimination.
D. Deny production because the client has an attorney-client privilege.

197. A female supervisor sued an employer for sex discrimination when the employer passed her over for promotion in favor of a male subordinate, after the female manager had refused the sexual advances of the plant manager. The supervisor sued in federal court under the court's federal-question jurisdiction. During jury draw, defense counsel used peremptory challenges to strike three female jurors, leaving an all-male six-member jury with two female alternates. Which of the following describes plaintiff's counsel's best strategic response?

A. Challenge the peremptory strike of female jurors, making the court constitute a jury of an equal number of male and female jurors.
B. Challenge the peremptory strike of female jurors, making defense counsel articulate non-discriminatory reasons for the strikes.
C. Argue in closing that the defense discriminated in its juror selection and that the jurors should avoid relying on sexual bias.
D. Insist that the court allow the two female alternate jurors to deliberate with the six male jurors after the close of proofs.

198. A telecommunications retailer contracted to service an accounting firm's telephone and internet systems after having sold the firm new telecommunications equipment. The retailer subsequently sold its service-contract business to a highly qualified vendor that effectively managed service contracts for multiple other retailers. The retailer assigned the accounting firm's service contract to the vendor, which effectively serviced the accounting firm's systems for an initial period of several months. The vendor then performed defectively in a way that caused substantial loss of service to the accounting firm. Which parties are liable to the accounting firm for damages associated with the loss of service?

A. Only the retailer with whom the accounting firm had a services contract.
B. Both the retailer on the contract and the vendor with the firm as third-party beneficiary.
C. Both the retailer and the vendor because either could make the accounting firm pay.
D. Only the vendor because the retailer assigned the vendor the contract.

199. An adult male runner encountered a younger female runner along a secluded country lane. They ran together for a few minutes before stopping, embracing, and then kissing. As the male runner began to undress himself and her intending to have sexual intercourse, the female runner suddenly said to stop and that she didn't want to go any farther. The male runner did not desist, though, until the female runner started to cry and then told the male runner that she was only fifteen years of age. The male runner then fled. Authorities soon indicted the male runner for attempted rape, assault with intent to rape, contributing to a minor's delinquency, and attempted statutory rape with sixteen years the age of consent. Under what circumstance could the court sustain the charge of attempted rape?

A. The court does not allow evidence of the male runner's flight.
B. The jury finds that the female runner was resisting the male runner's force seeking sex.
C. The male runner believed that the female runner was over the age of consent.
D. The jury finds the male runner not guilty of all of the other charges.

200. A conservationist borrowed money under mortgage to buy undeveloped lands to preserve before others could develop them. The lender required the conservationist to purchase standard title insurance covering both the lender and conservationist. The title insurer's search disclosed no liens, and its policy contained no exceptions. The conservationist soon paid the loan, extinguishing the mortgage. The conservationist then sold the land by full covenant and warranty deed to a nature conservancy. The nature conservancy later quitclaimed the lands by donation to a public trust. Following that conveyance, the public trust's manager discovered an unsatisfied old mortgage recorded against the lands, predating the conservationist's conveyance to the nature conservancy. The title insurer would have discovered the old mortgage if it had exercised reasonable care in its title search. On the public trust's demand, the conservationist paid the old mortgage. What result if the conservationist sues the title insurer for reimbursement?

A. Conservationist wins because the title insurer's obligation persists after sale.

B. Title insurer wins because the public trust took by quitclaim rather than warranty.
C. Title insurer wins because the conservationist conveyed away the insured title.
D. Title insurer wins because the conservationist repaid the insured lender.

B. Second MBE Practice Exam

1. Part I—Third 100 Questions (Questions 201-300)

201. A hotel had front and side entrances that were secured by card-entry systems after nightfall. The card-entry systems discouraged anyone from entering the hotel after nightfall, other than hotel guests with key cards issued for that night. In the back of one wing, the hotel had a service door that was not secured by card-entry system. The night supervisors knew about the unsecured back door. No guest had yet been hurt until a senior guest was seriously injured in the back wing by an intruder. What additional fact would increase the senior guest's likelihood of prevailing in a negligence claim against the hotel for his injuries?

A. The identity of the intruder who injured the senior guest remains unknown.
B. The hotel recently suffered several break-ins into rooms in that same wing.
C. The hotel's advertising was of a general nature not asserting anything as to security.
D. The senior guest had stayed in the hotel before on several occasions.

202. A criminal-defense lawyer arranged with a local provider to pay a significant sum for cable-television service in order to watch a televised murder trial in state court. Halfway through the state-court trial, the judge terminated the video-recording and display for disrupting the proceeding. The lawyer promptly filed suit in federal court seeking an injunction for the trial judge having deprived him of his property interest in the cable-television contract, without due process. Before the federal court could hear the lawyer's injunction action, the state-court criminal case concluded properly with the defendant's murder conviction and prompt sentencing. How if at all should the murder trial's conclusion affect the lawyer's pending federal-court action?

A. No affect until final appeal of the murder conviction, in case of remand for retrial.
B. No affect because state law would determine mootness based on state-court action.
C. Dismiss the federal action for mootness because no present or likely future controversy.
D. Proceed with the federal action to resolve an important, common constitutional question.

203. An estate sued a bar for its bouncer having killed the estate's decedent in a chokehold when attempting to eject the decedent from the bar. After the bar terminated the bouncer's employment, authorities convicted the bouncer of manslaughter for the decedent's death, despite that the bouncer testified in the criminal trial in his own defense that the bar's owner had told him to eject unruly patrons "no matter what it takes." The bouncer refused to testify at the civil trial of the estate's wrongful-death claim against the bar because the bouncer had appealed his criminal conviction. The estate thus offered in the civil trial a transcript of the bouncer's criminal-trial testimony about the owner's instruction to the bouncer. Should the court admit the transcript?

A. No because the transcript involves multiple hearsay not all within hearsay exceptions.

B. Yes because although hearsay, the transcript is former testimony.
C. Yes because the owner's instruction is not hearsay.
D. Yes because the bouncer's testimony is the statement of an agent of a party opponent.

204. A rancher sued a chainsaw manufacturer in federal court based on diversity jurisdiction. The rancher's claim was for products liability related to a personal injury that occurred while the rancher was repairing the chainsaw. The rancher maintained that the chainsaw's design was defective despite that the design met industry engineering standards. The court seated six jurors and two alternates. One of the two alternates was an engineer. At the conclusion of the proofs, the trial judge held a conference in chambers. The trial judge asked defense counsel what defense counsel preferred for deliberating jurors. Which of the following describes the best defense strategy with respect to deliberating jurors?

A. Request that both alternates deliberate, and insist on permitting a juror to dissent.
B. Request on permitting a juror to dissent, and insist that both alternates deliberate.
C. Request that both alternates deliberate, and insist on unanimity of jurors.
D. Request unanimity of jurors, and insist that both alternates deliberate.

205. A brother and sister together visited and cared for their elderly disabled father in a nursing home. When the brother left for an extended business trip, the sister told the disabled father that she was the better child of the two whom he should reward with a larger part of his assets than the brother. The father hesitated until the sister said that she, too, would stop visiting the father unless he conveyed his expensive collector car to her for only $5,000. The father agreed, completing the conveyance immediately. The father died shortly later. On what grounds could the brother best challenge the father's contract conveying his collector car to the sister?

A. Duress.
B. Lack of consideration.
C. Mistake.
D. Undue influence.

206. A chronic alcoholic developed severe and persistent hallucinations especially when drunk. Some of the hallucinations caused him to be violent, and given his declining state, sometimes the hallucinations even appeared when he was not drunk. On one particularly long and deep drinking binge, the alcoholic met a concerned neighbor at the alcoholic's door. The neighbor urged the alcoholic to get ahold of himself. As he spoke with increasing urgency, the neighbor reached forward to place a hand of concern on the alcoholic's shoulder. But in his hallucinogenic condition, the alcoholic thought that the neighbor was threatening him and so strangled the neighbor to death. What would be the best defense to a second-degree murder charge?

A. Intoxication.
B. Self-defense.
C. Insanity.
D. Absence of malice aforethought.

207. A homeowner used his $150,000 home on twin lots to finance a $50,000 business loan. The homeowner executed a

mortgage that the bank making the loan duly recorded. The homeowner later determined to borrow another $25,000 as a home-equity loan to renovate the home's kitchen. The homeowner once again executed a mortgage that the home-equity lender duly recorded. After meeting both mortgage obligations for a year, the homeowner fell ill, lost a job, and defaulted on both mortgages. The bank promptly commenced foreclosure proceedings. The homeowner and home-equity lender filed a motion showing that the mortgaged home and twin lots had increased to $200,000 in value and that the severable lot alone had a value of $75,000, enough to secure the bank fully. What result if the motion requested the court to restrict the bank's foreclosure rights to the $75,000 severable lot, over the bank's objection?

A. Motion granted because of marshalling's two-funds rule.
B. Motion granted because pro-rata foreclosure fully secures the bank.
C. Motion denied because the mortgage covered the entire property including the home.
D. Motion denied because the bank holds a purchase-money mortgage.

208. A laborer was part of a crew contracted to mow, trim vegetation, and do other maintenance alongside a busy urban road. The work required the crew to frequently cross the road with maintenance equipment. The laborer was seriously injured by a driver who had not noticed the work until it was too late to avoid the laborer. The laborer hired a lawyer to investigate a claim against the company that was responsible for the work area and had contracted the crew. Which of the following would most help the lawyer establish a standard of care for an action against that company?

A. A national standard that warning signs should have been placed around the area.
B. The driver's admission that he was uninsured, unemployed, and unlicensed.
C. Evidence that there were several close calls involving other crew members.
D. The laborer was crossing the road with a cumbersome piece of maintenance equipment.

209. A state legislature determined to increase income-tax revenue in the state by defining as income the value of any employer-supplied motor vehicle to the extent that the motor vehicle is available for the employee's personal, rather than merely employment-related, use. The federal government supplies motor vehicles to many of its federal employees, making those motor vehicles available for both personal and employment-related use. The federal government does not provide either way whether states may tax a federal employee's motor-vehicle benefit. Is the state income tax on the value of federal employees' personal motor-vehicle benefit constitutional?

A. No because the tax is effectively on the United States, from which it is immune.
B. No because the tax is primarily on employment activities for the United States.
C. Yes because the non-discriminatory tax is on employees rather than the United States.
D. Yes because exempting federal employees would deny equal protection to others.

210. Federal prosecutors charged a man with violating anti-trafficking laws relating to female minors found housed for

prostitution in a neighbor's home. At trial, the prosecutors called an undercover FBI agent to testify that when the neighbor introduced the defendant as "my partner" in the home's activities, the defendant merely shook the FBI agent's hand. Is the testimony admissible over defense counsel's objection?

A. Yes because a statement against the defendant's penal interest.
B. Yes because the defendant adopted the neighbor's statement as an admission.
C. No because prosecutors have not shown that the neighbor spoke for the defendant.
D. No because the neighbor's statement is hearsay outside of any exception.

211. A terminated teacher sued his former public-school employer for violation of due-process rights in the termination. The teacher claimed that the school did not give the teacher notice and a hearing on the grounds for termination. The teacher filed the suit in federal court under federal-question jurisdiction. The trial judge requested the parties to propose jury instructions to include in the final pretrial order. The teacher's counsel gave that task to an associate. Which of the following best describes the sources for proposed jury instructions?

A. Standard instructions adopted in the district, pattern instructions in formbooks, and special instructions based on research.
B. Standard instructions promulgated by statutes, pattern instructions promulgated by rules, and special instructions from cases.
C. The trial court's prior rulings on motions to dismiss and for summary judgment, establishing the law of the case for this trial.
D. The parties' motions, responses, and memorandum briefs, setting forth the disputed facts and applicable law for trial.

212. A creditor loaned $10,000 to a debtor for the debtor to consolidate and pay off high-interest credit-card obligations. The loan required the debtor to repay the full $10,000 within six months, the debtor expecting to sell personal property to do so. When the debtor shared that she was pregnant, the creditor had a change of heart leading to an offer to take just $7,500 in full satisfaction of the $10,000 loan obligation if the debtor paid in full within thirty days. The debtor responded that she would try to come up with the money by then. The creditor subsequently revoked the offer and demanded the full $10,000 payment at the end of the six months, when the creditor learned that the debtor was in fact not pregnant. What result if the creditor sues for the full $10,000 after the six months elapsed?

A. Debtor owes $10,000 because the debtor's response to the $7,500 offer was too indefinite to indicate assent.
B. Debtor owes $10,000 because the debtor did not get the $7,500 figure reduced to a signed writing.
C. Debtor owes $7,500 because the parties entered into an accord and satisfaction for the reduced amount.
D. Debtor owes $7,500 because the debtor accepted the reduction before the creditor revoked the offer.

213. An illegal-drug distributor wanted to eliminate a drug dealer who had not paid and who had threatened to turn in the distributor to authorities. The distributor approached an undercover agent who had infiltrated the drug distributor's network to

commit the killing for hire. The agent pretended to agree, taping that conversation and subsequent conversations in which the distributor shared plans and payment terms. In the last taped conversation, the distributor called off the whole thing because the dealer had paid up. What result if authorities charge the distributor with solicitation to commit murder?

A. Conviction because the agent agreed to commit the offense.
B. Conviction because the distributor completed the offense before cancelling the plan.
C. Acquittal because the distributor cancelled the plan before paying.
D. Acquittal because no one performed any substantial acts in furtherance.

214. A seller and buyer entered into a written, signed, contingency-free, and otherwise valid contract for the sale of a farmhouse and its farmlands. The agreement provided for a closing date within three months. The seller died suddenly and unexpectedly one month later, two months before the due date for closing. The personal representative for the seller's estate nevertheless executed a deed in the buyer's favor, placing the sale proceeds in the estate for distribution. The seller's will left all real property to a farmer daughter while leaving the estate's residue to a businessman son. If no other will provision affects the treatment of the sale proceeds, then what determines whether the farmer daughter or businessman son receives the sale proceeds?

A. Whether the probate court approved and ordered the closing of the sale.
B. Whether the applicable law follows the doctrine of equitable conversion.
C. Whether the closing date in the sale contract was before or after the seller's death.
D. Whether the will describes the farmland specifically or just all real property.

215. Through no fault of her own, a driver accidentally caused her vehicle to strike and knock over a road barrier. Road-construction crews had placed the barrier to keep vehicles from entering a construction area. The driver immediately realized that with the barrier down, other drivers would be at risk of injury from entering the construction area. The driver, a petite woman of unusually small size, did not have the strength to replace the barrier. The driver immediately called for help. Another driver was injured because of the missing barrier. That other driver sued the driver who had knocked over the barrier. Which of the following is the most accurate statement of the defendant driver's standard of care?

A. The actions of a reasonably prudent person of the defendant driver's knowledge, skill, and experience under the circumstances.
B. The actions of a reasonably prudent person of the defendant driver's physical characteristics under the circumstances.
C. The actions of a reasonably prudent person without respect to the defendant driver's physical or mental characteristics.
D. The actions of a reasonably prudent person of average height, weight, strength, knowledge, skill, and experience.

216. A city issued a taxicab operator's license to an applicant. Under the

authorizing legislation, no one is to operate a taxicab in the city without such a license. The city posted the applicant's approval to its website, giving thirty days for any member of the public to object, as the authorizing legislation also required. The legislation further provided that driving ability and knowledge of the city's streets were the only license criteria, and that city officials had the discretion to either grant or deny a hearing on any objection to a granted license. A currently licensed taxicab operator timely objected to the applicant's approval on the grounds that although the applicant was qualified, the competition would reduce the value of the operator's current license. The city refused a hearing on the operator's objection and instead finalized the applicant's approval, granting the applicant the license. What result if the current operator sues claiming that the city denied the operator due process when it refused the operator a hearing?

A. Operator prevails because due process required a hearing before the adverse effect on the operator's current license.
B. Operator prevails because the official whose action is subject to challenge must not have discretion to deny a hearing.
C. City prevails because the operator benefitted from the same licensing scheme that the operator now challenges.
D. City prevails because the licensing scheme creates no protectable property interest in freedom from competition.

217. An investor brought a civil fraud claim against four defendants in federal court. Prosecutors had convicted each of the four defendants of fraud in state-court criminal cases. In the federal civil trial against the four defendants, the trial judge admitted as evidence a different form of proof as to each of the four defendants' state-court criminal convictions. One form was a certified copy of the judgment of conviction, another the investor's own testimony when the investor was present at the conviction, another that defendant's admission to another witness of that defendant's conviction, and another by the trial judge's telephone call to the state-court clerk. Which of the four defendants has the best appeal argument that the admission of conviction was error?

A. The defendant shown convicted by certified copy of judgment of conviction.
B. The defendant shown convicted by the investor's testimony present at conviction.
C. The defendant shown convicted by admission to another witness of conviction.
D. The defendant shown convicted by the judge's telephone call to the clerk.

218. A driver in a white-out snowstorm ran her motor vehicle into a tractor-trailer that had jackknifed across both lanes of the freeway. The driver survived the crash but crouched prone on her vehicle's seat as others vehicles crashed into the pileup one after another. When the driver's serious injuries took months to heal, she accepted a settlement from the tractor-trailer company and then sued the operator of the first vehicle, a delivery truck, to strike her vehicle. At the conclusion of proofs, the trial judge met with counsel in chambers to decide on jury instructions. The trial judge adopted all of the injured driver's proposed instructions and none of the defendant's proposed instructions. Which of the following best describes what defense counsel should do regarding the trial judge's choice of instructions, several of which defense counsel believed to be erroneous?

A. Move for judgment as a matter of law, judgment notwithstanding the verdict, or new trial based on instructional error.
B. Argue to the jury in closing to disregard the erroneous instructions because they are not supported by law.
C. Object on the record to the erroneous instructions before the trial judge gives them to preserve appeal rights.
D. Ensure that defense counsel has filed rejected proposed instructions with the court to preserve appeal rights.

219. An entertainer retained a renowned chef to cater and cook at the entertainer's party celebrating the entertainer's receipt of an entertainment award. The entertainer expected prominent producers, directors, and other entertainers and artists with whom the entertainer had professional relationships to attend to enjoy the renowned chef's creations. The catering contract was silent as to either side's assignment or delegation. The renowned chef then accepted an offer to open a restaurant on another continent. In doing so, the chef sold the catering business to his longtime sous chef, assigning the sous chef the entertainer's catering contract while touting to the entertainer the sous chef's considerable skill. Must the entertainer permit the sous chef to perform the renowned chef's catering obligation?

A. Yes because the entertainer had adequate assurance of the sous chef's equivalent skill.
B. Yes because the contract included no prohibition against delegation or assignment.
C. No because the renowned chef's purported delegation constituted a contract novation.
D. No because the renowned chef's obligations were personal involving skill and taste.

220. Prosecutors charged several defendants with felony murder. One defendant committed a residential burglary that led to the homeowner's death. Another defendant committed attempted rape that led to the victim's death. Another defendant committed manslaughter, and another defendant committed arson leading to the death of a person within the building where the defendant set the fire. Which of these defendants will the court most likely acquit of the felony-murder charge?

A. Burglary.
B. Attempted rape.
C. Manslaughter.
D. Arson.

221. An elderly homeowner conveyed his home in fee simple to his caretaker. The homeowner's deed stated that the caretaker had paid $10 and other good consideration. The caretaker duly recorded the deed. A few days later, the homeowner executed and caretaker signed and accepted a trust instrument stating that the conveyance's purpose was that the caretaker hold the home in trust for the homeowner's granddaughter. No one recorded the trust. When the homeowner died shortly later, the caretaker rented out the home's main living quarters and paid the rent over to the granddaughter. A few years later, the caretaker sold the home to a young couple who had no knowledge of the trust. The young couple moved in while the caretaker moved with the market-value proceeds to warmer climates. No longer receiving rent payments, the granddaughter investigated and discovered the sale. What result if the granddaughter sues the young couple to perform the trust?

A. Young couple wins because the homeowner conveyed the home before creating the trust.
B. Young couple wins because they are bona fide purchasers who took free of the trust.
C. Granddaughter wins because parties need not record trusts creating equitable interests.
D. Granddaughter because a successor in title takes subject to the grantor's trust.

222. A contractor negotiated a snow-removal agreement with a retail store just as the snow season started. The contract began December 1st. It snowed on December 2nd. The contractor did not hire the personnel to perform the contract until December 3rd. A store customer slipped and fell on snow and ice on December 2nd, before the contractor had performed any aspect of the contract. The customer sued the contractor, whose lawyer moved to dismiss the lawsuit for no duty. How should the court rule?

A. Deny the motion.
B. Deny the motion if the contractor should have had the personnel in place already.
C. Grant the motion if the contractor is usually prudent in the performance of contracts.
D. Grant the motion.

223. In order to combat a significant increase in the distribution and sale of illegal drugs in elementary and secondary schools, Congress enacted legislation requiring states to adopt and enforce criminal laws prohibiting the distribution and sale within 1,000 feet of any such school, of controlled substances transported in interstate commerce in violation of federal laws. Several states joined in an action challenging the constitutionality of Congress's enactment. Which of the following options describes the likely outcome of the challenge?

A. Enactment held unconstitutional, Congress lacking power to compel states to adopt laws.
B. Enactment held unconstitutional, as not sufficiently related to interstate commerce.
C. Enactment held constitutional, as limited to actions affecting interstate commerce.
D. Enactment held constitutional, under Congress's power to act for general welfare.

224. Prosecutors charged a woman with murdering her on-and-off-again, adulterous boyfriend. The boyfriend had been married right up to his death by homicide. The prosecution then called the deceased boyfriend's wife as a witness at the criminal trial to testify that her husband had said to her, just the day before he died, that the defendant woman, a putative friend of his, had threatened his life. Is the wife's testimony admissible over defense counsel's objection?

A. No because hearsay and outside of any recognized exception.
B. No because inadmissible character evidence of a prior bad act.
C. Yes because an admission by a party opponent.
D. Yes because showing the defendant's state of mind.

225. An equipment-finance company leased a programmable die-cutting machine to an industrial manufacturer. The industrial manufacturer missed making several consecutive monthly lease payments before

filing for bankruptcy reorganization. The bankruptcy stay barred the finance company's action against the industrial manufacturer. So the equipment-finance company sued the industrial manufacturer's corporate parent instead. The finance company's answers to the corporate parent's admission requests confirmed that the finance company's only agreement was with the corporate parent's bankrupt industrial-manufacturer subsidiary. Which of the following describes the action defense counsel should take to bring the lawsuit to its earliest conclusion?

A. Request facilitative mediation.
B. Move to lift the bankruptcy stay.
C. File a motion for summary judgment.
D. Offer to assume the lease payments.

226. A cabinetmaker supplied custom furniture to an interior designer at a contract price of $12,500. The furniture met all contract specifications of the written contract terms. The designer mistakenly claimed that the furniture did not meet certain specifications. The designer proposed that the cabinetmaker accept $10,000 in full payment of the $12,500 contract amount. The cabinetmaker accepted, and the designer promptly paid the $10,000. What result if the cabinetmaker later sued the designer for the $2,500 contract balance?

A. Cabinetmaker prevails because the $10,000 payment was not additional consideration for the reduced obligation.
B. Cabinetmaker prevails because an oral agreement cannot modify the terms of a written contract.
C. Designer prevails because the cabinetmaker's acceptance of the $10,000 payment satisfied the accord.
D. Designer prevails because the cabinetmaker's acceptance of the $10,000 payment fulfilled a novation.

227. A hooded man robbed a teller of bank funds at the deposit window. Detectives believed that the robber may have been the same one who had robbed several other area banks in similar fashion. The detectives had obtained fingerprints and surveillance photographs of the suspect, from which they apprehended the suspect. A detective then showed the bank teller the mug shot of the recently arrested suspected robber, asking the teller whether the photograph depicted the suspect who robbed the teller. When the teller paused, the detective added that they were confident that the mug shot showed the robber. The teller then agreed. Prosecutors then indicted the suspected robber. If defense counsel moves to suppress the trial testimony of the teller as to the suspected robber's identification, then how should the court rule?

A. Grant the motion because the out-of-court identification tainted any in-court testimony.
B. Grant the motion unless the prosecution shows that in-court identification is reliable.
C. Deny the motion because the out-of-court identification was permissible preliminarily.
D. Deny the motion as tainted out-of-court identification doesn't bar in-court testimony.

228. A brother owned a rarely used resort vacation home on a golf course. His beloved sister visited the home often, calling it her own home. Facing financial difficulty, the sister secretly purported to convey the home to a buyer for valuable consideration.

The buyer recorded the sister's warranty deed in which the sister reserved an estate in the home for three years. The brother died two years later leaving the home to his beloved sister a deed for which the personal representative of the brother's estate promptly executed and recorded. Six months later, the sister purported to convey the home again to an unsuspecting friend for valuable consideration. The friend recorded the sister's warranty deed and then took possession of the home, moving in. The friend and buyer were surprised to meet one another at the home a few months later when the sister's three-year estate would have ended. What would be the grounds if litigation between them to quiet title resulted in a win for the friend and loss for the buyer?

A. The buyer's deed was not in the friend's chain of title.
B. The friend was first in possession of the home.
C. The sister's deed to the buyer took effect after her deed to her friend.
D. The sister had nothing to convey to the buyer.

229. A farmer maintained her crops using a large tractor. The large tractor had the tires and engine power to enter the fields at all times of year including when they were flooded from heavy rains, melting snow, and runoff. A gardener who lived next door to the farmer maintained his gardens with a small garden tractor and several pieces of associated small equipment. The gardens flooded severely early one spring, endangering the gardener's equipment. The farmer could have saved the gardener's equipment using the farmer's large tractor. What additional facts would be necessary for the farmer to be liable to the gardener for the loss of the gardener's equipment?

A. No additional facts.
B. The gardener asked the farmer to save the equipment, but the farmer declined without offering a reason.
C. The farmer knew that the gardener was detrimentally relying on the farmer's offer to save the equipment.
D. The gardener and farmer were old friends who often helped one another on the farm and in the garden.

230. Vaccinations under state child-health programs have declined significantly in recent times. To combat the recurrence and spread of serious childhood diseases readily controlled by vaccination, the president contemplated using funds that Congress had appropriated generally to the president's office to initiate a national health campaign urging vaccination of children. Congress has neither specifically nor expressly authorized the president to implement the contemplated program. Would the president have constitutional authority to act as contemplated?

A. Yes because of the president's plenary authority to act for general health, safety, and welfare.
B. Yes because the Constitution vests the president with executive authority not prohibited by federal statute.
C. No because the states hold traditional authority under the Tenth Amendment for family and child welfare.
D. No because Congress has not authorized the president's use of funds and office for such a national program.

231. A wife sued a husband for divorce. The parties tried the case to the bench to resolve child-custody and property-division issues. The trial judge refused the wife's

counsel's request to sequester the husband's witnesses from the courtroom during the wife's case in chief. The judge then allowed the husband's counsel to ask cross-examination questions of one of the wife's witnesses that went well beyond what the wife's counsel had covered on direct examination. The judge also let the husband's counsel cross-examine the witness on questions of the witness's credibility even though the wife's counsel had not sought on direct examination to endorse the witness's credibility. The judge later refused to allow the wife's counsel to cross-examine the wife's close sister using leading questions, when the husband called the sister as an adverse witness. If the wife appeals the judgment arguing each of these rulings as error, then which is the appellate court most likely to agree was error?

A. Refusing to sequester witnesses.
B. Cross-examination beyond the scope of direct.
C. Cross-examination on credibility despite no direct endorsing credibility.
D. Refusal to allow leading questions on cross-examination.

232. The buyer of a print-shop business sued the seller for allegedly misrepresenting the age and working condition of several pieces of printing equipment and the gross receipts of the business in the presence of a business broker. The seller filed a motion for summary judgment, supporting it with the seller's affidavit and an affidavit from the business broker. Both affidavits denied that the seller had made any statements whatsoever regarding the equipment or receipts. The buyer opposed the motion with an affidavit repeating the allegations and contradicting the seller's and broker's affidavits. Which of the following best describes how the court should evaluate and rule on the motion?

A. Disregard the affidavits because they cancel out, and require additional evidence.
B. Weigh the affidavits giving each witness equal credibility, and grant the motion.
C. View the affidavits in the light most favorable to the seller, and grant the motion.
D. View the affidavits in the light most favorable to the buyer, and deny the motion.

233. An entrepreneur hired a builder to renovate abandoned storefront retail location as a new business incubator and co-working space. The parties entered into a $200,000 contract in which the builder expected to incur $180,000 in labor and materials while realizing a $20,000 profit. The entrepreneur subsequently canceled the contract after the builder had spent $50,000 on labor and materials. The builder was able to use $10,000 of the materials on another job. How much would be the most that the builder could recover in a breach-of-contract action against the entrepreneur?

A. $70,000 representing the $50,000 spent on labor and materials plus the $20,000 profit.
B. $60,000 representing the $50,000 spent on labor and materials plus the $20,000 profit less the $10,000 in materials used on another job.
C. $50,000 representing the amount spent on labor and materials.
D. $40,000 representing the reasonable value of services provided.

234. Prosecutors charged a gang leader with conspiracy to commit murder. The judge held a preliminary hearing at which the prosecution called five witnesses whose

testimony was vague and contradictory. As a result, the judge ruled that the prosecution had not established probable cause to support the charge. After the judge dismissed the charge, the prosecution convened a grand jury at which the prosecution called the same five witnesses who testified in the preliminary hearing. The grand jury indicted the gang leader for the same charge of conspiracy to commit murder. What result if defense counsel moves to quash the indictment arguing the gang leader's double-jeopardy rights?

A. Motion denied because no prior conviction or acquittal.
B. Motion denied because defendant has not yet faced jeopardy of conviction.
C. Motion granted unless the prosecution presented newly discovered evidence.
D. Motion granted because the first dismissal on the merits bars the same charge.

235. A debtor owing $60,000 to a creditor inherited three contiguous vacant lots each having a $15,000 value for a total $45,000 total value. To pay down his debt, the debtor mortgaged all three lots to a bank in exchange for a $45,000 loan reflecting the mortgaged lots' full market value. The debtor used the $45,000 loan proceeds to pay the $60,000 debt down to $15,000. The debtor then forged and recorded the bank's mortgage release for one of the three lots in order to sell the released lot to an unsuspecting buyer. Relying on the forged release, the buyer paid the debtor the lot's full $15,000 value, recording the debtor's warranty deed under a recording act that protected bona fide purchasers without notice. The debtor used the $15,000 proceeds to pay off his debt, and then promptly skipped town. The bank and lot's buyer together soon discovered the debtor's forgery. What result if the bank and lot's buyer litigate whether the bank has a mortgage on the buyer's lot or the buyer owns the lot free of the bank's mortgage?

A. Bank wins because the debtor's forgery was ineffective to remove the mortgage.
B. Bank wins because the buyer should have discovered the forgery after reasonable inquiry.
C. Buyer wins because the buyer relied on the recorded release under the recording act.
D. Buyer wins because the bank should have discovered the recording of the forged release.

236. A boat captain negligently rammed the boat into bridge pilings. The bridge was closed to vehicular traffic for three days while the pilings were repaired. A manufacturer's outlet store near one end of the bridge had virtually no sales for the three days that the bridge was closed. The store usually had brisk sales that time of year. The manufacturer's chief operating officer sought advice from a lawyer regarding whether the manufacturer could sue the boat captain and company for negligence to recover the lost sales. Which of the following is the best evaluation?

A. The manufacturer has a claim.
B. The manufacturer has no claim.
C. The manufacturer has a claim only if the lost sales can be proven to a certainty.
D. The manufacturer has no claim unless the captain knew sales would be lost.

237. Congressional leadership vowed a new attack on racial discrimination in housing, employment, and education,

particularly against Americans of African descent. One proposal sought to punish conspiracies of two or more persons intending because of another's African race to deny the right to contract for housing, employment, or education. Which constitutional provision provides the strongest and clearest support for such a measure?

A. Article I, Section 10's obligation-of-contracts clause.
B. Article I, Section 8's general-welfare clause.
C. The Thirteenth Amendment's badges-and-incidents clause.
D. The Fourteenth Amendment's due-process clause.

238. A federal bankruptcy judge enjoined the debtor's former business partner from having any contact with the debtor after the debtor showed that the former business partner had harassed and threatened the debtor to extort property from the debtor's bankruptcy estate. The judge later held a contempt proceeding against the partner at which the debtor offered to testify that he received a call from someone with an accent just like the partner, threatening the debtor with bodily harm if the debtor did not release bankruptcy-estate property to the partner. The debtor, who recorded the call but did not bring the recording to court, believes that the partner made the call but could not to a certainty identify the partner's voice, which the debtor felt that the caller was distorting to conceal identity. Should the judge admit the debtor's testimony?

A. No because the debtor cannot positively identify the caller.
B. No because the call recording is the best evidence of the caller's identity.

C. Yes because the rules of evidence do not apply in contempt or bankruptcy proceedings.
D. Yes because the debtor's uncertainty goes to weight rather than admissibility.

239. A patient suffered serious, life-threatening infections following exploratory abdominal surgery. The infections so severely scarred the patient's abdominal region that the patient had severe pain and mild organ dysfunction. The patient sued the hospital for causing the infection. At trial, the patient called as an expert witness the surgeon who performed the surgery. The surgeon testified that she had never had an infection from a similar surgery when performed at the other hospitals where the surgeon had privileges. At the close of the patient's proofs, the hospital's counsel determined that the patient had not with the requisite expert testimony established the hospital's standard of care and breach of the standard. Which of the following best describes the action that the hospital's counsel can take to end the lawsuit in the hospital's favor?

A. Offer the patient a nominal settlement.
B. Request a jury instruction on the standard of care.
C. Move for new trial.
D. Move for judgment as a matter of law.

240. A landowner agreed to sell her land to a speculator. The landowner and speculator both signed a memorandum adequately describing the land, stating the type of deed that the landowner would convey, and providing for a closing date. The memorandum contained no conditions or contingencies. While the memorandum

did not include the land's sale price, the landowner will testify that the landowner and speculator agreed on a $250,000 purchase price just before they signed the memorandum. Does the landowner have an enforceable contract?

A. Yes because the landowner's testimony supplies the only missing written term.
B. Yes because the written memorandum adequately implies a market-value price.
C. No because the evidence does not show that $250,000 is a market-value price.
D. No because the signed memorandum lacked the price as an essential term.

241. A shooting occurred in the street where several eyewitnesses identified the fleeing suspect. Police soon obtained a warrant for the suspect's arrest for the shooting. Acting on information that the suspect was holed up in a certain private residence, the police waited until the middle of the night to quietly enter the residence's bedroom and with guns drawn awaken the sleeping suspect. When the suspect asked what they were doing, one officer replied that "we've got you now." A second officer asked if the suspect had committed the shooting, to which the startled and confused suspect promptly confessed. The first officer then told the suspect that he was under arrest. If authorities charge the suspect with the shooting crime, then what is the suspect's best argument for suppressing his confession?

A. His confession was involuntary rather than voluntary.
B. His confession came before he had his *Miranda* rights.
C. Police only told him of his arrest after his confession.
D. Police did not have a search warrant to enter the residence.

242. A retiring rancher conveyed fee-simple title to his ranch for valuable consideration to an outdoorsman "and his heirs" by warranty deed. The outdoorsman had a single adult son. A few years later, the outdoorsman conveyed fee-simple title to the ranch, for valuable consideration, to a cattleman, by warranty deed that only the outdoorsman, and not his son, signed. The cattleman was an unmarried and childless bachelor. Soon after the outdoorsman's conveyance to the cattleman, the outdoorsman died leaving his adult son as his only heir. Who now holds fee title to the ranch?

A. The cattleman in fee simple because of the outdoorsman's deed.
B. The adult son because the cattleman's life estate ended with the outdoorsman's death.
C. The adult son and cattleman as joint tenants because both survived the outdoorsman.
D. The adult son and cattleman as tenants in common with equal shares.

243. A mother was tossing a softball in the yard with her daughter when a car careened into the yard and struck and seriously injured the daughter. Police investigating the incident determined that the car's drunk driver had been speeding. Mother and daughter sued the drunk driver, whose lawyer moved to dismiss the mother's claim. Which of the following would be the most likely additional fact to affect the court's ruling on the motion?

A. The mother was so upset over witnessing her daughter's serious

injury that she had to get psychological help for her nightmares and medical care for her gastric distress.
B. The mother was so upset over witnessing her daughter's serious injury that she threatened to harm the drunk driver if he was not criminally convicted for the incident.
C. The mother and daughter were so socially and emotionally close that they were often seen together and mistaken for sisters.
D. The daughter was so severely distressed by her serious injury that she needed the mother's love, society, and companionship more than the usual daughter.

244. Responding to demographic studies showing significant long-term negative impacts on social-welfare programs from a decline in birth rates, a state enacted legislation limiting abortions after the first trimester to cases in which a physician had determined that the pregnancy threatened the woman's life or health. Abortions on demand would be available only during the first trimester. What result if a public-interest organization with standing raised a constitutional challenge to the enactment?

A. Held constitutional because of the state's rational basis for striking a balance between the compelling state interest of protecting fetal life and the woman's fundamental privacy right.
B. Held constitutional because after the first trimester states may recognize a fetus as a person protectable under the Fourteenth Amendment's due-process clause.
C. Held unconstitutional because the state has burdened unduly a woman's fundamental privacy right before fetal viability, without adequate justification.
D. Held unconstitutional because the statute arbitrarily treats women and unborn children differently, with inadequate distinction in conditions by trimester.

245. A steel supplier entered into a requirements contract with a construction contractor building a new office tower. The contract provided for a fluctuating market price but required the supplier to notify the contractor at the time of each change, whether increase or decrease, in that price. When the contractor did not pay for the last several steel shipments, the supplier sued. At trial, the supplier offered as evidence the testimony of its billing manager that the manager maintained a regular practice of notifying of price changes. The supplier also offered file copies of the mailed notices showing each price change. Are the letter copies admissible on the issue of notice to the contractor?

A. No because not the best evidence of notice.
B. No because hearsay not within any exception.
C. Yes because showing the supplier's routine practice.
D. Yes because business records within that hearsay exception.

246. A commodities broker sold several carloads of grain to a cereal company. When the cereal company failed to pay, the commodities broker brought suit in federal court under diversity jurisdiction. At trial, the commodities broker put on proofs showing the terms of the contract and that the broker had delivered the grain on time to the right destination. The broker then rested. For its case in chief, the cereal company produced some testimony that the grain did not meet all of its standards. When

the cereal company rested, the broker moved for judgment as a matter of law, but the court denied the motion. For its rebuttal case, the broker showed that the cereal company used all of the carloads of grain in the same processes that it used other carloads of grain purchased from other brokers, and that it sold the grain product for the same price. The cereal company put on no rebuttal case. The jury returned a no-cause verdict against the commodities broker and in favor of the cereal company. Which of the following best describes the procedural action that the broker may take to reverse the outcome?

A. Move for mistrial and new trial, and if necessary challenge on appeal adverse rulings on the motions.
B. Move for judgment as a matter of law after trial and challenge on appeal adverse rulings on the motions.
C. Move to compel arbitration given the unfavorable judicial forum and the greater likelihood of prevailing.
D. Offer to settle the claim for a substantial discount in lieu of an appeal, which is unlikely to succeed.

247. A demolition company promised a city in a single contract to demolition three abandoned homes for $5,000 each. The contract provided that the city was to pay the demolition company the $15,000 contract total when the company completed demolition of all three homes. The demolition company demolished the first home without payment request but demanded $10,000 after demolishing the second home and before beginning work on the third home. Must the city pay the demolition company $10,000 as demanded?

A. Yes because the contract has three divisible parts each for $5,000.
B. Yes because the demolition company has substantially performed.
C. No because the contract specified payment after completing all work.
D. No because the demolition company made no demand after the first home.

248. Authorities arrested a suspect for a brutal kidnapping, torture, and murder, charging the suspect with first-degree murder. State law provided that the charge involved a capital offense for which the only penalties were either death or life in prison without possibility of parole. At trial, four prospective jurors responded to the prosecutor's questioning during jury selection that they opposed the death penalty and were unlikely to be able to vote for it in the case. Over defense counsel's objection, the trial judge removed the four jurors on the prosecution's challenges for cause. Trial resulted in conviction and, in a separate sentencing phase, death sentence. What result if the defendant appeals on the sole ground that the prosecutor's removal of the four jurors denied him the constitutional right to a representative jury?

A. Reverse both the conviction and the death sentence.
B. Affirm the conviction but remand for a sentencing hearing before a new jury.
C. Affirm the conviction but remand for sentencing to life in prison without parole.
D. Affirm both the conviction and the death sentence.

249. A cabin owner had access to his land and cabin from a dirt road but wanted access instead to a paved road nearby, both for ease of use and to increase the cabin's value. The cabin owner negotiated with the neighbor for a driveway easement across the neighbor's land and out to the paved road.

For valuable consideration, the neighbor signed and delivered to the cabin owner a written driveway easement, one that the cabin owner did not record. The cabin owner promptly completed the driveway. The neighbor then mortgaged his property to borrow money from a bank to construct his own cabin. The bank promptly recorded the neighbor's mortgage. Learning of the neighbor's plans, the cabin owner recorded the driveway easement. The neighbor decided not to build a cabin and instead defaulted on the loan and absconded with the loan money. The bank filed suit to foreclose on the mortgage to recover the defaulted loan from the sale of the neighbor's land, in doing so seeking to extinguish the cabin owner's easement. What would be the strongest grounds on which the court would preserve the easement?

A. The bank had notice or constructive notice of the cabin owner's driveway use.
B. The driveway easement was appurtenant and attached to the neighbor's land.
C. The driveway easement was necessary for access to a paved public road.
D. The cabin owner's recording before the foreclosure action protects the easement right.

250. A shopper was inspecting the baking goods on the shelves of a grocery store. The shopper did not notice that cooking oil had leaked from one of the goods onto the aisle floor. The shopper slipped and fell in the oil, injuring herself. The shopper retained a lawyer who filed a negligence action against the grocery store. The grocery store's counsel moved to dismiss the action for no evidence of breach of duty. Which of the following facts should the shopper's lawyer offer as evidence of breach?

A. The oil on the floor appeared from its stickiness to have evaporated in part.
B. The shopper had never slipped and fallen before in any other store.
C. The grocery store had several clerks on duty at the time the shopper fell.
D. The grocery store had wet-floor signs posted near the entrance to the store.

251. Two minority candidates won election to a five-member drain commission that employed a signficiant-size staff and entered into many substantial contracts. The commission's work did not involve any federal contracting. At the commission's first meeting after the election, the two new minority commissioners and a third commissioner adopted by majority vote rules that required the commission to set aside 25% of all staff positions for minority hires and 25% of all contracts for minority-owned contractors. Although the drain commission had not discriminated against minorities in the past, the majority's stated purpose in adopting the set asides was to redress historical discrimination against minority groups in this country. What result if residents with standing challenged the constitutionality of the set asides?

A. Held unconstitutional in violation of equal protection of the laws.
B. Held unconstitutional as impairing the right to contract.
C. Held constitutional as assuring minorities equal protection of the laws.
D. Held constitutional because drain commissions are proprietary rather than governmental.

252. Federal prosecutors charged a protester in federal court with damaging a federal nuclear facility. The protester pled

not guilty, her counsel disputing the prosecution's evidence of her identification at the scene. At trial, the prosecution called several witnesses who identified the masked protester's clothing at the scene. The prosecution then called the protester's husband to testify as to the clothing that the protester wore when she left the house the morning of the protest. Both the protester and husband objected to the husband testifying. May the trial judge hold the husband in contempt of court if the husband refuses to testify?

A. No because the husband has a marital privilege not to testify against his wife.
B. No because the wife has a marital privilege to prevent the husband from testifying.
C. Yes because the husband's observation of the wife's clothing is not a communication.
D. Yes because the marital privilege does not apply in criminal cases and to contempt.

253. A pickup truck driver collided with a bicyclist at a stop sign, causing the bicyclist a traumatic brain injury. The bicyclist sued the driver for negligence, after the bicyclist's brain injury prevented the bicyclist from returning to work as a carpenter. At trial, the bicyclist presented the testimony of the bicyclist's treating neuropsychologist to the bicyclist's work disability based on extensive testing of the bicyclist's brain injury. The driver's counsel did not cross-examine the neuropsychologist, challenge the expert's qualifications, or present any contrary evidence regarding brain injury. In closing argument, the driver's counsel attacked the neuropsychologist as an unqualified quack practicing voodoo medicine, a prostitute testifying for money, and a hired gun for plaintiffs. The jury returned a no-cause verdict. Which of the following best describes the immediate action that the bicyclist's lawyer can take to address the effect of defense counsel's closing argument?

A. File a grievance alleging counsel's ethics violations.
B. Retain and call a more-qualified neuropsychologist.
C. Move for new trial based on misconduct by counsel.
D. Appeal the adverse verdict based on party misconduct.

254. A popular outdoor-dining restaurant placed placards in its order window indicating that any customer who placed an order and then had to wait more than twenty minutes for the restaurant to fill the order would get the meal free. Several customers placed orders one evening and began waiting. The restaurant's manager removed the twenty-minute-wait, free-meal placard from the window when cooking delays made it appear that the restaurant would be unable to fill within twenty minutes the waiting customers' orders. The restaurant filled the orders only after a half-hour wait. What result if the waiting customers complain, showing that they had read and relied on the placard before its removal?

A. Customers prevail because their placing orders and waiting notified of acceptance.
B. Customers prevail because placing orders and waiting commenced performance.
C. Restaurant prevails because it revoked the offer before the customers performed.

D. Restaurant prevails because its placard was a non-binding statement of gift.

255. Narcotics agents guessed that a business consultant was selling cocaine but had no firm evidence. One of the agents secretly entered the consultant's office when the consultant was out of town. The agent discovered there a bank-deposit bag filled with thousands of dollars in cash along with a list of names and telephone numbers. The agent left the deposit bag after taking a photograph of the list. Agents then used the names and numbers to interview witnesses who confirmed the agents' suspicions and described how the consultant made his cocaine sales. Using the latter information, an undercover agent tricked the consultant at a business networking event into bragging about his cocaine-sales ring. A grand jury returned an indictment on this information. What result if the consultant moves to dismiss the indictment based on violations of the consultant's constitutional rights?

A. Granted because an agent violated the consultant's right to counsel.
B. Granted because an agent made an unlawful search of the consultant's office.
C. Granted because much of the agents' testimony must have been inadmissible hearsay.
D. Denied because the indictment's dismissal is not the remedy.

256. Forty years ago, a landowner divided a large parcel of land in half, getting local-government approval to develop one half for residential housing and the other half for commercial use. The landowner duly recorded plats for each property that included the government-approved development plans, one development for commercial and one development for residential. The residential development contained over two-hundred individual lots that the landowner promptly sold under deeds that referenced the plat's single-family, residential restrictions as binding on grantees and their heirs and assigns. The express restrictions, though, were to last for only thirty years. Those thirty years passed. What result if an original homeowner in the residential development sued, seeking approval to convert to a commercial use?

A. Homeowner wins because the deed restrictions expired but must comply with zoning.
B. Homeowner wins because the deed restrictions expired and need not comply with zoning.
C. Homeowner loses to residential lot owners asserting an implied reciprocal servitude.
D. Homeowner loses because homeowner took the property while still restricted.

257. A vehicle owner had the vehicle's tires rotated by an experienced mechanic. On the owner's way home from the mechanic's shop, the vehicle's wheels fell off causing an accident that injured the owner. Damage to the vehicle left it unclear why the wheel had come off. The vehicle owner consulted a lawyer regarding whether the owner had a negligence claim against the mechanic. Which of the following is the best evaluation?

A. No claim because no duty.
B. No claim because no breach.
C. Plausible claim.
D. Certain liability.

258. To spur innovation in public programs, Congress substantially increased

grant-in-aid programs that required states to compete for federal funds. To provide a forum for states to air their concerns over losing out on those funds, Congress enacted a statute granting federal courts jurisdiction to hear disagreements over funding decisions, enter judgments on those decisions, and transmit the judgments to the federal-agency head for consideration in whether to adjust the funding. Is the statute constitutional?

A. Yes because disagreements over federal funds raise federal questions within the judicial powers.
B. Yes because congressional appropriation of funds necessarily includes authority to settle funding disputes.
C. No because a federal-court judgment in such cases would offend the Eleventh Amendment.
D. No because the statute would vest authority in a federal court to make an advisory opinion.

259. Authorities charged a man with the sexual assault of a woman. At the trial of the case, the prosecutor offered evidence that the man had committed a prior similar sexual assault, as proof on the contested issue of whether the man had the strength and ability to accomplish the charged assault. In contradiction, the man's defense counsel offered evidence that the woman had a character for promiscuousness and had consented to sex with the man on several prior occasions and the occasion of the charge. Which of this evidence is admissible over objection?

A. The prior similar sexual assault only and not the promiscuousness or prior consent.
B. The prior similar sexual assault and prior consent but not the promiscuousness.
C. The prior consent and promiscuousness but not the prior similar sexual assault.
D. The prior consent but not the promiscuousness or prior similar sexual assault.

260. Adjoining landowners disputed whether one landowner had in a series of parcel swaps granted the other landowner a vehicular-access easement that substantially increased the value of that landowner's lands. The landowner who claimed the easement produced and recorded a document purportedly signed by the other landowner to that effect. The trial of the case resulted in a verdict and judgment for that landowner claiming the easement, even though the other landowner maintained throughout that the easement document was a fake. Eight months later, the losing landowner located the notary who had purportedly notarized the landowner's signature on the easement document. The notary signed an affidavit that the notary's signature was a forgery and the notarization a fake. Which of the following best describes the losing landowner's recourse based on the notary's affidavit?

A. No recourse because the case concluded forever with a final judgment.
B. File a new action against the winning landowner challenging the old judgment.
C. Move to set aside the judgment for newly discovered evidence of fraud.
D. Move for judgment as a matter of law based on the notary's affidavit.

261. A college student married her high-school sweetheart, a young man whom the college student's mother despised. Near her college graduation, the student gained acceptance to medical school but was deeply

concerned about the substantial cost, which she and her sweetheart husband would have to finance with borrowing. The student's mother offered to pay for her daughter's medical education if her daughter would divorce her young husband. The daughter agreed, going through with the divorce after she and her mother signed a contract documenting their agreement. The mother paid for the daughter's first year of medical school but then died, leaving a substantial estate the executor of which refused to continue the medical-school tuition payments. What result if the daughter sues her mother's estate for the balance of her medical education?

A. Daughter prevails because she relied to her detriment on the mother's promise.
B. Daughter prevails because the parties signed a writing satisfying the statute of frauds.
C. Estate prevails because the mother died before performing the contract.
D. Estate prevails because the contract is unenforceable as against public policy

262. Prosecutors indicted a defendant for a sexual assault and murder that had occurred years earlier and for which investigators had long sought charges. Defense counsel filed a motion to dismiss based on alleged prejudice in the delay in charges. At arraignment, though, the defendant indicated through counsel that he was pleading guilty to the charges. The trial judge then inquired and confirmed on the record that the defendant understood the charges and possible defenses, and the maximum sentence, after having had the benefit of counsel. The judge also confirmed that the defendant understood that he need not plead guilty. After accepting the plea and finding the defendant guilty as charged, the judge sentenced the defendant to 25 years. Which of the following provides the strongest constitutional basis for setting aside the plea?

A. The judge did not confirm that the prosecutor had disclosed all exculpatory evidence.
B. The judge failed to confirm that the defendant knew he was waiving a jury-trial right.
C. The judge did not inquire into and confirm the factual basis for the guilty plea.
D. The judge did not rule on the pending motion to dismiss for unreasonable delay.

263. A retailer owned land along a public highway. The owner of a salvage yard behind the retailer's land negotiated with the retailer for a right of way for ingress and egress across the retailer's land. The salvage yard had other access from a side street, but the right of way across the retailer's land was significantly more convenient. The salvage-yard owner duly recorded the retailer's deed that expressly granted the right of way to the salvage-yard owner "and successors, heirs, and assigns." The deed did not include a description of the right of way's specific location across the retailer's land. The retailer and salvage-yard owner agreed on a route that the salvage-yard owner then used for five years. The salvage-yard owner then sold the business and land to a new owner. The retailer also sold to an investor who demanded that the new salvage-yard owner move the right-of-way route to a different but reasonable alternative location on the investor's land. What result if the new salvage-yard owner refuses and the investor sues to either terminate or move the right of way?

A. Investor loses because the deed granted the right of way, and use defined it.

B. Investor loses because successive use fixed the right of way's location by prescription.
C. Investor wins but only on moving the right of way to the proposed reasonable location.
D. Investor wins and the right of way is extinguished for lack of its location description.

264. A lawyer presented the plaintiff's proofs in a motor-vehicle negligence case involving a rear-end collision. The lawyer's only witness as to duty and breach was a police officer who testified to the violation of a statute requiring drivers to maintain an assured clear distance ahead. The defense lawyer moved for a directed verdict at the close of the plaintiff's proofs. What should the plaintiff's lawyer argue in response?

A. A police officer is the most credible witness available to any plaintiff, and the court must give such an impressive witness great deference.
B. The police officer was the only witness available to this plaintiff, and the court must respect that the plaintiff was at a loss to provide other evidence.
C. Courts construe the violation of a safety statute as evidence that the defendant must have done something wrong, which means that the defendant automatically loses.
D. Courts construe the violation of a safety statute as negligence per se or allow a presumption or inference of negligence, which satisfy the plaintiff's burden of production.

265. An intelligence consultant had a long-term contract with the U.S. Department of State to provide intelligence information on a war-torn foreign disputed territory. The contract included a termination clause in the event that the U.S. president recognized a new sovereign government over the territory with which the United States entered into diplomatic relations. A military-officer dictator seized control of the territory and declared a new country, which the U.S. president then recognized and with which the United States entered into diplomatic relations. Having lost the consulting contract, the intelligence consultant sued the president and secretary of state in an appropriate federal court, challenging the new country's recognition as contrary to the laws of a democratic republic. How should the court treat the action?

A. Dismiss the suit for the consultant's lack of standing.
B. Dismiss the suit for lack of adversity between the consultant and defendant parties.
C. Dismiss the suit as presenting a non-justiciable political question.
D. Proceed to hear and decide the suit on its merits.

266. A motorcyclist crashed and suffered serious injury trying to avoid running into a motor vehicle whose driver pulled out suddenly from a stop sign into the motorcyclist's path. At the trial of the motorcyclist's negligence claim against the driver, the motorcyclist testified to his safe 45 mile-per-hour speed just before the crash. In defense, the driver estimated the motorcyclist's speed as an unsafe and excessive 65 miles per hour. In rebuttal, the motorcyclist prepared to offer the testimony of a police officer trained and experienced in estimating speeds that the motorcyclist was going only 45 miles per hour, based on skid and slide marks examined at the scene.

Should the trial judge admit the officer's testimony?

A. Yes because the jury already has the motorcyclist's own first-hand testimony as to speed.
B. Yes because the officer has the skill, method, and basis to qualify the opinion as expert.
C. No because the officer cannot qualify the opinion as having the requisite scientific basis.
D. No because an issue cannot have first-hand, lay-opinion, and expert-opinion testimony.

267. A drill-press operator lost her scalp when her hair got caught in the drill bit. She sued the drill-press manufacturer for negligent design and failure to warn. The trial judge denied the manufacturer's summary judgment motion but indicated that there were serious doubts that there was a negligent-design claim. The parties tried the case. At the close of proofs, defense counsel moved for judgment as a matter of law on the operator's negligent-design claim. The trial judge denied the motion but again indicated strong reservations about the claim. The trial judge then requested counsel to submit proposed jury instructions and verdict form. Which of the following best describes how defense counsel can ensure trial and appellate review of the verdict on the operator's negligent-design claim?

A. Request an instruction to evaluate the negligent-design claim closely for lack of evidence.
B. Move for new trial after an adverse verdict, based on the insufficiency of the evidence.
C. Propose a general verdict form with one question covering both of the operator's claims.
D. Propose a special verdict form with a separate question for the negligent-design claim.

268. A small developer skilled in urban renewal purchased and began renovating a decrepit building. Impressed with the developer's work, the owner of a neighboring vacant lot agreed to gift the lot to the developer so that the developer could have parking for the renovated building. Before the owner deeded the lot over to the developer, the developer cleared the lot of refuse and paid to have it graded and covered with asphalt. The lot owner then received and accepted an offer to sell the lot to another abutting development. What result if the small developer sues the lot owner for specific performance?

A. Developer wins because the owner's appreciation supplies the contract consideration.
B. Developer wins because developer's detrimental reliance estops the owner.
C. Owner wins because the gift was incomplete and developer gave no consideration.
D. Owner wins because the developer's claim cannot satisfy the statute of frauds.

269. An adult playground basketball captain frequently brought expensive used and new items, like jewelry and electronics, to give away to teammates. A few teammates paid for the items, while a few other teammates paid for the items before directing the items to other friends. When a new teammate joined and asked about the source of the items, a few admitted that the items were stolen, while other teammates

professed not to know and instead to believe that the captain ran a surplus store. If authorities convict the captain of theft of the items and then charge the team members with receiving stolen goods, then which team members would have the best defense?

A. Those who paid for the items even though knowing they were stolen.
B. Those who only accepted items as gifts even though knowing they were stolen.
C. Those who only paid for the items while directing the items to others.
D. Those who did not know the items were stolen but believed they were surplus.

270. An uncle owned a vacant home at which his adult nephew often stayed with his uncle's permission. The uncle held the title to the home in fee simple, reflected in a deed duly recorded. Needing funds for drugs, the nephew purported to convey the home by warranty deed to a buyer. The buyer duly recorded the deed but allowed the nephew to remain in the home. The uncle then determined to aid his nephew by deeding the nephew the home in fee-simply title. The nephew duly recorded the deed. Needing yet more funds, the nephew then conveyed the home by warranty deed to a second buyer who duly recorded the deed and took possession. When the first buyer from the nephew discovered the nephew's second buyer in the home, suit ensued to determine which of the two buyers had title. Who prevails?

A. The first buyer because of the recorded deed senior to the second buyer's deed.
B. The second buyer because recording without notice of the first buyer's claim.
C. Depending whether the first buyer's deed was in the second buyer's chain of title.
D. Depending whether the court imposes an equitable division of title.

271. A vehicle driver was on the road for several hours late in the day. The driver's eyes adjusted as the sun gradually set, so that the driver did not turn on his vehicle headlights as state law required. A second driver drove her vehicle through a stop sign without stopping and directly into the side of the vehicle driven by the first driver without the headlights on. The second driver admitted that she would not have seen the first driver's vehicle and been able to stop in time, even if its headlights had been on. A vehicle passenger injured in the collision consulted a lawyer about the probable liability of the first and second drivers. Which of the following is the best evaluation?

A. The first driver and second driver are each liable.
B. The first driver and second driver are each not liable.
C. The first driver is liable and the second driver is not liable.
D. The first driver is not liable but the second driver is liable.

272. A youth and his parents practiced an established religion one tenet of which was that religious officials promptly bury the intact body upon a member's decease. The youth died suddenly of mysterious causes that his physicians could not immediately trace to natural causes. The county medical examiner insisted on an autopsy pursuant to a state statute requiring an autopsy in any instance in which the death was not obviously due to natural causes. What result if the parents file suit in a court of appropriate jurisdiction challenging the autopsy and seeking the body's prompt

intact burial, arguing as First and Fourteenth Amendment grounds the family's sincere exercise of an established religion?

A. Suit dismissed because dead persons have no constitutional rights.
B. Suit dismissed because the statute was generally applicable on a legitimate interest.
C. Suit sustained because the statute is not necessary to advance a compelling interest.
D. Suit sustained because the statute does not relate to an important state interest.

273. A maker and distributor of illegal drugs shot and killed one of his dealers who had not paid the distributor for the drugs that the dealer sold. The dealer's four-year-old child witnessed the shooting. Authorities charged the distributor with the dealer's murder. If the prosecutor calls the child to testify that the distributor shot and killed the child's parent, then how should the trial judge treat the offer of the child's testimony?

A. Exclude the testimony because it is more unfairly prejudicial than probative.
B. Exclude the testimony as insufficiently probative given the witness's tender age.
C. Admit the testimony if the child has personal knowledge and knows to tell the truth.
D. Admit the testimony if the prosecutor shows the child's competency under state law.

274. A university researcher sued a university over rights to research designs and related intellectual property that the researcher created during his university employment. Following discovery, the university moved for summary judgment of the researcher's claims. The trial judge ruled that although the researcher's claims were extraordinary in nature, it appeared that there was at least a little credible evidence in support of each element and the claims should go forward to trial. The trial judge made similar rulings at trial denying the university's motion for judgment as a matter of law at the close of the researcher's proofs. The jury later returned a stunning verdict in the researcher's favor for more in damages than the researcher had requested at trial. The university's counsel interviewed jurors after their discharge, learning from several that the jurors were confused over the substantive law and procedural burden of proof, and likely would have found in the university's favor but for their confusion. Which of the following best describes the university's recourse on that information regarding the jurors' deliberations?

A. No recourse because jurors may not impeach their own verdict.
B. The information establishes grounds for judgment as a matter of law.
C. The information establishes solid grounds for motion for new trial.
D. The information is a basis for reconvening the jury to correct the verdict.

275. A landowner orally promised to pay for a replacement used truck for a timber cutter if the cutter would harvest certain timber from the landowner's lands. The landowner did not specify from whom the timber cutter must buy the used truck. The timber cutter completed the timber harvest for the landowner and then bought a used truck for $6,500 on credit from a local used-vehicle dealer, notifying the landowner to pay for it. What result if the landowner refuses to pay and the used-vehicle dealer

seeks to enforce the agreement against the landowner?

A. Dealership prevails because the dealership is the landowner's intended beneficiary.
B. Dealership prevails because the dealership detrimentally relied on the promise.
C. Landowner prevails because the agreement did not name the specific beneficiary.
D. Landowner prevails because the statute of frauds requires a writing for suretyships.

276. A drifter enticed a youth into the back of the drifter's motor vehicle on the false premise that they were going to get something to eat. Because the drifter had removed the inside door handles, occupants of the back seat could not get out, even though the youth tried when he became scared and wanted to return home. The drifter went to a hotel instead of a restaurant, where the drifter tied up and gagged the youth in the hotel room. The drifter then left to get friends to join him in torturing the youth, but the youth died from suffocation due to the gagging, while the drifter was still away. After investigators confirmed these facts and identified and arrested the drifter, prosecutors charged the drifter with both kidnapping and felony murder. On which of the two crimes may a jury convict?

A. Both kidnapping and felony murder.
B. Only felony murder because kidnapping is a lesser included offense.
C. Only kidnapping because the drifter did not intend to kill the youth.
D. Neither because the drifter did not intend the youth's death, which also frustrated the kidnapping.

277. Two women owned a retail shop as tenants in common, each with an undivided one-half interest. One woman ran the shop, while the other woman conducted her unrelated profession in a distant city. The professional woman sold her interest to a property speculator. The woman who ran the shop soon passed away, leaving to her daughter her entire estate including any interest in the shop. The daughter also ran the shop but over the years so poorly as to fall into arrears on the real-property taxes. Taxing authorities duly arranged for the real property's sale at auction. Seeking to preserve the interest in the property's value, the speculator purchased the shop at auction for an amount sufficient to pay the back taxes. What result if the speculator then filed suit against the daughter to quiet title in the speculator's own name as sole owner of the real property in fee simple?

A. The speculator wins because he survived his co-tenant, the woman who ran the shop.
B. The speculator wins because the daughter defaulted in running the shop.
C. The daughter wins because the professional woman's interest was inalienable.
D. The daughter wins but only if she pays one-half the amount of the sale at auction.

278. A local river guide took two tourists canoeing in the tourists' own canoe. The guide carelessly navigated the tourists' canoe over some falls resulting in the canoe getting wedged by strong current among logs and boulders. A man who was clearing timber along the riverbank helped force the canoe free but in doing so carelessly applied too much force to it, cracking the canoe's bottom. The canoe instantly swamped when

freed, causing the canoe and its contents to be lost to the river. Which of the following best describes the relative liability of the guide and the man along the riverbank?

A. Neither is liable because it took each of their actions to combine to cause loss of canoe and contents.
B. Only the guide is liable as the first to carelessly set events in motion to cause loss of canoe and contents.
C. Only the man is liable as the last to carelessly complete events causing loss of canoe and contents.
D. Both are liable if each of their actions were substantial factors in the loss of canoe and contents.

279. Facing significant and devastating increases in deaths due to drug abuse, Congress appropriated $5 million for a competition soliciting original, fit, and feasible proposals to fight drug abuse. The legislation further authorized a panel of presidential appointees to evaluate the proposals and make multiple awards in amounts up to $1 million for the best proposals. The legislation prohibited federal employees from participating in the competition and authorized any citizen taxpayer to challenge the appropriation in any federal court. What result in such a taxpayer challenge?

A. Dismiss the suit as presenting a non-justiciable political question.
B. Hold the statute unconstitutional as a standardless delegation of legislative power.
C. Hold the statute unconstitutional as not necessary and proper for the spending power.
D. Hold the statute constitutional as providing adequate criteria related to general welfare.

280. A drunken driver struck and seriously injured a pedestrian. Authorities charged the driver with operating a vehicle while intoxicated. The driver, a first-time offender, pled guilty and received only a license restriction and fine despite that the law provided sentence of up to two years of incarceration. The pedestrian then sued the driver for negligence. At the trial, the pedestrian's counsel offered the driver's conviction as evidence. How should the court rule?

A. Admit the conviction as evidence of the driver's intoxication.
B. Admit the conviction to impeach the driver's character for truth telling.
C. Bar the conviction as hearsay outside of any recognized exception.
D. Bar the conviction because the driver pled guilty before any criminal trial.

281. Two former business partners sued and countersued one another for an accounting of the business that they had dissolved. Before trial, at the trial judge's order, counsel for each side submitted proposed findings of fact and conclusions of law, each side's proposals contradicting the other side's proposals. The former partners then tried their equitable claims for an accounting to the bench. Following the close of proofs, the trial judge asked the court's law clerk to draft a proposed opinion for the trial judge to consider. Which of the following best describes what the proposed opinion should include?

A. Legal research justifying conclusions of law.
B. Summary of evidence supporting findings of fact.
C. Statements of factual and legal issues to decide.

D. Findings of fact and conclusions of law.

282. A wealthy business executive opened a $20,000 bank account in the name of an over-achieving office intern who had impressed the executive. The executive intended to give the account to the intern but never did. Instead, the executive a few months later became enamored with the industrious efforts of a permanent company employee to whom the executive reassigned the $20,000 account with the bank's protocol approval. The intern only then learned of the executive's original designation of the $20,000 account in the intern's name. What result if the intern sues the bank as the original beneficiary of the $20,000?

A. Intern prevails because a constructive assignee of the executive's original rights.
B. Intern prevails because an intended beneficiary of the original account agreement.
C. Bank prevails because the intern's right as an intended beneficiary had not vested.
D. Bank prevails because the intern did not receive possession of the account book.

283. An imprisoned drug dealer developed clear indications of appendicitis including severe abdominal pain in the right lower quadrant with increasing redness and tenderness. Federal prison officials ignored the concern despite sick-call requests from the dealer and bunkmates, and efforts to show the worsening condition to disinterested guards. The condition continued to worsen through several days, treated only with aspirin, until the dealer was in seizures and vomiting up blood. Only when bunkmates wheeled the unconscious dealer on a property cart up to block the communal-cell door did prison officials remove the dealer under guard to a local hospital. The dealer, who nearly died, underwent multiple abdominal surgeries attempting to clean up the sepsis from the burst appendix, estimated to have burst several days before hospitalization. What constitutional right of the dealer, if any, did prison officials violate?

A. None because no prison official acted with any intention to inflict needless pain.
B. The Fourth Amendment's prohibition against unreasonable search and seizure.
C. The Eighth Amendment's prohibition against cruel and unusual punishment.
D. The Fourteenth Amendment's due-process clause as to procedural unfairness.

284. Brothers owned a cottage in fee-simple title, as equal tenants in common, on inheritance from their parents. One brother lived in the cottage for 25 years, paying the taxes and utilities, collecting occasional rents when renting the cottage out for especially desirable times in the summer, and performing all maintenance and repairs. The other brother, who lived across the country, never visited, contributed to costs, or received rent or other benefit from the cottage. Needing money to pay substantial medical expenses, the distant brother demanded that the brothers sell the cottage. What result if the resident brother refuses, and the distant brother files an action for partition and accounting for the net benefit that the resident brother obtained from 25 years of using the cottage?

A. Grant partition but provide no accounting or any adjustment for net benefit.
B. Grant partition and provide an accounting, ordering adjustment for net benefit.
C. Deny partition but provide an accounting, ordering adjustment for net benefit.
D. Deny partition, vesting title in the resident brother by adverse possession.

285. A woman saw an oncologist to determine if she had cancer. The oncologist misread a lab report, incorrectly reporting to the woman that she had no cancer. When the woman's symptoms persisted and she returned to the oncologist months later, a second lab report confirmed the cancer. The woman also discovered the misread lab report. The woman died shortly later despite heroic efforts at treatment. The woman's estate sued the oncologist for misreading the first lab report and failing to diagnose the woman's cancer. Which of the following would be the most helpful additional information in evaluating whether the oncologist is liable?

A. Expert opinion on the woman's probability of surviving with a prompt diagnosis.
B. Expert opinion on the standard of care for the oncologist reading the lab report.
C. Information on how many heirs or beneficiaries the woman left following her death.
D. Information on the cost of treatment if the woman had been promptly diagnosed.

286. A representative gave a floor speech in a U.S. House legislative session impugning the integrity of a federal agency's hiring processes on the basis that a named employee of the agency had a criminal record indicating the employee's unfitness for public service and danger to the public. The speech was in open session unrelated to any pending legislation. The representative's source was a memorandum that the representative's legislative assistant had prepared carelessly confusing the named employee with a person having a similar name but whom no federal agency employed. The federal employee sued the representative and legislative assistant for defamation. What result if the representative and legislative assistant move to dismiss on constitutional grounds?

A. Deny the representative's motion as a government actor but grant the assistant's motion as protected by free speech.
B. Grant the motion recognizing immunity as to both defendants under the Constitution's speech-and-debate clause.
C. Grant the motion recognizing immunity as to the representative but deny the motion as to the assistant who gave no speech.
D. Deny the motion rejecting immunity as to either defendant because the speech did not relate to pending legislation.

287. A customer slipped and fell on winter ice on a walkway in front of the candle shop that she was trying to enter at a strip mall. The fall caused the customer such serious injury that she sued the candle shop to pay for her hospitalization and work loss. The candle shop denied that the walkway was icy. The candle shop further denied that it owned, controlled, or maintained the walkway, claiming that the strip-mall owner owned, controlled, and maintained the walkway. At trial, the customer offered a witness's testimony that immediately after the customer's fall, the candle shop's manager had salted, sanded,

and scraped the walkway. Should the trial judge admit the testimony?

A. Yes to show that the shop was negligent and as to the candle shop's control.
B. Yes to show that the shop was negligent but not as to the candle shop's control.
C. No to show that the shop was negligent but yes as to the candle shop's control.
D. No to show either that the shop was negligent or as to the candle shop's control.

288. A home-security company sued a homeowner when the homeowner discontinued paying the small monthly amount for the company's services. At the close of the company's proofs at trial, the trial court granted the homeowner judgment as a matter of law based on the homeowner's statutory defense that the company had sold the homeowner the service by door-to-door sale without giving the homeowner the required statutory notice of a right to cancel. Six months later, the company filed suit against a neighbor on an identical services contract sold in the same manner on the same day. Which of the following describes the best way in which the neighbor can defeat the company's action?

A. Move to dismiss based on claim preclusion from the prior action.
B. Move to dismiss based on issue preclusion from the prior action.
C. Move for judgment as a matter of law at trial on the statutory defense.
D. Move to consolidate the second action with the first action.

289. An elderly widow living in her own home valued at $125,000 invited her adult granddaughter to move in with her and care for her in her last years until her demise, in exchange for the widow's agreement to give her granddaughter the home. The widow reduced her offer to a writing that she signed and conveyed to the granddaughter who promptly moved into the home and began doing the only chores then necessary for the widow's care. Just one month later, the widow suddenly died of a stroke. What result if the widow's son, who was the sole beneficiary of the widow's will conveying all of her estate to the son, refused to relinquish the home to the granddaughter?

A. Granddaughter prevails only if she can show that the parties foresaw stroke death.
B. Granddaughter prevails because the writing and her chores created a valid contract.
C. Son prevails because one month is inadequate consideration for a $125,000 home.
D. Son prevails if the estate pays the granddaughter the value of one month's services.

290. A tradesman owned an old building that he had rented out for years but that was currently vacant. He knew that the time had come either to demolish and replace the old building or to sell it. The tradesman made an enforceable sale contract for the building. Before the closing, the buyer demanded several expensive repairs to the building that the tradesman was unwilling to make. So, he instead went out to the property and set the building on fire. Which of the following is the best argument that the tradesman can make in defense of a charge of common-law arson?

A. The building was vacant rather than occupied at the time of the fire.
B. He gained no insurance or other benefit from setting the fire.
C. The buyer owned the property at the time that the tradesman set fire to it.
D. The property was commercial rather than residential.

291. A landowner executed and delivered a deed to his niece granting her and her heirs and assigns the land as long as used solely for residential purposes. The deed further provided that if occupants used the land for other than residential purposes, then title to the land would pass to a conservation charity. The landowner soon died, leaving all his real estate interests to his son and remaining assets to his daughter. The jurisdictions Rule Against Perpetuities treats future estates as it does possessory estates and interests. The landowner's niece and daughter then made a signed and delivered contract to convey fee-simple title to the land to a purchaser. The purchaser subsequently refused to close believing after investigation that the niece and daughter could not convey good title to the land. What result if the niece and daughter sue the purchaser for specific performance?

A. Purchaser wins because the charity has a valid interest in the land.
B. Purchaser wins because the son has a valid interest in the land.
C. Niece and daughter win because the niece alone owns fee-simple interest.
D. Niece and daughter win because niece and daughter together hold fee-simple interest.

292. A restaurant's kitchen manager left rat poison in a plastic container similar to a container that waiters used for sugar. Two waiters each negligently mixed a spoonful of the rat poison into glasses of iced tea one of which was then served to a patron who was poisoned. Both waiters had mistaken the poison for sugar, but the patron was unable to show which of them had made the glass from which the patron had been poisoned. Which of the following best describes the waiters' potential liability to the patron?

A. Each is potentially liable, shifting the burden of proof to them to disprove liability.
B. Neither is potentially liable because the burden of proof remains on the patron.
C. Only one is potentially liable, depending on whether the patron can prove which one.
D. Each is potentially one-half liable, provided that the patron rules out other causes.

293. A state enacted a statute prohibiting hunters from using, storing, or transporting dove traps in the state. The statute's purpose was to protect dwindling dove populations from hunters deploying dove traps. The statute permitted transport of dove traps only by carriers moving the traps through the state into other states that permitted dove hunting and trapping. A game warden confiscated and destroyed the dove traps of a non-resident of the state who happened to have been passing through the state on the way home after having lawfully purchased the traps in another state for lawful use in the non-resident's home state. What result if the non-resident challenges the constitutionality of the state statute?

A. Statute held constitutional because the traps were illegal contraband rather than a property interest.
B. Statute held constitutional because the state had a rational basis for distinguishing between private and carrier transport.

C. Statute held unconstitutional because the state had no compelling interest to distinguish between private and carrier transport.
D. Statute held unconstitional because the hunter had a fundamental right to travel through the state without confiscation.

294. A shooting occurred at an urban high-rise hotel. As the shooter fled in a vehicle waiting outside the lobby, a security guard read the vehicle's license number. The guard related the number to a desk clerk who called the police emergency number, relating the number in the guard's presence who confirmed that the number was correct. The guard later lost any recollection of the specific number that he and the desk clerk had accurately related to the police. At the criminal trial of the alleged shooter, the prosecution offered the guard to testify to these facts. Should the trial judge allow the prosecutor to play the audio recording of the desk clerk's call, over defense counsel's objection?

A. No because the desk clerk had no first-hand knowledge of the number she related.
B. No because the audio recording is hearsay and not within any recognized exception.
C. Yes because the audio recording is a public record or report excepted from hearsay.
D. Yes because the audio recording is a recorded recollection excepted from hearsay.

295. A hospital sued in federal court to enjoin a medical-equipment lessor from removing a critical piece of hospital equipment and for money damages regarding to the lessor's alleged breach of the equipment lease. The lessor counterclaimed for unpaid lease payments. The lessor agreed voluntarily not to remove the equipment while the parties litigated the damages claim and counterclaim. Following limited discovery, the trial court entered an order granting summary judgment to the lessor, dismissing the hospital's damages claim based on a contract clause limiting claims to repair or replacement of the equipment. The hospital instructed its counsel to appeal the trial court's ruling at the earliest opportunity. Which of the following best describes the earliest route to an appeal?

A. Request that the trial court certify its order for interlocutory appeal.
B. Stipulate to the dismissal of the hospital's claim for injunctive relief.
C. Appeal as of right because the court's decision was on an injunction.
D. Appeal as of right because the court's decision disposed of all claims.

296. A seventeen-year-old minor bought a gaming system on credit from the local game store, figuring that she would pay for it in a couple of months when her grandparents gave her cash on her eighteenth birthday as they usually did. The system's price was $500. When on her eighteenth birthday she received only $250 from grandparents rather than the $500 that she expected, the game buyer wrote the game store that she would pay the store the $250 for the gaming system. The gaming system's value in its used condition was then $350. What is the store's best result if the store sues the buyer, showing that eighteen years is the age of majority under the applicable state law?

A. Store wins $500 as the contract amount.

B. Store wins $350 as the present value.
C. Store wins $250 as the renewed promise.
D. Store wins nothing from the minor buyer.

297. A woman shared a home with a man who manufactured and sold illegal drugs out of the home. The woman wanted nothing to do with the man's illegal activity but did grow to like taking one of the drugs, a supply of which she kept in her dresser and nightstand drawers. She never sold or gave away any of the drugs. Authorities raided the home, arresting both the man and woman. Prosecutors charged the man with manufacturing, distributing, and selling drugs. They charged the woman only with drug possession. At trial, the prosecution presented the above evidence of the location of the drugs among the woman's personal effects and other strong circumstantial evidence of her drug use. The man, already convicted, testified in the woman's defense that she never made, sold, or distributed any drugs. May the jury convict the woman on these proofs?

A. Yes because possession for personal use is sufficient.
B. Yes because jurors may disbelieve the man's testimony.
C. No because personal use is insufficient to sustain a possession charge.
D. No because they did not catch the woman with the drugs on her person.

298. The owner of vacant land died. The owner's will devised the lands to her husband for life or until remarriage, and then to the owner's son. Not wanting anything to do with his deceased mother's affairs, the son promptly sold to an acquaintance, by properly drawn and recorded deed, whatever interest the son held in the land. The son soon died, with his father, the deceased owner's husband, as the son's only heir. With his son dead, the father (the deceased owner's husband) decided to remarry. He then executed a deed to the land purporting to convey the land to his new wife to assure her of his steadfast love for her. Who owns what interest in the land?

A. The husband's new wife owns the land in fee simple.
B. The husband's new wife has a life estate with the remainder in the son's acquaintance.
C. The husband owns the land in fee simple.
D. The son's acquaintance owns the land in fee simple.

299. Several hikers decided to take an early spring hike up a mountain that others knew to have occasional late-spring snowstorms. An outfitter worked with the hikers to prepare for the hike up the mountain. The outfitter was among the many who knew that the mountain had late-spring snowstorms. The outfitter negligently failed to warn the hikers, as did several friends, family members, park rangers, and other acquaintances. After several days of successful hiking, the hikers were trapped by a snowstorm. Several suffered severe frostbite injuries requiring amputation of toes and fingers. Those hikers sued the outfitter. Which of the following is the outfitter's best argument for dismissal of the hikers' action?

A. No duty.
B. No breach.
C. No proximate cause.
D. No damages.

300. Somalian terrorists attacked the U.S. president's Camp David compound, resulting in dozens of American deaths. Congress responded by authorizing the president to use all necessary and appropriate force against the attackers. Congress's legislative authorization included a separate provision allowing the president to detain indefinitely any individual participating in or supporting the attack. The detention provision further divested the federal courts of jurisdiction to hear the detainees' petitions for review of their detention. What result if a detainee nonetheless files suit in federal district court challenging the detention's constitutionality?

A. Hear the case as within the Supreme Court's original jurisdiction.
B. Hear the case because Congress did not invoke Article I's suspension clause.
C. Dismiss the case under the president's authority as commander-in-chief.
D. Dismiss the case because it presents a non-justiciable political question.

2. Part II—Fourth 100 Questions (Questions 301-400)

301. Neighbors sued one another over a fistfight that they had fallen into over a boundary dispute. At the trial of their civil assault and battery claims against one another, one neighbor called a friend as a witness. The friend testified that the other neighbor was the aggressor. The other neighbor then asked the witness on cross-examination whether the witness had recently lied on a motor-vehicle-insurance application. How should the trial judge rule on objection to the question?

A. Sustain the objection because the application itself is the best evidence.
B. Sustain the objection because impeachment here involved specific conduct.
C. Overrule the objection if the false insurance application resulted in conviction.
D. Overrule the objection because the specific conduct involved untruthfulness.

302. A client signed a fee agreement promising to pay two lawyers substantial hourly sums for their defense of a serious criminal charge up to verdict. The criminal case resulted in a hung jury, which reached no verdict. The two lawyers continued to defend the client through the retrial of the matter, without signing a new fee agreement and without the client paying. The lawyers later sued for their fees for defending in the retrial, claiming both breach of contract and quantum meruit for the equitable value of their services. A jury in the civil case returned a verdict for the lawyers on both the breach-of-contract and quantum-meruit theories. Research convinced the client's counsel in the civil case that the client should have had judgment as a matter of law on the breach-of-contract claim. Which of the following best describes the client's prospects for a successful appeal?

A. No prospects because an appeal cannot overturn a jury verdict.
B. Poor prospects because any error would have been harmless.
C. Good prospects because there should have been judgment as law.
D. Reversal is certain because there should have been just one theory.

303. A uranium processor made a contract with a centrifuge manufacturer to supply the processor with all of the centrifuges that the processor would need for a new plant. The contract required the manufacturer to supply the centrifuges on the date six months away that the plant's construction would conclude. Three months later, the processor demanded that the manufacturer reassure the processor that the manufacturer would be able to deliver all of the required centrifuges, even though the manufacturer had no reason to doubt the manufacturer's capability. The manufacturer refused to make any assurances because the contract was silent on that point. The processor promptly canceled the contract and obtained the centrifuges from another supplier. Will the manufacturer prevail in a breach-of-contract action against the processor?

A. Yes because the processor had no grounds to demand assurances.
B. Yes because the contract was silent on the right to demand assurances.
C. No because manufacturer anticipatorily repudiated the contract.
D. No because the contract did not specify a unit quantity.

304. A long-haul trucker bought methamphetamines at a truck stop in one state to sell at a truck stop in another state. State undercover agents arrested the trucker on his attempt to sell the drugs at the second truck stop. Federal agents had also been investigating the trucker but were not present at the attempted sale and arrest. Federal prosecutors contacted the state investigators indicating that they intended to press federal drug-distribution charges. State prosecutors opposed the federal intervention. In which proceeding, state or federal, may the arrested trucker successfully challenge jurisdiction?

A. Both federal and state because federal authorities were not involved in the arrest, and yet the crime occurred across state lines.
B. Federal only because federal authorities were not involved in the arrest, but not state because of intrastate effects.
C. State only because the crime occurred across state lines, and state arrest does not prevent federal prosecution.
D. Neither because both federal and state law address the crime, which had both interstate and intrastate effects.

305. An older woman who had never married deeded to a nephew with whom she was close the right to purchase for $1,000 per acre specific farmland that she owned. The deed further provided, though, the nephew would only have that right either at any time that woman should decide during her life to sell, or if she did not decide to sell, then within sixty days of her death. The nephew recorded the instrument, which did not constitute a will. What interest if any does the nephew now possess?

A. No interest because the nephew gave no valuable consideration for the instrument.

B. No interest because the first-refusal rights restrain the owner's alienation on death.
C. A valid option in the form of a right of first refusal on either of the two conditions.
D. A valid option in the form of a right of first refusal because the nephew recorded it.

306. An art museum hired a security company to protect its new building and grounds from vandalism. Vandals caused substantial damage to the museum's new building and grounds on a day that the security company's guard had failed to show up for work at the museum. The museum filed a negligence action against the security company for the damage. The security company's lawyer moved to dismiss the action on the basis of superseding cause. Which of the following is the best evaluation of the merits of that motion?

A. It will be denied because the vandalism's foreseeability was what made the company negligent.
B. It will be denied because the substantial nature of the damages due to vandalism warrants compensation.
C. It will be granted because the vandalism was intentional and criminal, and therefore less likely foreseeable.
D. It will be granted because security companies cannot prevent every act of vandalism and should not have to pay for the loss.

307. Recognizing the potential benefits and threats of bitcoins and other blockchain technologies, Congress created a new Electronic Financial Systems sub-agency

within the independent Consumer Financial Protection Bureau. The president appoints the Consumer Financial Protection Bureau chief with Congress's advice and consent but cannot remove the chief before the end of the chief's term. In creating the new Electronic Financial Systems sub-agency, Congress provided that the Consumer Financial Protection Bureau chief appoints the Electronic Financial Systems' three commissioners, whom only the chief can remove for cause. What result if a public-interest organization with standing challenged the constitutionality of the appointments provision of the new sub-agency?

A. Legislation upheld as within Congress's power of executive oversight.
B. Legislation upheld as within Congress's power over the currency and treasury.
C. Legislation struck as unduly limiting the president's appointments power.
D. Legislation struck as exceeding any express congressional power.

308. At trial, a prosecution witness identified the defendant as the thief who grabbed and stole a jewelry store's jewels. Over objection, the prosecution also elicited testimony from the witness that the witness had a good reputation for truthfulness and had also promptly identified the defendant to police at the scene. On cross-examination, and over the prosecution's objection, defense counsel attacked the witness's credibility by eliciting testimony that the witness was a close friend of the store's owner. Once again over prosecution objection, defense counsel impeached the prosecution witness by calling a defense witness to testify to the prosecution witness's reputation for dishonesty. Which party has the best argument for error in the admission of testimony?

A. Defendant for the prosecution rehabilitating reputation before impeachment.
B. Defendant for the prosecution using a prior consistent statement to rehabilitate.
C. Prosecution for defense counsel having impeached for friendship with the owner.
D. Prosecution for defense counsel having impeached as to reputation for dishonesty.

309. A local filmmaker developed a film project around the sinking of a Great Lakes freighter in November gales. During the early stages of the project, the filmmaker discovered that a major studio was planning a nearly identical project that would destroy the value of the filmmaker's project. The filmmaker sued the studio claiming the studio's conversion of the filmmaker's idea. The trial court dismissed the filmmaker's claim after discovery showed that the studio had arrived at the project independent of any knowledge of the filmmaker's work. The filmmaker asked counsel whether the filmmaker could appeal the decision in order to delay the production long enough to convince the studio to abandon the project or for the filmmaker to get his project finished first. Which of the following best describes the correct advice?

A. The filmmaker should take an appeal of right to delay the studio's project.
B. The filmmaker should weigh the cost of an appeal against the project's value.
C. A frivolous appeal for ulterior purpose may result in dismissal and sanctions.
D. The filmmaker has no appeal rights because the outcome was by dismissal.

310. An electronics store contracted to sell a $10,000 home-theater system to a homeowner. The homeowner paid the store a $2,500 down payment and a contractor $1,000 to modify the home for the system's installation. The electronics store then canceled the contract without reason. The homeowner's reasonable efforts secured the homeowner a replacement system at a cost of $15,000 including the cost of further modifications for installation. Which of the following options describe appropriate damages measures in the homeowner's action against the electronics store?

A. Expectation damages in the full $15,000 amount of the only available replacement home-theater system.
B. Expectation damages in the full $10,000 amount of the original home-theater system as bargained for.
C. Restitution of the $2,500 down payment, $1,000 in reliance damages, and $5,000 in expectation damages.
D. Restitution of the $5,000 cost difference, $1,000 for the home modification, and $2,500 in reliance damages.

311. A state statute required that any person who observes child abuse or has reasonable basis to believe in its occurrence must promptly report the observation or belief to appropriate child-protective authorities. Acting on their own investigation, police arrested a neighborhood recluse on suspicion of child abuse. Evidence indicated that the recluse had abused several neighborhood children over a period of years. Evidence further indicated that homeowners in the neighborhood, both with and without children, had long suspected that the recluse might be an abuser but had not reported their observations or suspicions. Do prosecutors have a basis for a failure-to-report charge?

A. Yes because the statute created a clear duty to act in these circumstances.
B. Yes because the homeowners lived in the neighborhood able to observe for years.
C. No because crimes must involve actions rather than mere failure to act.
D. Only as to those with children because the childless would have no duty report.

312. A landlord and tenant entered into a written, signed, and otherwise enforceable lease for an apartment unit near the university at which the tenant was a student. The lease term was for one year. The tenant stayed throughout the year, paying rent on time at the beginning of each month. The tenant had one year remaining at the university and so remained in the apartment at the end of the lease term. The tenant paid the landlord the next month's rent at the beginning of each of the next two months after the lease ended, consistent with the tenant's prior obligation and practice. At first, the landlord accepted the tenant's rent payments while tendering the next year's lease for the tenant's signature. The tenant did not sign, hoping that the landlord would accept rent each month instead so that the tenant could leave without obligation when school ended after nine months. But the landlord instead served a notice to quit. The tenant paid another months' rent, which the landlord accepted despite the notice. If during that month for which the tenant paid rent the landlord sues to evict, then what is the tenant's status?

A. Tenant at will with a month-to-month lease because the landlord accepted rent.
B. Tenant at sufferance with no possessory rights because of the landlord's notice to quit.
C. Tenant on a periodic tenancy from year to year because of the prior one-year term.
D. Trespasser subject to both contract damages under the lease and tort damages.

313. A large tent collapsed on a wedding party, injuring several guests. The wedding producer had retained a contractor to specify the tent. The contractor did so and then had retained a tent company to locate it on the wedding grounds. The tent company did so and then had retained a crew to erect the tent. The crew did so and then had left it to a caterer to secure shut certain tent door flaps. The injured guests retained counsel to investigate tort claims. Of the producer, contractor, tent company, crew, and caterer, only the tent company had liability insurance coverage. Which of the following research topics would most help determine the tent company's liability for negligent acts by the others?

A. The law of joint and several liability.
B. The law of vicarious liability.
C. The law of allocation of fault.
D. The law of satisfaction and release.

314. Congress passed a law allowing the Secretary of the Interior to designate game animals open to hunting on federal wilderness lands consistent with recognized conservation standards. The Secretary of the Interior reasonably determined that state game officials in each state on which those federal wilderness lands were located had the better knowledge of local conservation conditions within that state. So the Secretary of the Interior deferred to state game officials in each state to designate game animals open to hunting on federal wilderness lands. Congress's enactment further provided that majority vote of the House's Committee on the Interior would overrule any game-animal designation that the Secretary of the Interior made. What result in a proper action challenging the constitutionality of Congress's enactment?

A. Held invalid because Congress exceeded its delegation authority.
B. Held invalid as violating bicameralism and presentment requirements.
C. Held valid as a proper exercise of Congress's delegation authority.
D. Held valid because the Secretary of Interior consulted state officials.

315. Ambulance took a passenger in a motor-vehicle accident to the hospital emergency room. The physician on duty read radiographs of the passenger's fractures to a medical assistant who typed them into the emergency-room report. The passenger later sued the at-fault driver in a negligence action. At trial, the passenger called the hospital's medical recordkeeper to authenticate the emergency-room report as an exhibit for admission. How should the trial judge rule over objection?

A. Admitted as statement of then-existing physical condition and present-sense impression.
B. Admitted as statement of medical diagnosis and record of regular business conduct.
C. Barred as an expert opinion based on underlying facts not yet in evidence.
D. Barred because the proponent has not yet qualified the physician as an expert witness.

316. A hospital sued a patient and the patient's spouse for unpaid medical expense. The hospital based its claim against the spouse on the theory that one spouse has a legal duty to provide for the other spouse, on which a third party like the hospital can rely. The parties tried the case to the bench. The trial judge decided a fact dispute over the amount of expenses in the hospital's favor and also held in the hospital's favor on the issue of law that the non-patient spouse was liable for the patient spouse's expenses. The patient and spouse asked their defense counsel what the prospects for an appeal were. Before answering, defense counsel asked a law clerk to research the standard of review that the appellate court would apply to the trial court's factual determination and its ruling on the issue of law. Which of the following best describes the appellate court's review standards?

A. Decide the issue of law without deference to the trial court's decision but reverse the trial court's factual determination only if clearly erroneous.
B. Decide the fact issue without deference to the trial court's decision but reverse the trial court's determination of law only if clearly erroneous.
C. Decide both the fact issue and the issue of law under an abuse-of-discretion standard, reversing only if the trial court abused its discretion.
D. Decide both the fact issue and the issue of law under a clearly erroneous standard, reversing only on definite and firm conviction of mistake.

317. A clothier ordered from a commercial-equipment supplier for a new clothing store fifteen clothing racks at a cost of $1,000 each and a total contract value of $15,000. The clothier and supplier signed a contract requiring the supplier to deliver the racks on the specific date on which the new store's builder would turn the building keys over to the clothier. The supplier then orally requested that the clothier give the supplier an additional week within which to deliver the racks, to which the clothier orally agreed. When the supplier attempted to deliver the racks on the week-later date to which the parties had orally agreed, the clothier pointed to replacement racks and refused to accept them. What result if the supplier sues the clothier for contract breach?

A. Supplier wins because the clothier waived the earlier date in an enforceable modification.
B. Supplier wins because neither the original nor modified agreement required a writing.
C. Clothier wins because the parol-evidence rule bars evidence of the oral modification.
D. Clothier wins because no consideration supported the subsequent modification.

318. Prosecutors charged an executive with soliciting prostitution. At trial, and over defense counsel's objection, the judge incorrectly admitted hearsay evidence of a witness's statement at the scene of the alleged crime. The statement confirmed the time of the alleged crime, a fact that other witnesses had already confirmed and was not in dispute. The judge also incorrectly admitted an audio recording of the executive in custody admitting to the crime. Defense counsel was so shocked at the judge's admission of the damaging evidence that counsel forgot to object. If the jury convicts the executive, then what appeal rights does the executive have?

A. Appeal both the admitting of hearsay because counsel objected and the recording because of its affect on substantial rights.
B. Appeal the admitting of hearsay because counsel objected but not the recording because counsel failed to object.
C. Appeal the admitting of the recording because of its affect on substantial rights but not the hearsay for failure to object.
D. No appeal rights because admitting the hearsay was harmless, and counsel failed to object to the recording.

319. The owner of a small-town sandwich-shop business and the building housing the shop decided to rent the shop along with the apartment upstairs. The owner entered into a five-year written lease calling for the tenant, a youthful entrepreneur, to take possession in three months. Two months before the tenant took occupancy, the sandwich shop had a small fire the modest damage from which the owner took pains to clean up. At about the same time, the entrepreneur's inspection revealed some mold in the apartment upstairs. Thus, one month before the tenant was to take occupancy, the entrepreneur notified the owner that the entrepreneur was refusing to take occupancy but that he had a buddy who was interested in taking over the lease. The owner simultaneously discovered that the entrepreneur had joined the military and already left for training. If the owner sues the entrepreneur accelerating damages for the entire lease term, then what legal arguments should each side raise?

A. The entrepreneur the servicemembers' civil relief act, and the owner breach of the duty of occupancy and specific performance.
B. The entrepreneur the protection of the recording statute, and the owner breach of the warranty of habitability.
C. The owner breach of the duty of good faith and fair dealing, and the entrepreneur impossibility and impracticality, and the absence of any damage.
D. The owner anticipatory breach, and the entrepreneur breach of the warranties of habitability and suitability, and the obligation to mitigate damages.

320. A restaurant manager instructed a cook to drive the restaurant's catering van to the grocer for fresh produce for the night's fare. On the way back to the restaurant from the grocer's, the cook ran a red light, collided the van into the side of a sedan, and injured a passenger. The passenger retained counsel to plead the allowable tort claims in a jurisdiction that had no no-fault act. Which of the following best states those tort claims?

A. Negligence as to the cook and vicarious liability as to the restaurant.
B. Negligence as to the cook and vicarious liability as to the manager.
C. Negligence as to the cook, manager, and restaurant.
D. Vicarious liability as to the cook, manager, and restaurant.

321. Responding to public concerns over contamination of water supplies from drilling companies' hydraulic fracturing (fracking), Congress enacted the Federal Fracking Control Act requiring that drilling companies first obtain federal permits before conducting any fracking. Congress's legislation further provided that the federal permits issue only after the applicant demonstrate compliance with agency

regulations ensuring protection of water supplies in any fracking method. The legislation finally authorized federal agency post-permit review of fracking sites and substantial penalties on evidence of non-compliance. The legislation also specifically prohibited state laws from regulating fracking in any manner inconsistent with the Act's provisions including federal regulations adopted under the Act. A state legislature then enacted a state law providing for similar state oversight of fracking sites but permitting state officials to grant a waiver of all state or federal permitting for drilling companies that demonstrated substantial expertise in fracking. Would the state law survive constitutional challenge?

A. Yes because the statute includes similar oversight and is within a state's police power.
B. Yes because the statute does not discriminate against or burden interstate commerce.
C. No because the federal legislation specifically forbids inconsistent state regulation.
D. No because the statute discriminates against oil companies not located within the state.

322. Business partners disputed their rights on dissolution of the business. One partner sued the other, claiming breach of the partnership agreement and conversion of partnership assets. At trial, and with the plaintiff partner on the witness stand, plaintiff's counsel offered as an exhibit an accounting that the defendant partner had prepared and conveyed to the plaintiff partner. The trial judge and defense counsel both indicated that they were unsure of what use plaintiff's counsel intended for the exhibit. What should each lawyer do?

A. Plaintiff's counsel should take exception, and defense counsel should move to strike.
B. Defense counsel should take exception, and plaintiff's counsel should move to strike.
C. Plaintiff's counsel should object, and defense counsel should make an offer of proof.
D. Defense counsel should object, and plaintiff's counsel should make an offer of proof.

323. A tourist suffered serious injury on an amusement ride at a carnival. The tourist sued the carnival operator under diversity jurisdiction in federal court, claiming damages in excess of $75,000 for medical expenses, pain and suffering, and lost enjoyment of life. More than twenty-one days after proper service of the summons and complaint, the carnival operator had not answered, appeared, or otherwise communicated with the tourist or counsel. Which of the following actions should the tourist take to obtain a default judgment?

A. File a motion requesting that the court enter a default judgment, serving defendant with a copy of the motion.
B. Show the court clerk by affidavit or otherwise that defendant defaulted, asking the clerk to enter default judgment for a sum certain.
C. Show the court clerk by affidavit or otherwise that the defendant defaulted, while applying to the court for a default judgment and hearing on damages.
D. Take no action because the court will enter default on its own, scheduling a hearing on damages.

324. A medical group contracted in a signed writing to purchase a $2,500 imaging device from a medical-equipment distributor but then refused delivery on the contracted-for date. The medical group had no excuse for the refusal other than its own internal mismanagement for which the supplier was not responsible. The distributor managed to sell the specific device promptly to another customer for the same price, without notifying the medical group of the effort to resell. The distributor sells many such devices, which manufacturers make available to the distributor in any quantity that the distributor requires. What amount should the distributor recover if it sues the medical group for contract breach?

A. The $2,500 contract price for deliberate breach by repudiation.
B. The distributor's lost profit on the sale plus any incidental loss.
C. No recovery because the supplier sold the device at the same price.
D. No recovery because the supplier did not notify the group of resale.

325. A hacker took control of a private company's electronic systems, causing the company substantial embarrassment and loss until the company met the hacker's demand to pay for system's release. In response, the company hired an electronic-security expert who infiltrated the hacker's computer, intercepting a similar demand that the hacker made to another systems-hostage target. The security expert's intercept violated federal and state statutes against electronic surveillance by private individuals. The expert nonetheless turned the intercepted demand over to federal investigators with the company's request that federal officials pursue federal hacking charges. The investigators told the expert that they would need more evidence and directed the investigator to re-enter the hacker's electronic system to look for a list of things. The expert did so, finding hundreds of messages and files fulfilling each request of the investigator. In a federal criminal case against the hacker, how should the court rule on the hacker's motion to suppress the expert's evidence as a Fourth Amendment violation?

A. Grant the motion suppressing any evidence from the expert.
B. Grant the motion only in part, suppressing only the expert's second system entry.
C. Grant the motion only in part, suppressing only the expert's first system entry.
D. Deny the motion, allowing all of the expert's evidence.

326. A real estate agent contracted with a military veteran to sell the veteran's home. The selling agent's listing of the home caught the attention of a buyer's agent whose clients then made an offer on the home through their agent. The veteran accepted the offer through his agent. At the closing, the veteran took aside the selling agent complaining confidentially that he had just learned that the buyers had the same ethnicity as that of the combat opposition that had imprisoned and tortured the veteran. Also at the closing, the agents disagreed on how to treat the standard commission on sale of the home. How should both issues ordinarily resolve?

A. The veteran sells the home because now bound, and the agents increase the commission.
B. The veteran sells the home disregarding ethnicity, while the agents split the commission.

C. The veteran rescinds for unilateral mistake, while the selling agent gets the commission.
D. The veteran rescinds for misrepresentation, while the buying agent gets the commission.

327. A property owner leased a facility to a metal-coating shop. The shop went out of business. When the property owner tried to sell the property, soil testing showed toxic waste from the metal-coating shop. The property owner hired a contractor to clean up the toxic waste, but some of the toxic waste contaminated the neighbor's land during the contractor's clean up. The neighbor retained counsel to investigate tort claims. Investigation showed that the contractor was uninsured and without substantial assets but that the property owner had applicable liability insurance. Which of the following describes the best advice to the neighbor regarding claims against the property owner?

A. The property owner owes vicarious liability to the neighbor for an inherently dangerous activity.
B. The property owner owes vicarious liability to the neighbor for retaining control of the clean-up work.
C. The property owner owes direct liability to the neighbor for negligent hiring and entrustment.
D. The property owner owes contribution and indemnity to the neighbor for the contamination of the land.

328. Federal law expressly authorizes states to license credit unions operating within the state. The federal legislation expressly provides that a state may prohibit an unlicensed credit union from offering banking services within the state. Relying on the federal legislation, a state statute authorized a state agency to grant or deny credit-union licenses within the state on specific criteria and prohibited unlicensed credit unions from operating within the state. The state agency then denied a license to a credit union that already operated in approximately half of the other states. What result if the unlicensed credit union files suit in a proper court, challenging the constitutionality of the state law prohibiting it from offering banking services within the state?

A. Held constitutional because of the federal authorization of state law.
B. Held constitutional as a reasonable restriction on interstate commerce.
C. Held unconstitutional as an impermissible burden on interstate commerce.
D. Held unconstitutional as preempted by inconsistent federal legislation.

329. A seller of real property sued an alleged buyer for specific performance of the alleged sale contract. At trial, the seller offered as an exhibit the alleged sale contract, maintaining that the exhibit was the original sale contract and that it included the buyer's original signature. The buyer objected to the exhibit's offer, maintaining that the exhibit was not at all what the seller purported it to be, that it was not an original document, and that the signature was not the buyer's signature. Who between judge and jury decides how to treat the exhibit?

A. Judge decides whether to admit the exhibit and whether it is original.
B. Judge decides whether to admit the exhibit and jury decides whether it is original.

C. Jury decides factual conditions to admit the exhibit and judge decides whether original.
D. Jury decides factual conditions to admit the exhibit and whether it is original.

330. A Missouri citizen filed a civil-rights lawsuit in federal court in Missouri against a police officer who was a citizen of Iowa, relying on the federal court's diversity jurisdiction. The lawsuit maintained that the Iowa police officer had taken the Missouri citizen into custody in Missouri in violation of the Missouri citizen's due-process rights under the Missouri state constitution. The Missouri citizen claimed nothing other than that the Iowa police officer violated the Missouri citizen's due-process rights under Missouri's state constitution. Which law must the federal court apply?

A. The U.S. Constitution's due-process clause because of the U.S. Constitution's supremacy clause.
B. The U.S. Constitution's due-process clause because the Rules of Decision Act requires it.
C. The Missouri Constitution's due-process clause because the Rules of Decision Act requires it.
D. The Missouri Constitution's due-process clause because the Erie doctrine requires it.

331. A seller of a used motor vehicle told the buyer in advance of sale that the vehicle was free of rust. To the contrary, the seller had temporarily concealed substantial rust beneath paint and other material in a way that the rust would soon reappear after the vehicle's sale. Indeed, the buyer discovered the rust soon thereafter when it began once again to show through. The buyer sued, alleging both rescission of the contract for the seller's fraud and contract damages for the lost benefit of the buyer's bargain for a rust-free vehicle, worth many thousands of dollars more than the rusted vehicle that the buyer received, if the buyer decided to keep and repair the vehicle. What defense, if any, may the seller raise regarding the buyer's inconsistent claims?

A. No defense because a plaintiff such as the buyer may seek alternative remedies.
B. The gist or essence of the claim, which lies in fraud, not breach of contract.
C. Election of remedies, forcing the buyer to choose between breach of contract or fraud.
D. Failure to mitigate damages, in which the buyer must recover the lesser of the two claims.

332. A robber entered a methamphetamine lab in a homeowner's garage, demanding that the homeowner turn over all the meth that was ready for sale. The homeowner pulled a concealed weapon from his pocket and shot the robber dead. Not wanting authorities to discover his meth lab, the homeowner buried the robber's body in a wooded area near the home. The robber's spouse reported the robber as missing, giving authorities information leading them to the homeowner's lands. Stepping over the homeowner's wire fence, the authorities searched the woods where they discovered the robber's body. They then went immediately to the home where they tackled the homeowner in his garage. With the homeowner on the floor of the garage with one official on top of him, the other official demanded to know why the homeowner had killed the robber. The homeowner promptly admitted to the killing, while trying to explain the circumstances. What result if the homeowner's counsel moves to suppress both the evidence of the

body and the homeowner's admission, asserting Fourth Amendment rights?

A. Admit both evidence of the body and evidence of the admission.
B. Admit evidence of the body but not of evidence of the admission.
C. Admit evidence of the admission but not evidence of the body.
D. Admit neither evidence of the body nor evidence of the admission.

333. The owner of a rural home rented it out to a tenant who had bad credit. After a couple of years, the tenant convinced the owner to sell the home to the tenant on a land contract for a favorable price $50,000 below fair market value. Needing money to repair the home, the tenant then borrowed $25,000 from a private lender who demanded and received an absolute deed from the tenant as security against the loan. The tenant soon defaulted on the loan. The private lender promptly foreclosed. Instead of selling the home, though, the private lender wanted to occupy and improve the home as his own. The tenant wanted instead to remain in the home or receive the equity in it after payoff of the loan. The original owner wanted return of the home. Which of the following accurately states relative rights?

A. The tenant likely has a right to redeem the home or recover the home's net equity.
B. The tenant's interest depends on whether the tenant recorded the land contract.
C. The private lender owns the home by absolute deed free of any interest in the tenant.
D. The original owner has no remaining interest given the deed in lieu of foreclosure.

334. A motor-vehicle collision occurred at an intersection where one driver faced a stop sign and the other driver had a through route. The accident report showed that although the first driver had not stopped at the stop sign, the second driver had been speeding, contributing to the cause of the accident. The first driver, who was injured, consulted a lawyer regarding making a claim against the second driver based on the second driver's speeding. Which of the following is the best evaluation of the first driver's claim, in a contributory-negligence jurisdiction?

A. Valid claim because the second driver's speeding contributed to the accident.
B. Valid claim because the accident report is the best evidence of what happened.
C. No claim because the second driver's speeding probably had nothing to do with it.
D. No claim because barred by the first driver's running the stop sign.

335. A mentally disabled former student returned to his community college where he shot and seriously injured a professor, staff member, and administrator. In response, the state legislature enacted a gun-control statute imposing a week-long waiting period on the sale of a handgun to any individual having a history of mental illness. The statute further required the applicant to submit a mental-health treater's statement certifying competence to have a handgun. A homeowner with agoraphobia sought to buy a handgun following increased neighborhood crime but first had to comply with the waiting period and certification. What result if the homeowner files suit in federal court challenging the state statute's constitutionality?

A. Held constitutional because states may reasonably limit the right to bear arms.
B. Held constitutional as within the state's power to regulate in-state commerce.
C. Held unconstitutional as discriminating unduly against a protected class.
D. Held unconstitutional because the right to bear arms in the home is unlimited.

336. The prosecution in a criminal trial presented the investigating officer as a witness to testify to facts supporting the defendant's guilt. On defense counsel's cross-examination of the officer, counsel asked in a single question whether the defendant had denied responsibility at the crime scene and whether the officer had at that time believed the defendant's denial to be true. The prosecutor promptly objected to defense counsel's question. How should the trial judge rule?

A. Sustained as a compound question, requiring that counsel state separate questions.
B. Sustained as seeking irrelevant evidence of denial and belief at the scene.
C. Overruled because the reasonable juror would know what counsel is asking.
D. Overruled because counsel has the right to ask difficult questions requiring answer.

337. A consumer retained experienced counsel who filed a products-liability action for the consumer in federal court. Counsel then repeatedly requested extensions for more time to amend the pleadings, add new defendants, and name lay and expert witnesses beyond the schedule witness-list due dates. The court sanctioned counsel and his consumer client at a pretrial conference and warned of the strongest sanctions if the conduct persisted. Counsel and his consumer client were nonetheless late serving discovery responses, and then the consumer client missed her duly noticed deposition. These circumstances delayed the case for several years. The frustrated trial judge then duly ordered a status conference at which counsel failed to attend. As final sanction, the trial judge dismissed the case with prejudice on defendant's oral motion made on the record during the status conference. What result if counsel and his consumer client appeal the dismissal?

A. Reversed as an abuse of discretion for not providing a hearing on the sanction.
B. Reversed because most of the misconduct was counsel's fault, not the client.
C. Affirmed as an appropriate use of the trial court's discretion to enforce orders.
D. Conduct an appellate hearing to review the trial court's decision *de novo*.

338. A disabled veteran employed a caretaker both for personal assistance and household chores. Although the veteran privately paid and employed the caretaker, the caretaker worked at an hourly rate established as reasonable by a government agency responsible for the support and protection of disabled veterans. The caretaker soon told the veteran that although he would work for the established hourly rate, he would also need the veteran to convey household items of significant value to him from time to time or the caretaker would see that the veteran would never leave the house again. After yelling at the veteran and roughing him up until getting his assent, the caretaker presented a bill of sale and vehicle title for the veteran to sign the next day conveying to the caretaker the veteran's antique car for services rendered.

What result if the veteran's adult children soon noticed the missing car, convincing the veteran to fire the caretaker and file an action to rescind the car's conveyance?

A. Veteran recovers the car because the adult children had not authorized conveyance.
B. Veteran recovers the car because the caretaker induced assent through duress.
C. Caretaker keeps the car because the caretaker's services supplied consideration.
D. Caretaker keeps the car because the veteran and caretaker both completed performance.

339. To reduce the incidence of both illegal drugs and guns, police in a rural area notorious for illicit marijuana production, cocaine processing, and production of other drugs set up a checkpoint to stop vehicles at random. An officer motioned a van over at the checkpoint. The van's driver promptly stopped and, when asked, produced valid driver's license, vehicle registration, and proof of insurance. While the driver was securing the documentation from within the vehicle, the officer used a flashlight to look through the van's closed windows for contraband or other evidence of drug production. Seeing a handgun partly under the passenger seat and within the driver's reach, the officer ordered the driver from the vehicle, searched the van, and discovered both the unregistered handgun and evidence of illegal drug production. What result if in response to charges for the gun and drug violations, the van driver moves to suppress the vehicle evidence?

A. Motion denied because the gun's discovery in plain view justified the search.
B. Motion denied because the officer followed a department plan rather than acting alone.
C. Motion granted because the flashlight's use involved illegal search of the van's interior.
D. Motion granted because the plan to stop vehicles at random was itself unlawful.

340. An aunt who wanted to see her niece do well after college graduation agreed to help the niece buy a home by loaning the niece the home's down payment. The niece and aunt signed a loan agreement that required the niece to repay the loan on a specific schedule and that stated that the home would be the aunt's loan security. The niece told her commercial mortgage lender about the aunt's loan and even offered the lender a copy of the unrecorded loan agreement, but the lender declined. The lender made the loan and then duly recorded the niece's properly executed mortgage, which said nothing about the aunt's loan of the down payment. The niece subsequently moved out of the home and defaulted on both loans after she failed to pay utilities and the utility company shut off the heat and lights to the home in the freezing winter. Which of the following would be most pertinent to which creditor, the aunt or the commercial mortgage lender, has priority in foreclosure proceedings?

A. The jurisdiction follows the title theory for mortgages.
B. The jurisdiction follows the lien theory for mortgages.
C. The jurisdiction follows the intermediate theory for mortgages
D. The jurisdiction's recording act follows race rather than notice.

341. A claimant suffered injury when a forklift operator lowered a load of lumber on the claimant's arm. The claimant had carelessly reached under the forklift's load

to clear away some debris. The claimant warned the forklift operator when the claimant snagged his glove on the debris and couldn't withdraw his arm from under the load. Although hearing and understanding the claimant's warning, the forklift operator carelessly lowered the load anyway, seriously injuring the claimant's arm. If the claimant sues the forklift operator in a jurisdiction that recognizes the contributory-negligence defense, then which of the following describes the most-probable outcome?

A. The claimant prevails because the claimant was only in part at fault.
B. The claimant prevails because the operator had the last clear chance.
C. The operator prevails because the claimant was at least in part at fault.
D. The operator prevails because the operator was not at all at fault.

342. During a presidential election, the Federal Communications Commission received frequent complaints of biased media reporting including secret coordination between a candidate's campaign and commentators posing as news journalists. To address the complaints and promote media fairness, the Commission promulgated a rule prohibiting licensed television networks from endorsing political candidates and requiring them to remain neutral when reporting on elections. The rule further required that networks renewing licenses or applying for a new license must certify their compliance with the rule. What result if a network challenged the constitutionality of the rule in a court of competent jurisdiction?

A. Held constitutional as rationally related to a legitimate governmental interest.
B. Held constitutional as necessary to further a compelling governmental interest.
C. Held unconstitutional as a prior restraint on free speech and expression.
D. Held unconstitutional as a condition requiring First Amendment waiver for a license.

343. A patient suffered a devastating adverse reaction to a medical procedure. The patient later sued the physician who performed the procedure, claiming that the physician had committed medical malpractice. At trial, the patient's counsel offered the testimony of a hospital recordkeeper to authenticate medical exhibits that the judge had already admitted on stipulation. The patient's counsel also offered the testimony of a fourth expert witness on breach of the standard of care, after three similarly qualified expert witnesses had already given the same testimony. Defense counsel objected to both of those offers of evidence. How should the trial judge rule on the objections?

A. Admit both offers as within the patient's right to conduct the case as the patient chooses.
B. Admit the recordkeeper's testimony but exclude the fourth expert as cumulative.
C. Exclude the recordkeeper's testimony as wasting time but admit the fourth expert.
D. Exclude both offers as wasting time and needlessly presenting cumulative evidence.

344. A satirical journal repeatedly parodied a congressional representative in ways that deeply embarrassed and arguably defamed the representative under the law of the state that the representative represented in Congress. The representative determined

to file a defamation suit against the journal. Federal constitutional law requires public officials like the representative to prove actual malice as federal law defines actual malice, in order to make a defamation claim. Would a federal court have subject matter jurisdiction over the representative's defamation suit?

A. No because the federal issue is part of the defense rather than the claim.
B. Yes but only if the representative pleads federal malice in a well-plead complaint.
C. Yes because the state-law defamation claim embeds a federal question.
D. Yes because the First Amendment protection of free speech is fundamental.

345. A hunting enthusiast met with a gun collector at a gun show discussing the possible sale of a certain rare gun. The collector did not have the gun with him at the show. After significant negotiation, they agreed in a brief but complete signed writing that the hunting enthusiast would buy the rare gun from the collector for a specific cash price. When they met a week later to exchange the gun and cash, the collector had brought a different rare gun than the enthusiast had understood and expected. The collector and enthusiast had each in their negotiations and brief written description different guns reasonably in mind. What result if the collector sues the enthusiast to make the enthusiast complete the transaction?

A. Collector wins because of the complete signed writing.
B. Collector wins because of collector's tender of performance.
C. Enthusiast wins because of the mutual misunderstanding.
D. Enthusiast wins because the collector did not complete performance.

346. A prosecutor convened a grand jury to investigate a shooting. Autopsy and ballistics had shown that two bullets from two different guns rather than a single gun had caused or contributed to the victim's death. The prosecutor called as a witness one of persons rumored to have been present at the shooting. The witness, though, refused to testify, invoking the privilege against self-incrimination. The prosecutor then granted immunity to the witness from the use of the witness's grand-jury testimony. Relying on the immunity, the witness admitted to shooting the victim and identified the accomplice who also shot. After granting a plea deal with the accomplice, the prosecutor subsequently charged the grand-jury witness with the shooting, planning to call the accomplice to testify at trial. What result if the witness's defense counsel moves to suppress the accomplice's testimony, relying on the immunity?

A. Motion denied because the accomplice's testimony was voluntary and independent.
B. Motion denied because authorities knew the witness was present before his testimony.
C. Motion granted because the witness's testimony identified the accomplice.
D. Motion granted as prosecutors cannot bargain codefendant rights against one another.

347. A dentist owned a duplex residential property on which a bank had a recorded purchase-money mortgage securing a $100,000 loan balance that the dentist still

owed from his original purchase. The dentist lived in one side of the duplex and a tenant in the other side. The dentist decided to move and so sold the duplex to the tenant on a written and signed land contract in which the tenant agreed that the tenant was subject to the dentist's mortgage on the duplex. The dentist and tenant did not notify the bank because the mortgage included a due-on-sale clause. The bank, knowing nothing of the sale, assigned its mortgage to a real-estate investment trust. What are the obligations if the tenant defaults on the purchase-money loan now held by the trust?

A. The bank may foreclose, sell, and collect any deficiency from the dentist.
B. The bank may foreclose and sell but may not collect any deficiency from the dentist.
C. The trust may foreclose, sell, and collect any deficiency from the dentist.
D. The trust may foreclose, sell, and collect any deficiency from the tenant.

348. A woman had wanted to shoot the rapids on a river since she was a little child. She was pleased to learn that some young men had started a company that offered rides down the rapids. The woman did not hesitate to hire the company for a ride down the rapids, even though she had seen many rafts flip on the rapids. The woman was injured when her raft flipped. She sued the company. The company's liability insurer assigned defense counsel. What affirmative defense should defense counsel plead?

A. Implied assumption of risk.
B. Express assumption of risk.
C. Contributory negligence.
D. Comparative negligence.

349. A state education department promulgated a rule permitting high school students to choose their gender identity for purposes of using whichever public-school bathroom and shower facility that they deemed appropriate. A parent group concerned with the rule's negative effect on female students who had suffered sexual assault took out a full-page advertisement in the state's largest newspaper urging citizens to take any and all necessary steps to oppose the rule. The advertisement published the names and government addresses of the department officials responsible for adopting and enforcing the rule, urging citizens to deluge and pressure the officials to rescind the rule. The advertisement also included contact information for state legislative representatives whom the advertisement said must enact legislation reversing the rule. State officials wrote the parent group ordering that the group cease and desist from publishing any further such advertisement. What result if the parent group brings proper suit challenging the constitutionality of the state officials' order?

A. Officials prevail because the call to take any and all necessary steps incites violence.
B. Officials prevail because of the compelling interest in regulating subversive speech.
C. Parents prevail because media advertisements have greater First Amendment protection.
D. Parents prevail because the state has no substantial interest justifying the order.

350. A building collapsed shortly after completion of its construction. The building's owner sued the architectural firm in malpractice for the building's allegedly defective design. At the trial of the claim, the owner presented the testimony of a

qualified engineering expert who testified to the cause of the collapse, the engineering standard, and the firm's breach of the standard. Defense counsel objected, though, when the owner further offered the expert engineer's testimony that the firm's personnel committed engineering malpractice. How should the trial judge rule?

A. Inadmissible though opinion on an ultimate issue because not to criminal state of mind.
B. Inadmissible because not opinion on an ultimate issue and instead only state of mind.
C. Admissible though opinion on an ultimate issue because not to criminal state of mind.
D. Admissible because not opinion on an ultimate issue and instead only state of mind.

351. An accountant determined to sue a client for nonpayment of accounting fees. For convenience, the accountant chose the accountant's own state in which to file suit. The client resided in another state but had enough contacts with the accountant's state to satisfy personal jurisdiction. The accountant had his client's current address in the other state but chose to follow a state statute that permitted the accountant to serve the client only by publishing notice of suit in the local newspaper. If the client receives no notice of the suit, then what result if the client later attacks the default judgment by challenging the constitutionality of service by publication?

A. Client loses because state law authorized service by publication.
B. Client loses because client had minimum contacts with the jurisdiction.
C. Client wins unless the court had ordered substituted service after motion.
D. Client wins for the manner of service having failed to satisfy due process.

352. A boater determined to sell his boat over the winter while the boat was out of the water in dry dock. In early spring, the boater represented to a potential buyer that the boat was seaworthy in that the boat had indeed been fine on the water when moved in the fall into dry dock. The boater and buyer agreed on a sale price significantly below the market value for seaworthy boats of that type, which the buyer promptly paid. The buyer immediately had the boat put in the water, whereupon it promptly sank due to major cracks in the hull that experts opined had opened as the hull dried out of the water in winter. The buyer, who lived out of town and hadn't seen the boat in dry dock, was unaware of the cracks and that the boat was not seaworthy when he represented it to be so. The boat had only modest salvage value well below the purchase price. What is the most relief that the buyer may be able to obtain in an action against the boater?

A. Expectation damages of the full market value of the boat as if seaworthy.
B. Rescission of the contract including return of the full purchase price.
C. Only the difference between the purchase price and modest salvage value.
D. No relief because the boater had no knowledge that the boat wasn't seaworthy.

353. A supervisor and two subordinates finished work and headed out in the supervisor's vehicle for an evening of partying. Late in the night, and after much rowdy fun, the three were cruising slowly from one party to another when they got into

a heated argument with the driver of another cruising vehicle. The supervisor cut off the other driver, got out, pulled the driver from his vehicle, and choked him to death. The subordinates did nothing to either urge on the supervisor or to discourage the attack or aid the driver victim. They simply watched the event unfold. But then when the victim fell dead to the ground, the subordinates urged the supervisor to get quickly back in the vehicle and flee the scene, which the supervisor did with the subordinates. Detectives later arrested the supervisor and subordinates, following which prosecutors charged the supervisor with manslaughter and subordinates as accomplices. Do these facts justify the accomplice charges?

A. Yes because the subordinates made no effort to intervene.
B. Yes because the subordinates urged the supervisor to flee.
C. No because they did not encourage the supervisor to commit the crime.
D. No unless the supervisor first suffers conviction for the crime.

354. An employer agreed to back a key employee's credit so that the employee could qualify for a high-value home loan. The employee completed the purchase, duly executing a purchase-money mortgage that the lender duly recorded. While the employee was the sole named obligor on the promissory note, the employer agreed in an attached writing to act as the employee's surety for the home-loan-note obligation. Over the next two years, the employee made regular payments on the home loan plus, when receiving a year-end bonus, a substantial lump-sum reduction of the loan's principal. The lender, though, improperly applied the lump-sum reduction to a credit-card balance that the employee also owed the lender. The employee then quit for another job in a foreign company and abandoned the home without making another payment. If the lender sues the employer to recover the outstanding home-loan obligation, then what theories should each side pursue in the litigation?

A. The employer subrogates as to the employee's rights while the lender pursues suretyship.
B. The employer assigns the employee's rights while the lender pursues subrogation.
C. The lender should foreclose while the employer relies on the equity of redemption.
D. The lender should assign while the employer seeks the employee's indemnification.

355. A developer retained an excavator to dig foundations for an urban highrise. The excavator encountered rock that the excavator could only economically remove with blasting. The excavator, who had substantial experience in blasting, followed all reasonable precautions regarding the work. Nevertheless, an unpredictable blast scattered debris over a neighboring auto dealership, ruining the paint job on every vehicle. The dealership's insurer paid for the vehicle damage. The insurer then retained counsel to evaluate a tort claim against the excavator by subrogation into the dealership's rights. Which of the following is the best evaluation of the insurer's claim against the excavator?

A. The insurer has no strict-liability claim because the excavator followed reasonable precautions.
B. The insurer has no strict-liability claim because digging foundations is a reasonable necessity.

C. The insurer has a negligence claim because the excavator must have done something wrong.
D. The insurer has a strict-liability claim based on the conduct of an abnormally dangerous activity.

356. A Native-American advocacy group erected a tent city on federal land in the path of a pipeline that if completed would cross a site that some Native Americans consider sacred. The group's purpose in peacefully occupying the tent city was to protest the destruction of sacred Native-American sites. The federal Bureau of Land Management began to remove the tent city under a regulation the only purpose of which was to protect an endangered flower by prohibiting camping on the tent-city site. What result if the Native-American advocacy group challenges the regulation as violating the group's First Amendment rights?

A. Government wins because government owns the federal land and can do with the land as it determines will best promote energy policy.
B. Government wins because the neutral law directly and narrowly protects an important interest, leaving alternative speech avenues.
C. Advocacy group wins because the tent city constituted expressive conduct carrying a message of protest that the First Amendment protects.
D. Advocacy group wins because Native Americans must know best how to treat sensitive flora and fauna on their own sacred lands.

357. Surgeons mistakenly cut into a patient's nerve roots when performing cosmetic facial surgery. As a result, the patient lost sensation and control in one side of her face. The patient sued the surgeons for malpractice. To prepare for trial, the patient's counsel retained a medical illustrator to work with the plaintiff's retained expert-witness surgeon to draw an anatomical diagram of the surgery and nerve injury. At trial, the patient's counsel then offered the diagram to support the expert witness's testimony. If the trial judge permits use of the anatomical diagram, then which of the following would be the best grounds?

A. The diagram is real or physical evidence of the actual conditions and events.
B. The diagram is demonstrative evidence assisting the jury with visual context.
C. The diagram is testimonial evidence established through first-hand knowledge.
D. The diagram is documentary evidence reflecting records underlying the case.

358. A farm-equipment manufacturer is incorporated and has its principal place of business in a western state. An engine maker incorporated and with its principal place of business in a southern state supplied defective engines to the farm-equipment manufacturer giving rise to a $100,000 claim. The engine maker manufactured the defective engines in a northern state before shipping them to the farm-equipment manufacturer's home western state. Assuming that each of the involved western, southern, and northern states has only one federal judicial district, where would the farm-equipment manufacturer have federal-district court venue for the claim?

A. Only in the farm-equipment manufacturer's home western state.

B. Only in the engine maker's home southern state or the northern state where it made the engines.
C. Only in the farm-equipment manufacturer's home western state or the northern state where the engines were made.
D. In any of the involved western, southern, or northern states, or any other state of personal jurisdiction over the engine maker.

359. A marina owner negotiated with a jet-ski service for the service to lease use of the marina's lakeshore and docks to rent jet skis to water-sports recreationists. The parties agreed on a five-year lease. By the lease's third year, water levels in the lake had fallen to such historic lows that the service could no longer use the marina's shore and docks to operate its jet-ski services. The service therefore terminated the lease, moving its jet skis to another leased location. The marina was unable after reasonable effort to find any replacement lessee. What result if the marina owner sues the jet-ski service for the remaining lease payments?

A. Marina wins because the jet-ski service still had use of the lakeshore and docks.
B. Marina wins because the marina was unable with reasonable effort to re-lease.
C. Jet-ski service wins because of the impracticability of its performance.
D. Jet-ski service wins because of the contract's frustration of purpose.

360. A woman who needed money to pay her rent decided to steal jewelry from her friend and pawn it for money. Knowing that her friend was out of town, the woman broke the lock on a rear window on her friend's house and climbed her way in, under cover of night. The woman found and took her friend's jewelry box. She climbed out the back window with it, planning to cross the backyard and return to her vehicle parked on another street. Halfway there, though, the woman had second thoughts and decided to return the jewelry, opening the window again and tossing the box on a chair inside. On the friend's return and discovery of the broken window, the friend reported the matter to prosecutors who, to her friend's surprise and regret, identified and charged the woman. With what crimes may prosecutors convict the woman over the friend's objection?

A. No crimes because the friend did not complain and instead regretted prosecution.
B. Burglary but not larceny because the woman returned the jewelry before discovery.
C. Burglary but not larceny, which is a lesser included offense to burglary.
D. Burglary and larceny because the woman completed both crimes.

361. A mortgage broker obtained an appraisal on a new home that the broker knew was substantially more than the home's market value and then used that appraisal to loan an amount over the home's market value to an unsophisticated first-time homebuyer. The broker then sold the mortgage loan to a real-estate investment trust, which took an assignment. The homebuyer made several more payments on the loan to the broker, which had not notified the homebuyer of the broker's assignment to the trust. The homebuyer then refinanced with a bank for a lower interest rate but made no further payments because of job loss. How should the homebuyer defend if the broker sues on the loan and for foreclosure?

A. Plead novation, impossibility, and redemption.
B. Plead misrepresentation, assignment, credit, and discharge.
C. Plead poverty, immunity, release, and satisfaction.
D. Demand that the refinance company defend and indemnify.

362. A rancher bred, trained, and sold bucking bulls for use in rodeos often conducted to benefit charities. A rodeo producer purchased one of the rancher's bulls and kept it in a field. A neighboring farmer had his jacket blow off of his tractor and into the producer's field in sight of the bull. The farmer entered the field to retrieve his jacket, knowing that the bull might charge, having seen it do so on several prior occasions and knowing that the rancher had bred, trained, and sold the bull for its high spirit. The bull seriously injured the farmer in its charge. The farmer retained counsel who sued the rodeo producer for strict liability for a wild animal and abnormally dangerous activity. Counsel served the complaint on the producer who forwarded it to the producer's defense lawyer for answer. Which of the following defenses should the lawyer plead?

A. Assumption of risk and disclaimer of warranties of fitness.
B. Assumption of risk and contributory or comparative negligence.
C. Contributory or comparative negligence and consent.
D. Contributory or comparative negligence and charitable immunity.

363. A newspaper editor developed a deep mistrust for certain local public officials based on years of writing and editing stories relating to their suspected ineptitude and unaccountability. Finally, in an editorial published in the main edition of the local newspaper, the editor wrote that those local public officials must be cooperating with and supported and influenced by corrupt mobsters, given the latest evidence of their wrongdoing. Aggrieved at the editor's accusations, the officials filed suit in the proper court seeking an injunction against the editor publishing anything further regarding the officials' conduct. What result if the editor challenges the suit, asserting First Amendment protections?

A. Officials win because the publication editorialized rather than reported news.
B. Officials win because accusation of mobster influence is per se defamatory.
C. Editor wins because the requested injunction would be a prior restraint.
D. Editor wins because the press has the freedom to publish whatever it wishes.

364. An employee filed a civil suit against her employer and supervisor, alleging that the supervisor committed a sexual assault on her while at work. The employee alleged physical injury, sexual disease, and severe mental and emotional distress. The employee further alleged the employer's vicarious liability for ratifying the assault and direct liability for negligent hiring and entrustment. The employer's defense counsel sought medical records and psychological records of the employee's treatment before and after the alleged event, while the employee's counsel moved for protective order to deny production. How should the court rule?

A. Order production of the medical and psychology records.

B. Order production of the medical records but deny production of the psychology records.
C. Deny production of the medical records but order production of the psychology records.
D. Deny production of the medical and psychology records.

365. A commercial designer provides decorating services for the offices of multinational corporations. The designer has its state of incorporation and principal place of business in a large eastern-seaboard state close to many of its multinational clients. The designer also does significant design work in a large southeastern state where other multinational corporations maintain their office headquarters. The designer's service contract includes a clause providing for the parties to litigate any suits arising out of the contract in the designer's home eastern-seaboard state to the exclusion of any other forum. A multinational client nonetheless sued the designer in the southeastern state where the client had its headquarters, the designer was to provide the contract services, and the designer had other significant business. How should the designer proceed if it wants the dispute heard in its home eastern-seaboard state?

A. Ignore the action as improperly served, while filing a home-state action.
B. File a motion to dismiss the action because venue is improper.
C. File a motion to transfer venue because venue is inconsistent with the contract.
D. File a motion to dismiss the case because the forum is inconvenient.

366. A woman who wished to straighten her hair went online to read about various straightener products. She chose one the directions for which she could easily follow. The woman purchased the product and used it according to directions. The product nonetheless burned her scalp, causing hair loss and scarring. The woman retained counsel who filed a breach-of-express-warranty claim against the product's manufacturer. The manufacturer moved for summary judgment arguing that it had given no express product warranty. How should the woman's counsel best respond to the manufacturer's motion?

A. The law implies a warranty of merchantability.
B. The law imposes a warranty that a consumer product will not injure its user.
C. The product must carry the qualities of hair straighteners generally.
D. The product's description and directions expressly warranted that a fit product.

367. A homeless man fell asleep one night in a chair just inside the lobby entrance of a glamorous downtown hotel. As local authorities had approved, the hotel's desk clerk rousted the homeless man from his sleep, demanding that he leave the premises. As he got up to go, the homeless man cursed the desk clerk under this breath. In response, the desk clerk struck the homeless man several times about the head with a heavy brass doorstop that the clerk had brought along for protection. Impeded from leaving, the homeless man reached into his coat pocket for a mace spray that he kept to discourage attackers and sprayed the desk clerk in the face, causing the desk clerk serious eye injuries. Assuming that the jurisdiction defines aggravated assault as assault intending to commit serious injury, then what is the most-serious crime for

which prosecutors could convict the homeless man?

A. No crime.
B. Burglary.
C. Assault.
D. Aggravated assault.

368. A land-rich and cash-poor elderly testator executed a valid will devising to his nephew a farm that the testator had just purchased for its $1,000,000 fair-market value. The will further directed the sale after the testator's death of three other real properties valued at $3,000,000 in total, to fund out of those specific proceeds bequests of $1,000,000 to each of his three nieces. The will had no other applicable provisions. A severe recession shortly before the testator's death reduced by two thirds the value of the three specific properties that were to fund the nieces' bequests. The estate's sale of the properties realized only $1,200,000. The farm retained its $1,000,000 value right up until just before the testator's death, but the testator had to sell it to pay business losses associated with the recession. After the testator's death, the estate had no other remaining distributable funds, assets, or interests other than the $1,200,000 in proceeds from the sale of the three specific properties. What property or funds will the nephew and each niece realize under what law or doctrine?

A. The nephew gets nothing because of the doctrine of ademption, while the nieces each get $400,000 because of the operation of abatement.
B. The nephew gets $300,000 and the nieces each get $300,000 because of the operation of the doctrines of abatement and adjustment.
C. The nephew gets $1,000,000 and the nieces each get one third of the remaining $200,000 because of the doctrine of exoneration.
D. Neither the nephew nor the nieces get anything because the testator sold the properties or left insufficient value for full funding.

369. A woodworker purchased a new table saw from its manufacturer. The table saw came with a rip fence to guide wood into the saw parallel to the saw blade. The particular table saw that the woodworker purchased had the rip fence slightly twisted relative to the saw blade because of a manufacturing defect in the rip fence's alignment. With the table saw's rip fence twisted in manufacture, the saw had a propensity to violently kick back boards toward the saw's operator just as the boards were about to clear the saw blade. The woodworker was seriously injured by one such kickback before discovering the manufacturing defect. The woodworker consulted a lawyer who prepared a demand to the manufacturer in strict products liability. Which of the following best states the strict-products-liability standard?

A. The manufacturer is liable because the table saw as impliedly warranted was not reasonably fit for its ordinary and intended uses.
B. The manufacturer is liable because the table saw was in a defective condition unreasonably dangerous to the woodworker.
C. The manufacturer is liable because its assemblers and inspectors must have been negligent to twist the rip fence in manufacture.
D. The manufacturer is liable because a covenant of good faith and fair dealing is implied in every product-sale contract.

370. The energy industry developed experimental means to transport liquefied natural gas by container ship for overseas sale. An executive agency promulgated an emergency rule prohibiting any such transport and sale until the agency completed a review of the environmental effect and public safety of the proposed transport. Very late in the term, just before adjourning, both chambers of Congress passed legislation that would have reversed the executive-agency action prohibiting the foreign sale of domestic liquid natural gas pending agency review. However, the president did not either sign or veto the legislation, instead letting it lapse after Congress had adjourned. What result if a natural-gas exporter challenges the emergency rule based on Congress's action?

A. Exporter wins because Congress enacted legislation reversing the agency rule.
B. Exporter wins only if Congress overrides the president's veto after return from recess.
C. Agency wins because Congress has no authority to override an emergency rule.
D. Agency wins because the president's inaction constituted a pocket veto.

371. An employee threatened to sue her employer for race and sex discrimination relating to the employer passing her over for promotion. The employer denied any wrongdoing, maintaining that it had promoted more-qualified employees. The employer nonetheless offered to settle the employee's claim in exchange for a release and confidentiality agreement, believing that settlement was preferable to litigation from both management and morale standpoints. The employee rejected the offer and sued. At the trial, the employee's counsel offered the employee's testimony regarding the employer's pre-suit offer to settle. How should the trial judge rule on the employer's objection?

A. Overrule the objection and permit the evidence for any use.
B. Overrule the objection but permit the evidence only as evidence of bias or prejudice.
C. Overrule the objection but permit the evidence only as to the validity of the claim.
D. Sustain the objection and prohibit the evidence.

372. A citizen of a foreign country died when a pleasure boat operated by a local resort capsized on a lake in the country's dry region. The deceased citizen's personal representative sued the boat's American manufacturer for products liability for the death, bringing the suit in federal court in the state of the manufacturer's incorporation. The manufacturer moved to dismiss, invoking the doctrine of forum non conveniens, establishing that the physical evidence and fact witnesses were in the foreign country, which had the greater public interest in the matter in that the accident killed the citizen of that foreign country. What result if the personal representative showed in response that the foreign country had no civil justice system in which to maintain the suit?

A. Deny the motion for lack of an available alternative forum.
B. Deny the motion because the federal forum is also convenient.
C. Grant the motion and dismiss the case under forum non conveniens doctrine.
D. Grant the motion but rather than dismiss, hold court in the foreign country.

373. A local department store retained a commercial designer to decorate the store's several large street-level windows for the holiday shopping season for a design fee of $10,000 plus approved materials. The contract required the designer to complete performance before Thanksgiving Day. The contract further provided that the designer must pay $50,000 in liquidated damages, five times the contract amount, in the event of any delay in full performance. The designer finished ninety percent of the work before Thanksgiving Day but didn't complete the last ten percent until the day after Thanksgiving. What is the probable outcome if the store sues, claiming the $50,000 in liquidated damages?

A. Actual damages only because the clause is void as a penalty.
B. $5,000 in liquidated damages, representing the ten percent incomplete.
C. $10,000 in damages, representing the full design fee.
D. The full $50,000 in liquidated damages.

374. Boyfriend and girlfriend had just finished a fine meal in a downtown district and were walking a few blocks away to where they had parked their vehicle. An assailant jumped out at them from a vestibule, brandishing at the girlfriend what looked like a gun while demanding that the boyfriend give the assailant all the boyfriend's money or he would shoot the girlfriend. The boyfriend promptly did so, following which the assailant ran away with the money. Police caught the assailant, whom prosecutors prepared to charge to discourage a series of like incidents. Assuming the jurisdiction punishes robbery as a more-serious crime than assault or larceny, which is the most-serious crime for which prosecutors may convict the assailant?

A. Assault on the girlfriend.
B. Assault on the boyfriend and girlfriend.
C. Larceny from the boyfriend.
D. Robbery from the boyfriend.

375. An older brother fell ill, cared for in his own home by his younger sister. Although the brother had adult children of his own whom he loved, his sister's devoted care convinced him to devise his home to his sister in a will that he executed while nearing death. The brother's valid will left the residuary of his estate to his children. To everyone's surprise, the sister fell ill and died shortly before the brother's own demise. The sister, like the brother, also left adult children of her own, to whom she left her entire estate in her own valid will. To whom will the brother's home pass?

A. To the brother's children because the sister predeceased her brother and is not alive to receive and enjoy the devise.
B. To the sister's children because although the sister predeceased her brother, he wanted her to have it, and her children having it is next best.
C. To the brother's children if lapsed under the common-law doctrine, but to the sister's children if saved under an anti-lapse statute.
D. To the brother's children if saved under an anti-lapse statute, but to the sister's children if lapsed under the common-law doctrine.

376. A family bought a plastic hockey stick for a young boy. The family bought the stick from a national-chain dollar store. When the boy used the stick to hit a tennis

145

ball, the stick's plastic blade separated from the stick's plastic handle, flying into and seriously injuring the eye of a young girl. Inspection showed that only a defective plastic rivet had connected the blade to the stick. The girl's father could not identify the hockey stick's manufacturer but learned that the family had bought it at the dollar store. The father contacted the dollar store's national headquarters, which indicated that an unknown overseas manufacturer had manufactured the stick, which the dollar store bought from a certain distributor. The father consulted counsel, requesting that counsel sue a responsible party for strict products liability for the defective stick injuring his young daughter. What action should counsel take pursuing the father's lawful objective?

A. Counsel should not sue anyone until identifying the manufacturer.
B. Counsel should name the dollar store and distributor as defendants.
C. Counsel should name only the young boy as a defendant.
D. Counsel should name the young boy's family members as defendants.

377. In response to reports of increased voter fraud in state and national elections, a state legislature adopted a photo-identification requirement for all registered voters. The legislation required each voter to present photo identification when voting or within a ten-day period following the election. Reliable studies of such laws in other states showed no effect on voting patterns. The legislation included a requirement that voters who failed to present photo identification when voting and who instead relied on the post-election photo-identification process must also read and recite aloud in English a statement of compliance. The federal Voting Rights Act prohibits literacy tests that discriminate racially against voters, as would the photo-identification legislation's read-and-recite provision. What result if a voter with standing challenges the constitutionality of the state photo-identification legislation's read-and-recite provision?

A. Voter prevails because the federal Voting Rights Act carries out the 15th Amendment.
B. Voter prevails because the 26th Amendment guarantees nationally uniform voting rights.
C. State prevails because Congress may not regulate the qualifications for state voting.
D. State prevails because the read-and-recite provision relates to photo identification.

378. A regional clothing retailer sued a national clothing retailer for antitrust violations. In discovery, the parties exchanged voluminous printed and electronic financial records. The regional retailer retained accounting experts to analyze the national retailer's records from which he experts created summaries reflecting entries that supported the alleged anti-trust violations. The experts also created damages calculations from the regional retailer's own records exchanged in discovery. Should the trial judge admit the regional retailer's summaries and calculations into evidence over the opposing national retailer's objection?

A. No, bar admission of the summaries and calculations.
B. No, bar admission of the calculations, but yes, admit the summaries.
C. Yes, admit the summaries and compilations.

D. Yes, admit the summaries and compilations but only with the underlying records.

379. A former employee sued his former employer for age discrimination relating to the employee's termination from employment at sixty-five years of age. The employer produced evidence in discovery that the manager making the decision to terminate did so for the employee's excessive unexcused absences (no call, no show) and for physically assaulting a co-worker. The employer further produced evidence that the employer had not filled the employee's former job. For his part, the employee produced no evidence in discovery of any writing, statement, or other evidence of the manager's allegedly discriminatory animus or that the reasons for discharge were pretext. If the employer moves for summary judgment, then how should the court rule?

A. Deny the motion because the manager's state of mind presents a genuine fact issue.
B. Deny the motion unless the employer supports it with affidavits or other evidence.
C. Grant the motion if the employee fails to submit evidence of discrimination.
D. Grant the motion because the business-judgment rule protects the employer.

380. A software developer negotiated with a product distributor to design a new electronic inventory-control-and-tracking system for the distributor's Midwest region. The developer and distributor expressly agreed that the developer's work would not include system coverage for the distributor's much larger national network. Instead, the parties expressly agreed that the small Midwest region was to be a low-cost pilot project for later high-cost development of a full national system. The parties then reduced their oral agreement to a written and signed contract that mistakenly purported to require the developer to design a full national system. The developer completed and distributor accepted and paid for the Midwest-region system design. The distributor then prepared to retain the developer under a new contract for the national system but discovered that the existing written agreement already called for such work. What is the probable outcome if the distributor demands that the developer complete a national system under the existing written agreement?

A. The developer must now comply with the existing agreement as written.
B. The developer has the option of complying or returning all funds.
C. Reformation of the agreement to reflect the parties' original intent.
D. Rescission of the agreement because it did not reflect party intent.

381. A shopper approached a leather-goods store clerk asking about a certain expensive leather coat. Relying on the shopper's false statement that she was a good friend of the store's owner, the clerk approved that the shopper don the coat to walk outside to get a feel for the fit. Once outside, the shopper quickly slipped away with the coat. A couple of weeks later, the store's owner saw the same shopper wearing the same coat at a mall several miles away, identifying her from surveillance video back at the owner's leather-goods store. The owner approached the shopper demanding the coat back or that the shopper pay for it, but the shopper told the owner to get lost or her face would regret it. The owner called mall security who apprehended the shopper.

What is the most-serious crime with which prosecutors could convict the shopper, assuming the following options list crimes in ascending order of seriousness in the jurisdiction?

A. Embezzlement.
B. False pretenses.
C. Larceny.
D. Robbery.

382. An elderly couple took out a mortgage on their home to pay the wife's medical bills. The wife passed away shortly later. The elderly man was unable to retire the loan obligation that the mortgage secured before his own demise. Shortly before his death, the man by valid will devised the home to the couple's eldest child, leaving the residuary of the estate to the couple's other, younger child. The will said nothing about how to treat the mortgage on the home. The home and residuary estate have approximately equal value, while the mortgage-loan balance is about half the value of the home. If the estate has no other assets or obligations, then what disposition of home, mortgage obligation, and residuary estate would the law provide, assuming that the couple's children make no agreed-upon adjustment?

A. The younger child and eldest child will divide the estate equally after the estate pays the mortgage balance and treating the home as part of the estate.
B. The younger child and eldest child will divide the estate equally, while the loan balance lapses and mortgage is discharged by the elderly husband's death.
C. The eldest child receives the home encumbered by the mortgage, while the younger child receives the residuary estate free of the mortgage holder's claim.
D. The eldest child receives the home free of the mortgage, while the younger child receives the residuary estate after reduction to pay the mortgage-loan balance.

383. A child was seriously injured when cut by a very sharp metal bracket on the underside of a folding table. The child's parents eventually retained a lawyer who inspected and photographed the table. The lawyer promptly confirmed that the table's metal framework had a date stamped on it indicating the manufacturer and a manufacturing date 11 years earlier. The lawyer also learned from the parents that the accident had happened on the now-14-year-old child's 11th birthday. Which of the following best describes steps the lawyer should take to determine whether the child has a products-liability claim against the table's manufacturer and, if so, to preserve that claim?

A. Determine the jurisdiction's statutes of limitations, tolling, and repose, and preserve the table.
B. Determine the jurisdiction's statutes of products liability and warranty, and dispose of the table.
C. Determine the manufacturer's insurance carrier, and make a demand including the photos.
D. Open a probate case for the child so that the probate court can authorize the parents' action.

384. A state public-school superintendent ran for reelection while seeking the support of local superintendents and building principals throughout the state. After the state superintendent won, he demoted several local superintendents and building principals who had supported his opponent in the election to ensure that he had uniform

support in the next election. The state superintendent had no other reason for demoting these public employees. The state superintendent had the general authority to retain, promote, and demote local superintendents and, through them, building principals to carry out public-school missions. What result if the demoted employees challenge the constitutionality of their demotion in a court of appropriate jurisdiction?

A. Employees win because unless the state superintendent gave the employees a hearing.
B. Employees win because of the violation of their First Amendment free-speech rights.
C. State superintendent wins because of his supervisory authority over subordinates.
D. State superintendent wins because of right to freely associate with those of his choice.

385. A drunken driver struck and seriously injured a bicyclist. Authorities arrested the driver, whom prosecutors then convicted of the drunk-driving offense. Because the conviction was a third offense, the court sentenced the driver to extended jail time. The bicyclist then sued the driver in negligence. The bicyclist's counsel deposed the driver in jail. On deposition, the driver admit that the driver was not only drunk but also careless in not seeing the bicyclist, although the driver further testified that the bicyclist was also careless in weaving into the driver's lane of the road. At trial, the bicyclist's counsel offered as evidence those portions of the driver's deposition testimony tending to implicate the driver. The driver's counsel objected, asking the court to prohibit the deposition's use or, failing that, to admit into evidence the other portions showing the bicyclist's own carelessness. How should the court rule?

A. Grant the request to prohibit use of all or any part of the deposition.
B. Grant only the request to include other parts of the deposition.
C. Overrule the objection, denying request to bar or include other parts of the deposition.
D. Overrule the objection and allow the deposition only if the driver is still incarcerated.

386. Counsel for a pedestrian seriously injured by a motor vehicle filed a damages action in an appropriate federal court under its diversity jurisdiction. The defendant whom counsel duly served with the summons and complaint defends on mistaken identity. Defense counsel has filed a motion to dismiss pursuant to Federal Rule of Civil Procedure 12(b)(6). The Rule 12(b)(6) motion attaches a police report identifying a different person as the vehicle's driver and showing that the defendant was merely a passenger. Defense counsel also attaches affidavits of both the defendant and the actual driver confirming these facts. What is the court's proper ruling on the Rule 12(b)(6) motion?

A. Deny the motion as based on materials outside the cited rule.
B. Deny the motion as raising a genuine issue of material fact.
C. Grant the motion, dismissing with prejudice.
D. Grant the motion, dismissing without prejudice.

387. A chemical engineer took new employment with an agribusiness company to develop new fertilizer and pesticide

products. The engineer's employment agreement required the engineer to treat as trade secrets the company's formulas and other confidential information including the engineer's new-product work. After significant product development, the engineer left the company a year later to work for a competitor under circumstances suggesting that the engineer had on departure removed confidential company files to share with the competitor. The company demanded the files' return, to which the engineer replied that the engineer had removed and intended to share only personal files that belonged to the engineer as his personal work product. What is the best result that the company could obtain in seeking to enforce the contract's trade-secret clause?

A. Expectation damages in the full amount of the loss of any trade-secret materials.
B. Discovery of the full extent of the specific materials that the engineer removed.
C. Declaratory judgment, specific performance, and injunction against further breach.
D. An order enjoining the engineer from ever working in the industry again.

388. A moody panhandler walked up to the order counter of a coffee shop and discretely emptied the tip jar of approximately $25 in cash into his coat pocket. Noticing the panhandler's action, a customer blocked the panhandler's exit from the shop while loudly berating him to put the tip money back in the jar. When the panhandler hesitated, the customer reached into the panhandler's pocket while striking the panhandler in the face. The enraged and embarrassed panhandler grabbed the customer by the throat, choking him to death. At the panhandler's murder trial, defense counsel requested jury instruction on manslaughter as a lesser included offense. Should the court grant the request?

A. No because the panhandler's theft provoked the customer's assault.
B. No because the panhandler intended to kill or cause serious injury.
C. Yes because the strike to the panhandler's face could be adequate provocation.
D. Yes because the panhandler's actions may have been only reckless.

389. A husband and wife constructed a small home on one half of their own home's lot in which the wife's elderly mother then lived. When the mother passed away, the couple divided their lot and sold the small home to a college student. The couple later sold their own home to a surveyor. The surveyor promptly confirmed that the student's driveway to the small home was on the surveyor's main lot. The student pointed out that the surveyor's utility pole and line to the surveyor's house was on the student's lot. What rights if any do the surveyor and student have to continue their current uses on one another's lots?

A. Neither gets to continue use of the other's lot unless the lot owner grants an easement.
B. Neither gets to continue use of the other's lot unless able to prove necessity.
C. Each gets to continue use of the other's lot under quasi easement implied by use.
D. Each gets to continue use of the other's lot under implied reciprocal servitude.

390. A reptile collector determined to obtain a python. Local ordinance prohibited

the keeping of wild animals, specifically including the python species of snake. The collector nevertheless located a pet distributor from whom the collector purchased a python. The distributor indicated to the collector to feed the python nothing larger than rats. Some months later, the neighbor's little dog went missing. The neighbor took the occasion to report the collector's ordinance violation to police authorities, suspecting the python's involvement in the little dog's disappearance, even though there was no indication that the python had left the collector's home. Veterinarians examined the python, confirming for the authorities that the python had eaten the neighbor's little dog. The neighbor filed a small claim against the collector for loss of the little dog. A magistrate heard the small claim. How should the magistrate rule?

A. For the neighbor based on the collector's negligent failure to confine the python.
B. For the neighbor based on strict liability for property damage from a wild animal.
C. For the collector if he reasonably believed the python ate nothing larger than rats.
D. For the collector so long as he kept the python reasonably confined within the home.

391. A rancher fell into a dispute with state conservation officials over the rancher's use for livestock grazing of federal lands located within the state. The rancher maintained that federal regulations and licensing permitted the grazing, while state officials maintained that the grazing threatened fish in downslope streams. When the state officials finally ordered the rancher to desist and threatened an injunction action, the rancher brought a proceeding against the state in the federal agency's administrative tribunal both to decide the dispute and award the rancher damages. What result if the state officials challenge the constitutionality of the federal proceeding?

A. Proceeding dismissed because general police powers remain vested in the states.
B. Proceeding dismissed because of Eleventh Amendment state sovereign immunity.
C. Proceeding goes to hearing because the rancher would have no other judicial forum.
D. Proceeding goes to hearing on the relative merits of the rancher and state claims.

392. At the trial of a medical malpractice case, the plaintiff's expert physician testified that the defendant physician breached the standard of care established by the custom in that field. Defense counsel had available at trial the leading medical treatise in that field. The treatise clearly indicated that the customary practice under circumstances like those involved in the case was contrary to the expert's testimony and instead consistent with the defendant physician's care. How if at all may defense counsel use the treatise if plaintiff's counsel objects to any use?

A. In any manner that defense counsel wishes including as substantive evidence.
B. Only as substantive evidence in the defense case, and not to impeach the expert.
C. Only to impeach the expert, and only on evidence that the treatise is authoritative.
D. Not at all because a treatise is hearsay outside of any recognized exception.

393. Plaintiff's counsel in an employment-rights action based on federal law served the individual defendant in person with a federal summons and copy of the complaint. Defense counsel promptly discerned from the face of the summons that the federal court had issued the summons five months earlier than the date of the summons's service. The time stamp on the copy of the complaint confirmed that the plaintiff had filed the complaint that same day five months earlier than the date of the complaint's service. On these facts alone, does defense counsel have a basis for a motion to dismiss the case?

A. Yes for a motion challenging service as improper.
B. Yes for a motion challenging service as untimely.
C. No because in-person service on an individual is proper.
D. No because dismissal would be without prejudice and the complaint promptly refiled.

394. An employer entered into a contract with a caterer for the caterer to throw a party for an employee-of-the-year whom the employer subsequently duly designated. The employer at first chose a supervisor as employee-of-the-year, directing the caterer to prepare for the party, but before notifying the supervisor changed its decision designating a manager instead. The supervisor then discovered her own original designation. What right would the supervisor have if the supervisor sues the caterer for a party in the supervisor's favor?

A. Right to enforce specific performance as the intended third-party beneficiary.
B. Right to expectation damages as the incidental beneficiary.
C. No right to enforce the contract under any terms because not a party to it.
D. No right to enforce the contract absent expressly stated right or express assignment.

395. An employee broke into his employer's human-resources office at night to examine the employer's records on his compensation, performance, and attendance. The employee believed at the time of the break-in that he was committing a crime, although in fact his conduct did not constitute a crime. The employee examined records but did not remove any records. A night watchman caught the employee just as he was leaving the human-resources office to return to his night shift. Prosecutors charged the employee with burglary. How should the charge resolve, assuming the event occurred in a jurisdiction that has expanded the burglary crime to include all buildings, not just residences?

A. Conviction because impossibility is not a defense to this type of crime.
B. Conviction because the employee had the requisite mental state at the time.
C. Acquittal because what the employee intended to do and did was not a crime.
D. Acquittal because the employee did not complete the crime, only an attempt.

396. Adjacent landowners hunted and fished on one another's wild lands at first by courtesy and later by express written agreement. Seeking to maximize the value of each land by this mutually beneficial agreement, the owners made their written agreement not only for the benefit of one another but for successors, heirs, and assigns. After years of mutual use, each landowner sold to other owners. One of those owners began to sell licenses to

friends to come and hunt and fish on the both lands. The other owner protested and attempted to prohibit not only the other owner's friends but also the other owner from making any further use of the land. What result if the two owners seek a court declaration of their rights?

A. Each owner may hunt and fish on the other's land by profit but not extend that right to others.
B. Each owner must not hunt or fish on the other's land because any such right ceased on land transfer.
C. The owner who sold licenses to friends to use the other's land has lost all right, and so has the other owner.
D. The owner who sold licenses to friends must disgorge to the other owner half of the profits to retain the right.

397. A cleaning company received service of a complaint alleging that the company had negligently damaged a customer's wood floors some years earlier when using a buffing agent that the customer himself had supplied. In a short answer pleading no defenses, the cleaning company admitted the complaint's allegations, confident that the court would reject the claim anyway both because of the customer's own negligence and that the customer had waited too long to file the complaint. If the customer moves for judgment on the pleadings, then which of the following states the most-probable outcome?

A. The cleaning company wins for the customer's failure to state a claim.
B. The cleaning company wins based on its affirmative defenses.
C. The cleaning company loses for failing to raise affirmative defenses.
D. The cleaning company loses for having guaranteed a good result.

398. A gunman shot and seriously injured a state congresswoman at a political event held on the grounds of a local community college. Data discovered on the gunman's home computer suggested a possible link between the gunman's horrific act and hate-filled social-media posts directed at women and minorities. In response, the state legislature enacted a statute prohibiting statements on public property likely to trigger imminent violence against women or minorities. Will the statute survive constitutional challenge?

A. Yes because the statute punishes only content-neutral speech against specific groups.
B. Yes because the state can prohibit fighting words in any forum, public or private.
C. No because the state cannot restrict speech on public property used as a public forum.
D. No because laws affecting women and minorities receive heightened scrutiny.

399. While witnessing several shockingly brutal gang-related murders, a wounded bystander yelled to watch out because "Peanut" was coming back. The bystander then succumbed to his wounds. Working from that information related by a witness who heard the bystander's exclamation, investigators soon arrested a figure whom the neighborhood knew by the nickname "Peanut." Prosecutors then charged Peanut with the crimes based on substantial circumstantial evidence. At trial, the prosecution called the witness to testify to the bystander's exclamation, in support of other evidence of Peanut's crime. How should the trial judge rule on defense

counsel's objection to the bystander's exclamation?

A. Bar the testimony because it is hearsay not within any recognized exception.
B. Bar the testimony because the declarant bystander is unavailable.
C. Admit the testimony because the declarant bystander is unavailable.
D. Admit the testimony because the statement was an excited utterance.

400. A property insurer rejected a policyholder's $100,000 jewelry-theft claim, resulting in the claim's trial. At trial, the policyholder attempted to prove that the policyholder had recently purchased $100,000 of jewelry with cash, when the policyholder's tax returns showed that the policyholder had no more than $5,000 in income in any recent year. The policyholder had no receipts or other records for the $100,000 jewelry purchase and could describe the jewelry only vaguely. The person from whom the policyholder claimed to have made the purchase could not remember any details of the purchase whatsoever. The policyholder had no explanation for the alleged theft other than that the jewelry had mysteriously disappeared from the policyholder's locked safe to which only the policyholder had access. If the jury finds for the policyholder but the insurer moves for new trial, then how should the trial judge rule?

A. Deny the motion because the insurer has given no indication of procedural defect.
B. Deny the motion because jury-trial rights have constitutional dimension.
C. Grant the motion because the policyholder is entitled to judgment as a matter of law.
D. Grant the motion because the verdict was against the great weight of the evidence.

Part IV: Multiple-Choice Answers & Explanations

A. First MBE Practice Exam

1. Part I—First 100 Questions (Questions 1-100)

1. **Civil Procedure.** Option B is correct because under FRCP 14, a defendant may within 14 days of answering implead a third-party defendant who is liable to the defendant for all or part of the claim. The retailer should plead its indemnity claim in a third-party claim against the manufacturer, filed with or within 14 days after the retailer's answer. Option A is incorrect because the shopper need not dismiss the case but may proceed against the retailer who would also be liable, whether or not the shopper or retailer hold the manufacturer liable in the same action. The retailer's demanding dismissal is not an action that would enforce the retailer's indemnity rights. Option C is incorrect because a settlement of the shopper's claim without the retailer notifying the manufacturer and giving the manufacturer an opportunity to defend may compromise the retailer's right to indemnity. The retailer may not have indemnity for an excessive amount, particularly when the manufacturer had no opportunity to challenge liability and damages. Option D is incorrect because the retailer has no counterclaim against the shopper, and a counterclaim is not the way to invoke indemnity and bring in the third party who owes it. The retailer needs a direct claim against the manufacturer, not a claim through the shopper.

2. **Contracts.** Option C is correct because the parol evidence rule does not bar evidence of subsequent oral agreements made after parties sign a written agreement. The parol evidence rule bars prior oral statements altering a subsequent written agreement. Option A is incorrect because the parol evidence rule does not affect later oral agreements. Option B is incorrect because the integration of a prior written agreement would not affect a subsequent oral agreement. Option D is incorrect because non-integration would also have no effect on a subsequent oral agreement.

3. **Criminal Law & Procedure.** Option C is correct because under *Miranda v Arizona,* before commencing custodial interrogation and as an absolute prerequisite to the admissibility of any statement, law enforcement must provide an individual with *Miranda* warnings to combat the inherently coercive atmosphere. Custody means restricting freedom of movement, while interrogation means direct questioning or its functional equivalent, that is, words or actions designed to elicit an incriminating response. Here, the young man was under arrest and in the police car, and thus in custody. The officer's offer to protect the young man if he told the officer the name of his dealer was an attempt to elicit an incriminating response. Option A is incorrect because the Supreme Court presumes all custodial interrogation is inherently coercive. Option B is incorrect because interrogation alone is not a basis for suppression, while failure to read *Miranda* rights is. Option D is incorrect because to invoke the right to silence, an individual must clearly and unambiguously indicate he does not wish to speak to law enforcement. Simply refusing to disclose a name does not clearly and unambiguously assert a desire to remain silent.

4. **Real Property.** Option D is correct because an owner seeking relief from lawfully enacted zoning to conduct a new use not permitted in the district does so by request for variance. The resident was seeking a new non-permitted use in a district under lawfully enacted zoning. Variance is her only choice. Option A is incorrect because the resident was proposing a new use rather than attempting to preserve a prior non-conforming use. Option B is incorrect because the resident has no change in circumstance to plead but is simply seeking a new use. Change in circumstance is not a zoning doctrine but a doctrine relating to servitudes. Option C is incorrect because the doctrine of amortization has to do with phasing out a prior non-conforming use, when here the resident had no prior non-conforming use.

5. **Torts.** Option D is correct because to be actionable, a misrepresentation must be verifiably false, not merely conjecture, salesperson puffing, or opinion. A salesman's statement that a product is the best on the market is probably opinion or puffing that one would expect to hear rather than a verifiably true or false statement. Options A and B are incorrect because the statement would still have to be verifiably false. Just because a survey indicates otherwise does not mean that the consultant is incorrect in giving an opinion which would not be verifiably false in any case. Knowledge and reliance are necessary but alone not sufficient. Option C is incorrect because although the statement may be true that the musicians were sophisticated, the conclusion is a non-sequitur. The producer relied on the consultant, but the consultant's statement was probably merely an opinion and puffing.

6. **Constitutional Law.** Option A is correct because the Supreme Court recognizes marriage as a fundamental right that an individual protects as a matter of substantive due process. A law that interferes substantially with a fundamental right triggers strict scrutiny. The law's proponent must show that it is necessary to serve a compelling state interest. Option B is incorrect because strict scrutiny requires a higher standard than substantial relationship to an important interest. Option C is incorrect because laws having important public purposes may nonetheless violate fundamental rights when not necessary to serve compelling interests. Option D is incorrect because the strict-scrutiny standard protecting fundamental rights is much higher than this option's stated rational-basis test.

7. **Evidence.** Option C is correct because lay witnesses may give opinions on matters that are rationally based on the witness's perception, helpful to understanding the witness's testimony or determining a fact issue, and not based on scientific, technical, or other specialized knowledge. Lay witnesses have testified to vehicle speed absent unusual factors. Option A is incorrect because to estimate the motorcycle's speed would be to draw a conclusion. Option B is incorrect because while present sense impression can take a statement out of the hearsay prohibition, this statement is not hearsay but instead raises a question of the witness's capability to testify to conclusions. Option D is incorrect because speed can be a matter of lay testimony based on the lay witness's driving experience and knowledge.

8. **Civil Procedure.** Option B is correct because under FRCP 23, a judgment in a class action conducted in the name of one or more representatives who adequately represent numerous other class members will bind those members. Here, the court certified the class, establishing that the results of the homeowner class representative's action would bind class members. Option A is

incorrect because class-action judgments bind class members. Option C is incorrect because class members need not join as class representatives in order for the class-action judgment to bind them. Option D is incorrect because class members need not have retained the lawyer who prosecutes the class action. They are bound by the results and representation.

9. **Contracts.** Option A is correct because the perfect-tender rule requires full performance of the precise contract terms in lieu of which the non-breaching party may accept and sue or reject and sue. Option B is incorrect because the retailer may also reject all mixers under the perfect-tender rule. Option C is incorrect because the retailer may accept the mixers but still sue for damages for the rest. Option D is incorrect because the substantial-performance doctrine does not apply in sale-of-goods cases, and this response does not correctly state the substantial-performance doctrine.

10. **Criminal Law & Procedure.** Option A is correct because although a drug detection dog's sniff is not a search in and of itself, the Supreme Court has cautioned that a seizure that is justified solely by the interest in issuing a ticket to the driver can become unlawful if it is prolonged beyond the time reasonably required to complete that mission. Option B is incorrect because the facts do not indicate that the drug detection dog physically intruded the passenger compartment of the car. Option C is incorrect because a drug detection dog's positive alert can establish probable cause. Option D is wrong because while drug detection dogs are not infallible, police officers may rely on their positive alert to establish probable cause.

11. **Real Property.** Option A is correct because the owner of a chattel who affixes the chattel to real property only temporarily, intending that the chattel not remain as a fixture, may bequeath the chattel apart from a deed or devise of the real property to which the chattel is affixed, if the chattel can be removed without damage to the real property. The doctrine of accession, in which a tenant or life estate holder affixes a chattel to the real property in a manner that law prohibits its removal such that it passes with the real property, does not apply. Option B is incorrect because although the bank has a security interest in the mantel, and UCC Article 9 authorizes security interests in fixtures, the estate has plenty of cash assets to pay off the loan, and so the bank would receive cash rather than the mantel. Option C is incorrect because the elderly man only affixed the mantel temporarily with the intent to convey it to the daughter. The mantel was not part of the real property for the charity to inherit. Option D is incorrect because the elderly man gave everything by will to his daughter other than the home, and the mantel was only temporarily affixed with the intent that the daughter receive it. The charity has no basis to claim the mantel whether it pays the value or not.

12. **Torts.** Option D is correct because truth is a defense to defamation claims, or more accurately, the defamation claimant has the burden to prove falsity. Here, the newspaper published nothing false, so it has no duty to retract. Option A is incorrect because the newspaper did not defame the owner, having published nothing false. Also, retraction does not eliminate but only mitigates defamation. Option B is incorrect because nothing indicates that retraction is prudent business. Retraction may be imprudent when the newspaper published only the truth. Option C is incorrect because retraction does not establish defamation, even though it may tend to confirm that what was published was untruthful.

13. **Constitutional Law.** Option C is correct because Congress has power to regulate commerce among the several states. While residential rentals may be only local in individual effect, the Supreme Court has held that Congress may rely on the aggregate of local effects that have a substantial effect on interstate commerce. A is incorrect because the Fourteenth Amendment limits only state, not private action, and the Supreme Court has held that the Amendment's enforcement clause thus only authorizes Congress to regulate state rather than purely private action. Option B is incorrect because the privileges and immunities clause grants Congress no power. Option D is incorrect because the general-welfare clause only grants Congress the power to tax and spend for the general welfare, not to regulate generally.

14. **Evidence.** Option A is correct because a lay witness with personal knowledge of the handwriting of the person in question may testify as to whether the document is in that person's handwriting for purposes of authenticating the document. The roommate showed her personal knowledge. Option B is incorrect because the business-records exception applies to a hearsay objection, and the objection here is authentication, not hearsay. Option C is incorrect because a lay witness may authenticate handwriting on personal knowledge. Option D is incorrect for the same reason and because the court need not for authentication purposes certify a lay witness with personal knowledge, as an expert in handwriting.

15. **Civil Procedure.** Option D is correct because parties may mediate a dispute with the assistance of a trained professional who helps the parties fashion voluntary, compromise, alternative relief. Courts have express or inherent authority to order mediation. Mediation in this case may help unwind the dispute by addressing the underlying issues. Option A is incorrect because the court has no basis for dismissal. Parties have rights to pursue relief in court even if litigation is inefficient. Option B is incorrect because a judge has no authority to dispense with discovery and hearing in order to impose the judge's own terms. Option C is incorrect because there must first be a basis in law or contract for arbitration, which appears here not to be the case. The parties have a right to resolve their dispute in court.

16. **Contracts.** Option D is correct because performance that does not meet the substantial contract terms leaves the party without recovery and liable for contract-breach damages. Here, gold shingles are not substantial performance. The roofer may have a quantum-meruit recovery for any net-positive value to the partial performance. Option A is incorrect because the owner's expectations have not been fulfilled and the roofer has no excuse. Option B is incorrect because the owner is entitled to the bargained-for shingles. Option C is incorrect because shingling is not a sale-of-goods case, so the perfect-tender rule does not apply.

17. **Criminal Law & Procedure.** Option C is correct because under *Ash*, until adversarial judicial proceedings commence, an individual is not entitled to the presence of counsel during a quick on-the-scene showup. Option A is incorrect because although identification experts agree that this instruction is necessary protocol, the Supreme Court has yet to adopt it as a legal requirement. Option B is incorrect because an individual does not have the right to counsel until adversarial judicial proceedings commence. Option D is incorrect because the man was not entitled to a lawyer at this show-up stage, and if he had been entitled to a lawyer, he would not have had to request the presence of counsel.

18. **Real Property.** Option B is correct because tickets to a commercial event are a license revocable at the will of the licensor. Here, the producer may revoke the license for any reason or likely no reason but especially for violation of well-publicized rules. Option A is incorrect because the facts give no clear indication that either the producer or even the rowdy patron was violating the law, which would in any case not necessarily justify terminating the season tickets. Option C is incorrect because the law construes attending a commercial event as a revocable license notwithstanding the ticket purchase. The producer would have to pay damages if the revocation breached the purchase terms, but revocation would remain the producer's right. Option D is incorrect because the holder had several warnings, and even without warning the producer would have had a right to revoke the license.

19. **Torts.** Option C is correct because economic loss typically begins with medical expense and wage loss. Several weeks in the hospital would likely mean substantial medical expense and a period of complete disability from consulting work. Option A is incorrect because the more substantial economic losses would be the medical expense and work loss, and because although damage to the computer would be one economic loss, it would be measured by diminution in the computer's value, not what the consultant could have earned using the computer. She must mitigate her damages by acquiring another computer. Option B is incorrect because it omits the substantial medical expense as a typical form of economic loss and because lost earnings (the wage value of work that the injured person was unable to perform), not loss of business profits, is the general measure for work loss. Option D is incorrect because it describes non-economic rather than economic loss.

20. **Constitutional Law.** Option D is correct because the ex-post-facto clause prohibits states from enacting laws that criminalize and punish acts occurring before the law's adoption. The new law could apply only to acts occurring after its adoption, whereas here the official had acted only before the law's adoption. Option A is incorrect because the new law could pass the due-process clause's rational-basis test. Option B is incorrect because the new law does not address a fundamental right or burden a suspect class, as the equal-protection clause would require for any standard higher than the easy-to-pass rational-basis test. Option C is incorrect because the new law does not affect citizenship rights within the privileges-and-immunities clause.

21. **Evidence.** Option C is correct because testimony about what a witness observes is admissible generally and opinion testimony that a person was under the influence of marijuana is admissible if established that the witness is familiar with what people look and act like under the influence of marijuana. Testimony about the machine's malfunction is not admissible without counsel first qualifying the witness as an expert on machine malfunctions. Options A and D are incorrect because testimony about the machine's malfunction is not admissible without counsel first qualifying the witness as an expert on machine malfunctions. Option B is incorrect because testimony about what a witness observes is admissible generally and opinion testimony that a person was under the influence of marijuana is admissible if established that the witness is familiar with what people look and act like under the influence of marijuana.

22. **Civil Procedure.** Option A is correct because those who anticipate litigation have a duty to take reasonable steps to preserve (not to spoliate) evidence. A reasonable manufacturer would have known that it must preserve the valve as evidence of a potential claim. The sanction may

be up to the manufacturer's default on liability or an adverse jury instruction. Option B is incorrect because the valve's unavailability was not the business owner's fault. A court would punish the manufacturer, not the business owner. Option C is incorrect because a court would construe the manufacturer's spoliation of the valve as evidence for liability. Option D is incorrect because although cleanup crews traced the backup, that fact alone may not be sufficient evidence to determine the nature of the defect and trace it to the manufacturer.

23. **Contracts.** Option D is correct because under the Uniform Commercial Code, only parties that perform may enforce a contract that requires both parties to tender performance. Option A is incorrect because the sportsman had a duty to tender performance in order to trigger the captain's duty. Option B is incorrect because the captain had a duty to tender performance in order to trigger the sportsman's duty. Option C is incorrect because each party's performance was a condition of the other party's performance.

24. **Criminal Law & Procedure.** Option B is correct because law permits police as social invitees to approach a home to conduct a knock-and-talk procedure. Although this argument will likely fail here, it is the best one and only accurate one that a prosecutor could make. Option A is incorrect because although the dog handler and drug-sniffing dog never went inside the man's home, they did enter the curtilage specifically looking for evidence of a crime. Option C is incorrect because the front porch, as curtilage, would enjoy the same Fourth Amendment protections as the home. Option D is incorrect because although the Supreme Court ruled that narcotics-dog drug sniffs are not always searches, *Florida v. Jardines* sets forth at least one example of when a drug sniff by a narcotics dog would constitute a search.

25. **Real Property.** Option C is correct because a sublease is the lease of less than all of the property or for less than the full term, while an assignment is a lease of the entire property for the entire term. A sublease of less than the entire tenancy leaves only the tenant and not the subtenant liable to the property owner, while an assignment would make both tenant and subtenant liable unless the owner discharges the tenant. Here, the tenant remained liable for the last two unpaid years of rent. The subtenant would be liable only to the sculptor and only for the one unpaid year of rent. Option A is incorrect because the sculptor would owe both years of unpaid rent, not just the last year, and the subtenant would owe only the tenant, not the property owner. Option B is incorrect because the sculptor owes for all of the two unpaid years, and the painter owes only the tenant and would owe $12,000, not $6,000. Option D is incorrect because the sculptor also owes for the unpaid sublet year, although the sculptor would have an action against the subtenant for that year.

26. **Torts.** Option B is correct because when parties settle a tort claim, the plaintiff signs an agreement releasing the settling defendant and its insurers and agents from further liability, while attempting to preserve rights against non-settling defendants. The operator should release the equipment designer and its insurer and agents but reserve rights as to other defendants. Option A is incorrect because the operator wishes to preserve the remaining claims against the non-settling manufacturer and installer. Option C is incorrect because release liability for actions would not forestall suing the same defendants for other actions, and no defendant would settle for actions leaving open the possibility of liability for other actions. Releases are as to persons and entities,

not actions. Option D is incorrect because the release should be of the settling party, not as to the amount. The operator may wish to recover less than $20,000 from other non-settling parties.

27. **Constitutional Law.** Option A is correct because the statute singles out an easily ascertained group for punishment without trial, within the Supreme Court's definition for an unconstitutional bill of attainder. Option B is incorrect because the statute appears to give individuals fair and reasonable notice of whether the statute would outlaw their specific conduct. Option C is incorrect because states share with the federal government interests in regulating for safety and security. Option D is incorrect because while the provision regulates a right of freedom of association, the First Amendment does not protect association for the purpose of committing violent crimes.

28. **Evidence.** Option A is the correct answer because the marital-communications privilege protects confidential communications between spouses made during the marriage. Option B is incorrect because the marital-communications privilege does not end with one spouse's death. Option C is incorrect because the sought-after testimony would not relate a co-conspirator admission, the charges involved racketeering rather than conspiracy, and the marital-communications privilege would prohibit the testimony even if it reflected an admission. Option D is not an excited utterance because it does not indicate any excited state, and excited utterance is a hearsay exception when hearsay is not the issue here. The privilege is the issue.

29. **Civil Procedure.** Option B is correct because under FRCP 56, a party responding to a summary judgment motion must set out specific facts showing a genuine issue for trial, supported by affidavit or otherwise. The borrower must articulate the misrepresentation and statutorily inadequate notice and support that articulation by affidavit, exhibit, or otherwise. Option A is incorrect because although articulating legal authority may help and would certainly be something that the borrower's counsel would do, the lender's motion presumably already addressed the law, which the court likely knows or can readily discover. Rule 56 requires instead that the borrower set out the disputed facts and support those facts with affidavit or otherwise. Option C is incorrect because discovery is complete, and one must respond to a Rule 56 motion not with discovery requests but with discovered evidence. Option D is incorrect because request for extension does not avoid summary judgment, and stipulation would require the lender's agreement when the facts give no indication that the lender is willing to agree.

30. **Contracts.** Option B is correct because culpable parties may not recover on an illegal contract; only innocent parties to an illegal contract have a remedy in quasi-contract. Here, neither party is innocent, so the law leaves them as it found them. Option A is incorrect because the retiree knew the tradesman was unlicensed and would thus be culpable in seeking to capitalize on the tradesman's lack of license. Option C is incorrect because the contract is illegal and cannot be enforced in law or equity. Option D is incorrect because the contract is illegal and the tradesman not an innocent party.

31. **Criminal Law & Procedure.** Option B is correct because in *Moran v. Burbine*, the Supreme Court held that on egregious facts, police deception might rise to a level of a due-process violation. Here, police deception permeated the entire episode and substantially affected the young woman's rights. Option A is incorrect because a lawyer may not invoke an

individual's *Miranda* rights. Option C is incorrect because the woman's waiver was not voluntary given the level of police deception. Option D is incorrect because even if the young woman did not invoke her rights, the due process violation renders the statement inadmissible.

32. **Real Property.** Option B is correct because although trust deeds (a mortgage substitute used in some states in which the landowner grants a deed in the lender's favor for a trustee to hold and auction if the landowner defaults) are usually enforceable much like a mortgage, one taking an interest in land takes subject to easements over which one has constructive notice in a jurisdiction having a statute requiring recording or constructive notice. Here, the bank either would or should have seen the neighbor's paved driveway and driveway use, and known of the neighbor's easement interest, when loaning in exchange for a trust deed. The neighbor's completed easement thus has priority due to constructive notice. Option A is incorrect because the order of easement before trust deed is alone not enough without considering recording or constructive notice. Option C is incorrect because the neighbor does not lose the easement right over failure to record if as here the bank had constructive notice. The neighbor would have lost the right if the neighbor never built the driveway and the bank did not otherwise have notice. Option D is incorrect because no general rule places trust deeds ahead of easements. And by the way, the neighbor would likely not have the right to park vehicles on the landowner's land because the easement was for a driveway, driveways are generally for ingress and egress, and parking vehicles may be beyond the easement's scope.

33. **Torts.** Option B is correct because tort liability extends to protect against harm to commercial interests, either for the commercial disparagement form of injurious falsehood or for interference with business relations, including forms of unfair competition. The above facts describe several acts that could constitute one or more forms of injurious falsehood. Option A is incorrect because the facts do not describe actions in which either was trying to get the other to rely upon a false statement. They were not scamming one another but instead competing by improper means. Option C is incorrect because competition alone is not an improper motive, and here the cleaners were competing out of their own interest in surviving. The law protects competition of this type. Option D is incorrect because the common law, while protecting economic interests and liberty, does not protect improper and wrongful conduct of the type described that harm economic interests and liberty.

34. **Constitutional Law.** Option D is correct because the statute was content neutral and thus subject to mid-level review in that it need only have been narrowly tailored to further a significant governmental interest. Government agencies have significant safety interests in avoiding fires inside public buildings, making the ban narrowly tailored to further that interest. Option A is incorrect because the statute passes the applicable mid-level test. Option B is incorrect because the statute does not require and need not require property damage, making irrelevant whether such damage occurred. Option C is incorrect because the activist intended the conduct to communicate protest of state energy policies, thus potentially extending First Amendment protection.

35. **Evidence.** Option B is correct because a party challenging witness testimony may generally show the witness's bias or interest. The prosecutor is showing that the partner has the same interest to protect, to defeat a criminal charge, as the owner whom the partner's testimony

supports. Option A is incorrect because the question does not elicit extrinsic evidence of the charge such as a record or another witness. Also, the prosecutor may not use extrinsic evidence of specific acts to impeach a witness. Option C is incorrect because a charge alone would show the partner's interest or bias, not merely a conviction, and the testimony would in any case be admissible to show bias or interest. Option D is incorrect because simply being prosecuted for an act does not mean one is guilty of it under the law, and so answering the question about the charge would not require the partner to incriminate himself.

36. **Civil Procedure.** Option D is incorrect because the 7th Amendment defines federal jury rights by historical practice for suits at common law, while state constitutions and practices define state jury rights. The federal court would try the case to a jury based on the historical practice when the nation adopted the 7th Amendment. Option A is incorrect because the federal court would not try a case to a jury in federal court without a jury right, even if the plaintiff had chosen a jury before removal. Option B is incorrect for the same reason, because the federal court would not try a case to a jury in federal court without a jury right, even if the defendant chose a jury after removal. Option C is incorrect because state-court practice does not determine federal-court jury-trial rights. The 7th Amendment determines jury-trial rights in federal court by reference to historical practice at the time the nation adopted the 7th Amendment.

37. **Contracts.** Option C is correct because the conscious-ignorance doctrine assigns the risk of loss to the one who deliberately accepts it. The prospector knew that the rock might be valuable but knowingly accepted that risk. Option A is incorrect because the parties were not mistaken, knowing that the rock might be valuable. The parties recognized that they were ignorant of value and accepted the risk that came with it. Option B is incorrect because misunderstanding applies when the minds appear to have met but have not. Option D is incorrect because the prospector was not mistaken but instead accepted the risk, and both sides accepted that risk rather than one side acting unilaterally.

38. **Criminal Law & Procedure.** Option C is correct because while once an individual invokes his right to remain silent, all questioning must cease, police may resume questioning if the individual reinitiates communication. Here, the young man specifically asked to speak to the detective. Option A is incorrect because although the detective made a comment after the young man said he did not feel like talking, the detective's comment did not amount to direct questioning or its functional equivalent. Option B is incorrect because the *Miranda* rule does not dictate the manner in which police incarcerate suspects. Option D is incorrect because the public-safety exception does not apply to these facts, there being no indication of public danger.

39. **Real Property.** Option B is correct because while the statute of frauds requires a writing signed by the party to be charged relating to the conveyance of real property, part performance removes a case from the reach of the statute of frauds. Here, the young couple gave substantial performance in paying twenty percent and taking over the payments, taxes, and insurance, all of which the developer accepted, confirming the oral agreement. Option A is incorrect because the statute of frauds permits an exception for part performance. Option C is incorrect because the developer must convey title rather than keep title, earn the sale profit, but reimburse the young couple. Option D is incorrect because quantum meruit is a quasi-contract theory rather than a

real-property concept, and the young couple partially performed such that they have an enforceable oral agreement.

40. **Torts.** Option C is correct because while the invasion-of-privacy tort takes one of four forms, either appropriation, intrusion, disclosure, or false light, the public-disclosure form involves the disclosure to more than a few of private facts that would highly offend the reasonable person. Here, the former boyfriend disclosed shameful secrets, which would have been private facts, to several of the young woman's friends, which would have been public disclosure, satisfying the elements of that invasion-of-privacy tort. Option A is incorrect because the former boyfriend did not appropriate the young woman's likeness for commercial exploitation. Option B is incorrect because the former boyfriend did not intrude on the young woman's seclusion. They were close at one time, and she voluntarily disclosed the secrets to him. Option D is incorrect because the former boyfriend did not place the young woman in a false light. The secrets were true. He just should not have disclosed them.

41. **Constitutional Law.** Option B is correct because under Supreme Court case law, state funding and accreditation of private educational institutions is not sufficient to satisfy the state-action requirement of the First and Fourteenth Amendments. The Amendments protect only against state, not private, action. Option A is incorrect because if the college's actions were state action, then it would have no such absolute right to interfere with others' free-speech rights, only a limited right to promote its own efficient operations. Option C is incorrect because accreditation (regulation) and funding are not sufficient involvement to meet the state-action requirement, which the Supreme Court has indicated requires greater involvement. Option D is incorrect because the First and Fourteenth Amendments do not reach purely private conduct, although state and federal civil-rights statutes do reach purely private conduct. This question involved only constitutional, not statutory, rights.

42. **Evidence.** Option C is correct because extrinsic evidence of a specific prior act is inadmissible in most circumstances. The former roommate's testimony is extrinsic evidence of a specific act. Prosecutor could cross-examine the machinist but would have to take the answer or call a reputation witness as to the machinist's violent nature if the machinist opened the door by putting his character for peacefulness or violence at issue. Option A is incorrect because hearsay is not the issue and the roommate's testimony would not be as to state of mind. Option B is incorrect because the roommate's testimony would constitute impeachment by extrinsic evidence of a specific prior act. Option D is incorrect because the roommate's testimony would not implicate the machinist's or anyone else's Fifth Amendment privilege against self-incrimination.

43. **Civil Procedure.** Option A is correct because under FRCP 54 and similar state rules, a judgment is a court paper (whether or not titled "Judgment") disposing of all claims in a pending case, from which an appeal then lies. The Opinion and Order dismissed both counts of the complaint, deciding all claims, meaning that the order was a final judgment from which an appeal lies. Option B is incorrect because the Opinion and Order did not contain judgment language, and whether it did or not, it would not be a final judgment from which an appeal lies unless it disposed of all claims. Options C and D are incorrect because the Opinion and Order is a final judgment. Option C is also incorrect because a court paper need not be titled as a final judgment in order to be a final judgment. It need only dispose of all claims. Option D is also

incorrect because a judgment need not mention appeal rights to be a final judgment from which an appeal lies.

44. **Contracts.** Option A is correct because the law requires both procedural and substantive unconscionability to void an agreement as unconscionable. Here, while the price was grossly substantively unfair, the tourist's initials suggest that the tourist made the agreement from a procedural standpoint. Option B is incorrect because the tourist had procedural but not substantive fairness. Options C and D are incorrect because the law requires both procedural and substantive unfairness.

45. **Criminal Law & Procedure.** Option A is correct because although the *Miranda* warnings need not be stated in exactly the same way they were articulated in the *Miranda* opinion, the manner in which law enforcement provides the warnings must accurately convey these substantive rights and protections: you have the right to remain silent; anything you say can and will be used against you in a court of law; you have the right to the presence of a lawyer now and during interrogation; and if you cannot afford a lawyer, then one will be appointed for you at public expense. Option B is incorrect because asking her if she understood her rights is only one factor, not the deciding factor, to consider in determining whether a waiver was made knowingly, intelligently, and voluntarily. Option C is incorrect because a homicide exception to the *Miranda* rule does not exist. Option D is incorrect because the detective's warnings did not correctly advise the woman of her *Miranda* rights.

46. **Real Property.** Option A is correct because any property owner subject to reciprocal servitudes may enforce those servitudes against any other property owner also restricted. Here, any of the remaining 40 lot owners could object and prevent the investor from developing offices on the residential lots. The reciprocal restrictions were for the benefit of all lot owners, not only those who conveyed away to the investor. Option B is incorrect because the facts give no direct indication that the residential lots were restricted against office development. The district may have permitted both residential and office development. Option C is incorrect because the lot owners who sold were not the only ones with reciprocal restrictions. The remaining 40 lot owners could also enforce the restriction. Option D is incorrect because the investor owning both the office parcel and the 10 residential lots does not remove the restriction on the 10 lots. Unifying title in a single owner does not give the owner power to avoid reciprocal restrictions favoring other lots that the owner does not own or control.

47. **Torts.** Option C is correct because the tort of malicious prosecution requires plaintiff to show that defendant maliciously caused criminal charges to issue without probable cause, with the charges resolved in the plaintiff's favor. The father must show that the mother had no probable cause and instead acted with malice, meaning with ulterior purpose or ill will. Option A is incorrect because the prosecution need have no particular consequence beyond causing the father some damage such as his lowered reputation and criminal defense. Option B is incorrect because the tort does not require prior false reports. They may be helpful to prove lack of probable cause and malice, but they would not be necessary. Option D is incorrect because the question is the complaining-witness mother's lack of probable cause, not the prosecutor's basis or lack of a basis for the charge, and the mother's malice rather than the prosecutor's malice.

48. **Constitutional Law.** Option A is correct because although Article III grants Supreme Court jurisdiction over federal questions arising under the U.S. Constitution, the Supreme Court has no such jurisdiction when a state court decides the case on alternative adequate and independent state grounds. Supreme Court review here would be advisory only given the independent state grounds on which the state high court has the last decision. Option B is incorrect because the Supreme Court has jurisdiction not only over cases deciding the constitutionality of federal law but also the constitutionality (under the federal constitution) of state laws. Option C is incorrect because although the state high court applied the U.S. Constitution, it also applied the state constitution as an adequate and independent ground for decision. Option D is incorrect because although the U.S. Constitution protects abortion, when the state high court overturned the new state statute on state-constitution grounds, the Supreme Court no longer had jurisdiction because its decision on federal constitutionality would have been advisory only.

49. **Evidence.** Option D is correct because the declarant's testimony is hearsay as testimony of an out-of-court statement used to prove the truth of the asserted matter. The declarant would be testifying as to what the witness said to the declarant that would then establish the asserted control. The declarant could only testify that the declarant saw the proprietor fixing the sidewalk, which would prove control. Option A is incorrect because whether the witness is available or not is irrelevant. The declarant's testimony would still be hearsay. Option B is incorrect because the declarant's testimony would still be hearsay. If the declarant had seen the proprietor fixing the sidewalk, and if the fixing of the sidewalk had occurred after the fall, then the court could admit the declarant's testimony for the limited purpose of proving control only if the proprietor denied control. The testimony would be inadmissible to prove that the sidewalk had a defect at the time of the fall. Option C is incorrect because the fixing of the sidewalk took place before the fall, not after the fall. If the fixing had occurred after the fall, then the subsequent-remedial-measure rule would bar the testimony other than for the limited purpose of proving disputed control.

50. **Civil Procedure.** Option D is correct because claim preclusion (res judicata) bars a party from re-litigating matters the party could have litigated in a prior action that reached final judgment on the merits against the same party. The shareholder is raising the same or similar claims to those that the prior action raised, and the prior action was a final judgment on the merits after discovery when the shareholder could show no triable fact issue. Option A is incorrect because although there could potentially be questions over what duties the corporation owed, a shareholder would likely have a private right of action over misrepresentations in public filings. Re-litigating issues of law or fact would take more research, discovery, and expense than moving for summary judgment on the basis of claim preclusion. Option B is incorrect because although there may be some corporate shield of individual officers, directors, and other shareholders, corporate immunity is unlikely, and re-litigating issues of law and fact takes more research, discovery, and expense, than moving based on claim preclusion. Option C is incorrect because the trial court would have had to have decided the same issues for issue preclusion to apply. The issues in the second case were arguably slightly different, meaning that issue preclusion may not apply.

51. **Contracts.** Option D is correct because gratuitous assignments that have not vested terminate upon the death of the assignor. Option A is incorrect because the promise is

unenforceable regardless of the sorority sister's ability to prove it. Option B is incorrect because no facts support vesting here. Option C is incorrect because no statutes limit gratuitous gifts to certain amounts.

52. **Criminal Law & Procedure.** Option D is correct because under *Arizona v. Gant*, police may search a vehicle incident to a recent occupant's arrest only if the arrestee is within reaching distance of the passenger compartment at the time of the search or reasonable belief is that the vehicle contains evidence of the offense of arrest. When these justifications are absent, a search of an arrestee's vehicle will be unreasonable unless police obtain a warrant or show that another exception to the warrant requirement applies. Option A is incorrect because the officer arrested the woman for careless driving and disobeying a police signal, making unlikely that evidence supporting either of those charges would be found in the woman's car. Option B is incorrect because even if the woman was a fleeing suspect, the exigency ended once the officer placed the woman in the back of his cruiser. Option C is incorrect because the officer did not need to take inventory of the car, which is not an exception justifying warrantless search under these circumstances.

53. **Real Property.** Option C is correct because a grantee may enforce an express written grant for value of an undescribed easement later defined by use and acquiescence. The farmer granted the easement, which the herder then defined and as to which the farmer acquiesced. Note that although the herder used the easement for much longer than the period for adverse possession, a prescriptive easement would not have arisen because the use was by the farmer's consent rather than hostile. Option A is incorrect because the farmer's children had no right to exclude the heirs who succeeded to the enforceable easement. Option B is incorrect because the farmer's children may not relocate an easement that the parties to the grant had defined by use and acquiescence. The easement then is as good as if described. Option D is incorrect because the herder's children may keep the easement and would not have a theory for compensation in relinquishing it.

54. **Torts.** Option D is correct because interference with business relations is established by proof of intentional harmful interference with a contract or business expectancy by improper or wrongful means. The exterminator improperly induced the key employee to breach a confidentiality and non-compete agreement to obtain confidential customer list and other trade secrets, and then used that information in a successful campaign to take the competitor's customers. Option A is incorrect because the exterminator used the improper means of inducing a contract breach to disclose trade secrets. Option B is incorrect because the facts do not indicate any disparagement of the competitor's trade, only use of the trade-secret information. Option C is incorrect because the facts give no indication of the exterminator disparaging any title of anything the competitor owned.

55. **Constitutional Law.** Option A is correct because Article II's appointments clause authorizes the president, not the Senate, to nominate ambassadors and other federal officers, with the Senate's advice and consent. The proposed legislation would unconstitutionally restrict the president's nomination power while also removing the Senate's advice-and-consent power when it failed to act within forty days. Option B is incorrect because the president's foreign power is not plenary but instead restricted in several respects such as Senate approval of treaties and

Congress's regulation of foreign commerce. Option C is incorrect because the legislation would restrict presidential nominations to the Senate committee's list, when the Constitution has no such restriction on presidential power to nominate ambassadors. Option D is incorrect because although Congress has such power, legislation limiting ambassador appointments would not necessarily exercise that power and would instead limit the president's appointments-clause power.

56. Evidence. Option D is correct because although generally, extrinsic evidence of specific acts is inadmissible, and one proves character only through reputation, opinion, and records of conviction, when character is an element of the claim or charge, extrinsic evidence of specific acts showing character are admissible. The mayor's reputation for dishonesty, bribery conviction, and rezoning vote after paid-for cruise all go to the truth of the citizen's statement that the mayor would change his mind for the right price. Option A is incorrect because it omits the admissible rezoning vote after paid-for cruise. Option B is incorrect because it omits the admissible reputation for dishonesty. Option C is incorrect because it omits the admissible bribery conviction.

57. Civil Procedure. Option C is correct because under FRCP 4(e)(2)(B), a plaintiff effects service by leaving summons and complaint with a person of suitable age and discretion residing with the defendant. Option A is incorrect because cases including *Mullane* have softened this former condition of *Pennoyer*. Option B is incorrect because the federal rules do not have a legal-age requirement for receipt of service of process. Only the server, not the recipient of service, must be of legal age. Option D is incorrect because the facts do not indicate that the defendant debtor was dodging service, and the federal rules do not extend service to residents on condition of dodged service.

58. Contracts. Option B is correct because disclaiming implied warranties materially alters a contract, and a material alteration becomes part of a contract between merchants only when the other merchant accepts the alteration. Buyer did not accept the alteration, so the disclaimer did not become part of the contract. Option A is incorrect because under 2-207, an offeree's response to an offer for the purchase or sale of goods need not be the mirror image of the offer, and so the Acknowledgment could have become part of the contract but for its material alteration of the contact or if buyer had accepted the alteration. Option C is incorrect because buyer, not seller, will prevail and accepting goods is not the same as accepting a material alteration in the contract. Option D is incorrect for the same reason that Option B is correct that the other merchant must accept material alterations for them to become part of the contract, and here buyer did not accept the alteration.

59. Criminal Law & Procedure. Option A is correct because conspiracy involves an agreement between two or more to commit the crime, and evidence of agreement may be circumstantial. The younger man's statement implies that the two men had discussed entering together while agreeing to import the illegal substances. Option B is incorrect because importing the substance alone would not constitute agreement between the two men to do so. Option C is incorrect because the younger man did commit a conspiracy and his statement was circumstantial evidence of the agreement to import. Option D is incorrect because the younger man was not necessarily cooperating and cooperation alone would not absolve the younger man of the crime.

60. **Real Property.** Option B is correct because a life estate passes to the heirs of the last-surviving joint tenant in the remainder interest even if neither joint tenant in that remainder survive the person holding the life estate. The farmer's heirs take the farm. The farmer and rancher held an indefeasibly vested remainder as joint tenants. The facts neither state nor imply any condition that they survive the friend in order to take. Because the rancher predeceased the farmer, the farmer took the property interest under the right of survivorship that joint tenants have. Upon the farmer's death, the remainder passed to his heirs. In turn, the farmer's heirs took the farm on the death of the friend, the life tenant. Option A is wrong because the friend had only a life estate; he had no interest to pass to his heirs at his death. Option C is wrong because the farmer survived the rancher and thus owned all of the remainder at his death; the rancher owned nothing. Option D is wrong because the landowner, having granted a life estate and an absolutely vested remainder, retained no interest in the farm.

61. **Torts.** Option C is correct because mistake does not negate intent, whether or not the mistake is reasonable. The rancher committed a conversion of personal property, which is an intentional tort dependent on the actor having intended dominion and control, whether or not the actor knew the personal property was someone else's. Option A is incorrect because the subjective belief of an actor that the property was his does not give the actor a defense to conversion. Option B is incorrect because even a reasonable belief is not sufficient to negate intent. Option D is incorrect because the reasonableness of the mistake is of no consequence. Even a reasonable mistake does not negate intent. Also, the facts state that the mistake was reasonable, meaning that the option does not address the question.

62. **Constitutional Law.** Option C is correct because while the First Amendment protects commercial speech, it does so to a lesser extent than core political speech, not protecting commercial speech that is misleading or deceptive. State law could provide liability for false commercial claims on a strict-liability standard. Option A is incorrect because the actual-malice standard applies to protect against defamation claims by public officials and public figures. Actual malice is not a commercial-speech standard. Option B is incorrect because the First Amendment does not protect misleading or deceptive commercial speech, when the speech here was in fact false, as sales and use soon proved. Option D is incorrect because while the states do regulate drugs for health and safety, drug companies would still have commercial-speech protection for truthful advertising, even if not for false claims.

63. **Evidence.** Option D is correct because records created outside of the attorney-client relationship unrelated to the representation are not within any representation-related privilege simply because the attorney takes possession of those records. The records remain evidence in the attorney's hands rather than becoming privileged. Option A is incorrect because attorney-client privilege involves confidential communications between attorney and client, not records unrelated to the representation held by a third party. Option B is incorrect because attorney work product is confidential material created by or at the direction of the attorney in furtherance of the representation, not records unrelated to the representation held by a third party. Option C is incorrect because records created and held by a third party do not implicate the privilege against self-incrimination. No one is asking the client to testify against the client's own interest in avoiding criminal conviction.

64. **Civil Procedure.** Option D is correct because neither Article III of the Constitution nor 28 USC §1332 permits aliens to sue aliens in diversity in federal court. Option A is incorrect because under 28 USC §1332(a)(2), a permanent resident alien is a citizen only for purposes of defeating diversity, not creating diversity. Option B is incorrect because no facts and no law support this choice. Option C is incorrect because the $120,000 claim exceeds $75,000 as diversity jurisdiction requires.

65. **Contracts.** Option D is correct because under UCC 2-206, a seller can accept in any reasonable manner and by any reasonable medium an offer for the purchase of goods. The manufacturer's prompt shipment of non-conforming goods was acceptance of the retailer's offer to buy conforming goods. Because the manufacturer shipped without indicating that the non-conforming goods were an accommodation to the buyer, shipment was acceptance. Option A is incorrect because retailer, not manufacturer, wins, and the UCC requires no meeting of the minds for the sale of goods. Option B is incorrect because retailer, not manufacturer, wins, and shipment without notice of accommodation is acceptance, not counteroffer. Option C is incorrect because whether the shipped goods were obsolete or had a market is of no consequence to retailer prevailing when manufacturer shipped as acceptance without notice of accommodation.

66. **Criminal Law & Procedure.** Option D is correct because at common law, the intent to cause serious bodily injury satisfies the intent element of murder. A jury may accept circumstantial evidence of intent from factors such as choice of weapon and nature and apparent consequences of attack. The collector chose a heavy weapon and brought it down hard enough on the mechanic's head to fracture his skull. Option A is incorrect because the evidence supports the more-serious crime of murder. Option B is incorrect because the evidence of the weapon and hard strike to the head evidence intent. Option C is incorrect because while the collector might plead extreme provocation, a jury could easily reject unintentional property damage as extreme provocation and instead find intent to cause serious bodily injury, and hence convict of murder.

67. **Real Property.** Option A is correct because a third party's interest that arises only on the occurrence of a condition subsequent as to a fee-simple holder is merely an executory interest, not a remainder and not an interest having a right of entry. The grandson has an executory interest. The language of the grant to the granddaughter creates a fee-simple interest in the granddaughter but subject to a condition subsequent as to the granddaughter's interest. Options B and C are incorrect because the grandson and heirs do not take if the granddaughter and heirs comply with the use restriction. The grandson has no remainder interest. Although a right of entry normally follows a fee simple subject to condition subsequent, when the interest goes to a third party rather than the original owner, that third party has an executory interest.

68. **Torts.** Option B is correct because battery is an intentional harmful or offensive contact. The aide purposefully poisoned the resident intending the resident's harm, that poisoning constituting a sufficient contact to satisfy the battery tort. Option A is incorrect because the facts give no indication that the resident apprehended an imminent battery. Option C is incorrect because the facts give no indication of the degree to which the resident was emotionally distressed, when the IIED tort requires evidence of severe distress. Option D is incorrect

because the autopsy and investigation confirmed that the aide's actions were purposeful, not careless, the aide's homicide conviction confirming those findings.

69. **Constitutional Law.** Option B is correct because the Supreme Court recognizes a market-participant exception to the dormant-commerce-clause theory, which applies instead when the action is regulatory. The state owned the leased lands and as a market participant could favor local interests without violating the dormant commerce clause. Option A is incorrect because although if the dormant commerce clause applied the Supreme Court would apply strict scrutiny, here the market-participant exception took the case out of the dormant commerce clause's protectionism theory. Option C is incorrect because the state had a rational basis in lowering local gas costs, and rational-basis is not the test in any case for a dormant-commerce-clause challenge. Option D is incorrect because the market-participant exception took the case out of the dormant commerce clause's protectionism theory, which applies to regulators, not market participants.

70. **Evidence.** Option D is correct because a mandatory presumption would contradict the constitutional rule that prosecutors must prove each element of a charged crime beyond a reasonable doubt. Option A is incorrect because the reasonableness of the presumption does not overcome that the presumption is mandatory and would frustrate the constitutional rule for proof beyond a reasonable doubt. Option B is incorrect because the instruction as stated is mandatory rather than one that would allow the defendant to rebut the presumption. A jury would properly conclude that the juror had no choice but to presume death. Option C is incorrect because the reasonableness of the presumption is not the question but instead that the mandatory presumption defeats the constitutional rule for proof beyond a reasonable doubt.

71. **Civil Procedure.** Option C is correct because under the *home-state defendant rule* of 28 USC §1441(b)(2), a defendant may not remove an action to federal court from a state court of the state of which the defendant is a citizen. Option A is incorrect because the *home-state defendant rule* prohibits removal even when the federal court would otherwise have jurisdiction. Option B is incorrect because tort claims for medical malpractice depend on state rather than federal law. Option D is incorrect because under 28 USC §1446(b)(1), the time for removal is 30 days from service, not 21 days or any other shorter period.

72. **Contracts.** Option B is correct because under the UCC, parties to a contract for the sale of goods may modify the contract without consideration if the modification is made in good faith and for a commercially reasonable purpose. Both exist here. Option A is incorrect because a modification made by a seller simply to increase his profit is not deemed good faith. Option C is incorrect because contracts for the sale of goods may be modified without consideration. Option D is incorrect because buyer's signed check and accompanying note satisfy the statute of frauds.

73. **Criminal Law & Procedure.** Option D is correct because robbery is larceny from a person or in the person's immediate presence accomplished by force or fear, had the facts been as the defendant believed. The defendant's mistaken belief as to the person's mental state, and factual impossibility, are not defenses. Option A is incorrect because the defendant committed robbery. Option B is incorrect because robbery is more serious than larceny, and larceny is from a place

rather than person. Option C is incorrect because attempt at robbery is more serious than attempt at battery.

74. Real Property. Option C is correct because the first interest holder for value to record without notice prevails under a race-notice statute. Here, the buyer was a bona fide purchaser who recorded first without notice, under a race-notice statute. While the bank acquired its future-advance mortgage interest before the buyer, the buyer purchased the land for valuable consideration and without notice of the bank's interest. (A future-advance mortgage is one that the parties enter into but the mortgagor draws loan proceeds at a later date, like a line of credit secured by the mortgage.) Option A is incorrect because to prevail, the bank must also have recorded before the buyer. Option B is incorrect because even though a mortgage interest is security for a loan, it is still an interest in land and under the statute still required recording. Option D is incorrect because whether the jurisdiction follows the lien theory or a title theory is irrelevant to the question. The outcome is the same under either theory.

75. Torts. Option D is correct because false imprisonment is intentional unauthorized restraint against will. The mason intended that the assistant be restrained within the trailer against the assistant's will. Options A, B, and C are incorrect because there was no battery. The mason did not intentionally bring about a harmful or offensive contact with the assistant. Options A and B are also incorrect because there was no assault. The mason did not intend to bring about the assistant's apprehension of an imminent battery. Option A is also incorrect because the mason did not intend the assistant's severe distress nor know to a substantial certainty that it would occur.

76. Constitutional Law. Option D is correct because Congress may overturn an executive action only by enacting a statute. Congress may delegate authority to an executive agency, but Congress may not then retain a legislative veto over that agency that permits reversal of the executive action on less than approval by both legislative chambers and presentation of the legislation to the president for signature or veto. Option A is incorrect because the delegation of authority to the agency was in itself proper. Only the reservation of reversal authority was improper. Option B is incorrect because domestic action consistent with a rejected treaty does not interfere with the president's conduct of foreign affairs. Congress may control federal land uses. Option C is incorrect because Congress may require agencies to report to Congress when Congress delegates authority to those agencies.

77. Evidence. Option B is correct because hearsay is evidence as to an out-of-court statement offered to prove the truth of the matter that the statement asserts. Here, the regulators want to use the notes to prove what the notes record about the alleged fraud discussion. The notes record out-of-court statements and are thus hearsay. Option A is incorrect because immunity may reflect the secretary's bias or interest, and thus evidence of immunity would be admissible, but bias or interest would not make the secretary's testimony inadmissible, just arguably less reliable. Option C is incorrect because the notes are not a business record because the secretary prepared them on her own initiative, whereas business records must be a regular practice of that business activity. Option D is incorrect because the notes are not past recollection recorded, which only permits a party to have the recollection read into the record when the witness does not recall the recollection and has laid the foundation that they recorded the witness's observation accurately.

78. Civil Procedure. Option A is correct because the fact pattern reveals no contact that would yield personal jurisdiction in the forum state over the supplier, whether general or specific. Option B is incorrect because specific jurisdiction requires claim-related, purposeful contact with the jurisdiction, of which the facts indicate none. Option C is incorrect because general jurisdiction exists in the principal place of business and state of incorporation, neither of which are the forum state. Option D is incorrect because corporations are not subject to transient jurisdiction, corporations having no physical body.

79. Contracts. Option D is correct because a promise to buy all that one requires (a *requirements contract*) implies the buyer's good-faith purchase of reasonably specific amounts as consideration for the seller's promise to sell at the agreed-upon price. Option A is incorrect because mutuality exists when both sides promise value that the law recognizes as consideration. Option B is incorrect for the same reason that Option D is correct that agreement to purchase requirements in good faith provides a reasonably specific quantity term as consideration for the promise. Option C is incorrect because requirements contracts need consideration, supplied in the form of good faith to purchase requirements.

80. Criminal Law & Procedure. Option C is correct because common-law murder requires intent to kill or cause serious injury, or a reckless, depraved-heart indifference to the value of human life, requiring knowledge of a very high risk of death or serious injury. Here, the man intended only to embarrass the musician by an act that would not have endangered the health of a normal person. Option A is incorrect because the man only premeditated an act of embarrassment that would not endanger a person of normal health, not to kill or cause serious injury. Option B is incorrect because the man did not intend death or serious injury by poison, only to cause embarrassment through an act that would not endanger a person of normal health. Option D is incorrect because both Options A and B are incorrect.

81. Real Property. Option D is correct because the common law Rule Against Perpetuities voids an interest that could vest in possession more than 21 years after a life in being. While the matriarch attempted to give her daughter and heirs a fee simple subject to executory interest, the attempted gift to the niece and her successors fails because the niece's interest could vest in possession more than 21 years after the daughter's life. The court will rule for the matriarch's grandson who received a possibility of reverter through the matriarch's residuary clause. Option A is incorrect because when the daughter's husband ceased using the property for residential purposes, the possibility of reverter automatically enacted, taking the interest back to the grandson. Option B is incorrect because after the niece's interest voids, the daughter and her heirs have a fee simple determinable and the landowner a possibility of reverter, which passed to the grandson through the residuary clause. Option C is incorrect because the developer lost the interest when the daughter's husband vacated for the developer to build a shopping center.

82. Torts. Option D is correct because intentional infliction of emotional distress, also known as the outrage tort, involves the intentional infliction of severe distress by outrageous conduct beyond the bounds of all decency in civil society. Highly distressing an animal lover with strung-up animal carcasses and a telephone message is likely sufficiently outrageous conduct to satisfy the IIED tort given the landowner's high distress. Option A is incorrect because the hunter made no particular disclosure of any private fact. Option B is incorrect because the hunter did not cause an intrusion into the landowner's seclusion, which would form the basis for that form of invasion of privacy. Option C is incorrect because the facts do not show that the hunter portrayed the landowner in any false light in any publication seen by another.

83. **Constitutional Law.** Option D is correct because the ordinance permits picketing on only certain issues and is thus a content-based regulation subject to strict scrutiny. The ordinance is not likely a necessary means of advancing a compelling governmental interest, especially given that it permits some picketing while prohibiting others. Option A is incorrect because the ordinance was not content neutral. It permitted only picketing relating to the local zoning or land use. Option B is incorrect because the ordinance regulated both conduct and speech, not conduct alone. The ordinance regulated the kind of message that picketers could convey. Option C is incorrect because although the ordinance did distinguish among messages, the constitutional test is not discrimination but rather strict scrutiny of content-based regulation.

84. **Evidence.** Option B is correct because evidence of bias or interest is ordinarily admissible, whereas evidence that a party had liability insurance is ordinarily inadmissible other than to show bias, interest, agency, ownership, or control, when disputed. Option A is incorrect because the rules prohibit evidence of liability insurance to show that an insurer rather than the insured defendant would pay for all or part of any award. Option C is incorrect because the rules permit evidence of insurance when offered for some other purpose such as bias or interest, as here, or agency, ownership, or control. Option D is incorrect because the evidence would be admissible to show bias or interest of the testifying witness. Also, insurance is arguably relevant as to who would pay or whether insurance made the insured defendant less cautious, for both of which reasons the rules would bar insurance evidence.

85. **Civil Procedure.** Option B is correct under the *relation-back* doctrine, which construes the filing date of amended claims arising out of the same conduct, transaction, or occurrence as the date of the original complaint. *See* FRCP 15(c). Option A is incorrect because no discovery is necessary on the given facts regarding the limitations period. Option C is incorrect because the new claim arises out of the same conduct, transaction, or occurrence as the original claim, thus relating the date of the new claim back to the original filing date under the relation-back doctrine. Option D is incorrect because if as the facts indicate both claims arose out of the same transaction or occurrence, then the relation-back doctrine would save the added negligence claim.

86. **Contracts.** Option A is correct because an offeree accepts an offer for a unilateral bargain by completing the requested performance. The graduate's completing a term of college completed the requested performance for tuition reimbursement. The graduate did not complete the new-car performance because he did not earn all A grades in any term. Option B is incorrect for the same reason that Option A is correct. The graduate completed the tuition term, not the car term. Option C is incorrect because going to college was consideration. Option D is incorrect because the graduate could complete it within one year, thus falling outside the statute of frauds.

87. **Criminal Law & Procedure.** Option C is correct because in addition to aiding, encouraging, or assisting the crime, accomplice liability requires the culpable intent to do so. Here, the one who bought the beverage had no intent to facilitate the theft, as shown by his startled reaction and shaking head. His actions may have aided and assisted the crime, but he hald no intent to do so. Option A is incorrect because facilitation alone is not enough without the requisite intent to aid, encourage, or assist. Option B is incorrect because accomplice liability does not arise with failure to stop a crime, only with affirmative aiding, encouraging, or assisting plus the requisite intent. Option D is incorrect because accomplice liability does not require prosecution or conviction of the principal committing the underlying crime.

88. **Real Property.** Option D is correct because on mistake in a deed, physical description supersedes and corrects quantity description unless mutual mistake establishes a right of reformation, while reformation under mutual mistake requires that both parties have intended something other than the deeded description. Here, the parties intended to convey the parcel's western half to the apple grove, which the controlling physical description did actually convey notwithstanding the quantity error. Option A is incorrect because the parties were not mutually mistaken as to the deed's controlling physical description, which the parties actually intended. Option B is incorrect because the deed is valid and parole evidence could if necessary establish intent. Option C is incorrect because the buyer receives the intended physically described land, which was 229 acres, not 220 acres.

89. **Torts.** Option D is correct because consent is an agreement or permission defense to an intentional tort. The facts indicate that the gymnast requested and consented to, and did not at the time complain about, the stretching in the customary and usual fashion. Options A, B, and C are incorrect because the gymnast's request, compliance, and non-complaining indicate express and implied consent. Whether the gymnast has a professional negligence (malpractice) claim would depend on additional information on the standard of care and the coach's compliance with it, but the gymnast has no intentional-tort claims.

90. **Constitutional Law.** Option A is correct in that Article III, Section 2, expressly provides that the Supreme Court has appellate jurisdiction with such exceptions and under such regulations as Congress provides. Congress may limit Supreme Court appellate jurisdiction. Option B is incorrect because while states traditionally define crimes, federal constitutional rights provide substantial procedural protections over the interpretation of which the Supreme Court has had appellate jurisdiction, subject to Congress's power to limit that appellate jurisdiction. Option C is incorrect because federal review of state decisions on federal rights has been available both by Supreme Court appellate review and by habeas petition. Congress could limit appellate review but has not done so. Option D is incorrect for the same reason that Congress has permitted Supreme Court appellate review of state court criminal decisions implicating federal rights, even if those cases are not within the Supreme Court's original jurisdiction. So Option D, while correct on its face, does not address the question.

91. **Evidence.** Option A is correct because while a party may offer evidence of the reputation of the character of a witness when material to the case, the court will not admit evidence of specific conduct to prove character unless character is an element of the charge or defense. Option B is

incorrect because a criminal defendant's character for an honesty relative to a fraud charge is a material issue rather than a collateral matter. The evidence is inadmissible but for a different reason. Options C and D are incorrect because although an accused may offer reputation or opinion evidence on the accused's character when in issue, the character evidence may not take the form of specific instances of conduct, even though such specific instances are arguably probative.

92. **Civil Procedure.** Option D is correct because under Rule 12(h)(1)(B)(ii), a responsive pleading or Rule 15(a) amendment to a responsive pleading preserves the defense of lack of personal jurisdiction, and under Rule 15(a)(1), a party has 21 days after filing a pleading within which to amend once as a matter of course. Option A is incorrect because a defendant may raise a defense of lack of jurisdiction in either a Rule 12 motion or a responsive pleading. Option B is incorrect because a defendant preserves a defense of lack of jurisdiction by amending the responsive pleading once within 21 days as a matter of course. *See* Rule 12(h)(1)(B)(ii). Option C is incorrect because under Rule 15(a), a party may amend once as a matter of course within 21 days, without moving for leave to amend.

93. **Contracts.** Option B is correct because a promise to keep an offer open as an option contract is not enforceable without consideration for the option. The neighbor gave no consideration to keep the offer open for two weeks, meaning the owner could revoke the offer at any time before acceptance. Option A is incorrect because if an offer is irrevocable as an option contract, good reason does not make it revocable. The reason for revocation is not the issue. Lack of consideration for the option is the issue. Option C is incorrect because option contracts require consideration. Option D is incorrect because the neighbor gave no consideration for keeping the offer open, and the phrase *firm offer* applies in the context of sale of goods by a merchant, not sales by non-merchants like this classic-vehicle owner.

94. **Criminal Law & Procedure.** Option D is correct because common-law attempt must involve acts furthering the crime beyond mere preparation, beyond the model code's broader substantial-step standard. Here, the distributor did not do anything toward committing the crime, the talk of completing it in 24 hours not constituting furtherance or even a substantial step. Option A is incorrect because agreement does not constitute an act in furtherance or even a substantial step. Option B is incorrect because expressing an intention is not enough to qualify as an act toward committing the crime. Option C is incorrect because the intent of informants, undercover officers, or others is irrelevant as to whether the defendant has committed an attempt crime.

95. **Real Property.** Option D is correct because title is unmarketable where owners of present and future estates attempt to convey in fee simple absolute interests of the unborn or unascertainable. The title is unmarketable. The sister has a life estate, while the brother has a vested remainder subject to open because there may be other nieces and nephews born during the sister's life, who then become entitled to share in the remainder. The sister and brother can transfer their title to others, but the interest of after-born nieces and nephews could cloud title to the property, making it unmarketable. Option A is incorrect because while a quitclaim deed transfers whatever interest the grantor has, transfer does not assure marketability of title. Option

B is incorrect because a title unmarketable due to remainder interest subject to open is not freely alienable. Option C is incorrect because that doctrine does not apply here, the question having to do with the buyer refusing the purchase of unmarketable title, not whether the conveyance or the descent is the stronger interest.

96. **Torts.** Option C is correct because a child who is engaged in an adult activity will be held to an adult's standard of care. Operating a high-speed buffing gun is an adult activity for which the law would hold a seven-year-old boy to an adult standard. Option A is incorrect because although the boy may be a sympathetic defendant, sympathy does not determine the standard of care. Option B is incorrect because children performing adult activities owe adult duties. Option D is incorrect because the question asks for a recommendation based on the boy's standard of care, not the neighbor's interests.

97. **Constitutional Law.** Option D is correct because one has the First Amendment right to associate freely as long as one does not intend to further an organization's illegal aims. Option A is incorrect because the past membership would not necessarily alone constitute the necessary specific intent to endorse illegal goals. The Supreme Court protects membership, just not the endorsement of illegal aims. Option B is incorrect because an integrated bar that one must join for law practice would constitute state action against which the First and Fourteenth Amendments would protect. Option C is incorrect because it overstates the First Amendment protection. The First Amendment would not protect membership if it denoted endorsement of the organization's illegal goals.

98. **Evidence.** Option A is correct because testimony of a hearsay statement by an unavailable declarant is admissible if against the declarant's interest. The against-interest requirement ensures the statement's trustworthiness. Here, the derelict is dead and thus unavailable. The derelict's statement would have implicated the derelict in the arson and insurance fraud such that the statement is against the derelict's interest and thus admissible as an exception to the hearsay rule. Option B is incorrect because while courts may construe a co-conspirator's admission as an admission by the party opposing the testimony, and thus admissible under the party-admission exception to the hearsay rule, the exception does not apply if the declarant made the statement after the conspiracy ended or not in furtherance of the conspiracy. The derelict's statement was after the conspiracy and not in furtherance of the conspiracy, but the statement was admissible as an admission against interest. Option C is incorrect because the statement falls within the admission-against-interest exception to the hearsay rule, for unavailable declarants. Option D is incorrect because the testimony is admissible under a different exception to the hearsay rule than the co-conspirator-statement exception, which would be the statement-against-interest exception.

99. **Civil Procedure.** Option D is correct because oral statements are outside the scope of Rule 11 sanctions. Option A is incorrect because Rule 11 applies to pleadings, written motions, or other papers presented to the court. Option B is incorrect because while sanctions must be limited to deter, no sanction is appropriate here because oral statements are outside Rule 11's scope. Option C is incorrect because under Rule 11(c)(2), the safe-harbor window is 21 days, and the plaintiff's lawyer waited longer than 21 days.

100. **Contracts.** Option A is correct because forbearance of bringing a claim and payment of a disputed debt both have value the law recognizes for purposes of consideration. The passenger's promise to forgo a case he honestly and reasonably believed had merit was an act having value that the law recognizes done in exchange for the driver's promise to pay a disputed debt, which also has value the law recognizes. B is incorrect because the driver's promise required consideration to be enforceable, and the promise had the above consideration. Option C is incorrect because the promise was definite enough and implies payment within a reasonable time. Option D is incorrect because other witnesses disputed the driver's belief, making for a disputed claim, and the law does not void contracts based on belief or disbelief in responsibility.

2. Part II—Second 100 Questions (Questions 101-200)

101. **Criminal Law & Procedure.** Option B is correct because to be an accomplice to crime, the underlying crime must have been committed, and robbery requires larceny from a person or in the person's presence under force or fear. Here, the merchant showing the shotgun, tossing a quarter, and telling the gang leader to get lost show that the merchant was not under force or fear. The new member cannot be an accomplice to robbery when the gang leader did not commit robbery. Option A is incorrect because the new member did not actually withdraw in the required renunciation, only got scared and drove off, and withdrawal is effective only when the crime can still be stopped. Option C is incorrect because the new member had already set the planned crime in motion before seeing the police vehicle and did not renunciate it. The police would have had to deter the gang leader from committing the crime, which the police did not—the merchant prevented the crime. Option D is incorrect because the new member could not be an accomplice to a crime that did not occur and because the new member did not actually withdraw, certainly not effectively.

102. **Real Property.** Option A is the correct answer because accretion is the increase of riparian land by the slow change of a river over time, in which any resulting deposit of soil belongs to the owner of the abutting land. The owner of the ranch owns the 10 acres because accretion belongs to the riparian owner. Option B is incorrect because adverse possession doesn't apply here. Option C is incorrect because it misstates the law and reaches the wrong result. Option D is incorrect because although avulsion does not change property rights, avulsion is a sudden loss or addition to land, while here we had slow addition.

103. **Torts.** Option B is correct because violation of industry standards may give rise to an inference of negligence. Option A is incorrect because the supervisor's failure to train would not help an action against the chipper manufacturer, nor would it give rise to a negligence action against the employer because of the worker's compensation exclusive-remedy provision. Option C is incorrect because the co-worker's not knowing about the operator would not aid the action against the manufacturer. Option D is incorrect because it tends to place responsibility on the worker and employer rather than machine manufacturer.

104. **Constitutional Law.** Option A is correct because the ordinance prohibits some protected conduct, and is thus overbroad, while also leaving the public unclear about which conduct is permitted and which forbidden, and is thus vague. The First Amendment's doctrine of overbreadth prohibits the former while its doctrine of vagueness prohibits the latter. Option B is incorrect because it misstates a version of the former test for obscenity, and neither the former obscenity test nor the current patently offensive obscenity test apply here, where overbreadth and vagueness are instead the concerns, not obscenity. Option C is incorrect because the treatment of graphic versus text content does not implicate a suspect classification (those buying either material are not historically discriminated against) and thus needs only a rational basis, which this distinction can probably satisfy in that pictures may be more emotive than words. Option D is incorrect for the same reason that because the classification of adults versus minors does not implicate a historically suspect classification, the ordinance need only have a rational basis,

which it probably does in protecting minors more than adults when minors may be more subject to influence.

105. Evidence. Option A is correct because a party may impeach a witness with a prior inconsistent statement on any material issue. A second witness may contradict a prior witness on any material issue, just not collateral issues. Here, the coach's drug dealing was the charge, and thus the prosecutor may use another witness to contradict the coach's testimony and impeach the coach on that material issue. Option B is incorrect because the rules bar evidence of prior bad acts to prove character (in this instance character for breaking the law) and ordinarily allow only reputation and opinion evidence of character when character is in issue. Option C is incorrect because the prosecutor is offering the evidence to contradict and impeach the coach, not to establish the coach's character. The rationale is correct that one or more specific instances would not be admissible to prove disputed character, but the conclusion is wrong, and the rationale does not apply here. Option D is incorrect because the officer's testimony would contradict on the material matter of whether the coach distributed drugs. The matter is material, not collateral.

106. Civil Procedure. Option B is correct because the supplemental jurisdiction statute has been interpreted to require the maintenance of complete diversity when jurisdiction is based upon diversity. As to Option A, the supplemental jurisdiction statute, 28 USC §1367, as interpreted by the Supreme Court in *Exxon v Allapattah Services*, allows the court to overlook the jurisdictional minimum, as long as the claim is related and there is no loss of complete diversity. As to Option C, the hypothetical presents no federal question. As to Option D, a related claim is a necessary but not a sufficient condition of supplemental jurisdiction. The federal court must also have subject-matter jurisdiction through diversity or federal question.

107. Contracts. Option B is correct because a promise to pay an existing debt that is either due or would be due except for the expiration of the statute of limitations is enforceable without consideration. Option A is incorrect because the executor is just as bound by the statute of limitations as the sportsman would have been had he lived. Option C is incorrect because no consideration is required for a promise acknowledging a prior debt still due or not due only because the statute of limitations has expired. Option D is incorrect because the promise being enforced is the new one, not the old one.

108. Criminal Law & Procedure. Option A is correct because larceny is complete with the taking and carrying away of personal property of another without consent with intent to permanently deprive, and concealing and moving property from its original location constitutes taking and carrying away. The young woman completed the crime when she hid the item and moved toward the door, even if she didn't move very far with it. Option B is incorrect because the young woman more than attempted larceny. She completed larceny, even though she did not leave the store. Moving the item from its original location was a sufficient carrying away. Option C is incorrect because she did commit larceny and the facts say nothing about her possibly buying the item. She intended to steal the item and only put it aside out of fear of getting caught. Option D is incorrect because she need only have moved the item from its original location, not gotten all the way out of the store.

109. **Real Property.** Option B is the correct because a condition subsequent is valid even as to a gift. The collector has the present right to possession because he gave the son the painting subject to a condition subsequent that the son return it if he no longer hung it. Option A is incorrect because the buyer purchased from a thief, and the thief's title is void. If the buyer had purchased from the art dealer, the result may have been different. Option C is incorrect because the son held subject to the condition subsequent that he return the painting to the collector if he did not hang it. Option D is incorrect because the art dealer was in a bailor-bailee relationship with the son. The dealer did not own the painting.

110. **Torts.** Option B is correct because extraordinary, unforeseeable, independent events that bring about the harm will supersede prior negligence and cut off proximate cause. The hardware store was clearly at fault as the facts plainly recite in that the managers should have detected and deterred the theft. The facts readily satisfy cause in fact in the terrorist's stealing the items from the store, so as to be able to make a bomb. Yet proximate cause is problematic at best, given the intentional and extraordinary nature of the act. Options A and C are incorrect because proximate cause is not strong. Options C and D are incorrect because breach is not weak. Options C and D are incorrect because cause in fact is not weak.

111. **Constitutional Law.** Option C is correct because while states retain the general power over traditional state matters such as family law including marriages and divorces, and Congress is limited to powers that the Constitution enumerates, the Constitution grants Congress express power to govern the District of Columbia, giving it state-like control over that district. Option A is incorrect because the marriage or divorce of a military member is not sufficiently close to Congress's military power to support the legislation as an enumerated power. Option B is incorrect because while Congress has power over federal-court jurisdiction, that power would not likely extend to the point of authorizing Congress to control marriage and divorce through federal jurisdiction, where family law is a traditional state matter. Option D is incorrect because an executive agreement could not extend Congress's powers beyond those that the Constitution enumerates. Congress would need to find other express power, of which the Constitution offers none.

112. **Evidence.** Option B is correct because a witness has a Fifth Amendment privilege against self-incrimination not to testify in ways that could subject the witness to criminal prosecution. The likelihood of prosecution, that the witness has already testified to other matters, and that the witness is not a party, all do not matter to the privilege. Option A is incorrect because counsel is not trying to impeach as to character for truthfulness but trying to show the unreliability of observation. Option C is incorrect because a witness waives the privilege only when testifying to matters within the privilege. Here, the motorcyclist has not testified to state of influence and thus may still invoke the privilege. Option D is incorrect because although drugs could influence observation, the motorcyclist still has a privilege against self-incrimination.

113. **Civil Procedure.** Option D is correct because the Erie Doctrine requires following the state's substantive law in federal-court diversity-jurisdiction cases. The duty question is one of substantive, not procedural law, and thus is a state-law question. Option A is incorrect because although the Erie Doctrine would have federal courts follow federal procedural law, the duty question is substantive law, and so state law applies under the Erie Doctrine. Option B is

incorrect as the opposite of the Erie Doctrine. Option C is incorrect because although state law applies, the duty question is not procedural but substantive, and if the question were procedural, then federal law would apply.

114. **Contracts.** Option C is correct because indirect revocation is effective on notice from a reliable source of an offeror's definite and inconsistent act. The gardener's sale to the farmer indirectly revoked the offer to accept $600 within one month when neighbor learned about the sale from the farmer. Option A is incorrect because the offer *was* revocable. The neighbor gave no consideration for an option contract, and the gardener's counter was not a firm offer because the gardener was not a merchant. Option B is incorrect because the gardener didn't have to notify the neighbor. Indirect revocation is effective on a reliable source's notice of an offeror's definite and inconsistent act. Option D is incorrect because the gardener's letter wasn't just a rejection but also a counteroffer.

115. **Criminal Law & Procedure.** Option D is correct because robbery involves the taking of another's personal property from the other's person or presence by force or intimidation, intending to permanently deprive, rather than mistaken taking of property that one believes, reasonably or unreasonably, is one's own. Here, the traveler was only mistaken about which computer the man had, thinking it the traveler's own computer, and thus was not intending to deprive the burly man of what the traveler believed was the man's own computer. Option A is incorrect because mistake does defeat specific intent to commit the crime. Option B is incorrect because while the traveler use force, the traveler did not have the requisite intent because of the traveler's mistaken belief that the computer was the traveler's own. Option C is incorrect because robbery is by force or intimidation and does not require use of a weapon. Fists are enough.

116. **Real Property.** Option C is correct because most courts hold that an engagement ring is a gift in contemplation of marriage and therefore conditional until complete on marriage. The gambler gets the ring back as a conditional gift. Option A is incorrect for that same reason. She doesn't get the ring unless it were other than an engagement ring, in which case all the elements of an *inter vivos* gift would have been met. Option B is incorrect because even though the gambler purchased the ring, he conditionally gave it away, did not then own it, and could not demand its return but for the marriage getting called off. Option D is incorrect because no court takes a split-the-proceeds approach.

117. **Torts.** Option B is correct because the professional's standard of care ordinarily requires expert testimony by a similarly qualified professional, except in the rare case when the breach is obvious. Mistakenly operating on the wrong limb is an obvious breach that does not require expert testimony as to the custom for ensuring operation on the correct limb. Option A is incorrect because reasonableness is not the professional's standard. Customary practice is the standard. Jurors are not generally permitted to determine the professional's custom without expert testimony from similarly qualified professionals. Option C is incorrect because the breach was sufficiently obvious not to require expert testimony as to the custom. Option D is incorrect because although the second surgery was successful, the first surgery was unnecessary.

118. **Constitutional Law.** Option D is correct because the Fifth Amendment prohibits government taking without just compensation, including regulatory takings that destroy all economically beneficial use of property including the owner's investment-backed expectations, which this regulation accomplished. Option A is incorrect because retaining title is not the takings test. When government destroys all beneficial use through regulation, the regulation can constitute a taking even when the owner retains title. Option B is incorrect because physical intrusion is not necessary to accomplish a taking when the government by regulation deprives the owner of all beneficial use. Option C is incorrect because how compelling is the government's objective is not the takings test. The government would owe compensation even for a compelling taking.

119. **Evidence.** Option B is correct because evidence of out-of-court statements used to prove the truth of the matters that the statements assert is inadmissible hearsay, but a proponent may use out-of-court statements to prove other matters such as knowledge or notice. The letter show that the manufacturer was aware of allegations of defect before selling the oven to the homeowner. Option A is incorrect because the letters are hearsay as to their assertions that the ovens were defective but not hearsay if used only to prove the manufacturer's notice of the allegations. Option C is incorrect because if the letters are hearsay if used to prove defectiveness, then the court should not let counsel read the hearsay into evidence. Reading them rather than admitting them makes no difference to the hearsay objection. Option D is incorrect because although the letters are hearsay when used to prove defects, the letters are not hearsay when used to prove notice of allegations.

120. **Civil Procedure.** Option A is correct because under *Pennoyer v. Neff*, due process requires that a defendant domiciled in another jurisdiction and served only by publication have claim-related contact with the forum jurisdiction in order to extend full faith and credit to the judgment. As to Option B, while the lack of notice may be a valid reason for relief from this judgment, this judgment will be set aside whether or not the notice was valid because there was no sufficient contact with Michigan for personal jurisdiction. As to Option C, judgments are not entitled to full faith and credit if they are entered without due process of law. Option D is incorrect because a party may collaterally attack a judgment given by a court that lacked personal jurisdiction.

121. **Contracts.** Option D is correct because a counteroffer rejects an offer, a subsequent attempt to accept a rejected offer is a counteroffer that requires acceptance, and silence must fall into a special category, of which none apply here, to constitute acceptance. The contractor's $325 counteroffer rejected the homeowner's $300 offer, so that the contractor could not later accept it. The contractor's $300 putative acceptance was actually an offer, one which the homeowner never accepted. Option A is incorrect because the homeowner had no obligation to respond, and the silence doesn't fall into any of the categories recognizing acceptance by silence such as prior dealings accepting silence, agreement to accept silence, or the silent party's action on the agreement. Option B is wrong because the contractor, not the homeowner, had the standing offer. The contractor cannot accept his own offer by performing. Option C is incorrect because the homeowner did nothing to imply assent.

122. **Criminal Law & Procedure.** Option C is correct because the right of self-defense ends when the threat ends, and a jury may properly determine whether or not heat of passion

continues across a few moments and steps to convict only of manslaughter or whether a reasonable person would have cooled off and the defendant in fact did cool off before killing. The shooter may have acted in the heat of passion or may have cooled off as a reasonable person would have cooled off, making either murder or manslaughter a possible conviction. Option A is incorrect because the killing shot may have been in the heat of passion and thus warranting only manslaughter, not murder. Option B is incorrect because the shooter may have cooled off as a reasonable person would have cooled off, making the killing shot murder. Option D is incorrect because the fallen leader was face down and defenseless, no longer a threat to the shooter.

123. **Real Property.** Option B is correct because tacking periods of adverse possession requires privity between successors. The hunter and naturalist were not in privity, meaning that the naturalist cannot tack on the hunter's period. Without privity, the naturalist's statute of limitations began running only 15 years earlier when she entered. She must hold for six more years before the statute of limitations has passed to acquire the property by adverse possession. Option A is incorrect because the naturalist cannot tack without privity. Option C is incorrect because the hunter long ago relinquished possession, and the statesman need only sue the naturalist for ejectment. Option D is incorrect because adverse possession does not require entering under color of title. While color of title can help shorten the statute of limitations in some cases, none are applicable here.

124. **Torts.** Option A is correct because invitees, who enter another's premises with permission for pecuniary purposes or accompany another who does so, are owed duties of reasonable care. The supplier was benefitting the store in a commercial transaction, such that the store owed the supplier a duty of reasonable care as an invitee. Option B is incorrect because the supplier was an invitee, not a licensee, and the duty to a licensee is to warn of known hidden dangers, not to cure them. Option C is incorrect because the supplier was an invitee, not a licensee, and the invitee duty is higher and more applicable to this condition, which was not a hidden defect. Option D is incorrect because the store owed the supplier a higher duty as an invitee, and landowners do not owe a duty to anyone to warn of hidden dangers. Trespassers are owed no duty.

125. **Constitutional Law.** Option C is correct because Article III requires that a plaintiff in federal court establish standing to maintain the suit, an association's standing requiring an injury in fact that would give at least some individual members the right to sue. Here, the association represented business professors rather than commodities traders, with the business professors having academic interests rather than substantive rights at stake. Option A is incorrect because standing requires more than the challenge of a federal statute. Standing requires injury in fact. The federal question would be pertinent to jurisdiction, not standing. Option B is incorrect because the conclusiveness of the relief is not the standing test, which instead involves sufficient injury. Option D is incorrect because whether the plaintiff has suffered injury yet involves a question of ripeness rather than standing, and even under the ripeness standard, a plaintiff may challenge a statute before its enforcement if enforcement was at all likely.

126. **Evidence.** Option A is correct because evidence that makes a material fact in issue more likely or less likely is probative and therefore admissible as relevant evidence. The carpenter's own experience of his abilities and back condition not only after the accident but also before

would be highly probative of the cause of his post-accident disability. Option B is incorrect because although lay witnesses may give opinions based on their own observations and helpful in deciding a fact issue, when not based on specialized knowledge, here the carpenter need not even qualify to give a lay opinion because the carpenter is relating direct testimony on a fact in issue, which is whether the carpenter had any disabling back condition before the accident. Option C is incorrect because the carpenter need not qualify as an expert if able to give a lay opinion as just described, but also the carpenter need not even qualify to give a lay opinion because the testimony is directly on a fact issue. Option D is incorrect because the testimony is admissible and because the possibility that the post-accident pain is from a pre-existing condition would not bar direct evidence addressing the carpenter's pre-accident condition.

127. **Civil Procedure.** Option B is correct because a defendant may join (permissive) counterclaims that do not arise out of the same transaction or occurrence as the opposing claim. The dairy farmer should file a trespass counterclaim in the grower's pending unpaid-hay lawsuit even though it would be unrelated to the unpaid-hay claim. Option A is incorrect because a separate lawsuit would be inefficient, and the court might in any case consolidate it with the pending unpaid-hay claim between the same parties. Option C is incorrect because an affirmative defense does not raise an unrelated claim. Option D is incorrect because the dairy farmer wants to raise the trespass claim and has an efficient means to do so as a counterclaim in the pending lawsuit.

128. **Contracts.** Option B is correct because although the general rule is that an offeree doesn't have to notify the offeror of an acceptance by performance, if the offeree has reason to know that the offeror won't know about the performance, then he must use reasonable diligence to notify the offeror. Here, the painter knew that the retailer was gone, he had her cell number, and he didn't call her to notify her that he was starting the work in acceptance of her offer. Option A is incorrect because setting aside the notice issue, starting to perform in acceptance creates an option contract, making the offer irrevocable for a reasonable time. Option C is incorrect because of the notice issue, and Option D is incorrect for the same reason.

129. **Criminal Law & Procedure.** Option D is correct because in *Hudson v. Michigan*, the Supreme Court ruled that although knock and announce is an ancient common law rule, exclusion of evidence is not the proper remedy for a knock-and-announce violation. Option A is incorrect because although the knock-and-announce rule is constitutional in nature, the Court ruled that because the interests violated have nothing to do with the seizure of evidence, suppression is not the appropriate remedy. Option B hints at one of the purposes of the knock-and-announce rule, to ensure the safety of the officers and those inside, but that conclusion is unsupported by the facts. Even if the officers did create a risk of harm by failing to knock and announce, that violation does not implicate the exclusionary rule. Option C is incorrect because good faith is a consideration when the officers relied on the authority of a search warrant later declared invalid, to execute a search. The good-faith exception is inapplicable to a knock-and-announce violation.

130. **Real Property.** Option C is correct because tenants in common may lease their concurrent right of possession, but the tenant gains only the owner's concurrent, not exclusive, right of possession. The investor can convey by lease but only the investor's concurrent right of use, not

an exclusive right that the investor does not have. Option A is incorrect because the investor may lease his concurrent right of possession to a tenant. Option B is incorrect because the tenant gains only the investor's concurrent, not an exclusive, right of possession. Option D is incorrect because the court would determine the disputed interests given the actual controversy over substantial rights.

131. **Torts.** Option A is correct because comparative negligence does not bar a plaintiff's action but reduces the plaintiff's claim by the percentage of plaintiff's fault compared to defendant's fault. The owner was comparatively negligent in leaving open the valves, while the pilot was also negligent in leaving open the valves. The negligence of one would be compared to the negligence of the other, and the owner's claim reduced by his own percentage negligence. Option B is incorrect because comparative negligence reduces the award by the plaintiff's, not the defendant's, negligence. Option C is incorrect because comparative negligence does not bar, but only reduces, a claim. Option D is incorrect because the negligence of two or more actors can combine to cause harm, and both will be liable (or, in this case, the negligence of the plaintiff will reduce the recovery by comparative-negligence rules).

132. **Constitutional Law.** Option D is correct because Congress may tax to raise revenue for the general welfare, which is all that this tax accomplishes, as long as the tax has no prohibited extraneous purposes. Option A is incorrect because although federal taxes must be uniform in provision, this tax is uniform in its provision. That a tax falls disproportionately or solely on one state in its effect is not the text, as long as the tax on its face does not discriminate among the states. Option B is incorrect because the commerce clause merely empowers Congress to act to promote interstate commerce. The clause does not prohibit Congress from taxing in a way that reduces interstate commerce. Option C is incorrect because the question involves the power to tax, not the power to regulate federal lands. The power to regulate lands does not authorize taxation of a good.

133. **Evidence.** Option B is correct because evidence that makes a material issue of fact more probable or less probable is probative evidence and therefore relevant, and relevant evidence is generally admissible. Option A is incorrect because a court can exclude images when, although relevant, their unfair prejudice substantially outweighs their probative value. The screenshot here is highly probative of a disputed issue, and the manufacturer has not shown unfair prejudice, but the statement is simply wrong that the court cannot an image. Option C is incorrect because the best-evidence rule, while requiring the original evidence to prove its contents, permits a duplicate as evidence unless inauthentic or unfair. Here, the screenshot may actually be an original insofar as it doesn't necessarily duplicate the video recording but is a part of it. Even if a duplicate, the screenshot represents a part of the video accurately, and the operator wasn't involved in the video's destruction, so its admission would be fair. Option D is incorrect because no rule requires using a duplicate or showing that a duplicate is unavailable. The best-evidence rule requires using an original only when an available duplicate may be inauthentic and admitting the duplicate would be unfair.

134. **Civil Procedure.** Option D is correct because a defendant must plead or lose a counterclaim that arises out of the same transaction or occurrence as the claim. The federal courts apply a flexible and generous logical-relationship test to define compulsive counterclaims.

The claim is barred because as a counterclaim it would have borne a logical relationship to the original claim. Option A is incorrect because a defendant must raise or will lose counterclaims arising out of the same transaction or occurrence as the claim, defined as bearing a logical relationship to the claim. Option B is incorrect because the claim and counterclaim are connected and also because the federal courts apply a logical-relationship test, not an immediate-connection test. Option C is incorrect because the law bars only those counterclaims that arise out of the same transaction or occurrence, not all counterclaims that are available between the same two parties.

135. **Contracts.** Option C is correct because an offer to buy goods is accepted either by promise or by the prompt shipment of the goods, which is what occurred here. Option A is incorrect because no notice is required when prompt shipment occurs. Option B is incorrect because under UCC §2-204, acceptance occurs upon shipment. Option D is incorrect because no firm offer to hold the offer open for a certain period was made here. The offer simply required delivery within two weeks.

136. **Criminal Law & Procedure.** Option D is correct because under *Terry v. Ohio*, while an officer may on reasonable and articulable suspicion of crime and that a person is armed and dangerous briefly stop the person to confirm or dispel the officer's suspicion and conduct a pat-down frisk of the person's outer clothing to check for weapons only, if the patdown dispels the suspicion then the individual must be free to go unless the patdown reveals contraband without manipulation, in which case the officer may seize the contraband based on the plain-feel doctrine but must not manipulate the item. Here, the young man running away late at night probably justified the stop and frisk. However, after the officer determined that the young man did not possess a weapon, the officer should not have manipulated the item to confirm that it was a pill bottle. Option A is incorrect because it reflects an incorrect statement of the facts. The officer had reasonable and articulable suspicion. Option B is incorrect because it presents both an incorrect statement of the facts and an incorrect statement of the law. The officer was performing a lawful patdown, but a patdown is not a full search. Option C is incorrect because an officer may seize an item even if the officer does not feel a weapon while conducting a lawful patdown if the officer detects something that without manipulation feels like contraband.

137. **Real Property.** Option B is correct because a deeded and recorded servitude that touches and concerns both the dominant and servient lands remains enforceable by and against successors in interest who take with notice. Option A is incorrect because no common-law right of lake view arises without satisfying the intent conditions of an equitable servitude. The right here is contractual, not common law. Options C and D are incorrect because a deeded and recorded servitude does survive the grantor's and grantee's deaths.

138. **Torts.** Option A is correct because products liability includes not only negligence claims but also claims based on breach of express and implied warranty and strict products liability for design, manufacture, and warning defects. The facts here appear to support possible claims under each theory. Option B is incorrect because although each of those phrases helps define a possible theory, other theories (negligence, warning failures, etc.) are left out. Option C is incorrect because breach of contract and misrepresentation are not products-liability theories, and the given facts do not appear to support those claims. Option D is incorrect because those

theories are not products-liability theories, and the given facts do not appear to support those claims.

139. **Constitutional Law.** Option B is correct because the Fifth Amendment's due-process clause incorporates the Fourteenth Amendment's equal-protection clause as a restriction on federal powers. A suspect classification such as that along nationality lines invokes strict scrutiny under which the classification must be necessary to a compelling governmental interest. Option A is incorrect because the commerce clause grants Congress power rather than restricting that power and thus would tend to support the legislation rather than void it. Options C and D are incorrect because the privileges-and-immunities clauses prohibits states from discriminating against citizens of other states, not the federal government from discriminating against suspect classes.

140. **Evidence.** Option B is correct because although hearsay, meaning an out-of-court statement used to prove the truth of the matter the statement asserts, an exception to hearsay is statement by an opposing party offered against the party, or a statement made by the party's agent without the agency relationship while the relationship existed. Here, the driver's apology could be evidence of his admission while employed of his carelessness while driving, offered against his employer. Option A is incorrect because the then-existing-state-of-mind exception applies to a statement that describes a current statement of mind, not one that refers to prior carelessness. Option is C incorrect because the declarant-admission-against-interest exception applies to a witness's testimony about an unavailable declarant's statement. Here, the driver is available. Option D is incorrect because prior inconsistent statements are for impeachment purposes, not for substantive evidence in the manner that counsel offered the apology here.

141. **Civil Procedure.** Option A is correct because under FRCP 65 and similar state rules, for a preliminary injunction, the party must show likelihood of success, irreparable harm if no injunction, inadequacy of damages, and a balance of greater harm. Here, with no clear legal basis for the claim, the small-business owner is unlikely to prevail on the merits. Defense counsel should argue no likelihood of success on the merits. Option B is incorrect because the small-business owner showed irreparable harm in the destruction of the business. Option C is incorrect because the small-business owner showed inadequacy of money damages in the ruining of the owner's reputation. Option D is incorrect because the small-business owner showed a loss of local jobs, and no harm is suggested as to the national corporation.

142. **Contract Law.** Option B is correct because a contract induced by material misrepresentation including active concealment of a material condition becomes voidable at the fraud victim's election. The homeowner actively concealed the roof leak and water damage, which at a $30,000 cost was a material condition. Option A is incorrect because the buyer did know the material terms other than the roof leak and water damage, and not knowing material terms would alone not excuse performance without misrepresentation or active concealment. Option C is incorrect because homeowner loses and because active concealment is an exception to the usual rule of buyer beware. Option D is incorrect because material misrepresentations including active concealment are actionable even when one has an opportunity for greater due diligence.

143. **Criminal Law & Procedure.** Option B is correct because burglary is the breaking and entering of the dwelling of another at night time while intending to commit a felony within. The girlfriend did not intend a felony when entering. Nor did she initially intend larceny when borrowing the recordings. Yet larceny may occur under the continuing-trespass doctrine in which one commits a trespassory taking of another's property while intending to return it but while continuing that trespass decides and acts to deprive the owner of the property permanently. Option A is incorrect because the girlfriend committed larceny under the continuing-trespass doctrine. Options C and D incorrect because the girlfriend only committed larceny. She did not commit burglary because she did not intend a felony when entering the boyfriend's home.

144. **Real Property.** Option B is correct because any party with the lease right to possession may enforce that right. The landlord retains the right to terminate the prior lease while the new tenant has the right to actual possession that the new tenant may enforce under the new lease. Option A is incorrect because the new tenant also has a right under the new lease to actual possession. Option C is incorrect because the landlord retains a right to enforce the prior lease. Option D is incorrect because no circumstances suggest any right of the prior tenant to remain as a holdover.

145. **Torts.** Option C is correct because an assault is the reasonable apprehension of an imminent harmful or offensive contact (an imminent battery) with the actor's apparent present ability to carry it out. The landowner's actions probably satisfy each of those elements. Option A is incorrect because an assault likely was committed and because the forester's fainting was not determinative. The forester's jumping back apparently in fear of the axe swing would have been enough to show the apprehension of an imminent battery. Option B is incorrect because an assault likely was committed and because there is no tort-law requirement that individuals submit to assault and battery. Option D is incorrect because there is no requirement that the forester faint and come into contact with the land. Apprehension of an imminent battery would have been enough without the fainting and fall.

146. **Constitutional Law.** Option D is correct because the Constitution's Article III authorizes federal-court federal-question jurisdiction, and the alien would be making an equal-protection challenge under the Fourteenth Amendment. Option A is incorrect because the Constitution gives Congress the power to create lower federal courts with the Supreme Court's jurisdiction, the Supreme Court has jurisdiction to hear cases against a state, and Congress expressly authorized the federal courts to hear cases brought by aliens against states. Option B is incorrect because although states typically control property rights to in-state lands, the Constitution's individual rights, including rights of equal protection under the Fourteenth Amendment, limit state powers. Option C is incorrect because Article III and Congress determine federal-court jurisdiction, such as for diversity of citizenship and federal questions, and neither Article III nor Congress grant the federal courts jurisdiction over matters involving international law.

147. **Evidence.** Option D is correct because an opposing party has the absolute right to examine documents that a witness uses to refresh recollection while testifying, but the court may permit examination of documents refreshing recollection before trial if justice so requires. Option A is incorrect because parties have an absolute right to examine documents used while testifying, and the court may permit examination of documents refreshing recollection before trial. Option B is

incorrect because the court may permit examination of documents refreshing recollection before trial if justice so requires. Option C is incorrect because the rule does not depend on the witness having contributed to the document and does not limit inspection to only those contributions.

148. **Civil Procedure.** Option C is correct because under FRCP 65 and similar state rules, a party may seek a temporary restraining order, even ex parte (without notice), and then move for preliminary and permanent injunction. Counsel should take immediate action filing an action with the court seeking an ex parte restraining order to serve on the local bank and then the other partner. A is incorrect because any notice to the other partner may precipitate the action that counsel is supposed to prevent. A letter to the other partner would have no force or effect if the other partner is an embezzler intending to abscond with funds. B is incorrect because a letter by regular mail would arrive too late and because a letter would not require the bank to refuse to extend the funds. The bank may or may not pay attention to the letter. D is incorrect because a motion would not prevent the bank or other partner from taking action. It would only serve to give the other partner notice.

149. **Contract Law.** Option B is correct because the defense of impracticability applies when through no fault of its own a party cannot fulfill the contract terms because of the occurrence of an event that frustrated a basic assumption of the contract. The architect was not to blame for his disability that prevented him from performing the construction-site inspections. Option A is incorrect because document review would not have replaced on-site inspections as a reasonable substitute, and the lender may in any case insist on performance as agreed. Option C is incorrect because the architect was unable through no fault of his own to perform the contract, raising the impracticability defense. Option D is incorrect for the same reason that the personal nature of the performance did not matter if the architect was unable to perform through no fault of his own.

150. **Criminal Law & Procedure.** Option A is correct because conspiracy is an agreement between two or more persons to commit a crime. While some jurisdictions also require an overt act in furtherance, that element is not an issue here because both had carried the contraband off the boat. Option A is incorrect because the crime was already complete when the first mate gave the 1statement implicating both of them in agreeing to import the cocaine. Also, cooperation with authorities afterward is not withdrawal, which instead requires action communicating a voluntary and complete renunciation to co-conspirators. Option B is incorrect because the first mate's statement is circumstantial evidence of their agreement. Option C is incorrect because possession alone is not sufficient to establish conspiracy, which instead requires agreement.

151. **Real Property.** Option C is correct because a sale contract purporting to sell an interest that the seller does not yet have is still enforceable, and the retailer appears to have promptly sought specific performance of that promise as soon as the investor obtained the title from the farmer. Option A is incorrect because a buyer need not have an agreement directly with the owner of land, when as here the owner agrees to sell to an intermediary who promises to sell to the buyer. The buyer may still enforce the agreement. Option B is incorrect because the retailer need not have sued the investor when the investor notified the retailer that the investor's closing with the farmer was delayed. The retailer need only have sued reasonably promptly when the investor had the title to convey. Option D is incorrect because a sale contract does not merge

into a deed. The actual doctrine of estoppel by deed applies when a seller purports to convey title that the seller does not actually have but later receives. Here, the retailer had no deed yet from the investor, and so the retailer had nothing into which the investor's deed from the farmer later could merge.

152. **Torts.** Option B is the correct answer because mistaken entries are still trespass as long as they are intentional, even if the boundaries are not known and are mistakenly assumed. Option A is incorrect because the knowledge or innocence of the homeowner is irrelevant. An intentional entry is sufficient, and the homeowner intended to construct the deck. Option C is incorrect because it is not established that the homeowner should have known, and whether or not the homeowner should have known is not a determinative factor as to the intentional entry. Option D is incorrect because the substantiality of the construction is not established and is not a determinative factor. Damages are presumed, and the deck's construction precludes the neighbor's alternative use of his land and may be a substantial interference.

153. **Constitutional Law.** Option B is correct because although individuals have the right to the free exercise of their religion, the right is not absolute, and a strong state interest may place a lighter burden on the practice. States have strong interests in preventing animal cruelty, and preventing animal torture is a relatively lighter burden. Option A is incorrect because sincere belief in an established religion warrants protection. Recognized ceremonies within regular religious practices constitute established and therefore protected practices. Option C is incorrect because while the priest has a free-exercise right, the right is not absolute, as the explanation for the correct Option B articulates. Option D is incorrect because the courts will not judge the reasonableness of a belief but instead only whether the one claiming the free-exercise right holds the belief sincerely and whether the burdened practice is established within the religious belief.

154. **Evidence.** Option A is correct because although the records are hearsay, they fall within the business-records exception because maintained in the regular conduct of business, and the exception includes the absence of record entries. Option B is incorrect because the declarant of the statement against interest must be unavailable for that hearsay exception to apply. Here, the facts give no indication of any witness being unavailable, and the statement would only be against the physician's interest, with the physician available. Option C is incorrect because the best-evidence rule applies to bar a suspect duplicate of an original record, not to require testimony over an original record. The nurse's testimony probably would not, in any case, be the best evidence. The record would be better evidence. Option D is incorrect because the records fall within the business-records exception to the hearsay rule.

155. **Civil Procedure.** Option C is correct because parties may discover evidence from non-parties only by deposition and document request, not interrogatories or medical examination. The estate's counsel should subpoena the driver to a deposition to inquire about any epileptic condition and may accompany the subpoena with a document request for any statement, report, notes, or other document relating to the cause of the accident. Option A is incorrect because although it may produce helpful information, the driver may not cooperate, would be under no compulsion to do so, may not tell the truth, and would not be under oath. The investigator's report may also be inadmissible, and the effort may not produce any admissible evidence. Option B is incorrect because non-parties need not submit to medical examination, which is only

for parties. Option D is incorrect because non-parties need not answer interrogatories, which are only for parties.

156. **Contract Law.** Option C is correct because the crop loss was foreseeable, and under *Hadley v Baxendale,* damages that the parties have reason to foresee are recoverable on breach. A commodities broker would be knowledgeable about commodities risks, and the contract provided for bringing in the crop as soon as dry. The loss was therefore likely foreseeable. Option A is incorrect because the contract provided for bringing in the crop as soon as dry. Option B is incorrect because explicit warning is unnecessary when the breaching party has reason to know of the probable result. Option D is incorrect because losses occurring during the contract term are not recoverable unless the breaching party had reason to foresee those losses. This option's rationale is overbroad.

157. **Criminal Law & Procedure.** Option A is correct because the intent to do serious bodily harm, provable circumstantially, satisfies the intent to commit murder, when the serious injury directly causes the death. Also, while provocation can be a defense to downgrade the crime to voluntary manslaughter (an intentional killing without deliberation, premeditation, and malice), the provocation must be reasonable to make that reduction. Here, the modest property damage would not provoke the reasonable person into intending serious injury. Yet even if a jury could find the provocation here sufficient, the jury need not do so. Option B is incorrect because murder is a more serious crime on which to convict. While provocation could reduce the crime to voluntary manslaughter, it need not do so. A reasonable juror could find that the property damage should not have provoked the strike. Option C is incorrect because involuntary manslaughter is a negligence or recklessness crime, whereas here the hunter intended serious injury. Option D is incorrect because all of the above crimes are more serious, even though a jury could convict the hunter for assault, a threat of imminent bodily harm with the apparent present ability to carry it out, and also battery, the carrying out of the assault.

158. **Real Property.** Option D is correct because joint tenants with rights of survivorship have only a joint interest in the property, a judgment lien or recording of judgment lien would not alone sever that interest, the death of a joint tenant leaves the property with the surviving joint tenant, and one joint tenant does not owe another joint tenant's debts, before or after the death of the debtor joint tenant. The stepchild's death extinguished the creditor's rights, whether by judgment or judgment lien. Option A is incorrect because one joint tenant does not owe another joint tenant's separate debts, whether before or after the debtor joint tenant's death. Option B is incorrect because devises may create joint tenancy provided that the devise so states and intends. Option C is incorrect because recording of a judgment lien does not sever a joint tenant's interest. The joint tenants continue to share the property interest, although only the debtor tenant remains obligated for the judgment debt. Recording the judgment lien simply secures the creditor's right against the judgment debtor.

159. **Torts.** Option A is the correct answer because intangible entries (noise, smell, light, etc.) may be addressed through the tort of nuisance, which involves unreasonable interference with use and enjoyment rather than exclusive possession. The violation of law may provide a stronger basis on which to maintain that the noise was unreasonable. Option B is incorrect because there was no interference with exclusive possession (no entry). Option C is incorrect because there

was no invasion of privacy (no exploitation, intrusion, false light, or public disclosure). Option D is incorrect because there may be a nuisance remedy.

160. **Constitutional Law.** Option A is correct because the federal courts apply intermediate scrutiny to gender-based discrimination, meaning that to survive, the challenged action must substantially relate to an important government interest. The Supreme Court has held that gender discrimination in the selection of jurors does not survive intermediate scrutiny and instead violates equal protection. Arbitrators are in this instance likely equivalent decision makers as to whom the employee would have equivalent constitutional protection. Option B is incorrect because an arbitration panel is not, strictly speaking, a jury, and so a jury of peers is not the standard on which to judge arbitrators. Option C is incorrect because intermediate scrutiny rather than strict scrutiny applies to gender distinctions and also because the discrimination here would not survive strict scrutiny, not even intermediate scrutiny. Option D is incorrect because gender discrimination faces intermediate scrutiny, not the rational-basis test.

161. **Evidence.** Option B is correct because an out-of-court statement used to prove the truth of the matter it asserts is inadmissible hearsay, while a prior inconsistent statement is still admissible to impeach the credibility of the inconsistent declarant. Here, the bystander's two statements are directly inconsistent. Once the court admitted the first statement, whether hearsay or excepted because a present sense impression, the second statement then became admissible to impeach credibility. Option A is incorrect because the bystander's statement would be hearsay if used to prove the pedestrian's fault but may still be used to impeach the bystander's credibility for having made a prior inconsistent statement. Option C is incorrect because the motorist may still use the bystander's statement to impeach the bystander's credibility. Option D is incorrect because prior inconsistent statements are admissible to impeach credibility whether the declarant gets to explain them or not.

162. **Civil Procedure.** Option A is correct because sampling, cost-shifting, quick-peek, and claw-back provisions may be appropriate practices for discovery of difficult-to-access electronically stored information. Option B is incorrect because there has been no misconduct or inappropriate request of the kind that would warrant these sanctions. Option C is incorrect because there are no multiple claims or parties to sever, and severance and bifurcation are not measures that reduce and balance the burden of discovery. Option D is incorrect because it describes alternative forms of dispute resolution, not measures to reduce and balance the burden of discovery.

163. **Contract Law.** Option C is correct because the parties' original oral agreement manifested assent to the contract's bargained terms, as more than mere preliminary negotiations, making the subsequent documentation unnecessary for enforcement. Option A is incorrect because the law does not inquire into the consideration's adequacy relative to the market value if some consideration supports the contract. Option B is incorrect because the parties had already assented to the bargained terms orally, making documentation of the oral agreement unnecessary to its enforcement. Option D is incorrect because the landowners' consent was not the issue, which was instead whether the parties had bargained to the point of mutual assent before documenting the agreement in writing.

164. **Criminal Law & Procedure.** Option B is correct because involuntary intoxication can be a defense where the intoxication results from an innocent mistake as to the intoxicating character of the substance taken, and where the intoxication prevents the suspect from having the required mental state or conforming his conduct to the law. Option A is incorrect because the law treats addiction as voluntary rather than involuntary for these purposes. While voluntary intoxication is a defense in most states when the intoxication directly negates the required mental state, battery, defined as an intentional harmful or offensive touching of another without consent, requires only recklessness rather than the intent to injure. So an addiction defense would not defeat the requisite mental state of recklessness, addiction being reckless and raging a foreseeable consequence of the recklessness. Option C is incorrect because taunts are not sufficient provocation to commit a battery. One should be able to resist taunts and insults. Option D is incorrect because testimony about raging would not defeat the recklessness of taking a substance that causes raging. Recklessness is sufficient to convict for battery.

165. **Real Property.** Option D is correct because a grantee who accepts a deed that expresses the terms of acceptance agrees to perform those terms including any promise that would protect the grantor, such as to pay a mortgage. Payment of a mortgage would include not just the value of the security but also the deficiency. Option A is incorrect because while the speculator would remain secondarily liable to the lender on the deficiency for having made the note, the court would enforce the hunter's promise by acceptance to pay the loan obligation. Option B is incorrect because a grantor may make a deed signed only by the grantor and not the grantee, and yet bind the grantee by the deed's express terms on the grantee's acceptance. The law calls this form of deed a *deed poll*. Option C is incorrect because making payments on an obligation would not alone make the payor liable on the remaining obligation. The payor must make a binding promise for the recipient of those payments to have an enforceable right against the payor.

166. **Torts.** Option A is correct because trespass to chattels is the intentional interference with the exclusive possession of another's personal property, compensated by lost-use value. Probably, the deleting of the files and perhaps even if the changing of the background and screen interfered with the staff member's use of the computer, even if the staff member was not deprived of its use for any period. Interference could also come from alteration or damage rather than solely deprivation of use. Option B is incorrect because there must be some interference. A de minimis handling of another's personal property would ordinarily not constitute interference. Option C is incorrect because interference with the computer's use would constitute trespass to chattels. Option D is incorrect because alteration or damage could also constitute interference.

167. **Constitutional Law.** Option D is correct because Congress's power to regulate interstate commerce carries the negative implication under the dormant commerce clause that states not discriminate against out-of-state interests in favor of local interests. The tax has expressly that purpose to diminish purchase of out-of-state components while increasing purchase of in-state components. Option A is incorrect because equal treatment of local assemblers wouldn't save the tax if the treatment nonetheless discriminates against out-of-state purchases. Option B is incorrect because promoting in-state interests is alone insufficient to overcome the dormant commerce clause's negative implication that states must not discriminate against interstate

commerce. Option C is incorrect because although taxes reduce commerce, they may do so as along as the reduction does not discriminate between in-state and out-of-state producers.

168. **Evidence.** Option D is correct because the confrontation clause bars admission of an out-of-court testimonial statement unless the declarant is available for cross-examination before or during trial. A testimonial statement includes one made during police investigation. The timecards are business records admissible as an exception to the hearsay rule and not testimonial statements. Options A and C are incorrect because the workers are both unavailable for confrontation and cross-examination, and their statements, whether written or video, were both made during investigation and are thus testimonial. Option B is incorrect because although the detective is available for confrontation and cross-examination, the worker who made the photo-lineup identification is not available, and the identification is the material testimonial statement. The detective's testimony that a photo lineup occurred would not be objectionable but also would not be material without the identification.

169. **Civil Procedure.** Option A is correct because under FRCP 26, federal-court parties must disclose experts, witnesses, supporting documentation, damages computations, and insurance after discovery conference 21 days before Rule 16 conference. The idea is to exchange basic discovery before requests for discovery begin. Option B is incorrect because the parties will discern disputed issues through the course of discovery, not before discovery. Option C is incorrect because the parties will discern discovery issues as they engage in discovery, not before discovery. Option D is incorrect because initial disclosures do not include settlement information.

170. **Contract Law.** Option B is correct because express contract terms prevail over course of dealing or usage of trade in both UCC and non-UCC cases. The contract contained an express term for 20% of earnings, which remained the agreement when the parties renewed the contract on the same terms. Option A is incorrect because one looks to course of dealing only when the contract does not supply an express term. Option C is incorrect because one looks to usage of trade only when the contract does not supply an express term or course of dealing does not define the unexpressed term. Option D is incorrect because quantum meruit applies only when the parties have not formed an express agreement and one party accepts services knowing that the other party expects compensation for value received.

171. **Criminal Law & Procedure.** Option A is correct because murder is an unlawful killing with malice aforethought, meaning either premeditated intent to kill or seriously injure, or reckless indifference to human life (depraved heart). Reckless indifference requires knowledge (in most states) of a very high risk of death or serious injury. Here, the worker had no knowledge of the manager's medication, and the laxative did not present a very high risk without the medication. The laxative should have caused only some discomfort. The medication mix was the cause of death, and the worker did not know of the risk of mix. Options B, C, and D are incorrect because the charge fails for not meeting the requisite mental state. The worker simply did not believe and even need not reasonably have believed that a double dose of laxative would cause death, only a little discomfort.

172. **Real Property.** Option C is correct because a tenant in common has only concurrent right of possession and can lease that right, but the lessee obtains only what the lessor tenant in common conveys, which at most is a right of concurrent possession. The therapist could lease up to all of her tenancy in common, which would be concurrent use of the whole building, but could not grant exclusive possession of any part of it. Option A is incorrect because a tenant in common can form a lease for a tenant to share all or any part of the tenant in common's concurrent rights of possession. Option B is incorrect because the other tenants in common could not evict the masseuse from the common rooms if as here the therapist had leased that access to the masseuse. Option D is incorrect because while the lease purported to convey use of the office suite to the masseuse, the therapist only had concurrent use of the whole possession and so could not lease exclusive possession to the masseuse.

173. **Torts.** Option C is correct because one may use reasonable force in self-defense of physical injury. The bank manager, when confronted with a man brandishing a knife, could reasonably shove the man back and lock the door, even if it caused the man to cut his head. A brandished knife threatens death or serious injury. Option A is incorrect because the bank manager is not liable and a poor strategic move to encourage a frivolous claim. Option B is incorrect because motive is not an element and a poor strategic move to encourage a frivolous claim. Option C is incorrect because there is no reason to be concerned about suit and no real reason to apologize. The man should apologize to the bank manager, who gave the man what he had coming to him.

174. **Constitutional Law.** Option D is correct because federal courts only have power to hear justiciable cases or controversies, and this case is not yet ripe for decision because it is not yet concrete enough for effective adjudication. Anticipated harm must be reasonably likely and specific, whereas here one cannot yet know at such an early stage whether the agency will adopt a specific pasteurization requirement. Option A is incorrect because the matter is not yet ripe, and the federal court would only be interfering with the agency rulemaking process, which would likely provide for hearings and comments. Option B is incorrect for the same reason that brewers would presumably have an opportunity in the rulemaking process to make these showings, which the federal court should not preempt in this lawsuit. Option C is incorrect because federal courts must dismiss rather than stay non-justiciable actions and because proposed rules would likely also not yet present a ripe case or controversy. Rules often change due to hearing and comment. The matter may not be ripe until the agency actually adopts rules.

175. **Evidence.** Option B is correct because the rules exclude party admissions from the definition of hearsay, and the best-evidence rule bars evidence of the contents of a document when the document is available, not testimony as to other matters, based on first-hand knowledge. The officer's testimony as to the co-conspirator's admissions is admissible even though the recording is available and in part inaudible. Option A is incorrect because the availability of an audio recording, whether audible or in part inaudible, does not affect the admissibility of testimony based on first-hand knowledge. Option C is incorrect because the best evidence rule, bar evidence of the contents of a document when the document is available, does not bar testimony as to other matters, based on first-hand knowledge. Option D is incorrect because hearsay by definition does not include a party admission.

176. **Civil Procedure.** Option B is correct because under FRCP 16 and equivalent state rules, trial courts issue a scheduling order for pleading amendment, discovery, witness and exhibit lists, motions, and other case management, and hold pretrial conferences. A trial court may enforce its pretrial order with appropriate sanctions up to default or dismissal, particularly when an opposing party suffers prejudice by an order's violation. Here, barring unlisted witnesses and exhibits would be an appropriate sanction, particularly if the corporation counsel's neglect prejudiced the minority shareholder, as it may have for lack of notice of evidence. Option A is incorrect because the corporation should be sanctioned, not the minority shareholder whose lawyer did nothing wrong. Option C is incorrect because to dismiss the lawsuit would sanction the minority shareholder whose lawyer did nothing wrong. Scheduling orders are for the benefit of the opposing parties, not just the court. Option D is incorrect because a trial court may enforce its scheduling orders by appropriate sanction.

177. **Contract Law.** Option C is correct because third-party beneficiaries have claims only when the promisee expresses an intention that they benefit from the contract. Here, the clinic did not expressly indicate any clear intent to benefit patients, certainly not to give them the right to sue the custodial service, such that the patients' benefit was instead only incidental to the contract. Option A is incorrect because public policy would not be grounds on which to extend contract liability to protect non-parties to the contract. Violating hospital standards does not create third-party beneficiary liability. Option B is incorrect because the facts give no indication that the clinic intended anything other than to satisfy hospital standards, not to benefit patients or give patients a right of action against the custodial service. Option D is incorrect because a contract's failure to name a person as a party to the contract would not prevent that person's third-party beneficiary claim if the contract otherwise expressed the intent to benefit the third party.

178. **Criminal Law & Procedure.** Option B is correct because the prosecution must prove beyond a reasonable doubt every element of the charged crime. Because the crime theory was the brother's presence at the scene, the prosecution must retain the burden of proof on that element rather than shift it to the defendant claiming an alibi. Option A is incorrect because an affirmative defense on which the defendant must have some evidence is one that adds additional mitigating circumstances, not a challenge to the prosecutor's theory. An alibi here is not an affirmative defense but a way of saying that the brother had additional evidence. This instruction incorrectly places the burden on the brother to show reasonable doubt, when the burden must instead remain on the prosecution to show the absence of reasonable doubt. Option C is incorrect for the same reason that alibi here is not an affirmative defense but instead a direct challenge to the prosecutor's theory and proof. Option D is incorrect for the same reason that it places a burden on the brother when he should have no burden of proof, all of which must remain on the prosecution.

179. **Real Property.** Option D is correct because while a gratuitous death escrow (placing an executed deed in escrow for delivery on death) ordinarily effects delivery on escrow, delivery only occurs on death if the grantor reserves a right of return. The woman reserved a right of return, and so escrow did not deliver the deed. When the daughter died before the woman died, the escrow terminated. The woman retained title to the home, which then passed to the charity on the woman's death. Option A is incorrect because the daughter did not receive the home to

convey to the boyfriend. The woman reserved a right of return, so that only the woman's death would have effected delivery, and instead the escrow terminated on the daughter's death. Option B is incorrect because the daughter's estate did not receive the home on the woman's death to convey to the daughter's husband, because the daughter predeceased the woman, terminating the escrow before delivery of the deed. Option C is incorrect because the woman willed her entire estate to the charity, and the son has no theory to obtain the home.

180. **Torts.** Option D is correct because one may use reasonable force to defend property, as long as the force is not likely to cause death or serious injury. Guns are likely to cause serious injury or death. A store owner risks civil (not to mention criminal) liability for injuring or killing others with a gun, even if those are others are looting the owner's store and goods. Options A and B are incorrect because there is no privilege to use deadly force to defend property and, as to Option A, certainly none when one is mistaken. Option C is incorrect because one is not entitled to shoot in defense of property even if those threatening the property can shoot in their own defense. One would only have a right to use deadly force on deadly threat to the person, not property.

181. **Constitutional Law.** Option B is correct because federal grants for buildings constructed for secular (non-religious) purposes do not advance or inhibit religion, or foster excessive entanglement in religion, simply because a religious institution owns the building. The grants have a secular purpose, do not advance religion, and do not excessively entangle government in religion. Option A is incorrect because secular grants do not promote sectarian purposes. School, hospital, and other aid for secular purposes can flow to those institutions even when operated by religious organizations. Option C is incorrect because secular aid for secular purposes to a religious institution does not promote religion. Option D is incorrect because building aid alone does not create excessive entanglement, particularly when the buildings are for secular purposes.

182. **Evidence.** Option C is correct because although an out-of-court statement used to prove the truth of the matter the statement asserts is inadmissible hearsay, prior inconsistent statements are admissible as a hearsay exception to impeach, and the rules permit extrinsic evidence of prior inconsistent statements if the declarant has an opportunity to explain the inconsistency. Here, the audio recording is double hearsay. The recording records an out-of-court statement, and the statement involves an admission by a party opponent. But the rules permit use of both levels of hearsay for the reasons just given. Option A is incorrect because the confrontation clause bars testimony as to statements by unavailable declarants, when used to prove an element of a criminal charge. This case is instead a civil case, the recording does not prove any element of a criminal charge, and the declarant has just testified and is available. Option B is incorrect because hearsay exceptions explained above warrant the recording's admission. Option D is incorrect because the recording is admissible only as a prior inconsistent statement to impeach, not as substantive evidence.

183. **Civil Procedure.** Option A is correct because under FRCP 16, at a pretrial conference, a federal court may dismiss insupportable claims and defenses, refer matters to a magistrate or master, and encourage settlement. Here, the court lacked subject-matter jurisdiction because the amount in controversy was under the $75,000 jurisdictional limit. When the parties admitted that

fact, the court could promptly dismiss the case at the Rule 16 conference. Options B and C are incorrect because the parties admitted those amounts in controversy. They did not agree to a settlement at those figures, and there would have been no other basis for the court to order money judgment other than a settlement. Option D is incorrect because the court lacks jurisdiction, and referral to a magistrate judge would not end the case at the Rule 16 conference. Also, the court would lack jurisdiction to hear and decide dispositive motions. The court should dismiss the case.

184. **Contract Law.** Option D is correct because a party whom another induces by fraud to form a contract has the right to void the contract, whether the party suffers economic damages or not, if the other's actions satisfy the elements of fraud. Here, the family justifiably relied on the builder's knowing false misrepresentation, to its detriment in not gaining the wilderness setting for which the family bargained. Option A is incorrect because the family acted as soon as it learned of the misrepresentation, making its action timely. Only undue delay would bar an action. Option B is incorrect because the party voiding the contract for fraud need not show economic or other harm if the conduct otherwise satisfies fraud elements. Option C is incorrect because the contract was enforceable at its outset but only voidable for fraud. The family could have retained the home if it wished notwithstanding the fraud. Fraud makes a contract voidable at the fraud victim's election, not void for all purposes.

185. **Criminal Law & Procedure.** Option B is correct because misdemeanor manslaughter is a killing occurring from a *malum in se* (sufficiently bad) misdemeanor, criminal negligence, or a felony not sufficient for felony murder. Here, the driver's failure to renew a license did not cause the killing at all, making any misdemeanor or negligence of no consequence. Option A is incorrect because misdemeanor manslaughter does not require intent, only a *malum in se* misdemeanor or criminal negligence. While failing to renew a license is not sufficiently bad (*malum in se*) to justify criminal charges, and nor is it criminally negligent, other circumstances not present here might have satisfied the *malum in se* or negligence conditions, such that the rationale here is wrong. Option C is incorrect because failing to renew the license didn't cause the death, and the charge requires proof of connection (causation). Option D is incorrect for the same reason that failing to renew the license didn't cause the death.

186. **Real Property.** Option C is correct because a valid equitable servitude arises when touching and concerning both the benefitted and burdened properties, the parties intend that it bind others, the servitude satisfies the statute of frauds such as here by poll deed, and owners of the burdened land take with notice such as here by recorded deed. The outcome makes no difference that the initial sale agreement was oral. Once the executive reduced the agreement to a poll deed and the friend accepted that deed, all terms of the oral agreement that the written deed later recorded, whether contrary or inconsistent to the deed, would have merged into the deed so that only the deed terms were enforceable by either party. Option A is incorrect because a poll deed, one signed only by the grantor, binds the grantee and successors if the grantee accepts and especially, as here, the grantee records the deed. Even though not signed by the grantee, a poll deed satisfies the statute of frauds under these conditions. Option B is incorrect because servitudes meeting the above conditions including that they indicate the intent to bind successors in interest run with the land. Option D is incorrect because who builds first would not matter unless the deed so indicated, which it clearly did not do so here.

187. **Torts.** Option C is correct because public necessity is a complete defense to property-damage torts, where the damage was reasonably necessary to protect a public interest. Destruction of a cattle herd because of a disease that threatens the entire beef industry is a public necessity. Options A and B are incorrect because of the public-necessity defense to a conversion action. Option D is incorrect because it was a public necessity (a broad public interest) rather than a private necessity (the specific interest of one or small number of individuals) that warranted the action.

188. **Constitutional Law.** Option B is correct because unless the display primarily celebrated a secular holiday, an observer would reasonably construe it as official endorsement of its religious message in violation of the First Amendment's anti-establishment clause. The display would need other non-religious secular-holiday context to remove its religious-endorsement message. With that context absent, the display is unconstitutional. Option A is incorrect because ownership of the display is not the test. The state can own religious displays permissibly used to celebrate primarily secular holidays, or private citizens can own religious displays that a state impermissibly uses to celebrate a religious holiday. Option C is incorrect for the same reason that the source of the display or of the funds used to purchase it are not the test. The test is one of endorsement and thus of establishment of religion. Option D is incorrect because the other permanent displays do not give this religious display a secular context. They would instead need to relate to the purportedly secular holiday that the religious display would then celebrate.

189. **Evidence.** Option C is correct because character evidence based on prior bad acts is inadmissible to prove that the person acted in conformity with that character, which is exactly what the prosecutor is doing here. Option A is incorrect because although evidence of a prior act may be admissible to prove motive, preparation, or plan, prior bad acts are not admissible to prove character and action conforming to that character. Option B is incorrect because propensity for violence would be a character trait subject to the prohibition on prior-bad-acts evidence to prove character and action conforming to that character. Option D is incorrect because prior-bad-acts evidence to prove character and conforming action is inadmissible whether on direct examination or cross-examination.

190. **Civil Procedure.** Option B is correct because under the 7th Amendment, there are jury-trial rights for torts, contracts, and other legal damages cases but not for equitable claims seeking injunctive relief or family-law cases. The jury will decide all three claims because they are each damages claims. Only if the software company claimed declaratory and injunctive relief would the judge try that claim. Options A, C, and D are incorrect because the jury would try all claims, and the judge would try no claims.

191. **Contract Law.** Option D is correct because when a contract states a condition within one party's control, the law will imply that the party make reasonable efforts to satisfy the condition. Here, the investor never applied for financing when financing might have been available, thus preventing the investor from relying on the unfulfilled condition to avoid the contract. Option A is incorrect because whether the investor obtained financing or not would not have been the dispositive question, if financing might have been available on reasonable effort. Option B is incorrect because the law would imply reasonable effort to satisfy the condition.

When the condition is within a party's control, the party must make reasonable efforts to satisfy the condition. Option C is incorrect because although the law may excuse a condition to avoid disproportionate forfeiture, here the owner faces no forfeiture. The owner still has the property to sell to another buyer.

192. **Criminal Law & Procedure.** Option B is correct because a person who is not the aggressor may use reasonable force as appears necessary to protect against imminent unlawful force. The person may be reasonably mistaken and still have the defense. Option A is incorrect because public-welfare offenses not involving significant moral impropriety or severe penalty, like selling alcohol to a minor, are generally strict-liability crimes for which mistake is not a defense. Option C is incorrect for a related reason that most statutory rape statutes impose strict liability because suspects so often plead mistake in ways that prosecutors find hard to rebut. Option D is incorrect because mistake of law is not a defense to most crimes, only those crimes, like tax evasion, that specifically require knowledge of the law. Reliance on counsel's advice would not be a defense in most cases including to a charge of bigamy. Ignorance of the law is generally no excuse.

193. **Real Property.** Option D is correct because the statute of frauds requires agreements for the sale of lands to be in a writing signed by the charged party, and thus a party cannot compel specific performance of an agreement missing an essential term. While the courts are generous in finding agreements sufficiently complete, the agreement must adequately describe the conveyed lands. Option A is incorrect because equitable powers cannot satisfy the statute of frauds, if as here the parties have not agreed in a signed writing to an essential term. Option B is incorrect because even assuming an obligation of good faith and fair dealing relating to the contract, that obligation cannot satisfy the statute of frauds, if as here the parties have not agreed in a signed writing to an essential term. Option C is incorrect because while price is an essential term of a contract for the sale of land subject to the statute of frauds, a reasonably certain method of calculating the price satisfies the price term, as here providing for a price per acre and the number of acres.

194. **Torts.** Option D is incorrect because a negligence claim requires proof of duty, breach, causation, and damages. The duty element of a negligence claim asks whether a person or entity should have been exercising ordinary or reasonable care toward another. The company owed no tort-based duty to competitors and members of the local community with respect to the safety of the company's own workers. The company's actions were not creating a risk of harm to competitors and members of the public. Option A is incorrect because the motion should be granted for lack of a duty. Option B is incorrect because some public effect from crew-member injuries would not give rise to a duty to competitors or the members of the public. It might be the cause for legislation or regulation but not a tort action. Option C is incorrect because competitive effects are irrelevant to duty. One company would not owe a duty in negligence to its competitors, with respect to the treatment of its own crew members.

195. **Constitutional Law.** Option A is correct because a person has a property interest in the ability to earn income from work for which the person is otherwise qualified, such that state license proceedings must provide those persons with the Fourteenth Amendment's due process. While the contours of due process can vary, revocation of an occupational license based solely

on a redacted and therefore anonymous affidavit would not likely satisfy minimum due process standards. Option B is incorrect because the criminal charge did not reach a judgment, and so state license proceedings could in no way implicate the Constitution's full-faith-and-credit clause. Option C is incorrect because the Constitution says nothing of state administrative powers on state issues. Article III proscribes federal judicial powers, not state judicial powers. Option D is incorrect because federal drug laws are not so extensive as to occupy the field and entirely displace state regulation of drug-related activity. States also regulate drugs heavily. Congress gave no indication of intending to displace state licensing regulations.

196. **Evidence.** Option B is correct because although confidential communications between attorney and client are usually privileged, when the client uses the communication to attempt to advance a crime or fraud, the client loses the privilege. Option A is incorrect because although the client holds the privilege, the lawyer must respect the privilege, and the client has the right to invoke the privilege to prevent the lawyer's production of the letter. Option C is incorrect because the privilege against self-incrimination ordinarily applies to compelled testimony, not to documents that a defendant voluntarily creates. Option D is incorrect because although the client has an attorney-client privilege for confidential communications made to the attorney, the client loses the privilege for communications furthering a crime or fraud.

197. **Civil Procedure.** Option B is correct because the court and counsel voir dire prospective jurors for the court on challenge to strike the biased, leaving each side three racially and sexually non-discriminatory peremptory challenges. Plaintiff's counsel should challenge the defense's strike of female jurors, making the defense articulate non-discriminatory reasons. If the defense cannot, or if the court finds the reasons pretextual, then the court would seat the challenged jurors. Option A is incorrect because there is no absolute right to a jury of an equal number of males and females. The Constitution simply bars sexually discriminatory action. Option C is incorrect because the court may not allow such an argument without evidence and to suggest to jurors that they are probably biased is not likely to help. Option D is incorrect because a party has no right to insist that alternates deliberate, and the defense would likely refuse to consent to the female alternate jurors deliberating.

198. **Contract Law.** Option B is correct because the retailer remains liable to the accounting firm on the original contract, the firm not having released retailer, while the retailer delegated its duty to the vendor, which accepted the delegation with the firm as an intended beneficiary. Both a delegating party and the party accepting delegation remain liable unless the one to whom they owe the obligation releases the delegating party. Option A is incorrect because the vendor accepted assignment and provided service to the firm as intended beneficiary, giving rise to a third-party beneficiary liability. Option C is incorrect because mutuality of remedy is insufficient to extend liability to parties or non-parties, and the retailer could no longer make the firm pay, having assigned the contract to the vendor who had the only right to enforce the firm's agreement. Option D is incorrect because the retailer would also remain liable on the contract unless the firm released the retailer, of which the facts give no such indication.

199. **Criminal Law & Procedure.** Option B is correct because attempted rape is attempted unlawful intercourse with one other than one's wife and without the victim's consent. If the female runner did not resist the male runner's force seeking sex, when the facts indicate

inferences to the contrary, then the facts would not satisfy the charge but would instead indicate consent to sex. Note that the question asks about the charge of attempted rape, not attempted statutory rape, which is unlawful intercourse with an underage minor whether the perpetrator knows of the minor's age or not. Lack of consent is not part of the statutory-rape crime, so the male runner could be convicted of that attempt crime without the female runner having to resist. Attempt involves intent to commit the crime plus an overt act done in furtherance of the intent, beyond mere preparation. Option A is incorrect because abandonment is only a defense when voluntary, not due to problems completing the crime or risk of getting caught, and representing a full renunciation of the criminal purpose. The male runner had already completed the crime of attempted rape by continuing after the female runner said no and resisted. Fleeing because she said she was underage would not exonerate the male runner after he had already committed the attempt crime. Option C is incorrect because the question asks about attempted rape, not attempted statutory rape, so the male runner's belief would not matter, which it would not even as to the attempted statutory rape crime, which is a crime of strict liability. Option D is incorrect because although one cannot convict of both a charge and its lesser included offense, meaning an offense that includes only elements also included in the more-serious offense, the contributing-to-a-minor charge could well include different elements, so that acquittal on that charge would not be necessary for conviction on the attempted-rape charge.

200. **Real Property.** Option A is correct because standard title insurance policies cover an insured landowner's warranties when conveying away the lands. The title insurance persists after sale to protect the insured seller. Option B is incorrect because the conservationist properly met the public trust's demand to pay off the old mortgage. The conservationist gave a warranty deed to the nature conservancy and so owed the conservancy the obligation to remove the undisclosed old mortgage. The public trust took the conservancy's rights by quitclaim. Option C is incorrect because an owner insured under a standard title policy remains insured after conveying away the title. Option D is incorrect because although the lender no longer retained an insurable interest after the conservationist paid the mortgage, the conservationist still had an insurable interest in holding title and also in then conveying the title under warranty deed.

B. Second MBE Practice Exam

1. Part I—Third 100 Questions (Questions 201-300)

201. **Torts.** Option B is correct because the disputed duty to protect against crime may depend on several factors including the past experience of crime, offers of security, available means of protection, and foreseeability. That the hotel recently suffered several break-ins into rooms in that same wing increase the foreseeability of the senior guest's injury. Option A is incorrect because the intruder's identity is irrelevant to the hotel's negligence liability. Not knowing that identity does not make the hotel's liability any more likely or less likely. Option C is incorrect because general advertising without reference to security does not increase the likelihood of proving foreseeability. If the hotel had advertised security, then the guest's claim might have been stronger. Option D is incorrect because the senior guest's having stayed in the hotel on other occasions would not increase the hotel's foreseeability of the guest's injury.

202. **Constitutional Law.** Option C is correct because for an action to present a justiciable case or controversy as Article III requires, ongoing events must not deprive the litigant of the stake or interest that the litigant presented at the litigation's onset. Here, the lawyer has no remaining interest in watching a proceeding that has now terminated, making the controversy moot. Option A is incorrect because the criminal case concluded properly (as the facts state), indicating no likelihood of a renewed or continuing controversy over the trial's televising. The lawyer would have to show more than a remote likelihood that the controversy remains ongoing. Option B is incorrect because federal law, not state law, determines mootness for a federal proceeding as is this pending proceeding presenting only a federal constitutional question. Option D is incorrect because no matter whether the proceeding presented an important issue when filed, it no longer presents any ongoing controversy. The lawyer no longer has a stake in the outcome.

203. **Evidence.** Option A is correct because an out-of-court statement used to prove the truth of the matter that the statement asserts is inadmissible hearsay, and hearsay at multiple levels must satisfy an exception at every level, not just one level. While the owner's instruction was not hearsay because it was used to prove something (state of mind) other than what it asserted (that one may do whatever it takes), the bouncer's prior testimony is hearsay because used to prove what the statement asserted, which was that the bouncer acted on the owner's instruction. Option B is incorrect because prior testimony is admissible only against a party who had opportunity and motive to challenge it in the prior proceeding. As a non-party to the prior proceeding, the bar had no such opportunity or motive in the prior criminal trial against the bouncer. Option C is incorrect because although the owner's instruction is not hearsay because not used to prove what the statement asserted, the transcript of the bouncer's testimony of that statement is hearsay and under no exception as explained above. Option D is incorrect because the bouncer's criminal-trial testimony came after the bouncer was no longer the bar's employee and thus not an agent.

204. **Civil Procedure.** Option C is correct because the federal rules, particularly FRCP 48, require unanimity of jurors unless the parties stipulate otherwise, although many states permit one or more dissenting jurors. Here, one of the alternate jurors, the engineer, may favor the manufacturer's defense that the chainsaw met all engineering standards. Defense counsel should

request that alternates deliberate so that the engineer alternate deliberates. Defense counsel should then insist on unanimity so that the other jurors cannot overrule the engineer. Option A is incorrect because a party has no right to insist on juror dissent in federal court. FRCP requires unanimity unless there is consent to dissent. Also, the manufacturer would not benefit from permitting dissent because the engineer might well be the dissenting juror. The manufacturer would want the engineer to be able to prevent an adverse verdict. Option B is incorrect because the manufacturer has no right to insist on alternates deliberating. The federal rules require seating only six jurors in civil cases. Also, there is no strategy in the manufacturer asking for dissent. Option D is incorrect because the manufacturer can insist on unanimity, not merely request it, and because the manufacturer has no right to insist on alternates deliberating.

205. **Contract Law.** Option D is correct because the sister used her manipulation and domination of the father to induce him to do that which the father did not want to do but for her influence. Undue influence can arise from unfair persuasion through domination of the influenced party within a relationship and manipulation of the relationship against the influenced party's welfare. Option A is incorrect because duress requires a threat of improper action such as crime, but here the only action that the sister proposed was not to visit, which would not have been sufficiently improper. Option B is incorrect because the sister gave consideration in both the $5,000 and visits, even if less than the car's probable market value. Option C is incorrect because neither the father nor the sister were mistaken as to their agreement's terms. They both understood the facts of the exchange.

206. **Criminal Law & Procedure.** Option C is correct because the insanity defense's most-common test, the M'Naghten rule, requires a diseased mind that caused a defect of reason in that defendant either did not know his act was wrong or didn't understand the nature of his actions. Option A is incorrect because voluntary intoxication is only a defense as to certain specific-intent crimes but not general-intent crimes such as common-law murder of the depraved-heart variety. Voluntary intoxication cannot be a defense when the *mens rea* is only recklessness or negligence. Option B is incorrect because self-defense has both an objective element that the defendant must be reasonable in belief of the threat and a subjective element that the defendant must actually believe. The objective element was absent here. Option D is incorrect because an unjustifiably high risk to human life satisfies the depraved-heart form of intent, even without a subjective element. Choking someone carries such an unjustifiably high risk, and thus no-malice-aforethought is not the best defense.

207. **Real Property.** Option C is correct because senior lenders may foreclose on the entire interest despite that the owner and junior lenders have contrary interests. Option A is incorrect because marshalling's two-funds rule applies when a mortgage covers multiple parcels one of which is subject to a competing mortgage. In that case, the court could restrict foreclosure to the other property or properties if the foreclosing lender remained fully secured. Here, though, the junior lender only has a mortgage over the whole property just like the senior lender, and so the two-funds rule doesn't apply. The home-equity lender is subordinate to the bank. Option B is incorrect because only under the two-funds rule as just explained would full security under a portion of the mortgaged properties make a difference in the outcome. Here, the bank may foreclose on the whole mortgaged property. Option D is incorrect because the bank does not

hold a purchase-money mortgage used to buy the home but instead loaned for business. Also, the type of mortgage, purchase-money or not, here makes no difference to foreclosure rights.

208. **Torts.** Option A is incorrect because standards of care may depend on a variety of particular factors including custom, published standards, experience, and the likelihood and foreseeability of injury. A national standard that warning signs should have been placed around the work area would tend to establish that the company should have done so in order to alert the inattentive driver to a potential hazard to the work crew. Option B is incorrect because it does not establish a standard of care for the company and tends only to implicate the driver rather than the company. Option C is incorrect because although several close calls involving other crew members might help prove that drivers were unaware of the work crew's activities, it does not indicate the conduct in which the company should have engaged to protect the workers. It is helpful evidence on causation, more so than on standard of care. Option D is incorrect because it does not identify conduct in which the company should have engaged.

209. **Constitutional Law.** Option C is correct because federal employees have no immunity from state taxes, as long as the tax's legal incidence is on the employee rather than the federal government. Only the federal government itself is immune from state taxation. Option A is incorrect because the tax is in fact on employees rather than the federal government when only the federal government itself would be immune. Option B is incorrect because the Constitution grants no immunity against taxation of federal employees. While the Constitution might prohibit state taxation of the value of a federal vehicle's federal-business use, because doing so would effectively tax the federal activity, the Constitution would not prohibit taxation on the value of personal use of a motor vehicle as compensation for employment income. State income taxes are constitutional. Option D is incorrect because a state likely would have a rational basis for distinguishing between federal and other employees simply to promote federal-state relations, and rational basis is all that would be necessary for this non-suspect class.

210. **Evidence.** Option B is correct because an admission by a party opponent is not hearsay, and a party makes an adoptive admission by manifesting belief that the admission is true. Here, the defendant's handshake and silence showed that the defendant adopted the neighbor's statement as true. Option A is incorrect because although a statement against the declarant's penal interest fits an exception to the hearsay rule, here the defendant did not make the statement, and thus the statement was not against the defendant's penal interest. Option C is incorrect because prosecutors need not show authorization to speak if as here the defendant manifests by conduct and silence belief that the statement is true, as an adoptive admission outside of the hearsay rule. Option D is incorrect because the statement is not hearsay because it is instead an adoptive admission that lies outside the hearsay definition.

211. **Civil Procedure.** Option A is correct because under FRCP 51 and equivalent state rules, judges instruct jurors preliminarily at the case's beginning and then give final instructions after all evidence based on standard and special instructions proposed by counsel. The associate may find some instructions adopted by the district and other pattern instructions in formbooks, and may research statutes and case law to draft other special instructions. Option B is incorrect because statutes do not promulgate standard jury instructions, rules do not promulgate pattern instructions, and cases do not state special instructions. Statutes, rules, and cases may provide

the basis for the associate to draft special instructions. Option C is incorrect because although prior rulings may have indicated the court's position on disputed law, they would not have provided for jury instructions. Option D is incorrect because although the parties' motions, responses, and briefs may have included disputed law and fact, they would not have articulated jury instructions.

212. **Contract Law.** Option A is correct because a manifestation of assent must be sufficiently clear and specific to constitute an acceptance and promise. Here, the debtor only indicated a willingness to try to get the money together, which was not clear assent to the new terms. The constructive condition of first getting the money together made the reply too indefinite to constitute assent. Option B is incorrect because the modified agreement would not have been subject to the statute of frauds and thus would not have required a signed writing. Option C is incorrect because the debtor would owe $10,000, not $7,500. The debtor did not assent to the reduced payment within the shortened period. Option D is incorrect because the debtor did not accept the reduction but instead only committed to trying to get the money together, which was not sufficiently definite to constitute acceptance.

213. **Criminal Law & Procedure.** Option B is correct because the crime of solicitation involves inciting, inducing, or urging another to commit a felony with the specific intent that the solicited person commit the crime. Solicitation is complete when made whether the solicited person agrees or not, and follows through or not, and whether the solicited person only pretended to agree or actually did agree. Option A is incorrect because the solicited person need not agree. The offense is complete with the inciting or urging. Option C is incorrect because the offense is complete with the inciting, inducing, or urging, and attempt to withdraw from the actual plan does not correct the prior complete offense. Option D is incorrect because the solicitation crime does not require an act in furtherance.

214. **Real Property.** Option B is correct because at the seller's death, the doctrine of equitable conversion converts the seller's interest into personal property (the cash sale proceeds) and the buyer's interest into real property. The seller's death means that the seller no longer holds the real property but instead the interest in the coming sale proceeds, while the buyer gains a right to the real property. Option A is incorrect because a court order makes no difference. The law determines the rights, and the court would need to follow the law. Option C is incorrect because the doctrine of equitable conversion, not the anticipated sale date, determines the outcome, as here where the scheduled sale date was for after the date of death, but the buyer still received the real property. Option D is incorrect because the doctrine of equitable conversion determines the outcome as to all real property whether the will specifically describes it or not.

215. **Torts.** Option B is correct because in determining the standard of conduct, the reasonably prudent person takes on the physical characteristics of the one whose conduct is in question. There is no expectation that a driver too small or weak to take an action should be liable for failing to do so. Option A is incorrect because the subjective knowledge and individual skill and experience of the defendant is not the standard. Standards are objective except with respect to physical characteristics. Option C is incorrect because the standard does account for physical characteristics. Option D is incorrect because the standard does not contemplate an average

person, especially as to physical characteristics. The standard is the reasonably prudent person, not the average person, and the standard accounts for the defendant's physical characteristics.

216. **Constitutional Law.** Option D is correct because a due-process challenge must show deprivation of a property or liberty interest, and the operator here can show neither. The operator has no property interest in freedom from competition because the legislation did not limit the number of licenses. Anyone meeting the criteria could qualify. Option A is incorrect because due-process challenges require a protectable property or liberty interest, not just a showing of potential adverse effect. Option B is incorrect because the operator had no protectable property right and thus no right to a hearing, and so has no claim that the officer deprived the operator of a hearing. The official had no obligation to offer a hearing and thus violated no right when refusing a hearing. Option C is incorrect because benefit from legislation does not bar a due-process challenge. The question isn't benefit but whether the person making the challenge has a protectable property or liberty interest.

217. **Evidence.** Option D is correct because although a judge may take judicial notice of a matter the accuracy of which a party cannot reasonably question, a reasonable person could question a clerk as a reliable source of information for judicial notice. Option A is incorrect because certified copies of public records are self-authenticating. Option B is incorrect because testimony of a witness with knowledge is one means to authenticate a conviction, meaning to show that the matter is what its proponent claims it to be. Option C is incorrect because a party admission is admissible as outside of the hearsay rule. The rules define hearsay to exclude a party admission.

218. **Civil Procedure.** Option C is correct because under FRCP 50 and similar state rules, counsel object on the record to erroneous instructions before the court gives them or can lose appeal rights to all but plain error affecting substantial rights. Defense counsel should object on the record before the trial judge reads the erroneous instructions. Option A is incorrect because the trial judge has already effectively ruled that the instructions are not erroneous. Moving for relief based on them is pointless. The effort should be to alert the trial judges to the objections before the judge gives the erroneous instruction, and to preserve appellate review. Option B is incorrect because the judge determines the law, not counsel. The judge would not permit counsel to argue in closing that the judge's instructions were wrong. Option D is incorrect because filing the instructions would alone not demonstrate objection. Sometimes counsel bargain over proposed instructions, and filing them does not indicate insistence that they be given and others not be given.

219. **Contract Law.** Option D is correct because a party cannot assign and delegate obligations of a personal nature that depend on reputation, skill, and taste. Here, the entertainer chose the renowned chef, not the sous chef, depending on the renowned chef's reputation to impress other professionals. Option A is incorrect because assurance of equivalent skill is not the question. The entertainer chose the renowned chef, not any equivalent. Option B is incorrect because while an express prohibition would have clarified the contract, no such prohibition is necessary when the performance is plainly personal. Option C is incorrect because only the entertainer owed the obligation could have accomplished a novation. The one due performance must assent for a novation to occur. Here, the entertainer did not assent.

220. **Criminal Law & Procedure.** Option C is correct because felony murder requires an underlying felony that is inherently dangerous to human life while sufficiently independent from the homicide itself, and so not manslaughter (a homicide) or aggravated battery (leading to death and thus homicide). Examples of sufficiently independent but inherently dangerous felonies include rape, robbery, arson, burglary, and kidnapping. Option A is incorrect because burglary is both inherently dangerous while also sufficiently independent from the homicide, and thus a felony likely to support felony murder. Option B is incorrect because attempted rape is inherently dangerous and sufficiently independent, and so a felony within felony murder. Option D is incorrect because arson is inherently dangerous and sufficiently independent, and so a felony within felony murder.

221. **Real Property.** Option B is correct because a recording act protects bona fide purchasers who take fee title without notice of the unrecorded encumbrance while paying valuable consideration. The young couple didn't know of the unrecorded trust. Option A is incorrect because the timing of the trust's creation doesn't matter when the recording act requires notice. Option C is incorrect because recording acts do require recording of trusts creating equitable interests just as they require recording of other instruments. Option D is incorrect because although successor ordinarily do take only the title that the grantor possesses, the recording act would require that the encumbrance on the title be of record in order to bind bona fide purchasers. The young couple were bona fide purchasers protected by the recording act.

222. **Torts.** Option D is correct because ordinarily, the promisor on a contract owes a tort-based duty to a third party only when the promisor has undertaken some act performing the contract (misfeasance, not nonfeasance). Here, the contractor had not yet performed. The contractor's only duty was therefore a contract duty owed the store, not a tort-based duty owed the customer. Option A is incorrect because the court should grant the motion for lack of a duty. Option B is incorrect because whether the contractor should have started sooner or not does not change the duty issue. The contract clearly indicated so, but it made no difference if the contractor had not performed some part of the contract. Option C is incorrect because whether the contractor is usually prudent or not does not affect whether there was a duty in this instance.

223. **Constitutional Law.** Option A is correct because the Tenth Amendment reserves to the states powers not expressly delegated to Congress, by Supreme Court decision leaving a negative implication that Congress may not compel states to adopt specific state laws. Congress may coerce state legislation by offering or denying federal funds, but this legislation requires specific state laws. Option B is incorrect because the legislation does create a nexus to drugs moved in interstate commerce, thus relying on Congress's commerce-clause power. Option C is incorrect because although the legislation limits its reach to actions affecting interstate commerce, it still runs afoul of the Tenth Amendment limit on Congress's power, not to compel state laws. Option D is incorrect because Congress has no power to act for the general welfare, only to tax and spend for the general welfare. This provision does not tax or spend and thus draws no authority from the Constitution's general-welfare clause.

224. **Evidence.** Option A is correct because multiple hearsay must find an exception at every level to be admissible, and although an admission by a party opponent (here the inner level that

the defendant threatened the decedent's life) lies outside the hearsay rule, an out-of-court statement (the husband's statement to his wife) that another made a party admission (the defendant's threat on the decedent's life) would still be hearsay outside of any exception. Option B is incorrect because the inner statement (the defendant's threat on the decedent's life) would be an admission rather than a prior bad act. Option C is incorrect because the outer level of hearsay, the wife testifying to the deceased husband's statement, is not an admission by the defendant woman and thus not under any hearsay exception. Option D is incorrect because although the woman's threat may have fallen within the then-existing-state-of-mind exception to the hearsay rule, the other hearsay of the wife repeating the deceased husband's statement does not fall within that or any other exception.

225. **Civil Procedure.** Option C is correct because a party may move for summary judgment under FRCP 56 and equivalent state rules when there is no genuine issue of material fact and the party is entitled to judgment as a matter of law. The finance company's admissions establish beyond dispute that it has no claim against the corporate parent, which should file a motion for summary judgment. Option A is incorrect because the parent has no apparent reason to settle a claim on which it has no liability. The case would not end at mediation unless the parties agree. Option B is incorrect because there is no apparent basis to lift the stay, and lifting the stay would not end the current litigation against the parent. Option D is incorrect because assuming the lease payments would create an obligation on the parent's part that it does not appear that it wants. It might end the litigation, but not on the corporate parent's terms.

226. **Contract Law.** Option C is correct because the parties reached an accord, which the obligor satisfied by payment. Accord and satisfaction around a substitute performance bar enforcement of the original obligation. Option A is incorrect because although the pre-existing duty rule ordinarily prevents partial payment of a liquidated debt from discharging the obligation, here the designer raised a good-faith dispute, and the cabinetmaker's agreement to forgo enforcement of the original obligation constituted consideration for the reduced payment. Option B is incorrect because the designer fully performed the contract, taking it out of the statute of frauds, even assuming the written contract prohibited oral modification, of which the facts give no indication. Option D is incorrect because the facts do not state a novation, which instead occurs only when one owed an obligation accepts that someone other than the promisor will fulfill it while relieving the promisor of the obligation. This scenario does not involve novation.

227. **Criminal Law & Procedure.** Option B is correct because due process may bar out-of-court evidence of identification from a procedure that was unnecessarily suggestive. An especially egregious identification procedure may even bar the witness's in-court testimony unless the prosecution can show that the testimony is reliable outside of the taint. Here, the teller may have seen enough of the hooded suspect's face to make an identification apart from the tainted out-of-court procedure. Option A is incorrect because the prosecution may be able to show the testimony is reliable outside of the taint of the out-of-court procedure, such as by eyewitness observation at the scene of the crime. Option C is incorrect because a preliminary out-of-court identification may be so unnecessarily suggestive as to bar in-court testimony from its taint. This out-of-court procedure was very suggestive in that the detective used a mug shot, showed only one photograph rather than a photo lineup, and told the teller that they were

confident that it was him when the teller hesitated. Option D is incorrect because tainted out-of-court identification can in egregious cases bar in-court testimony.

228. **Real Property.** Option A is correct because a bona fide purchaser for value without notice gains the protection of the recording act as to deeds not in the chain of title. The buyer's deed is not in the friend's chain of title because the buyer took from the sister before the sister had title, whereas the friend took from the sister after the sister had recorded title. The chain from brother to sister to friend gave the friend notice of only that chain and not the sister's deed to the buyer before the sister had become part of that chain of title. Option B is incorrect because possession does not bear under these circumstances on who has good title. Option C is incorrect because nothing delayed the buyer's deed taking effect. The buyer either had title or did not, the latter being the case because the sister then had nothing yet to convey. Estoppel by deed could give the buyer good title relating back to the date of the sister's conveyance, but the recording act gives the friend bona fide purchaser the valid title. Option D is incorrect because the doctrine of estoppel by deed would work in the buyer's favor to gain title from the sister once she came into possession of it but for the workings of the recording act in the friend's favor.

229. **Torts.** Option C is correct because absent a special relationship or other exception, tort law generally imposes no duty to act such as to come to the rescue of another, unless one's actions created the need for rescue. The farmer's offer to help, and the gardener's detrimental reliance on that offer, and the farmer's knowledge of the detrimental reliance, would establish a special relationship. Option A is incorrect because the farmer did not owe the gardener a duty. Option B is incorrect because one person cannot create a duty on the part of another simply by asking. A person need not give reasons for refusing to come to another's rescue. Option D is incorrect because it does not describe the kind of special relationship that would give rise to a duty of aid or rescue.

230. **Constitutional Law.** Option B is correct because the president holds executive powers as long as using funds only as Congress appropriates and not violating any federal statute. Here, Congress appropriated funds generally to the president's office, which the president may use within the executive function such as for a national health campaign. Option A is incorrect because the president does not hold plenary power to act for health, safety, and welfare but instead depends on Congress for funding while deferring to the express constitutional powers of Congress. Option C is incorrect because while the states do hold authority to act for families and children, the Tenth Amendment does not limit the federal government from acting other than to prohibit Congress from expressly directing states to enact certain legislation. Option D is incorrect because Congress here authorized funding generally to the president's office, and the president has executive power to act to carry out the executive function.

231. **Evidence.** Option A is correct because the rules require a judge to sequester witnesses when a party so requests. Option B is incorrect because the rules give the judge discretion to allow cross-examination beyond the scope of direct examination as if on direct examination. Option C is incorrect because the rules provide that cross-examination may include matters affecting credibility whether raised on direct or not. Option D is incorrect because cross-examination of a witness whom the opposing party called under the adverse witness statute would effectively be like direct examination of a friendly witness and thus inappropriate for

leading questions. The wife's close sister would have favored the wife, not the husband who called her under the adverse witness statute.

232. Civil Procedure. Option D is correct because under FRCP 56 and equivalent state rules, the court must view the evidence in the light most favorable to the party opposing summary judgment. The buyer was opposing summary judgment, so the court must view the affidavits in favor of the buyer. The buyer's affidavit establishes a genuine issue of material fact, meaning that the court must deny the motion. Option A is incorrect because the affidavits do not cancel out, and the court may not require more evidence. Option B is incorrect because courts are not to weigh the evidence on summary judgment. They are to view evidence in favor of the party opposing summary judgment. Option C is incorrect because the seller filed the motion, meaning that the court must construe the evidence in the buyer's favor, not the seller's favor.

233. Contract Law. Option B is correct because $65,000 represents the builder's contract expectation. Expectation is the most common damages measure. The builder bargained for $20,000 in profit, spent $50,000 on labor and materials for which the builder should have restitution, but recouped $10,000 by using materials on another job, the net of which is $60,000. Option A is incorrect because while it recognizes the $50,000 in restitution and $20,000 in anticipated profit, it fails to account for the builder's using $10,000 in materials on another job. Option C is incorrect because it fails to account for the $20,000 profit for which the builder bargained or the $10,000 in materials that the builder saved by using on another job. Option D is incorrect because it fails to account for the $20,000 in bargained-for profit. The amount would serve as restitutionary damages but not account for the full expectation of the bargain.

234. Criminal Law & Procedure. Option B is correct because although double jeopardy bars the prosecution from trying the same defendant twice for the same charge, double jeopardy does not attach until the trial begins, which is when the selected jurors take their oath or in a bench trial when the court swears the first witness. Option A is incorrect because double jeopardy does not require a prior conviction or acquittal, only that the prior trial begin. Option C is incorrect because once jeopardy attaches in the first trial, no further prosecution on the same charge is permitted, whether the prosecution has new evidence or not. New evidence isn't the standard. Attaching of jeopardy for conviction is the standard for when double-jeopardy rights arise. Option D is incorrect because the first trial did not begin, and thus jeopardy did not attach. Dismissal on the merits is a preclusion condition for civil cases, not a standard for double jeopardy in criminal cases.

235. Real Property. Option A is correct because a forger cannot convey title that the forger never had, based on the forgery, and the forger's grantees get no advantage from the forgery. Recording acts protect against unrecorded interests but not against forgeries. Option B is incorrect because the law places no obligation on buyers who examine recorded title to discover forgeries, although they would certainly want to do so because they cannot gain title based on forgery. This option gives the right result for the wrong reason. Option C is incorrect because a buyer cannot gain interests purporting to arise based on the seller's forgery. Option D is incorrect because the law places no obligation on mortgagees or other holders of recorded interests to discover subsequent forgeries even if recorded. One has no duty to continue to examine recordings against an interest already acquired.

236. **Torts.** Option B is correct because the economic-loss doctrine limits tort duties to those instances where there is some direct injury and bars pure economic loss claims by those who have suffered no physical impact. The doctrine bars the manufacturer's claim because the manufacturer had solely economic loss without physical impact. Option A is incorrect because there is no claim, the only plausible claim being barred by the economic-loss doctrine. Option C is incorrect because the claim is barred by the doctrine whether or not the lost sales were certain. Certainty of loss is not the proof burden in any case. Option D is incorrect because the captain's knowledge of the lost sales would not create a duty to prevent them, when the claim is barred by the economic-loss doctrine.

237. **Constitutional Law.** Option C is correct because the Thirteenth Amendment empowers Congress to act to prohibit private action that imposes a badge or incident of slavery on a person. Here, Congress intends to reach private action and so would best use the Thirteenth Amendment as a source of powert to do so. Option A is incorrect because the obligation-of-contracts clause limits state power, prohibiting states from passing laws that impair the obligations of contracts, rather than empowers Congress to act. Option B is incorrect because the general-welfare clause empowers Congress to tax and spend, not to regulate private behavior as the proposed statute would here. Option D is incorrect because the Fourteenth Amendment's due-process clause limits state action rather than private action as the proposed statute would here. Congress would need a source of power that authorizes regulation of private rather than state action.

238. **Evidence.** Option D is correct because identification requires only evidence that the person is who the witness purports the person to be. Here, the debtor is able to authenticate the caller's voice as the partner. The rules do not require certainty for identification. Option A is incorrect because the rules do not require certainty for identification. Option B is incorrect because the best-evidence rule applies to evidence of a document's contents, whereas here the testimony is as to identification. The availability of the recording makes no difference to the testimony's admissibility. Option C is incorrect because the evidence rules do apply in both contempt and bankruptcy proceedings.

239. **Civil Procedure.** Option D is correct because under FRCP 50 and similar state rules, after a party rests, the trial judge may grant judgment as a matter of law (direct a verdict) where the evidence does not support a claim or defense. When the patient failed to present evidence on elements of the patient's case by the time of the close of the patient's proofs, defense counsel should move for judgment as a matter of law. Option A is incorrect because a nominal settlement offer is unlikely to resolve the case and would not resolve it as favorably as a dismissal on judgment as a matter of law. Option B is incorrect because the hospital would not want the case to go to the jury. It should be dismissed now before the hospital is put to proofs from which the patient may be able to establish the standard of care and breach. Option C is incorrect because the hospital would not want a new trial, and there is no basis for new trial. A failure in the patient's proofs does not warrant a new trial. This trial should end now with dismissal.

240. **Contract Law.** Option D is correct because agreements for the sale of real property must under the statute of frauds be in a writing signed by the charged party and containing all essential

terms. While the memorandum identified the parties, the land, and the buy-sell promise, the memorandum did not identify the price, the landowner's evidence for which was thus only oral testimony not satisfying the statute of frauds. Option A is incorrect because the statute of frauds requires that all essential terms be in writing. Option B is incorrect because the facts do not suggest any such implication of a market price and because the facts do not indicate whether $250,000 is in fact a market price. Option C is incorrect because while true, even if $250,000 was a market-value price, the facts give no indication of any indication in the memorandum that the parties had agreed to use a market value. The memorandum still would not supply an essential price term.

241. **Criminal Law & Procedure.** Option B is correct because police must give *Miranda* warnings before subjecting a suspect to custodial interrogation, or the court will ordinarily bar any resulting confession. A custodial interrogation is questioning when the suspect believes that he is not free to leave. Option A is incorrect because voluntariness or involuntariness of a statement involves a higher standard of threat, coercion, or duress, whereas *Miranda* offers a lower bright-line standard of custodial interrogation without duress. Option C is incorrect because *Miranda* does not require that police first tell a suspect that he is under arrest. If the suspect believes that he is not free to go, then the questioning is custodial, and *Miranda* rights apply. Option D is incorrect because an arrest warrant authorizes police to enter a residence without consent or warning. They do not need a search warrant to make an arrest within the residence.

242. **Real Property.** Option A is correct because the law construes a grant to a named person "and his heirs" not as creating any right in the heirs but instead as conveying fee-simple title to only the named grantee. The law construes "and his heirs" as intent to convey fee-simple title rather than as intent to create a current interest on the heirs' part. The outdoorsman took fee simple title clear of any interest on his adult son's part, making his conveyance to the cattleman likewise of fee-simple title. Options B, C, and D are incorrect because the adult son never gained any interest from the "and his heirs" language. Options C and D are incorrect because the law does not support any theory for the adult son and cattleman sharing tenancy interests.

243. **Torts.** Option A is correct because courts may require those who claim negligently caused emotional distress (without physical impact) to also show that they were contemporaneous witnesses, were a family member of the person physically injured, and suffered severe distress with physical manifestation. Psychological help indicates severe distress, and gastric distress may qualify as physical manifestation. Option B is incorrect because threats by the mother would have no relevance to whether she had a claim against the drunk driver. Option C is incorrect because the social and emotional closeness of mother and daughter would only be relevant to the extent that it contributed to the mother's severe distress over her daughter's injury. Direct evidence of the severe distress (Option A) is better than evidence of a reason for it (Option C). Option D is incorrect because the daughter's distress would only increase the daughter's damages, not give rise to a claim by the mother.

244. **Constitutional Law.** Option C is correct because a state must not unduly burden a woman's fundamental privacy right, which in the case of pregnancy continues up until the child is viable. The Supreme Court has held that the abortion right continues up until viability and that

a state may regulate to protect the woman's health and child's life only if not imposing an undue burden on the abortion right, which a life-or-health-only restriction clearly would under Supreme Court caselaw. Option A is incorrect because the Supreme Court has held that protecting fetal life is not compelling until the child is viable. Option B is incorrect because the Supreme Court does not recognize unborn children as persons and grants substantial protection to them only after viability. Option D is incorrect because the Supreme Court uses substantive due process to analyze abortion-rights cases rather than equal protection.

245. **Evidence.** Option C is correct because routine-practice testimony is admissible to show that the proponent followed the practice here. The letter copies are simply part of the routine-practice testimony, not used to prove the truth of what the letters assert. Option A is incorrect because the supplier is not trying to use the letters to prove their contents, which would be to prove the fact of a price change. Rather, the letters are to prove notice. Because the letters are not to prove their contents, the best-evidence rule does not apply to bar a disputed copy. Also, no dispute exists as to the reason that the original is not available. The supplier mailed the original, so that a copy is the supplier's only available evidence even if the best-evidence rule applied. Option B is incorrect because the letter copies are not hearsay because the supplier is not offering them to prove the truth of what they assert, which is that the steel price changed. They are instead to supply proof of notice to the contractor. Option D is incorrect for the same reason that the letter copies are not hearsay at all and so do not need a business-records exception.

246. **Civil Procedure.** Option B is correct because a party who moves for judgment as a matter of law before jury deliberation may renew the motion after losing at trial (also known as a motion for judgment notwithstanding the verdict or JNOV) and then also challenge rulings on appeal. When the broker moved the first time for judgment as a matter of law at the close of the cereal company's proofs, the broker preserved the same motion for after trial and preserved the right to appeal adverse rulings on the motions. A is incorrect because there are no apparent grounds for mistrial (no irregularity in the proceedings), and a new trial is not as favorable as a judgment as a matter of law. The broker would prefer judgment as a matter of law to another trial. C is incorrect because there are now no grounds to compel arbitration given that the court has already tried the case and the broker has lost. D is incorrect because the cereal company is unlikely to pay a settlement, and a settlement is not as favorable as judgment as a matter of law.

247. **Contract Law.** Option C is correct because when a contract specifies the order of performance and requires complete performance before payment, then the party having the express obligation to perform first and complete the work must do so before payment. Option A is incorrect because the contract expressly indicated the opposite that the company must perform all of the work, demolishing all three homes, before the city must pay. Option B is incorrect because under the contract terms, finishing two thirds of the work would not have been substantial performance. The contract required demolition of all three homes before the city must pay. Option D is incorrect because the company never had a right to payment after each demolition, and so making a demand after the first home would have made no difference.

248. **Criminal Law & Procedure.** Option D is correct because although a defendant has a Sixth Amendment right for trial by a representative jury drawn from a fair cross-section of the

community, qualifying jurors on the question of the death penalty does not violate that right, even in a bifurcated trial where the prosecution removes the juror only from the guilt phase. Prosecutors may remove those jurors from either the guilt or sentencing phase. Option A is incorrect because the Supreme Court has held that the Sixth Amendment permits death-qualifying a jury for either phase. Options B and C are incorrect because prosecutors may death qualify jurors even during the sentencing phase so that the appellate court would not reverse the death sentence on these grounds.

249. **Real Property.** Option A is correct because a recording act ordinarily protects only bona fide purchasers who take and record without notice of superior rights. Purchasers who are or should be aware of the superior right, in this case the driveway easement, take subject to that right. Here, the cabin owner had a written easement but just hadn't recorded it. The bank knew or should have known of the easement because of the driveway's construction. Option B is incorrect because although an appurtenant easement, one pertaining to a particular benefitted parcel, ordinarily passes with the property, the question here is not whether the easement continues but which interest, mortgage or easement, is superior under the recording act. Because the bank took the mortgage with notice or constructive notice of the driveway, the bank does not get the protection of the recording act. Option C is incorrect because access to a paved road doesn't matter when the cabin owner already had access to a dirt road. Easements by necessity do not arise simply to improve access but rather to create access that doesn't exist. Option D is incorrect because recording before foreclosure would not matter. Recording before the bank recorded would matter, except that the bank had notice in any case.

250. **Torts.** Option A is correct because proof of breach may be by direct or circumstantial evidence, including (for instance) constructive notice as to how long an unreasonably dangerous condition existed. The oil's stickiness from evaporation would tend to show that it had been on the floor long enough for the grocery store personnel to observe it and clean it up before the shopper slipped. Option B is incorrect because it would not tend to prove the grocery store's breach. Constructive notice is the breach issue, not the shopper's reasonable care. Option C is incorrect because it tends to show adequate staffing levels and thus work against breach of duty. Option D is incorrect because the wet-floor signs at the store's entrance would not have alerted the shopper to the oil on the floor of an aisle and would, if anything, tend to show the store's reasonable care rather than lack thereof.

251. **Constitutional Law.** Option A is correct because equal protection requires race-based affirmative action plans to satisfy strict scrutiny as necessary to achieve a compelling government interest. The Supreme Court has held that minority set-aside programs satisfy strict scrutiny only when enacted to remedy prior discrimination by the enacting agency. Option B is incorrect because the contracts clause prohibits states from impairing obligations of existing contracts, not from altering the conditions under which parties may enter into new contracts. Option C is incorrect because the enactment would not satisfy strict scrutiny without a record of prior discrimination by the drain commission. Option D is incorrect because equal protection and other rights apply to state actions generally whether or not those actions are governmental or proprietary.

252. **Evidence.** Option A is correct because a current spouse of a criminally charged defendant has a marital privilege not to testify against the charged spouse and is therefore immune from contempt proceedings for refusing to testify. Option B is incorrect because only the testifying spouse holds the privilege not to testify. If the testifying spouse wants to testify, then he may do so. The non-testifying spouse holds only a confidential-communications privilege to prevent the other spouse from testifying to those communications. Clothing testimony is not a confidential communication. Option C is incorrect because the husband has immunity from contempt and testifying under the marital privilege. Option D is incorrect because the marital privilege does apply in criminal cases, not civil cases, and holds the spouse immune from contempt for refusing to testify.

253. **Civil Procedure.** Option C is correct because trial judges can order new trial for misconduct by a party, counsel, witness, or juror. For defense counsel to argue against the neuropsychologist's qualifications without evidence and using inflammatory words and arguments could be the basis for a new trial. The neuropsychologist was a treating physician, not a retained expert, and there was no contrary evidence that he was not practicing sound medicine or was testifying for plaintiffs for the money. Option A is incorrect because although conduct of this kind may violate ethics rules, filing a grievance will not address the effect of counsel's argument (as the call of the question asks). It will only potentially affect defense counsel's license, not the outcome of trial. Option B is incorrect because the trial is over, it is too late to retain and call another expert, and there is no indication that a more-qualified neuropsychologist would have fared any better with opposing counsel. Option D is incorrect because although an appeal based on misconduct is possible, the bicyclist's lawyer should first move for new trial, and the lawyer would base an appeal on counsel misconduct, not party misconduct.

254. **Contract Law.** Option B is correct because once a party commences performance in reliance on a unilateral offer that a party accepts only by performance, the offeror can no longer revoke the offer. Once the customers placed orders and waited, they had commenced performance in reliance on a unilateral offer that they would have accepted only by such performance. Option A is incorrect because one accepts a unilateral offer by commencing and completing performance, not by notice of intent to perform. Telling the restaurant that they were relying on the placard would not have been necessary or even helpful. The customers would instead need to commence performance showing reliance on it, at which point the restaurant could no longer revoke, and then complete performance, waiting the full twenty minutes, to accept the offer, which they did. Option C is incorrect because the restaurant would have had to refuse the orders or remove the placard before taking the orders to avoid breach-of-contract liability. The restaurant could no longer revoke its unilateral offer once the customers commenced performance. Option D is incorrect because the placard was not a statement of gift but instead a unilateral offer that customers could secure by commencing performance and accept by completing performance.

255. **Criminal Law & Procedure.** Option D is correct because although the Fourth Amendment requires a warrant issued on probable cause, to enter and search a house, and the warrantless entry without probable cause violated that right, the trial court need not dismiss a facially valid indictment that prosecutors obtained on inadmissible evidence including evidence obtained in violation of constitutional rights. Option A is incorrect both because the suspect did not have the

right to counsel and because dismissal of the indictment would not be a remedy. The Sixth Amendment right to counsel attaches only when formal proceedings such as an indictment commence against the defendant. Even the Fifth Amendment *Miranda* right to have counsel present attaches only in custodial interrogation. Option B is incorrect because although once the officer made a warrantless entry without probable cause in violation of Fourth Amendment rights, the subsequent connected statement may well have been the fruit of that entry and thus also inadmissible, dismissal is not a remedy. Option C is incorrect because even though hearsay without an applicable exception is inadmissible, the dismissal of an indictment is not the remedy.

256. **Real Property.** Option C is correct because property owners may enforce an implied reciprocal servitude that existed expressly in prior deeds from a general plan, when the owner challenging the restriction has actual, constructive, or implied notice of the restriction. Option A is incorrect for the same reason because the law will imply a reciprocal servitude not expressly present in the deeds on the conditions just recited. Option B is incorrect for the same reason and also because even if no deed or implied reciprocal servitude restricted the owner, then the owner would still have to comply with zoning. Zoning restrictions do not depend on deed restrictions. Option D is incorrect because simply taking a restricted property would not continue to restrict the owner once the restriction expired. The restriction would continue only under an implied reciprocal servitude, not because the owner had taken while restricted. The restriction would, though, establish the owner's actual notice.

257. **Torts.** Option C is correct because the doctrine of res ipsa loquitur provides an inference of negligence when the injury-causing event speaks of negligence, the plaintiff cannot obtain evidence of negligence, and the circumstances are within the defendant's control. There is likely an inference that the mechanic negligently failed to secure the wheel's lug nuts or otherwise contributed to the occurrence. Option A is incorrect because the mechanic clearly had a duty. Option B is incorrect because of the effect of the doctrine of res ipsa loquitur. Option D is incorrect because res ipsa loquitur provides an inference of negligence, not certain liability.

258. **Constitutional Law.** Option D is correct because Article III gives Congress the power to extend federal-court jurisdiction only over cases and controversies, not to give advisory opinions. A judgment recommending adjustments to a federal-agency head would be only an advisory opinion and not the resolution of a case or controversy. Option A is incorrect because a federal question alone would not be enough to overcome the advisory-opinion problem that federal courts have judicial power only over cases or controversies. Option B is incorrect for the same reason that appropriating federal funds does not authorize Congress to give federal courts jurisdiction over advisory matters. Option C is incorrect because the Eleventh Amendment bars citizens from suing a state in federal court, not suits among states or between a state and the federal government.

259. **Evidence.** Option B is correct because prior sexual assaults by a defendant to a criminal charge are admissible if otherwise relevant, as are prior specific sexual acts of the victim with the defendant if offered to show consent, but not the sexual predisposition of the victim. Option A is incorrect because the victim's prior consent to sex with the defendant would be admissible. Option C is incorrect because the victim's promiscuousness would not be admissible. Option D

is incorrect because the prior similar sexual assault would be admissible as relevant to the defendant's strength and ability to accomplish the charged assault.

260. **Civil Procedure.** Option C is correct because parties may seek relief from judgment for newly discovered evidence, fraud, clerical mistakes, excusable neglect, and other grounds. The notary's attestation may be newly discovered evidence and evidence of the winning landowner's fraud, forming the basis for an evidentiary hearing to determine whether the judgment should be set aside, new trial, or other relief. Option A is incorrect because the losing landowner may seek relief from judgment for new evidence, fraud, clerical mistake, neglect, and similar grounds. Option B is incorrect because the prior judgment would bar a new action. The losing landowner must seek relief from the prior judgment in the same action by moving to set it aside for newly discovered evidence of fraud. Option D is incorrect because the notary's affidavit only raises a fact issue. The court could not order judgment as a matter of law simply based on the affidavit. The court would have to hold a hearing, take the notary's testimony, and allow cross-examination and contrary evidence.

261. **Contract Law.** Option D is correct because a contract the consideration for which is an agreement to divorce is unenforceable as against public policy. Public policy must not encourage divorce, as this contract would do. Option A is incorrect because reliance is irrelevant if as here the contract is against public policy. The issue wasn't whether the parties had entered into a contract. They clearly had. The issue was the contract's enforceability. Option B is incorrect because the statute of frauds is not the issue. The issue is instead that the contract was against public policy and thus not enforceable. Option C is incorrect because while death of an offeror would terminate the offer, the daughter had already accepted the offer by performing (divorcing), and death does not terminate a contract. The estate would be liable but for the contract being against public policy.

262. **Criminal Law & Procedure.** Option B is correct because a guilty plea must be both intelligent and voluntary. The defendant must understand the nature of the charge, the maximum and mandatory-minimum penalties, and the right to jury trial. Here, the judge did not inform the defendant of the Sixth Amendment right to jury trial. Option A is incorrect because while a prosecutor must disclose exculpatory evidence for fair trial, constitutional rights do not require disclosure at the plea stage. Option C is incorrect because although federal and some state courts inquire as to the factual basis, no constitutional rule requires that they do so, unless the defendant claims innocence and indicates an unacceptable reason for pleading guilty such as to avoid a harsh sentence. Option D is incorrect because no right requires that the trial judge first rule on pending motions.

263. **Real Property.** Option A is correct because use can establish the location of a deeded but undescribed right-of-way easement, and once use establishes the location, the restriction at that location persists. Option B is incorrect because the facts suggest only five years of use, which would not meet the typical statute on prescriptive use for ten years or more, and here the use was not adverse and prescriptive but instead by grant, so that prescriptive-use rights would not arise. Option C is incorrect because once the grantor and grantee fix the granted and deeded easement's location, the easement remains fixed. The grantee need not move it whenever the

grantor shows an alternative reasonable location. Option D is incorrect because a grantor and grantee may establish an easement's location in addition to by express description.

264. **Torts.** Option D is correct because courts construe the violation of a safety statute as negligence per se (the majority position) or allow a presumption or inference of negligence. Any of these positions satisfy the plaintiff's burden of production. Option A is incorrect because officers, though often credible, are not necessarily the most credible witnesses for any plaintiff, and deference to impressive witnesses is not the directed-verdict standard. Option B is incorrect because the facts do not indicate that there were no other witnesses, and whether there were other witnesses or not is irrelevant to the directed-verdict standard. Option C is incorrect because the violation is not construed as the defendant doing something wrong or that the defendant must lose. The proper terms are negligence per se or a presumption or inference of negligence, each of which permit the defendant to offer explanations.

265. **Constitutional Law.** Option C is correct because one of the constitutional limits on federal judicial power is that the federal courts may only hear justiciable issues and must not hear political questions that the Constitution commits to another branch of government, lack manageable resolution standards, interfere with finality in the political branches, and offer little judicial remedy. Recognition of foreign states is an executive power and nonjusticiable. Option A is incorrect because the consultant's loss of the contract is a sufficient injury on which to claim standing. Option B is incorrect because the parties are sufficiently adverse, the president having taken action that terminated the consultant's contract. Option D is incorrect because the case presents a non-justiciable political question under the above standard.

266. **Evidence.** Option B is correct because an expert opinion is admissible when the witness has specialized knowledge to assist the factfinder and the opinion is based on a reliable method applied to sufficient data or facts. Options A and D are incorrect because expert opinions do not depend on the absence of other forms of evidence. Expert opinions may corroborate or contradict other evidence. Option C is incorrect because because the facts indicate the officer's training and experience in estimating speeds, indicating a reliable method applied to the data at the scene.

267. **Civil Procedure.** Option D is correct because a trial court may take special verdicts requiring jurors to answer specific controlling questions or general verdicts deciding which party wins. Defense counsel should propose a special verdict form that separates the negligent-design claim from the failure-to-warn claim. If the jury returns a verdict for the manufacturer on failure to warn but against the manufacturer on negligent design, the manufacturer may get the trial judge or appellate court to grant judgment as a matter of law on that claim without granting new trial on the other claim. Option A is incorrect because an instruction to evaluate a certain claim closely would be argumentative and rejected. Option B is incorrect because before accepting a verdict and moving for a new trial, defense counsel should ensure that the verdict reflects the jury's evaluation of the negligent-design claim. Also, if the evidence was insufficient, then the motion would be for judgment as a matter of law, not new trial. Option C is incorrect because a general verdict form would not reflect the jury's evaluation of the negligent-design claim. If the operator prevailed and the trial court or appellate court decided that the manufacturer should have had judgment as a matter of law on the negligent-design claim, then the parties would have

to retry the case because the courts could not tell on which claim or claims the operator prevailed.

268. **Contract Law.** Option B is correct because although the owner could ordinarily have rescinded the uncompleted gift for lack of consideration, here the developer may claim promissory estoppel supported by the developer's detrimental reliance on the owner's lot gift. The developer's reasonable and detrimental reliance provides a substitute for the missing consideration. Option A is incorrect because while the facts do say that the developer's work impressed the lot owner, that appreciation would alone not serve as consideration. The lot remained a gift lacking in consideration. Option C is incorrect because although one ordinarily needs consideration to enforce an agreement, which without consideration would be a gift, detrimental reliance can serve as a substitute for the missing consideration in a claim of promissory estoppel. Option D is incorrect because while a real-property contract would ordinarily be subject to the statute of frauds, the developer's claim is for promissory estoppel based on detrimental reliance rather than for breach of contract. Even if the claim were for breach of contract, then the developer's partial performance would satisfy the statute.

269. **Criminal Law & Procedure.** Option D is correct because the crime of receiving stolen goods requires that the defendant receive the stolen property knowing it was stolen while intending to deprive the owner of it. A person may receive stolen property by acquiring it, although some states require the defendant to take physical possession of it. Some states require proof of actual knowledge that the goods were stolen, while other states hold the defendant responsible if defendant should have known, applying a reasonable-person standard, and still other states presume knowledge from unexplained possession of recently stolen goods. Option A is incorrect because payment for stolen goods does not relieve the defendant of the crime if all elements are present. Option B is incorrect because not paying for stolen goods does not relieve the defendant of the receiving charge. Option C is incorrect because controlling the goods is the key element, and paying for the goods while directing the goods to others would constitute control.

270. **Real Property.** Option C is correct because how the register of deeds indexes the titles can determine whether a deed from a grantor who only later obtains title appears in a later grantee's chain of title. A recording act protects a bona fide purchaser for value without notice of superior claims. If the second buyer's chain of title did not reflect the first buyer's deed because the indexing system only supported tracing chain from those who hold title when conveying, then the second buyer would win. But if the indexing would have revealed the first buyer to the second buyer, then the second buyer would lose the recording act's protection. Option A is incorrect because the grantor nephew did not have title when conveying to the first buyer, and so the first buyer's deed might not appear in the second buyer's chain of title, giving the second buyer the recording act's protection. Option B is incorrect because the second buyer could have had notice depending on the indexing system. Option D is incorrect because courts have no authority to impose equitable divisions when the deeds and law will determine title.

271. **Torts.** Option D is correct because the causation element of a negligence claim requires that the plaintiff show a cause-and-effect connection between the negligence and the injury. The plaintiff must show that but for the negligence, the harm would not have occurred. Here, the first

driver's negligence in not having his lights on was not a cause-in-fact of the collision and passenger's injury because the second driver would not have seen the first driver's vehicle even if the first driver had his vehicle's headlights on. Options A and B are incorrect because the first driver is not liable. Options B and C are incorrect because the second driver is liable.

272. **Constitutional Law.** Option B is correct because First and Fourteenth Amendment free-exercise-of-religion rights yield to generally applicable statutes advancing legitimate governmental interests. The state has a criminal-justice and public-health interest in determining the cause of suspicious deaths, which the autopsy statute directly advances. Option A is incorrect because although the dead may not enjoy constitutional rights, the parents are still living, have an interest in their child's burial, and brought the action. Option C is incorrect because strict scrutiny is not the standard to evaluate a statute of general applicability against a free-exercise claim. One gives only rational-basis review to such a statute and challenge. Option D is incorrect for the same reason that the Supreme Court gives only rational-basis review to such a statute, not mid-level review as this option suggests.

273. **Evidence.** Option C is correct because the rules presume competency with only personal knowledge and the willingness to tell the truth as limitations. Option A is incorrect because while the testimony is prejudicial to the distributor, it is not unfairly prejudicial and is instead very highly probative as eyewitness testimony. Option B is incorrect because as eyewitness testimony, the evidence is very highly probative of identification. The child's young age would go to the testimony's reliability and weight rather than probative value. Option D is incorrect because the evidence rules require only personal knowledge and willingness to tell the truth rather than competency under other law.

274. **Civil Procedure.** Option A is correct because jurors may speak after trial about their deliberations but under FRE 606 and similar state rules may not impeach their own verdict as a ground for new trial. The university has no recourse regarding this kind of juror information, which is information impeaching the jurors' own deliberations and verdict, rather than the kind of juror misconduct that might be grounds for relief. Options B and C are incorrect because juror interviews regarding confusion and dissent over the verdict are not grounds for judgment as a matter of law or new trial. A verdict binds the jurors to their decision. There must be an end to litigation, and jurors regretting, impeaching, or otherwise failing or refusing to endorse their verdict later are simply not grounds for relief. Option D is incorrect because courts do not reconvene juries after discharge. Discharge means the end of the jury's service. A new jury must be convened if the court is to re-try any matter.

275. **Contract Law.** Option A is correct because an intended beneficiary may enforce a promise that the parties intended to pay money to the beneficiary even when the promise does not identify the specific beneficiary but identifies beneficiaries only by class. When the landowner promised to pay for a used truck, the landowner intended to benefit the truck's seller with payment, making the promise enforceable by the dealership. Option B is incorrect because the facts give no indication of detrimental reliance (the dealer may instead have relied on the timber cutter's credit) and detrimental reliance is a condition for a promissory estoppel claim, when the landowner made no promise directly to the dealership. Option C is incorrect because a promise need not identify the specific intended beneficiary if the promise adequately identifies

the beneficiary class. Option D is incorrect because the dealership is not trying to enforce a direct promise to it, and the landowner did not promise to act as a surety, only to pay for a truck that the timber cutter purchased. The statute of frauds does not apply.

276. **Criminal Law & Procedure.** Option A is correct because kidnapping is the abduction, confining, or unlawful transportation of a person to hold the person against the person's will. The drifter plainly kidnapped the youth. Then, a dangerous felony such as kidnapping satisfies the intent element for felony murder. Kidnapping is not, however, a lesser included offense of felony murder because it requires proof of those other elements just stated, and a lesser included offense includes only elements of the superior charge. Option B is incorrect because kidnapping has different elements from the superior charge. Option C is incorrect because the felony of kidnapping supplies the intent to kill in felony murder. Option D is incorrect because kidnapping supplied the felony-murder intent, and the kidnapping occurred before the youth died. The death of the kidnap victim does not defeat the crime.

277. **Real Property.** Option D is correct because tenants in common have no rights of survivorship. The other woman's interest would pass to her daughter rather than expire. Option A is incorrect because tenants in common have no rights of survivorship and while living would owe one another fiduciary duties and duties of contribution. The daughter took her mother's interest in the shop but would have failed in her fiduciary duty as to taxes and would preserve her half interest as tenant in common only if fulfilling her duty of contribution as to her co-tenant's tax sale payment. Option B is incorrect because default on taxes and breach of fiduciary duty alone would be insufficient to extinguish the interest if the daughter made good on her duty of contribution. Option C is incorrect because the interest of a tenant in common is alienable. The professional woman did not extinguish her interest when selling it to the speculator. The daughter would only have to pay half of the tax-sale amount to preserve the interest.

278. **Torts.** Option D is correct because when two or more causes would each have brought about the harm independent of the other, a substantial-factor test will determine whether any one of those defendants contributing to the harm is liable. The actions of the guide and man appear to each have been a substantial factor in the loss of canoe and contents. Option A is incorrect because negligent actions that are substantial factors can result in liability even if it took other actions to cause the loss. Options B and C are incorrect because cause in fact does not follow first-action or last-action tests. The order of the actions is unimportant so long as each was a substantial factor.

279. **Constitutional Law.** Option D is correct because Congress has power to spend for the general welfare as long as any delegation of that power includes intelligible principles for following Congress's purposes. The competition adequately defined both the fight-drug-abuse purpose and the original, fit, and feasible criteria. Option A is incorrect because the competition does not implicate an unmanageable political question that the Constitution clearly commits to another branch for finality. Option B is incorrect because the statute provides three standards that the proposals be original, fit, and feasible. Option C is incorrect because Congres may spend for the general welfare, and a competition for proposals to fight drug abuse would be necessary and proper to the general-welfare issue of fighting drug abuse. The provision need only reasonably relate to the general welfare.

280. **Evidence.** Option A is correct because relevant evidence is admissible, and intoxication makes the driver's negligence more likely. While the conviction is hearsay, conviction of a crime punishable by imprisonment for more than one year is admissible to prove any fact essential to the conviction, which in this instance would have included intoxication. Option B is incorrect because drunk driving does not have an aspect of dishonest act or false statement to it and thus would not be probative of the driver's character to tell the truth. Option C is incorrect because although the conviction is hearsay, the rules except conviction from the hearsay rule when the conviction is punishable by more than one year and the conviction is to prove a fact essential to the conviction. Option D is incorrect because convictions are admissible or inadmissible without respect to whether obtained after guilty plea or after trial.

281. **Civil Procedure.** Option D is correct because in a bench trial, the judge must make findings of fact and conclusions of law, usually from proposed findings prepared by counsel. The law clerk should include findings of fact and conclusions of law in the proposed opinion. Option A is incorrect because the trial judge must make findings of fact, not merely conclusions of law, and conclusions of law need not be (although often are) supported by legal sources justifying conclusions. Option B is incorrect because the trial judge must reach conclusions of law, and findings of fact need not be (although often are) supported by a summary of the evidence. Option C is incorrect because the trial judge must do more than state fact and law issues. The trial judge must find facts and conclude as to the law.

282. **Contract Law.** Option C is correct because while the intern would have been an intended beneficiary under the original account agreement, the right of a donee beneficiary who had given no consideration for the benefit would have to vest either with detrimental reliance or at least with assent implied from knowledge of the donation. Intended beneficiaries who are mere donees not having given consideration can enforce agreements only after their rights vest. Option A is incorrect because no one assigned the intern anything, and even if the original account agreement was an assignment, the intern would have had to have shown consideration, reliance, or receipt of payment or symbol of assignment. Option B is incorrect because although the intern was an intended beneficiary, the intern was only a donee who had not given consideration, and donee intended beneficiaries have enforceable rights only after detrimental reliance or assent drawn from knowledge. Here, the intern didn't know until after the executive changed the agreement. Option D is incorrect because receipt of a symbol of the agreement is one way for a party taking an assignment to show a right to enforce the assignment. Transfer of the account book wouldn't have been necessary for the donee intended beneficiary's enforcement if the beneficiary could prove detrimental reliance or at least assent inferred from knowledge.

283. **Criminal Law & Procedure.** Option C is correct because cruel and unusual punishment under the Eighth Amendment, the unnecessary and wanton infliction of pain, includes deliberate indifference to a known serious medical need, not just intentional injuries. Deliberate indifference means the official knows of the need but recklessly disregards a high risk of serious harm. Option A is incorrect because cruel and unusual punishment does not require intention but recognizes recklessness in the manner just described. This event was a clear Eighth Amendment violation meeting the standard for protection. Option B is incorrect because no search of any

private area was involved, and officials did not seize any property. The dealer's seizure was a medical condition, not an official act. Option D is incorrect because federal officials were involved, not state officials, and the violations were substantive (cruel and unusual) rather than procedural (notice and opportunity to be heard).

284. **Real Property.** Option B is correct because tenants in common have rights of both partition and accounting at any time. The court would order adjustment for any net benefit based on the accounting and would attempt to divide the property, or if not feasible, then order sale and equal division of proceeds. Option A is incorrect because tenants in common have the right to both partition and accounting. Options C and D are incorrect because tenants in common have a right to partition at any time. Option D is also incorrect because the resident brother's possession was not adverse but by the knowledge and consent of the distant brother. Adverse possession must be hostile in order for the statute to apply. Tenants in common who consent to equitable use are not hostile.

285. **Torts.** Option A is correct because expert testimony may be required to establish cause-in-fact on medical, legal, technical, and scientific matters. To establish cause in fact, the estate must have expert opinion on what difference a prompt diagnosis would have made in the woman's survival. Option B is incorrect because although expert testimony on the standard of care may ultimately be required, the facts state that the oncologist misread the lab report, which is an obvious breach, making the causation issue the critical issue. Option C is incorrect because information on heirs or beneficiaries may be relevant at most to damages, not liability, depending on the jurisdiction's wrongful-death act. Option D is incorrect because treatment costs may be relevant at most to damages, not liability.

286. **Constitutional Law.** Option B is correct because Article I, Section 6's speech-and-debate clause protects both the legislator making the speech and aides supporting a legislator making the speech. Options A, C, and D are each incorrect because they do not extend the speech-and-debate immunity to both the legislator and assistant, when both would have immunity under the speech-and-debate clause. Option A is incorrect because the legislator would have immunity, while Option C is incorrect because the assistant would have immunity and Option D is incorrect because both would have immunity.

287. **Evidence.** Option C is correct because evidence of subsequent remedial repairs is admissible only to show ownership or control and not to prove negligence or wrongdoing. Options A and B are incorrect because the subsequent-remedial-repair rule would bar the witness's testimony that the manager salted, sanded, and scraped the walk to prove the shop's negligence in leaving an icy walkway, although it would not bar the evidence to prove ownership or control. Option D is incorrect because the testimony would be admissible to show the candle shop's control. The trial judge would give a limiting instruction to the jury.

288. **Civil Procedure.** Option B is correct because issue preclusion (collateral estoppel) bars a party from relitigating an issue that the prior litigation actually decided. The homeowner established in the first action that the services contract was unlawful. That ruling precluded the company from raising the same issue of an identical contract's enforceability in a subsequent action against the homeowner's neighbor. The parties need not be identical for issue preclusion

to bar relitigation. Option A is incorrect because the parties need to be the same for claim preclusion to apply, and here, the second action was against a different defendant. Option C is incorrect because although the court should grant judgment as a matter of law at trial on the statutory defense, the more efficient and less expensive way would be to raise the defense by motion. Option D is incorrect because the first action has concluded, the court would likely not grant consolidation of a new case with a concluded case, and consolidation would not end the case efficiently in the manner that a motion would end the case, based on issue preclusion.

289. **Contract Law.** Option B is correct because the recipient of a unilateral offer accepts by performance, and the granddaughter fully performed by moving in with the widow and doing all necessary chores. Option A is incorrect because the agreement assigned risks to each side, the granddaughter that the widow would live long and the widow that she would die quickly. They foresaw general risks but need not have foreseen specific causes. Option C is incorrect because when within a contract each party takes the risk of a lopsided bargain, the contract remains enforceable even if the contract ends up grossly favoring one or the other party. The widow took the risk that she would die early, while the granddaughter took the risk that the widow would live long. Option D is incorrect because the contract was an exchange of the home for the services, not for the reasonable value of the services. The granddaughter would prevail for the home, not the value of one month's services.

290. **Criminal Law & Procedure.** Option D is correct because arson at common law is the malicious burning or exploding of the dwelling of another, where malice involves action involving a great risk of harm. This option is the only one that clearly names a condition, commercial rather than residential structure, outside the common-law definition of arson. Burning a commercial structure is not within the common-law definition of arson, which goes instead to the personal invasion of burning a residence instead of the property loss. Option A is incorrect because whether the building is occupied or not goes to the degree of arson, such as aggravated arson under some statutes, not to whether common-law arson occurred. Arson includes burning vacant structures. Option B is incorrect because the presence or absence of insurance or other benefit from the action is not part of the common-law definition of arson, although it may under some statutes increase the degree. Option C is incorrect because while statutes may expand the definition to include burning one's own building or even personal property rather than buildings, the common-law definition goes to dwellings.

291. **Real Property.** Option B is correct because the Rule Against Perpetuities requires that an interest vest or fail within a life in being plus 21 years. The facts provide that the jurisdiction's Rule Against Perpetuities treats future interests just as it does other interests, which would be more like the common law Rule rather than the Rule as modified by the doctrine of cy pres or even abolished, in a modern trend. A future interest cannot follow a defeasible fee because the executory interest may never vest or fail, thus violating the Rule Against Perpetuities. Here, the landowner's conveyance violated the Rule Against Perpetuities because the land might at any time outside a life in being plus 21 years revert to the charity because of a non-residential use. Thus, the landowner held a possibility of reverter until he died, after which his son held that interest under the will. Thus, a person holding a possibility of reverter under the Rule must join in any conveyance to ensure marketable title. The son would have to sign the deed to the purchaser for the purchaser to have good title, which the niece and daughter had not assured,

making their title not marketable. Option A is incorrect because the Rule Against Perpetuities invalidates the charity's interest as just explained. Option C is incorrect because the niece does not hold the full title but is instead lacking the son's interest in the possibility of reverter. She thus holds only a fee simple determinable, a type of defeasible fee that in this case terminates on use of the land for charity. Option D is incorrect for the same reason and because the daughter holds no interest.

292. **Torts.** Option A is correct because when two individuals both act negligently, and only one has brought about the harm, but the plaintiff cannot determine which one, then the courts may shift to the defendants the burden of disproving causation. Each waiter is potentially liable, with the burden of proof shifted to them to disprove their liability. Options B and C are incorrect because the courts may shift the burden of proof to the two waiters. Option D is incorrect because the liability would not be divided equally but shifted to the waiters to disprove.

293. **Constitutional Law.** Option B is correct because state statutes need only be within the state's police powers, not burden a constitutional right, and not interfere with interstate commerce. This statute related rationally to protecting dove populations, did not burden a constitutional right, and recognized and protected interstate commerce. The state could distinguish rationally between private transport, which could be for unlawful use within the state, and carrier transport, which would be to protect interstate commerce, which the state must recognize and must not burden. Option A is incorrect because the traps were not contraband if transported through the state by carrier for lawful sale in other states. The state only prohibited private transport, which would have related reasonably to enforce the ban on private use within the state. Option C is incorrect because the facts do not implicate a suspect class or fundamental right, and so the Constitution would not require strict scrutiny of this type. Option D is incorrect because while the right to travel is indeed a fundamental right, as are First Amendment rights and rights to vote and for privacy, this statute does not unduly burden that travel right. Non-residents were still free to travel, just not to transport dove traps through the state.

294. **Evidence.** Option D is correct because the rules except from hearsay a record that relates to a fact that the witness once knew, the record arose when the witness had a fresh memory, the witness cannot now recall, and the record correctly reflects the witness's prior knowledge. Option A is incorrect because the past-recollection-recorded exception does not require that the witness be the one who made the record if the witness adopted the record while still having a fresh memory. Here, the guard confirmed that the desk clerk had made a correct report. Option B is incorrect because the recording falls within the past-recollection-recorded exception to the hearsay rule. Option C is incorrect because although a public record or report is an exception to the hearsay rule, the public official must make the record. Here, the desk clerk reported the number and thus made the record, and the desk clerk is not a public official.

295. **Civil Procedure.** Option A is correct because under 28 U.S.C. §1292, parties in federal court may appeal decisions on injunctions, or when the trial court certifies an interlocutory appeal, and some other decisions, before final judgment. Option B is incorrect because although dismissing the injunction claim by stipulation would remove the last claim, it would not decide the counterclaim, and there will be no appeal of right until all claims including counterclaims are dismissed. Option C is incorrect because although parties may appeal decisions on injunctions

before final judgment, this decision was not on an injunction. Option D is incorrect because the decision did not dispose of the injunction claim and the counterclaim. The decision must dispose of all claims including claims for injunction and counterclaims in order to constitute a final judgment from which appeal lies.

296. **Contract Law.** Option C is correct because while minors do not have the capacity to contract, and a minor is not obligated to pay for non-necessary items for which the minor contracts before the age of majority, the minor would owe any amount that the minor ratifies at the age of majority. Option A is incorrect because minors do not have the capacity to contract, and parties contracting with minors for non-necessary items such as a gaming system have no enforceable right of recovery for the minor's promise, which the minor may treat as voidable. Option B is incorrect because while minors must pay for the reasonable value of necessaries, the gaming system was not a necessary item, and so its present value is not the recovery measure. Option D is incorrect because the minor ratified $250 of the contract amount at the age of majority. If the store wouldn't accept that amount, then the buyer may treat the contract as voidable.

297. **Criminal Law & Procedure.** Option A is correct because in general, drug possession is the crime of having one or more illegal drugs in one's possession, either for personal use, distribution, sale or otherwise. Possession for personal use alone rather than manufacture, sale, or distribution is generally sufficient. Option B is incorrect because jurors would not need to disbelieve the man's testimony to convict the woman. Her personal use would be enough. Option C is incorrect because personal use is sufficient. Option D is incorrect because police need not catch the drugs on the person to sustain a possession charge. Possession can include circumstantial evidence of personal control and use.

298. **Real Property.** Option D is correct because the words "for life" create a determinable life estate and "or until remarriage" create a condition terminating the life estate, while the interest following that life estate is a vested remainder. Thus, the son held that vested remainder. The owner of a future interest in land, such as the son, may convey that interest, which the son did to his acquaintance. When the husband remarried, his life estate terminated, vesting the remainder in the son's acquaintance. Option A is incorrect because the husband's remarriage terminated the life estate by condition not to remarry. Option B is incorrect because the new wife cannot take an interest after its termination by the husband's remarriage to her. The husband no longer had anything to convey. Option C is incorrect because the husband only ever had a life estate, and his remarriage terminated that life estate by express condition. The son successfully conveyed his remainder interest to the acquaintance, who succeeded to it when the husband's remarriage terminated the life estate.

299. **Torts.** Option C is correct because proximate cause asks whether, as a policy matter, the cause-in-fact connection between the negligence and the injury is close enough to hold the defendant liable. There may have been too remote and tenuous of a connection between the outfitter's failure (among the failure of several others) to warn the hikers and the eventual occurrence of the snowstorm. Option A is less likely correct because the outfitter may well have owed a duty on the basis of superior knowledge and expertise, and the special relationship.

Option B is incorrect because the failure to warn would be a breach of a duty to warn. Option D is incorrect because there were severe frostbite injuries and amputations.

300. **Constitutional Law.** Option B is correct because Congress must formally invoke Article I, Section 9's suspension clause to deny the federal courts jurisdiction over habeas corpus petitions. While not granting habeas rights to individuals, the suspension clause expressly prohibits Congress from suspending the habeas corpus writ unless invasion or rebellion threaten public safety. Option A is incorrect because Congress has express Article III power to establish the jurisdiction of the inferior federal courts. Option C is incorrect because the right to a habeas writ is ordinarily a limit on the president's detention power. Commander-in-chief powers do not authorize detention in violation of constitutional rights. Option D is incorrect because the habeas writ does not raise a political question committed to another branch other than the judicial branch and is instead a historical judicial remedy.

2. Part II—Fourth 100 Questions (Questions 301-400)

301. **Evidence.** Option D is correct because the rules permit impeachment by evidence of bad character for truthfulness including intrinsic evidence of bad acts. The other neighbor could not bring in another witness or exhibit to prove the false insurance application but may ask the testifying witness about it to show the witness's bad character for truthfulness. Option A is incorrect because the other neighbor is not offering the testimony to prove the contents of the document but to impeach on bad character for truthfulness, and so the best-evidence rule does not apply. The best-evidence rule bars other evidence to prove the contents of a document when the document itself is available. Option B is incorrect because a party may impeach using specific instances of prior untruthful conduct if the party uses only intrinsic rather than extrinsic evidence. Option C is incorrect because the conduct need not result in conviction to use intrinsic evidence of the conduct to impeach. Impeaching by certain convictions involves a different rule.

302. **Civil Procedure.** Option B is correct because the harmless-error rule, which has constitutional dimensions, prevents appellate courts from reversing for errors that did not affect the outcome. The jury returned a verdict on quantum meruit, too, so that even if there was error on the breach-of-contract theory, the verdict would stand on quantum meruit. Option A is incorrect because appeals can overturn a jury verdict. Option C is incorrect because even if there should have been judgment as a matter of law on breach of contract, there would still have been a sustainable verdict on quantum meruit. Option D is incorrect because multiple theories can go to the jury. Sending two theories to the jury is not certain error.

303. **Contract Law.** Option A is correct because one owed an obligation under a contract for the sale of goods may demand assurances, and may suspend performance in the absence of such assurances, only when having reasonable grounds for insecurity. The processor had no such grounds, meaning that the processor had no basis for suspending the contract. Option B is incorrect because a contract's silence on assurance demands has no effect on the appropriateness of a demand. A party may still make a demand if having reasonable grounds for insecurity, the common law and UCC both providing for that right. Option C is incorrect because the refusal to give assurances is not an anticipatory repudiation when the demanding party has no reasonable grounds for insecurity. One may refuse the demand under those circumstances. Refusal to assure would be anticipatory repudiation only with grounds for insecurity. Option D is incorrect because the absence of a stated quantity does not void a requirements contract like this one to supply all of the needed quantity. The UCC expressly recognizes requirements contracts.

304. **Criminal Law & Procedure.** Option D is correct because while federal courts have exclusive jurisdiction over federal offenses, and state courts have exclusive jurisdiction over state offenses, some conduct qualifies as both a state and federal offense. Federal criminal jurisdiction commonly arises where the crime occurred on land owned or controlled by the federal government or the crime crossed state lines or involved interstate commerce, as the transport across state lines here. But state law may regulate conduct within the state's borders, such as the sale here. Option A is incorrect because federal authorities need not make the arrest to pursue federal charges, and state authorities may prosecute for in-state conduct even when relating to interstate conduct. Option B is incorrect because federal authorities need not make

the arrest to bring federal charges. Option C is incorrect because in-state conduct can give rise to state charges even when relating to interstate conduct.

305. **Real Property.** Option C is correct because a landowner creates a valid option in the form of a right of first refusal when conveying the interest in an executed deed. Option A is incorrect because while an option holder must ordinarily give consideration to secure the option against the grantor's termination, a deeded interest requires no consideration. Option B is incorrect because the rule against unreasonable restraints on alienation does not apply to a grantor offering rights of first refusal but instead only to grantor restraints on further conveyances of the property after the grantor conveys. Unreasonable restraints on alienation of fee-simple title are void, while disabling restraints on life estates may be void depending on the type of restraint, but restraints on leaseholds are generally permissible. The rules against restraints on alienation have nothing to do with preserving rights to alienate on death. Option D is incorrect because recording does not validate an otherwise invalid instrument. Recording simply ensures the priority of the recorded interest under certain circumstances.

306. **Torts.** Option A is correct because if the occurrence of a foreseeable criminal or intentional act is what makes the other person negligent, then the criminal or intentional act is less likely to cut off proximate cause. The museum hired the company to prevent foreseeable vandalism, making negligent the company's failure to do so notwithstanding that the vandalism was intentional and criminal, and therefore potentiality superseding. Option B is incorrect because the substantiality of the damage does not make proximate cause more likely. Option C is incorrect because although intentional and criminal acts are more likely to cut off proximate cause, the security company was specifically hired to prevent vandalism, which was specifically foreseen. Option D is incorrect because the security company was hired to prevent vandalism. That not all vandalism can be prevented would go to the standard of care and whether the company breached it, not whether it was a superseding cause when it actually occurred.

307. **Constitutional Law.** Option C is correct because Article II, Section 2's appointments clause empowers the president to appoint certain administrative-branch officials, and granting an independent commission's chief the power to appoint an agency head without the president's control unduly limits that power to control the agency. Option A is incorrect because Congress's power to oversee the executive branch would not extend to unduly limiting the president's appointment power. Option B is incorrect because while Congress has power to issue money and regulate its value, Congress's currency powers would not authorize it to unduly limit a presidential appointment power. Option D is incorrect because Congress would have interstate-commerce power to establish a financial-systems sub-agency within a federal consumer bureau.

308. **Evidence.** Option A is correct because while the rules permit a party to rehabilitate a witness's reputation for truth telling, after the opposing party has attacked the witness's credibility, the rules do not permit a party to rehabilitate a witness before the credibility attack. The prosecution violated the rehabilitation rule when bolstering the witness's credibility before defense counsel's credibility attack. Option B is incorrect because a party may use a prior consistent statement to rehabilitate. The party just may not do so until the opposing party attacks the witness's credibility. This option's conclusion is correct but its rationale wrong. Option C is

incorrect because a party may always use bias or interest to impeach. Option D is incorrect because a party may use reputation for dishonesty to impeach.

309. **Civil Procedure.** Option C is correct because under FRAP 38 and similar state rules, an appellate court may sanction a party who takes a frivolous appeal. The filmmaker should not pursue an appeal for ulterior purposes when the appeal has no merit. A frivolous appeal without merit but for delay purposes may result in dismissal of the appeal and sanctions against the lawyer and filmmaker. Option A is incorrect because to take an appeal for purposes of delay without merit in the appeal grounds would subject the lawyer and filmmaker to sanctions. Option B is incorrect because although economic considerations are important, when there are no grounds to appeal and any appeal would be frivolous and for ulterior purposes, then the party should not take the appeal because the outcome may be dismissal and sanction. Option D is incorrect because the filmmaker would still have appeal rights notwithstanding that the outcome was by dismissal. The question is whether there are grounds to appeal, not whether the right to appeal exists.

310. **Contract Law.** Option C is correct because restitution would restore the $2,500 benefit that the homeowner conferred on the electronics store, reliance would have the store pay for the $1,000 cost preparing the home for the installation, and expectation would have the store pay the $5,000 difference between the $10,000 bargained-for system and its $15,000 replacement. Option A is incorrect because expectation damages would be the $5,000 lost-bargain amount, not the full $15,000 value of the replacement system, while the option incorrectly omits the restitution and reliance damages. Option B is incorrect for the same reasons. Option D is incorrect because while it includes the correct damage total, it misnames the individual damages components.

311. **Criminal Law & Procedure.** Option A is correct because while generally crimes involve an act (the *actus reus* or guilty act with the *mens rea* or guilty mind), some statutes define a failure to act as criminal. The statute must clearly place on the individual the duty to act. Child neglect and reporting terrorism are other examples. Option B is incorrect because the statute does not limit reporting duties to those who live in the neighborhood or to conduct that goes on for years. Anyone would have the duty to report, and a single observation of a single incident would be sufficient. Option C is incorrect because statutes may create a duty to act and punish with criminal sanctions for failing to do so. Option D is incorrect because the statute makes no distinction between those who have children and those who do not have children.

312. **Real Property.** Option B is correct because although a tenant is at will month to month when the landlord accepts monthly rent after the lease term expires, the tenant is at sufferance with no possessory rights once the landlord protests the tenant's continued occupancy, such as by serving a notice to quit. Option A is incorrect because although the tenant was initially at will month to month when the landlord accepted rent and offered a lease, the tenant became at sufferance when the landlord served the notice to quit. Option C is incorrect because a periodic tenancy, one that adopts the prior lease's term, follows the rental payments (monthly, not yearly, here) rather than the full prior lease's term unless the lease specifies the same term for a tenant holding over after the original term. The lease term would be month to month, not year to year, but for the notice to quit making the tenancy at sufferance. Option D is incorrect because the

tenant had consent for possession and the landlord has accepted rent although having served a notice to quit and filed suit to evict. The tenant would remain liable for lease damages but likely not damages in tort.

313. **Torts.** Option B is correct because vicarious liability holds one party liable for the torts of another. Research on that topic would help the lawyer determine whether the tent company was liable for the negligence of the others. A is incorrect because joint and several liability has to do with the direct liability of multiple parties, not the liability of one party for the negligence of another. C is incorrect because allocation of fault involves determining relative percentages of fault among negligent parties, not the liability of one party for the negligence of another. D is incorrect because satisfaction and release involves the settlement of one party's liability, not the liability of one party for the negligence of another.

314. **Constitutional Law.** Option B is correct because the Constitution's Article I requires that both chambers of Congress approve laws (bicameralism) and that Congress present approved laws to the president for signature or veto. Allowing a House committee to overrule designations without action by both chambers of Congress and presentment to the president would violate those provisions. Option A is incorrect because Congress could delegate authority to an executive-branch official and agency but just must not have less than the full Congress after presentment reserve override authority. Option C is incorrect because of the committee override violating the Constitution's bicameralism and presentment requirements. Option D is incorrect because consulting state officials would not cure the violation of bicameralism and presentment requirements.

315. **Evidence.** Option B is correct because multiple hearsay is admissible if an exception applies to each level, and statements for medical diagnosis and records of regularly conducted business activity are both hearsay exceptions. The physician's diagnosis and assistant's record each satisfy those respective exceptions. Option A is incorrect because although a person's statement of their then-existing condition is a hearsay exception, as is a statement of present-sense impression, the record states the physician's medical diagnosis rather than the patient's statement of the patient's physical condition. Option C is incorrect because the physician is not testifying as an expert, and even if the physician were testifying, the rules permit the physician to rely on data on which experts reasonably rely even if not admitted or admissible. Option D is incorrect because the physician is not testifying. The passenger is only offering the record under recognized hearsay exceptions.

316. **Civil Procedure.** Option A is correct because under FRCP 52 and similar state rules, appellate courts review decisions of law on a no-deference de novo standard, fact decisions on a clearly erroneous (definite-and-firm-conviction-of-mistake) standard, and docket-management issues for abuse of discretion. The appellate court would review the legal-duty issue de novo but reverse the fact issue as to the amount of expense only if the trial court decided that fact issue in a manner clearly erroneous. Option B is incorrect because it has those two review standards backwards. There would no deference to the law decision but substantial deference to the fact determination under the clearly erroneous standard. Option C is incorrect because abuse of discretion is the standard for docket-management decisions, not law and fact decisions. Option D is incorrect because the appellate court would decide the law issue de novo, without deference.

317. **Contract Law.** Option A is correct because although the original contract fell within the statute of frauds as a contract for goods having a value in excess of $500, and the contract's modification was only oral, the clothier's oral consent acted as a waiver of the term for the earlier date. Waiver occurs when a party manifests willingness to forgo the benefit of a bargained term before the substitute condition fails to occur. The supplier tried to deliver the racks in what would have been a timely delivery under the waived term and modified contract. Option B is incorrect because the UCC's statute-of-frauds provision requires a goods-sales contract over $500 to be in writing. Waiver is what makes the oral modification enforceable. Option C is incorrect because the parol-evidence rule only bars evidence of prior oral agreements inconsistent with the subsequent written agreement. Here, the oral waiver occurred after the parties formed the written contract. Option D is incorrect because the UCC does not require consideration to modify an existing contract.

318. **Criminal Law & Procedure.** Option C is correct because a defendant may appeal errors that affect the defendant's substantial rights. Parties may not appeal harmless error not affecting substantial rights. Defense counsel must ordinarily bring the error to the trial judge's attention by objecting, but failure to object does not defeat an appeal when the trial judge made a plain error affecting the party's substantial rights. Option A is incorrect because admitting the hearsay was harmless error as not affecting any substantial right. Option B is incorrect because admitting the recording was plain error for its affect on substantial rights. The executive may appeal even though counsel did not object. Option D is incorrect because the executive may appeal the admission of the recording because even though counsel did not object, the error affected the executive's substantial rights.

319. **Real Property.** Option D is correct because a landlord may sue for anticipatory breach whenever a tenant refuses to perform a lease before the lease term begins or it reasonably appears that the tenant has made it impossible to perform the lease. On the other hand, a landlord owes a residential tenant a warranty that the apartment is habitable, a commercial tenant a warranty that the premises is suitable for the anticipated business, and also owes a tenant a duty to mitigate damages. The facts implicate each of these legal theories. Option A is incorrect because although the servicemembers' civil relief act ordinarily holds immune from civil suit a servicemember whom authorities call up for active duty, here the entrepreneur apparently just voluntarily joined rather than received a call up. Even if the relief act applies, the law doesn't recognize a duty of occupancy or give the landlord a right of specific performance to force the tenant to occupy. Option B is incorrect because the recording act does not in any way apply, and the landlord doesn't have a claim against a tenant for breach of the warranty of habitability. It would be the other way around that the landlord owes the residential tenant that duty. Option C is incorrect because the landlord would sue for anticipatory breach, not breach of the duty of good faith and fair dealing. The entrepreneur would not defend on impossibility (the premises could with appropriate repair or cleaning still be occupied) or impracticality (the facts give no indication of occupancy being impractical other than the need to complete any clean up after the fire and remediate any dangerous mold). And the landlord hasn't found another tenant yet, even if the entrepreneur had an interested friend, so the landlord may well suffer damage.

320. **Torts.** Option A is correct because vicarious liability includes the respondeat-superior liability of an employer for the negligent acts of employees within the course of employment. The cook was negligent in running the red light. The cook was acting with the course of restaurant employment making the restaurant vicariously liable. B is incorrect because the manager did not employ the cook. The restaurant employed the cook and owned the van. Respondeat-superior liability would not extend to the manager. C is incorrect because the manager and restaurant were not negligent on the given facts. D is incorrect because the cook would have no vicarious (only direct) liability, and the manager would have no vicarious or other liability.

321. **Constitutional Law.** Option C is correct because federal law is supreme over state law, and Congress may specifically preempt state law in enacting federal legislative schemes. Here, the federal legislation expressly prohibited inconsistent state laws, and yet this state law purported to grant a waiver contrary to the federal scheme. Option A is incorrect because although a state would have power to regulate, this particular state regulation expressly offered a waiver inconsistent with the federal legislative scheme, which included an express prohibition on inconsistent state regulation. Option B is incorrect because the constitutional challenge does not involve interstate commerce but rather preemption and the supremacy clause. Option D is incorrect because the state statute actually does not discriminate and discrimination is not the issue. Preemption and the supremacy of federal law are the issues.

322. **Evidence.** Option D is correct because counsel properly objects to evidence the purpose, relevance, and admissibility of which is unclear, while counsel properly makes an offer of proof to demonstrate the offered evidence's admissibility. Options A and B are incorrect because taking exception traditionally means to alert the trial judge that counsel believes the ruling to be erroneous, but here the judge hasn't yet ruled. The rules also do not require a party to take exception to a ruling. Also, a motion to strike testimony has no purpose when the judge has not yet admitted any evidence, and the offer here involves an exhibit rather than testimony. Option C is incorrect because plaintiff's counsel would not object to evidence that plaintiff's counsel offered. Defense counsel would object. And defense counsel would not make an offer of proof on evidence that opposing counsel offered. Opposing counsel would make the offer of proof.

323. **Civil Procedure.** Option C is correct because FRCP 55 prescribes a two-step process first for the clerk's entry of default and only then for default judgment, with a hearing when damages are not for a sum certain and cannot be calculated as a sum certain. Option A is incorrect because the rule requires no motion and no service on a non-appearing defendant. Option B is incorrect because the clerk cannot enter a default judgment when damages are not for a sum certain and cannot be calculated as a sum certain. Option D is incorrect because Rule 55 requires plaintiff to request default entry, although some state courts use this procedure.

324. **Contract Law.** Option B is correct because lost-volume sellers of goods readily available for sale in any quantity recover lost-profits damages plus incidental expenses incurred in the specific lost transaction. That the seller sold the specific unit to another buyer for the same price makes no difference if the seller lost sale volume. Option A is incorrect because the supplier sold the device to another buyer and so recovered the device's cost plus profit. Recovery of the full contract price would give the supplier a windfall recovery. Option C is

incorrect because the supplier was a lost-volume seller of readily available goods, making the supplier's loss the profit on another sale. Option D is incorrect because the UCC requires notice only if the damaged party seeks cover damages as the difference in price on private resale. The distributor suffered no loss on resale and so wouldn't seek cover damages but instead the lost profits of a lost-volume seller.

325. **Criminal Law & Procedure.** Option B is correct because while private action that violates privacy rights, including statutory rights, does not intrude on Fourth Amendment rights, action that the government takes does implicate those rights. The expert's first intrusion was private, but the subsequent search that the federal investigators directed constituted government action implicating Fourth Amendment rights. The investigators should have obtained a warrant. Option A is incorrect because the expert's first entry was on his own, without government involvement. Although a statutory violation, it did not implicate Fourth Amendment rights that depend on government involvement. Option C is incorrect because the first entry would be admissible as not involving government action, while the second entry would be inadmissible as a violation of Fourth Amendment rights. Option D is incorrect because the first entry would be admissible as entirely private action to which the Fourth Amendment does not apply.

326. **Real Property.** Option B is correct because fair-housing laws prohibit discrimination based on race, ethnicity, and other protected classes. Also, selling agents and buying agents ordinarily split the commission equally, the selling agent for having marketed the home and the buying agent for having brought the buyers to it. Option A is incorrect because the veteran would under fair-housing laws have to sell the home disregarding ethnicity even if not yet bound under sale contract. Also, agents owe fiduciary duties to their own clients and would not ordinarily be able to increase a commission beyond the contract amount to resolve their own dispute. Option C is incorrect because unilateral mistake is ordinarily not grounds to set aside a contract, and the buyer's ethnicity is not one of those grounds that would warrant such relief because sellers must not in any case discriminate based on race or ethnicity. Also, the agents usually split the commission. Option D is incorrect because the facts give no indication that the buyers deliberately concealed their ethnicity, which would not be a material fact and instead would be a fact on which the veteran must not discriminate. Also the agents usually split the commission.

327. **Torts.** Option A is correct because there may be vicarious liability for the acts of independent contractors, where the one hiring the contractor retains control or has nondelegable duties or inherently dangerous activities, or the contractor has apparent authority. Here, the cleanup of toxic waste was probably an inherently dangerous activity not delegable to another without liability. B is incorrect because there is no evidence that the property owner retained control. C is incorrect because there is no evidence of negligence in hiring or entrustment. D is incorrect because contribution depends on direct liability of which there is none here, and indemnity depends on a relationship not present here. Neither contribution nor indemnity apply.

328. **Constitutional Law.** Option A is correct because although the dormant commerce clause would ordinarily prohibit state interference with interstate commerce, Congress in its power to regulate interstate commerce may expressly authorize a state to so discriminate, which the federal legislation did here. Option B is incorrect because without federal authorization, the

dormant commerce clause would prohibit the state from burdening interstate commerce. Option C is incorrect because the federal legislation expressly authorized the state to act, and Congress has power to so regulate interstate commerce through a state. Option D is incorrect because the federal legislation is consistent rather than inconsistent with the state act, in fact expressly authorizing state action.

329. **Evidence.** Option B is correct because the rules provide that the judge decides whether the exhibit's proponent has satisfied the factual conditions for admission, while the jury decides whether the exhibit is the original. Option A is incorrect because the jury decides whether the exhibit is the original. Option C is incorrect because the judge decides factual conditions for admission, while the jury decides whether it is original. Option D is incorrect because the judge decides factual conditions for admitting the exhibit.

330. **Civil Procedure.** Option C is correct because the federal court must apply the law of Missouri under the unambiguous language of the Rules of Decision Act. Option A is incorrect because the supremacy clause requires the court to follow federal law, and federal law requires the court to use state laws, constitutions and treaties where they apply. Option B is incorrect because it offers the wrong result. Missouri law would apply. Option D is incorrect because Erie did not reach the question of state statutes, treaties, or constitutions. The Rules of Decision Act alone addresses the question.

331. **Contracts.** Option C is correct because the doctrine of election of remedies holds the plaintiff to have the right to choose one of two coexistent but inconsistent remedies, in which event the plaintiff loses the right to exercise the other. If two or more inconsistent remedies exist, as here, then a party's choice of one remedy prohibits pursuit of the other. A plaintiff must not obtain duplicate and inconsistent recoveries. Option A is incorrect because the seller may defend based on the doctrine of the election of remedies. Option B is incorrect because the doctrine of the gist or essence of the claim would have the court reject a claim that law recognizes only in another form, such as rejecting a negligence-breach-of-contract claim when the cause is instead breach of contract. Fraud and contract breach are in this instance both sound claims not subject to the doctrine of gist or essence. Option D is incorrect because the defense of failure to mitigate does not limit a plaintiff to the lesser of two claims but instead requires a plaintiff to take such reasonable action as will minimize damages. The plaintiff may still plead multiple theories and choose among them.

332. **Criminal Law & Procedure.** Option B is correct because *Miranda* rights arise on custodial interrogation. Without *Miranda* warnings, the statement is inadmissible. Yet open woods are not within the curtilage, and so no reasonable expectation of privacy arises. Search of the woods did not violate Fourth Amendment rights, and so the doctrine of fruit of the poisonous tree does not arise. *Miranda's* public-safety exception does not apply because it must involve an overriding consideration of public safety such as by imminent danger. Option A is incorrect because the statement is inadmissible without *Miranda* rights. Option C is incorrect for the same reason and because search of the open woods did not implicate Fourth Amendment rights. Option D is incorrect because evidence of the body would be admissible because the woods were not within the curtilage.

333. **Real Property.** Option A is correct because foreclosed homeowners generally have rights to redeem, and the law discourages private actions that clog the equity of redemption. Here, the tenant has around $25,000 in equity in the home, and the private lender should not by absolute deed take that equity doubling the loan's amount. Trust deeds are for sale of the home at auction so that the borrower recovers any net equity. The lender should get the loan repaid out of the home's sale and then the tenant recover the net equity. Option B is incorrect because although one may record a land contract or notice of the contract, the outcome here would not matter whether the tenant recorded the land contract but instead whether the tenant had a right to redeem or if not then to recover the home's equity net of the loan obligation. Option C is incorrect because of the tenant's redemption right and net-equity interest. As above, the law will construe an absolute deed taken as security as it would a mortgage or trust deed to preserve the equity of redemption or auction sale. Option D is incorrect because the tenant only supplied an absolute deed as security for the loan, not a deed in lieu of foreclosure, which would have been an offer and acceptance of a deed to the home after default on the loan, not as security for the loan before the loan. Moreover, the tenant had not completed the land contract and obtained a deed from the original owner, so that the tenant could not convey clear title by absolute deed as security or later by deed in lieu of foreclosure. The recording act won't help, either, because the private lender's search of the chain of title would not have shown any interest on the tenant's part unless the tenant recorded the land contract and then would have only shown the land contract obligation to the original owner. A check of title by property location would have shown that deeded title remained in the original owner.

334. **Torts.** Option D is correct because the traditional contributory-negligence defense bars a plaintiff's negligence claim if the plaintiff was at fault in part in the plaintiff's own harm, unless the defendant acted wantonly. The first driver's running the stop sign was contributory negligence that would bar the first driver's claim against the second driver even though the second driver was also negligent. Option A is incorrect because of the contributory-negligence defense that the second driver would have to the first driver's claim. Option B is incorrect because the accident report, although some evidence, is not necessarily the best evidence, and because the claim would be barred by the contributory-negligence defense. Option C is incorrect because the accident report indicates otherwise, that the speeding contributed to the accident. Speeding could have made it harder to slow, brake, evade, and yield.

335. **Constitutional Law.** Option A is correct because while individuals have a Second Amendment right to bear arms, states may place reasonable limits on that right, furthering public safety. Background checks and waiting periods can be reasonable regulations within the right. Option B is incorrect because the state's proper justification would be the police power to provide for public safety, not a right to regulate commerce, which the dormant commerce clause would restrict when touching on interstate commerce, which this provision may do. Option C is incorrect because the regulation reasonably limits purchases for public safety rather than unduly discriminating. The regulation would likely pass constitutional muster. Option D is incorrect because the right to bear arms has limits even within the home.

336. **Evidence.** Option A is correct because the evidence rules provide that the trial judge controls the mode of examination. A party may object to a compound question that asks for two or more answers, could be unfair to answer, and may confuse the jury. Here, the compound

question may be one that the officer would need to both admit (the denial) and deny (the belief), and that yes-and-no answer could be unfair to the officer in trying to articulate accurately and could confuse jurors. Option B is incorrect because statements and beliefs at a crime scene are not per se inadmissible as this option suggests. For instance, the officer's prior prompt belief in the defendant's innocence could directly contradict and impeach the officer's current testimony. Option C is incorrect because whether a juror would understand a compound question is not the issue. The issue is the compound question that may require both a yes and no answer that jurors may find confusing. Option D is incorrect because the judge has the authority to control the mode of examination including to prohibit compound questions.

337. **Civil Procedure.** Option C is correct because FRCP 41(b) permits the trial court to dismiss an action with prejudice for failure to prosecute a case or comply with a court order. The common law that has evolved under Rule 41(b) generally holds that a sanction as grave as dismissal with prejudice should not be the first sanction, which this sanction was not. Option A is incorrect because counsel would have had an opportunity to be heard if he had attended the conference as ordered. Option B is wrong because the client chooses his representative whose actions then bind the client, although the client may have a malpractice claim against her counsel. Option D is incorrect because decisions entrusted to the trial court's discretion are reviewed for abuse of that discretion, not *de novo*.

338. **Contract Law.** Option B is correct because duress makes a contract voidable, and threats of physical violence, deprivation of liberty, and mental stress can constitute duress. Option A is incorrect because the facts give no indication that the veteran was mentally incompetent or that the children were his conservators. Option C is incorrect because a contract formed under duress is voidable even if made with consideration. Option D is incorrect because the contract's completion would not bar a claim that the caretaker induced it by duress.

339. **Criminal Law & Procedure.** Option D is correct because a random stop of vehicles without reasonable articulable suspicion of illegal activities violates Fourth Amendment rights. The only permissible plans would have been to either stop all vehicles or only those vehicles as to which officers had such a suspicion. A random stop gives officers too much discretion and is too invasive. Option A is incorrect because while the plain view of the gun could have warranted its seizure, the stop itself was illegal for having been at random. Option B is incorrect because following a plan does not justify a stop when the plan itself is illegal, as here where random stops gives officers too much discretion and are too invasive. Option C is incorrect because a flashlight augmenting an officer's vision does not constitute a search. The stop itself was illegal, not the plain-view looking through the van's windows.

340. **Real Property.** Option D is correct because a race recording act gives priority to the first to record. Because the lender loaned to help the niece buy the home, the lender held a purchase-money mortgage. When the lender recorded, it was the first and only to record, because the aunt did not record her loan agreement with the niece. The facts are not even clear that the aunt has a mortgage because the facts only refer to a loan agreement including a statement that the home would be security. A mortgage is the recordable document in which the borrower formally grants the lender a security interest in the real property, and the aunt and niece may not have prepared such a document. Options A, B, and C are incorrect because the jurisdiction's

mortgage theory likely wouldn't matter. The title theory, recognized in a minority of jurisdictions, treats a mortgage as the borrower's conveyance of title to the lender. The lien theory, the majority rule, treats the borrower as retaining title but granting a lien on the property. The intermediate theory treats the mortgage as a lien until default and as conveyance of title after default. Whether the aunt's security was a lien or conveyance of title would be less significant than whether the lender had the advantage of a race recording act. Note that the niece may have not only defaulted but breached her other duties before foreclosure by not maintaining heat to the home in the freezing winter. The lender would have the right to inspect and take action to ensure that freezing pipes or other conditions diminish the home's value.

341. **Torts.** Option B is correct because jurisdictions following the old contributory negligence also recognize ameliorating doctrines like the last clear chance. Contributory negligence will not bar the plaintiff's claim if the defendant knew or should have known that the plaintiff's negligence had exposed the plaintiff to risk of the defendant's harm, and the defendant had the last clear chance to avoid the plaintiff's harm. Option A is incorrect because the claimant's partial fault would bar the claim in a contributory-negligence jurisdiction. Options C and D are incorrect because under the last-clear-chance doctrine, the operator would not prevail. Option D is also incorrect because the operator was at least in part at fault.

342. **Constitutional Law.** Option D is correct because the Constitution prohibits the federal government from requiring a waiver of constitutional rights in order to obtain a right or benefit. Here, the rule requires networks to waive First Amendment rights of free speech regarding support of political candidates, violating the unconstitutional-conditions doctrine. Option A is incorrect because the problem with the rule is the condition that it places on the exercise of First Amendment rights. The rule would have a rational basis but remains an unconstitutional condition. Option B is incorrect for the same reason that the rule places an unconstitutional condition of the exercise of First Amendment rights. The rule may not satisfy strict scrutiny, but the level of scrutiny and ability to satisfy it is not the concern, which is instead the unconstitutional condition for a license. Option C is incorrect because the rule is not a prior restraint, which instead occurs with government censorship before the speech occurs. This rule does not directly implicate the general prohibition on prior restraints.

343. **Evidence.** Option D is correct because the rules permit the judge to exclude evidence that would waste time or needlessly present cumulative evidence. The recordkeeper's testimony is a complete waste of time once the parties stipulated to the records' admission. The fourth expert testifying to the same opinions would be needlessly cumulative. Civil trial courts traditionally limit experts to three on any one expert issue. Option A is incorrect because the trial judge has the authority to exclude wasteful and cumulative evidence as just indicated. Option B is incorrect because the recordkeeper's testimony is a complete waste of time. Option C is incorrect because a fourth expert on the same issue is needlessly cumulative. One can make an argument that more experts always mean more credibility, but civil trial courts traditionally limit parties to three experts on any one issue.

344. **Civil Procedure.** Option A is correct because Supreme Court precedent holds that the federal question on which a party bases federal-court subject-matter jurisdiction must arise on the face of a well-plead complaint. A federal defense does not create a federal question for

subject-matter jurisdiction. Option B is incorrect because plaintiffs do not plead defenses, defendants plead defenses, and a federal defense would not invoke federal-question subject-matter jurisdiction. Option C is incorrect because although the claim embeds a federal issue, the issue arises under a First Amendment defense rather than from the claim itself. Option D is incorrect because the Supreme Court has rejected the argument that First Amendment interests create federal-question jurisdiction in public-official defamation cases.

345. **Contract Law.** Option C is correct because an agreement is void ab initio (from the start) due to mutual misunderstanding when each party has a different understanding in mind from an objective ambiguity in the terms of the agreement. Option A is incorrect because a writing can be complete but still be objectively ambiguous and void for mutual misunderstanding if the parties had different understandings of the terms. Option B is incorrect because tendering performance does not change that the agreement was void ab initio. The parties would not have known of the mutual misunderstanding until tender of the gun. Option D is incorrect because the collector did bring the gun for delivery, and whether or not the collector completed performance would not matter if the as here the enthusiast promptly brought the mutual misunderstanding to the collector's attention.

346. **Criminal Law & Procedure.** Option C is correct because when a person testifies under the prosecution's grant of use immunity, the agreement means that prosecutors must not use the testimony or information derived from it. Use immunity differs from transactional immunity in which prosecutors grant immunity from prosecution for any crime related to the same event. Here, the witness's testimony identified the accomplice, such that the accomplice's testimony derived from using the witness's testimony. Prosecutors cannot use the accomplice's testimony because it derived from using the witness's testimony. Option A is incorrect because the fact that the evidence came from a different witness doesn't matter if the testimony led authorities to the other witness because they would then have used the testimony. Option B is incorrect because suspicion before the testimony does not mean that prosecutors can use the testimony to locate the accomplice. The use immunity still prevents that use. Option D is incorrect because no law prevents a prosecutor from bargaining rights between codefendants, which is instead a common strategy.

347. **Real Property.** Option C is correct because while a mortgagor may sell the mortgaged property, the mortgagor remains personally liable unless the lender grants a novation. The buyer of the mortgaged property takes with the property subject to the mortgage, but the buyer does not have personal liability for the mortgage loan unless expressly assuming that obligation. Here, the tenant only took subject to the mortgage rather than assuming the mortgage. Indeed, a transferee cannot assume a mortgage that includes a due-on-sale clause triggering the loan's acceleration with sale. Options A and B are incorrect because once a party assigns an interest such as a mortgage and loan receivable, the assignor loses the right to benefit from that interest. By taking assignment, the trust secured the right to foreclose. Option B is also incorrect because the dentist remains personally liable to the bank. The bank didn't know about the dentist's conveyance to the tenant and so could not have given a novation. Option D is incorrect because a person purchasing a mortgaged property does not become liable on the mortgage note unless expressly assuming that obligation.

348. **Torts.** Option A is correct because the assumption-of-risk defense bars plaintiff's negligence claim if plaintiff voluntarily encountered and accepted the hazards of a known risk. Assumption of risk was implied here from the woman having observed many rafts flip. Option B is incorrect because there is no indication of the woman having expressed her acceptance of the risk by, for instance, signing a liability waiver. Options C and D are incorrect because there is no indication of the woman's contributory or comparative negligence or of which of those defenses would apply in this jurisdiction.

349. **Constitutional Law.** Option D is correct because the state cannot show any compelling or substantial interest that would justify restricting the parents' First Amendment rights. The parents have not, for instance, incited imminent violence or inflicted injury through defamation. Urging citizens to take any and all necessary steps is not an incitement to violence, and nor is deluging and pressuring representatives inflicting injury. Option A is incorrect because the statement does not advocate any violence particularly in the context of statements to deluge and pressure officials, and contact representatives. Option B is incorrect because the speech is not subversive but political, and so the state has no compelling interest in its regulation. Option C is incorrect because media advertisements do not have greater First Amendment protection. If the advertisement incited violence or inflicted injury, then the state could restrict it even if published in media.

350. **Evidence.** Option C is correct because the evidence rules expressly permit opinion testimony on an ultimate issue other than an expert opinion on whether a defendant in a criminal case had the mental state required to satisfy an element of the crime. Option A is incorrect because expert opinions on ultimate issues are admissible if not as to requisite criminal state of mind. Option B is incorrect because the testimony was on an ultimate issue and not as to state of mind, and was admissible. Option D is incorrect because the rules permit opinions on ultimate issues, just not expert opinions on whether a defendant in a criminal case had the requisite state of mind.

351. **Civil Procedure.** Option D is correct because although a state may in certain cases authorize service by publication, and FRCP 4(e)(1) permits service in accordance with state law, service must still satisfy due process. The Supreme Court has held that service on an individual by publication does not satisfy due process when the plaintiff knows the individual's address but makes no attempt at service at that address. Option A is incorrect because neither state law nor federal rule can co-opt the Constitution. Option B is incorrect because it confuses the minimum-contact requirement of personal jurisdiction with the notice requirement of due process. While Option C correctly describes what a party should do when service cannot be made in accordance with the rules, no court could properly grant such a motion without first confirming service efforts satisfying due process.

352. **Contract Law.** Option B is correct because innocent nondisclosure of a material term under circumstances requiring disclosure, or innocent misrepresentation of a material term, may give rise to a rescission remedy in a contract-breach action. Option A is incorrect because expectation damages would only be available in fraud for a knowing misrepresentation, not for an innocent misrepresentation, for which rescission would be the strongest remedy. Option C is incorrect because the rescission remedy would restore the full purchase price to the buyer, not

just the amount net of salvage value. In rescission, the boater would have the salvaged boat, while the buyer would have return of the full purchase price. Option D is incorrect because courts will recognize rescission remedy in some innocent-misrepresentation cases.

353. **Criminal Law & Procedure.** Option C is correct because an accomplice is one who aids, counsels, or encourages the principal to commit a crime with the intent that the crime occur. Here, the subordinates just watched as the supervisor completed the crime. Option A is incorrect because one generally has no duty to prevent a crime or aid a crime victim if not having induced the crime or standing in other special relationship to the perpetrator or victim. Option B is incorrect because urging a suspect to flee after the crime is not acting as an accomplice because the principal has already committed the crime. Option D is incorrect because the principal need not suffer conviction for the accomplice to be liable.

354. **Real Property.** Option A is correct because one may subrogate to another's rights when paying a debt or other obligation that the other owes. Here, the employer may subrogate to the employee's rights to have the lender account properly for the lump-sum reduction of the loan balance. Also, one pursues suretyship principles when one party guarantees, or acts as a surety for, the obligations of another. The lender would be suing the employer on the employer's suretyship for the employee. Option B is incorrect because the lender is not assigning (giving away) the employee's rights but instead seeking to exercise those rights. Also, the lender is not subrogating to any party's rights but instead seeking to pursue the employer's suretyship. Option C is incorrect because the lender has sued the employer to recover the loan balance rather than pursuing foreclosure and sale of the home to recover the loan balance. Also, the employer has no need for exercising the employee's right of redemption because the lender has not foreclosed. Option D is incorrect because the lender has nothing to gain by assignment, presumably meaning assigning the right of recovery. The lender is exercising that right and would not want to give it away. Also, while the employer might well seek the departed employee's indemnification, doing so may be fruitless with the employee out of the country and owing other debt, when the employer's first action should be to minimize the obligation owed the lender.

355. **Torts.** Option D is correct because strict liability exists for abnormally dangerous activities, defined generally by the inability to eliminate a high risk of harm from uncommon activities of uncertain value. Most likely, blasting in an urban area is sufficiently uncommon of an activity that there would strict liability for resulting injury, even when done with reasonable care. Option A is incorrect because strict liability does not require proof of unreasonable actions. The liability is strict, not contingent on proof of fault. Option B is incorrect because although digging foundations may be necessary, blasting is probably a sufficiently unusual means that it would give rise to strict liability for resulting injury or damage. Option C is incorrect because the facts state that the excavator followed all reasonable precautions.

356. **Constitutional Law.** Option B is correct because while the tent city may constitute a symbolic protest carrying a message that the First Amendment would protect, the government may neutrally regulate the message's location to protect important interests through narrowly tailored means. Option A is incorrect because the mere fact that the federal government owns the land does not mean that the government may ignore First Amendment rights. Option C is incorrect because while the tent city may have constituted protected expressive conduct, the

government may neutrally regulate the conduct to protect important interests through narrowly tailored means. Option D is incorrect because greater environmental knowledge, if true, would not warrant ignoring federal regulations.

357. **Evidence.** Option B is correct because demonstrative evidence, such as a diagram, animation, or model, is admissible when illustrating a witness's testimony. Evidence is either real (physical evidence), demonstrative, testimonial, or documentary. Demonstrative evidence is admissible when useful for assisting the factfinder in gaining context for the testimony. Option A is incorrect because physical evidence would be the actual tissue rather than a depiction of the anatomy and injury. Option C is incorrect because while the expert's testimony is testimonial, the anatomical diagram is a visual depiction rather than testimony. Option D is incorrect because while the patient's medical records would be documentary evidence, the anatomical diagram is instead an illustration created for the trial of the case.

358. **Civil Procedure.** Option D is correct because venue is proper in any federal forum where any defendant resides, if all defendants reside in the same state, with corporate defendants residing for this rule in each jurisdiction where subject to personal jurisdiction. Because the engine maker is subject to general jurisdiction in its home southern state and specific jurisdiction in the western state into which it sold engines and northern state where it made those engines, the federal district courts in any of those states have venue. Because the suit has only one defendant and all defendants therefore reside in the same state, the federal district court of any other state having jurisdiction over the engine company would also have venue. Options A, B, and C are each incorrect for having ruled out at least one of the three western, southern, and northern states.

359. **Contract Law.** Option D is correct because circumstances beyond either party's control frustrated the purpose of the contract, which both parties knew was for the service to operate a jet-ski business. The marina fulfilled its duty in making the lakeshore and docks available to the jet-ski service, but the low water levels frustrated the purpose. Option A is incorrect because while the marina complied, the low water frustrated the jet-ski service's purpose. Option B is incorrect because while the marina would have a duty to mitigate its damages by attempting to re-lease the lakeshore and docks if the jet-ski service had breached, here the low water level frustrated the service's purpose, relieving the service from contract liability. Option C is incorrect because the doctrine of impracticability, which excuses performance when performance becomes impracticable, does not apply here. The jet-ski could readily perform by paying the lease amounts, and the marina also performed by making the lakeshore and dock available. The low water level simply frustrated the contract's purpose.

360. **Criminal Law & Procedure.** Option D is correct because burglary is the breaking and entering of a dwelling of another intending to commit a felony therein, while larceny is the trespassory taking and carrying away of another's personal property with the intent to deprive its owner of it. The woman completed both crimes. Option A is incorrect because the victim's reports, complaints, or preferences do not negate the crimes, even if the victim forgives and later condones the actions. Option B is incorrect because renunciation of a completed crime does not absolve the criminal of conviction. Option C is incorrect because larceny is not a lesser included

offense of burglary. A lesser included offense involves only elements that the superior offense requires. Larceny has different elements from burglary.

361. **Real Property.** Option B is correct because a lender that misrepresents material terms of the finance transaction causing loss is liable for misrepresentation, a lender who assigns to another loses the right to pursue the assigned obligation, a borrower who pays part of the obligation deserves a credit for those payments, and a borrower who refinances with a different lender paying off the prior obligation should have a discharge of the mortgage-loan obligation. Option A is incorrect because a novation would be a lender's agreement to release a borrower in favor of a new borrower assuming the obligation, impossibility would be if other events made a party unable to perform, and redemption regains a home after foreclosure. Option C is incorrect because poverty is not a defense, the facts suggest no immunity, the facts give no indication of the broker or trust having released the homebuyer, and while the refinance should have paid off the loan obligation, the defense would likely be payment and discharge rather than satisfaction, which refers to payment of a judgment rather than a loan obligation. Option D is incorrect because while the refinance company might owe defense and indemnity if it purposely, carelessly, or in breach of contract duties failed to pay and discharge the prior mortgage, right now the homebuyer needs to defend the pending action, and a demand on a non-party would not alone accomplish that defense, even if it might soon advance the homebuyer's interests.

362. **Torts.** Option B is correct because assumption of risk and comparative negligence may be defenses to strict liability. The farmer knew of and voluntarily encountered the bull's charging risk. The farmer was also careless for the farmer's own safety. Option A is incorrect because there is no indication of disclaimers or limitations, which would not be defenses to strict liability but only warranty claims. Option C is incorrect because consent is a defense to an intentional tort, and here the rodeo producer had no intent to injure the farmer. Assumption of risk would be the defense for voluntarily encountering a known risk, not consent. Consent goes not to known risks but permitting intentional actions. Option D is incorrect because a rodeo producer is not a charity, even if rodeos are often conducted to benefit charities. Rodeo production is a commercial activity. Charitable immunity has also been abolished in most jurisdictions, and the farmer would not have been a patron of the charity if charitable immunity exists and applies only to patrons.

363. **Constitutional Law.** Option C is correct because the Supreme Court presumes prior restraints of unspecified publications to violate First Amendment freedom of the press except in special circumstances such as when presenting a clear and present danger to national security or law enforcement. The officials have not yet even proven the publication defamatory and yet seek a broader injunction than one that would restrict repeated defamation. Option A is incorrect because editorials receive First Amendment protection, too, not just news stories. Option B is incorrect because the facts do not establish that the publication is false and therefore defamatory and because prior restraint as requested here would be broader than limiting republication of defamatory material. Option D is incorrect because the freedom of the press faces some limits even under the First Amendment, such as not to publish material that would present a clear and present danger to national security or law enforcement.

364. **Evidence.** Option A is correct because a party whose litigation places their own physical or mental condition in dispute must waive the physician-patient or other medical-care-provider privilege within the litigation. The court could enter a protective order limiting use of the records to the litigation, but here the protective-order motion sought to deny production. Options B and C are incorrect because the rules do not distinguish among medical, psychological, psychiatric, or other mental-or-physical health records. Option D is incorrect because all records of mental and physical treatment are discoverable within the litigation.

365. **Civil Procedure.** Option C is correct because venue remains proper where a substantial part of the events giving rise to the claim occurred, notwithstanding a contrary forum-selection clause, but the courts give controlling weight to a forum-selection clause on motion to transfer in all but exceptional circumstances. Options A is incorrect because venue remains proper, and ignoring the action could result in default. Option B is incorrect because venue remains proper, and the court would not dismiss. Transfer is the appropriate remedy, not dismissal. Option D is incorrect because the doctrine of forum non conveniens applies only when the appropriate forum is outside the federal judicial system.

366. **Contract Law.** Option D is correct because manufacturers and retailers may expressly warrant a product's fitness for the product's advertised, described, and directed purposes. Option A is incorrect because the woman's claim is for breach of express warranty, not implied warranty, although the woman could also have relied on the implied warranty. Option B is incorrect because manufacturers make express warranties, which law does not impose. Warranties imposed by law are implied, not express, warranties. Also, law does not impose a warranty that products will not injure, which would constitute a guarantee of personal safety regardless of the product's use and fitness. Option C is incorrect because it makes no reference to express warranty and is thus not responsive to the manufacturer's summary-judgment motion. It would instead be an argument relying on an implied warranty of merchantability.

367. **Criminal Law & Procedure.** Option A is correct because a suspect must have the requisite mental state (*mens rea*) for conviction of crime. Assault is the attempt to commit a battery or placing another in a well-founded fear of imminent battery, which is an unauthorized and intentional harmful or offensive contact. Self-defense is a defense to assault and battery. Here, the homeless man acted in self-defense. Also, burglary is the breaking and entering at night of the dwelling of another with the intent to commit a felony therein. The homeless man did not break to enter and did not intend any felony. Option B is incorrect because for the reason just given that the homeless man did not break to enter or intend any felony. Option C is incorrect because of the homeless man's self-defense. Option D is incorrect because the homeless man acted in self-defense using force appropriate to the threat. A brass door stop strike on the head threatens serious injury, justifying use of substantial force in self-defense.

368. **Real Property.** Option A is correct because ademption, or ademption by extinction, is the common-law doctrine that voids a devise of a specific piece of real property when the testator no longer had the real property at death. The testator sold the nephew's anticipated property, leaving the nephew nothing because of ademption. Abatement is the common-law doctrine for proportionally reducing legacies when the funds and assets of the estate are insufficient to pay them in full. The three nieces get $400,000 each rather than $1,000,000 each because the estate

had insufficient assets. Option B is incorrect because while equal shares seems equitable, interests follow the will and law, not equity. The nephew gets nothing because of ademption by extinction as to his specific devise. The nieces get $400,000 each, not $300,000 each, because they divide equally the $1,200,000 without sharing with the nephew. Option C is incorrect because exoneration entitles a devisee of an encumbered property to have the estate pay the encumbrance out of personalty in the estate, if any, rather than passing the encumbrance along with the property to the devisee. Exoneration does not apply here. Option D is incorrect because the doctrine of lapse applies when a devisee under a will died before the testator died such that the estate cannot accomplish the devise. No devisee is around to take it. Lapse does not apply here.

369. **Torts.** Option B is correct because strict products liability provides that merchants who sell products in a defective condition unreasonably dangerous to users are liable for resultant injury. Option A is incorrect because it suggests a breach-of-warranty theory like that of merchantability, not a strict-liability theory as the call of the question requests. Option A is otherwise a reasonable answer. Option C is incorrect because it suggests a negligence theory, not a strict-liability theory. Option C is otherwise a reasonable answer. Option D is incorrect because it suggests a breach-of-contract theory, not a strict-liability theory. Also, the facts do not suggest a violation of good faith and fair dealing.

370. **Constitutional Law.** Option D is correct because under Article I, Section 7, legislation that Congress has approved before adjournment but on which the president refuses to act after Congress's adjournment does not become law. The president has exercised a pocket veto that Congress cannot override. Option A is incorrect because Congress's legislation would not take effect unless the president signed it or Congress overrode the president's veto, which Congress cannot do once it adjourns. Option B is incorrect because once the president exercises a pocket veto after Congress has adjourned, the legislation dies. Congress cannot override a pocket veto. Option C is incorrect because Congress can reverse an administrative-agency action if passing legislation through both chambers and presenting the legislation to the president who signs it.

371. **Evidence.** Option D is correct because offers of compromise and settlement are inadmissible to prove or disprove the claim. While the rule provides that such offers are admissible to prove a witness's bias or prejudice, the rule refers to the potential influence of compromise and settlement on the witness's credibility when testifying, not to any party's racial or sexual bias or prejudice. Option A is incorrect because the evidence is in admissible here and even if admissible would only be admissible to show a witness's bias or prejudice, not as to the validity or invalidity of the claim. Option B is incorrect because while the rule provides that such offers are admissible to prove a witness's bias or prejudice, the rule refers to the potential influence of compromise and settlement on the witness's credibility when testifying, not to any party's racial or sexual bias or prejudice. Here, the employer is not testifying, and so the evidence would not show offer's influence indicating the employer's bias or prejudice relating to settlement or compromise. Option is C incorrect because the rule expressly prohibits use of the evidence to prove or disprove the claim. The policy is to encourage settlement and compromise offers rather than to hold them against a party.

372. **Civil Procedure.** Option A is correct because while forum non conveniens is a common law doctrine that permits a court to dismiss an action when a forum outside the federal system provides an adequate remedy, and public and private interest factors favor the outside forum, here the personal representative has no alternative forum. Option B is incorrect because forum non conveniens would hold here for the foreign forum based on convenience alone, if the foreign forum were available, which the facts indicate that it is not. Option C is incorrect because the foreign country has no available forum for an adequate remedy, which the forum non conveniens doctrine requires. Option D finds no support in any law for a federal court to hold a trial in another country.

373. **Contract Law.** Option A is correct because while a court will enforce a liquidated-damages clause that attempts to estimate difficult-to-determine damages, the court will not enforce a penalty clause disproportionate to the probable damages. The court would in the latter case only award actual damages. Fifty-thousand dollars is disproportionate to the contract amount and probable loss, making the amount an unenforceable penalty. Option B is incorrect because the courts either enforce liquidated-damages clauses or void penalty clauses, rather than awarding a percentage of liquidated damages. Liquidated damages are to avoid having to calculate damages. Option C is incorrect because the facts and law give no basis for denying the designer any part of the $10,000 fee or making $10,000 the damages amount. Option D is incorrect because the $50,000 is very likely disproportionate because five times the $10,000 contract amount and much more than a day's delay in completing the last ten percent of the work would have caused in loss. The law does not enforce a penalty clause.

374. **Criminal Law & Procedure.** Option D is correct because robbery is larceny from a person accomplished with violence or intimidation, while larceny is a trespassory taking and carrying away of another's personal property with the intent to deprive the other of it permanently. Here, the assailant plainly used the threat of violence against the girlfriend to take and carry away the boyfriend's money. The threat of violence need not be against the property's owner to satisfy the intimidation element. Option A is incorrect because criminal assault, either an attempted battery or placing another in well-founded fear of imminent battery, is a less-serious crime than robbery. Option B is incorrect for the same reason that robbery is a more-serious crime, even though the incident probably did accomplish an assault on the boyfriend as well as the girlfriend. Option C is incorrect because while the assailant did commit larceny, the assailant further committed the more-serious crime of robbery.

375. **Real Property.** Option C is correct because the minority of jurisdictions that still follow the doctrine of lapse hold that property devised to a person who predeceases the testator passes to the testator's residuary estate, in this case the brother's children. In the majority of jurisdictions that have adopted an anti-lapse statute, the same property would pass to the devisee's issue, here the sister's children, rather than the testator's issue. Option A is incorrect because the answer would depend on the jurisdiction's law, and that law does not depend on whether a devisee is alive to enjoy the property. Option B is incorrect because again the answer depends on the jurisdiction's law, and that law does not depend on the children being the next best beneficiaries of the devise. Option D is incorrect because it gets the effect of the lapse doctrine and anti-lapse statutes exactly backwards.

376. **Torts.** Option B is correct because all merchants within the chain of distribution bear the same strict products liability to the injured user as the manufacturer, as do suppliers of defective component parts. Counsel should name the dollar store and distributor, both of whom are merchants within the chain of distribution. Option A is incorrect because the father's objective is to sue a responsible party, and waiting to identify an unidentified manufacturer does not achieve that objective. Counsel may never identify the manufacturer. Option C is incorrect because the young boy would not be liable in products liability. The young boy is not a merchant. Option D is incorrect for the same reason, that the family members are not merchants to whom strict products liability would attach.

377. **Constitutional Law.** Option A is correct because the 15th Amendment prohibits racial discrimination in voting, and the federal Voting Rights Act carries out that prohibition as the Amendment impliedly authorizes Congress. Option B is incorrect because the 26th Amendment only set a nationally uniform voting age while not dictating other uniform voting rights. States differ on other voter qualifications such as registration and identification. Option C is incorrect because while Congress may not regulate the qualifications for state voting in general, the 15th Amendment prohibits racial discrimination in voting even at the state level, and Congress may carry out that prohibition with federal legislation as it has done in the Voting Rights Act. Also, the state legislation applies to national elections. Option D is incorrect because while the read-and-recite provision ostensibly serves to carry out a permissible photo-identification provision, the read-and-recite provision separately serves as a racially discriminatory and therefore impermissible literacy test.

378. **Evidence.** Option C is correct because a proponent may use a summary, chart, or calculation to prove the content of voluminous writings or records that the factfinder cannot conveniently examine in court, if the proponent makes the underlying records available to other parties at a reasonable time and place including, if ordered, in court. Option A is incorrect because summaries, charts, and calculations are admissible to prove the contents of voluminous records not conveniently examined in court. Option B is incorrect because calculations are also admissible along with summaries on the terms explained just above that the records are available. Option D is incorrect because the rule does not require that the underlying voluminous records also be in evidence.

379. **Civil Procedure.** Option C is correct because the moving party on a motion for summary judgment need only show no genuine issue of material fact, while the party opposing the motion must come forward with evidence by affidavit or otherwise. While in a civil-rights case the plaintiff may rely on a prima facie case if also able to show employer pretext, here the employee has not even made out a prima facie case, no less shown that the employer's proffered reasons are pretext. Option A is incorrect because the party opposing the motion   Option B is incorrect because the movant need only show no genuine issue and does not need to attach evidence by affidavit or otherwise. Option D is incorrect because the facts do not raise a question of business judgment such as to lay off employees or close a plant. The issue is the specific treatment of this employee and whether the employee has any evidence of age discrimination.

380. **Contract Law.** Option C is correct because contract law supports an equitable reformation of a contract when the written document does not conform to the actual agreement of the parties,

and one party seeks to take undue advantage of the non-conformity, as long as reformation will not disadvantage any non-party. Option A is incorrect because the written agreement mistakenly incorporated terms different than those to which the parties had agreed. The distributor is clearly trying to take undue advantage. Reformation would not harm any non-party. Option B is incorrect because the developer completed the work as intended, receiving due payment, and would have no obligation to comply with a mistakenly documented written agreement. Option D is incorrect because the parties have completed the agreement as intended. Rescission is no longer possible, and neither party would desire rescission, because the agreed-upon design work is done, tendered, accepted, and paid for.

381. **Criminal Law & Procedure.** Option C is correct because larceny is the trespassory taking and carrying away of the personal property of another intending to deprive the person of it. The shopper met these elements when taking the coat from the store. Option A is incorrect because embezzlement involves a fraudulent conversion of personal property of another by one who is already in possession of it. Here, the shopper was not yet in possession when she committed larceny of the coat. Option B is incorrect because false pretenses involves a false representation of a material fact that causes the person to whom the perpetrator makes the representation to pass title to the property to the perpetrator who knows the representation is false and intends the scheme. Here, the shopper did not obtain title to the coat, just momentary possession of it until quickly leaving the premises. Option D is incorrect because the shopper took the coat by trickery rather than force or threat of force. Robbery is larceny with the addition of force or threat of force against the property's possessor. The shopper's latter threat against the owner did not deprive the owner of the coat, which the shopper had already stolen by larceny from the clerk.

382. **Real Property.** Option D is correct because exoneration entitles a devisee of an encumbered property to have the estate pay the encumbrance out of personalty in the estate, if any, rather than passing the encumbrance along with the property to the devisee, if as here the will makes no contrary provision. Option A is incorrect because the will devised the home to the eldest child, and treating it as part of the estate would frustrate that devise. Option B is incorrect because secured loans do not typically disappear with the debtor's death but remain attached to the security unless the loan agreement provides otherwise. The estate would owe the loan balance, which once satisfied would result in the mortgage's discharge. Option C is incorrect because exoneration would pay off the loan balance out of the residuary estate. Otherwise, the obligor's death would free the obligor to bequeath other assets (here, the residuary estate) without paying the mortgage-loan balance that the obligor owed before death, which would be contrary to the obligation and the policy supporting it.

383. **Torts.** Option A is correct because the statute of limitations and statute of repose are common products-liability defenses. The limitations period may be affected by a tolling statute. Preserving the product is essential to avoid a spoliation defense. Option B is incorrect because the first critical step is to determine time periods, and the table should be preserved, not discarded. Option C is incorrect because there would be no point to making a demand until the periods of limitations and repose are confirmed, and the claim preserved. Making a demand does not toll the limitations period, which in the absence of a tolling statute may be running.

Option D is incorrect because there would be no point to opening a probate case until it was confirmed that there was a viable action not barred by a limitations period or statute of repose.

384. **Constitutional Law.** Option B is correct because public officials must not adversely affect the terms of public employment based on the exercise of First Amendment rights other than for the highest political appointments. Here, the state superintendent made the demotions for no reason other than politics, violating the free-speech rights of the employees to support candidates of their choice. The state superintendent did so while exceeding his supervisory authority only to retain, promote, and demote for mission purposes. Option A is incorrect because due process is not the challenge (other than invoking the Fourteenth Amendment's due-process clause to incorporate First Amendment rights). Rather, First Amendment free-speech rights are the employees' basis for protesting their discriminatory treatment relative to other employees who supported the state superintendent's campaign. Option C is incorrect because the state superintendent's supervisory authority does not include violating free-speech rights by considering political positions. Option D is incorrect because the state superintendent's associational rights are not in question. The demotion of the employees calls into play the employees' free-speech rights.

385. **Evidence.** Option B is correct because under the rule of completeness, when a party introduces part of a writing or recorded statement, the adverse party may require the introduction at that time of any other part that in fairness the factfinder ought to consider at the same time. Option A is incorrect because a party may use the deposition of an opposing party for any purpose. Option C is incorrect because the rule of completeness requires that the court permit the opposing party to include parts of the writing or recorded statement that in fairness the factfinder should consider at the same time. Option D is incorrect because when the deposition is that of a party, the party's availability or unavailability makes no difference to the opposing party's use for any purpose of the deposition.

386. **Civil Procedure.** Option A is correct because motions under Rule 12(b)(6) are facial attacks on the pleadings alone and do not properly attach other materials. The court must accept the complaint's allegations as true and only grant the motion if the complaint as pled fails to state a claim. Rule 12(d) provides that when a motion presents matters outside the pleading, the court must treat it as a motion for summary judgment under Rule 56, giving the responding party time to develop the facts. Option B is incorrect because it cites the Rule 56 summary-judgment standard, not the Rule 12 pleading standard. Options C and D are incorrect because Rule 12(b)(6) does not authorize the court to look to the other materials behind the complaint to evaluate the complaint's allegations. The court must accept the complaint as pled. If the court treated the Rule 12(b)(6) motion as one for summary judgment under Rule 56, then the court would have to give the plaintiff time to develop and present evidence raising a genuine issue of material fact in the plaintiff's favor.

387. **Contract Law.** Option C is correct because a court will order specific performance of a contract obligation when damages would be inadequate, and may simultaneously enjoin further contract breach after having declared the rights of the parties. Here, damages would not likely be sufficient if the engineer removed and shared confidential trade secrets the value of which the action would forever destroy. A court may well declare the materials to be trade secrets, enforce

specific performance of the trade-secret clause with an order for return of the secret materials, and enjoin further distribution. Option A is incorrect because expectation damages would be hard to determine, when injunction against sharing or other unauthorized use of trade-secret materials would preserve whatever value they had to the company. Option B is incorrect because while identifying the removed materials would be key relief, it would only be a first step toward determining who owned the materials and preventing the misuse of trade secrets. Option D is incorrect because it would not prevent distribution or other use of trade-secret materials and would not in any case be likely relief because not meeting a rule of reasonableness. The allegedly breaching party, the engineer, would retain a right to work, just not to use any trade secrets. The company was not seeking to enforce a non-compete clause but instead a trade-secret clause.

388. **Criminal Law & Procedure.** Option C is correct because voluntary manslaughter is murder committed with adequate provocation, while murder is an unlawful killing committed with malice aforethought. A jury could find that a strike in the face along with grabbing the coat was provocation. Option A is incorrect because the perpetrator's involvement in causing the provocation does not affect the provocation's adequacy. The customer may have had a defense of recovery of property to an assault and battery claim by the panhandler, although the customer's force sounds more than reasonable and instead excessive. But here, the question is instead whether the customer's action was adequate provocation, which it clearly enough was. Option B is incorrect because while the panhandler likely did intend at least serious injury and perhaps even death, the provocation would by definition reduce the crime to voluntary manslaughter. The jury gets to decide adequacy of provocation if reasonable jurors could so decide. Option D is incorrect because voluntary manslaughter involves provocation, not recklessness. Recklessness is an aspect of depraved-heart murder, not manslaughter.

389. **Real Property.** Option C is correct because apparent uses that existed when a landowner divides the land and that benefit the divided lots may exist as quasi easements implied by use even when not confirmed in the landowner's deed or other signed writing. Option A is incorrect because the law will imply a quasi easement by the evident use that existed at the time the owner divided the lots. Option B is incorrect because necessity is not a condition for an implied quasi easement by use to arise. Easements by necessity typically apply to landlocked lands. Here, the surveyor may be able to run utility lines or the student build a driveway on their own lots, but the evident use when the owner divided the lots is sufficient to establish the quasi easement. Option D is incorrect because the utility line and driveway are different uses rather than reciprocal (same, mutual) uses. Reciprocal servitudes typically arise by common plan, whereas here the two lots have different servitudes requiring different easements.

390. **Torts.** Option B is correct because there may be strict liability for property damage or injury from wild animals, generally defined as those not common to the region. Here, the python was surely a wild animal not common to the region, insofar as ordinance prohibited its keeping. There would thus have been strict liability for the property damage constituting loss of the little dog. Option A is incorrect because there is no evidence of negligent failure to confine the python. The facts state that there was no indication the python left the home. Option C is incorrect because fault and reasonableness are of no consequence when, as here, there is a claim

for strict liability. Option D is incorrect because whether or not the collector confined the python, strict liability would apply for the loss.

391. **Constitutional Law.** Option B is correct because the Eleventh Amendment bars persons from suing a state in federal court and also has been interpreted to bar federal administrative proceedings. Option A is incorrect because while states retain police powers, those powers are not generally a positive limit on federal powers. A federal administrative tribunal could ordinarily hear a dispute involving use of federal lands except for state sovereign immunity under the Eleventh Amendment. Option C is incorrect because the rancher would from the state's threat of an injunction presumably have a state-court or state-administrative forum, and even if the rancher had no forum the Eleventh Amendment would bar a federal forum against the state. Option D is incorrect because of the Eleventh Amendment immunity against actions against a state in federal proceedings.

392. **Evidence.** Option C is correct because a statement contained in a learned treatise is admissible under a hearsay exception only when called to an expert's attention and established as reliable authority by the expert, other testimony, or judicial notice. The proponent may read the statement into evidence but not make it an exhibit. Option A is incorrect because defense counsel would first have to establish the treatise as authoritative in one of the above three ways and then could only use it to impeach without making it an exhibit in evidence. Option B is incorrect because defense counsel may not use the treatise as substantive evidence and may only use it to impeach. Option D is incorrect because the hearsay rules include an exception for use of a learned treatise as indicated just above.

393. **Civil Procedure.** Option B is correct because FRCP 4(m) requires plaintiff to serve summons and complaint within ninety days from filing the complaint. Here, plaintiff's counsel served the summons and complaint five months after the complaint's filing, making service untimely. Option A is incorrect because this challenge is as to the timeliness of the service, not that service itself is improper. In-person service of an individual defendant would ordinarily be proper. Option C is incorrect because while in-person service on an individual is ordinarily proper, the timing of the service here was too late. Option D is incorrect because although dismissal would be without prejudice, the plaintiff could refile, and a defendant may well choose to waive the late-service defect, counsel would still have a basis to move for and obtain dismissal, which is all that the question asks. Defendant may have other reasons to seek a technical dismissal.

394. **Contract Law.** Option D is correct because third parties do not generally acquire rights under others' contracts, and the contracting parties may impair or extinguish third-party rights unless the contracting parties expressly agree to grant those rights under the contract or a party assigns rights to an intended third-party beneficiary. Here, the employer and caterer did not state in the contract that the chosen employee would have rights, and the employer did not assign the right to a party to the supervisor. Option A is incorrect because the supervisor gained no right to enforce the employer-caterer contract in the absence of a contract statement to that effect or an actual assignment. Option B is incorrect because the supervisor gained no right and would not have any right as an incidental beneficiary. Option C is incorrect because while non-parties or third-party beneficiaries ordinarily do not have rights to prevent the parties from altering the

contract, they can acquire rights if the contract so states or one of the parties makes an assignment.

395. Criminal Law & Procedure. Option C is correct because the elements of burglary involve the breaking and entering of a dwelling (and in this modern jurisdiction any building) intending to commit a felony therein. Thinking that one is committing a crime is not enough to satisfy the intending-felony element. Option A is incorrect because conviction is not possible. While factual impossibility, that the circumstances are not as the defendant believes, is no defense to a crime of this type, legal impossibility, that the defendant misunderstands what is or is not a crime, is a defense. The defendant's wrong thinking cannot create a crime. Option B is incorrect because while the employee had the intent to commit an act that he thought was a crime, he was wrong in his thinking, and intending an act that is not in fact a crime cannot satisfy the intent element here. Option D is incorrect because the employee would have completed the crime upon breaking and entering if the employee had intended what was in fact a felony. And the employee would also have been guilty of an attempt if in fact intending a felony. But he did not intend a felony, only an act that he thought was a felony. So the employee would not even be guilty of an attempt.

396. Real Property. Option A is correct because a profit is a right to take from the land, including the right to enter the land to do so, but is not an interest in the land itself. A profit arises by express agreement or by prescription, and can be either appurtenant to adjacent land or in gross and transferable. Profits terminate by voluntary release, merger of the benefitted lands, waste, or terms of the agreement. Here, the profits appear to be appurtenant and thus not transferable in gross but only on conveyance of the land. Option B is incorrect because the original profits by their terms were also for the benefit of successors, heirs, and assigns. The rights appurtenant to each land may run with the land where, as here, so provided. Option C is incorrect because although one could make an argument that the sale of licenses was a sufficient waste of the profit as to terminate it, depending on the damage to the fish and wildlife, the rest of the answer is incorrect because the other owner committed no waste and should have a continued right. Option D is incorrect because the profits were for the benefits of the landowners and their successors, heirs, and assigns, not the benefit of friends or for commercial licensing to friends. So disgorging half of the profits would not perfect such a right.

397. Torts. Option C is correct because a defendant must plead, produce evidence of, and prove affirmative defenses to a negligence claim. Having defenses such as contributory or comparative negligence and the statute of limitations is insufficient if the defendant does not affirmatively assert them because the defendant carries the burden of pleading, production, and prove on affirmative defenses. Options A and B are incorrect because the customer states a negligence claim, and the cleaning company would lose for having failed to plead affirmative defenses. Option D is incorrect because the facts do not state that the cleaning company guaranteed a good result.

398. Constitutional Law. Option A is correct because a state may in content neutral manner prohibit speech that targets specific groups for imminent violence, without abridging First Amendment rights, which have reasonable limits. Option B is incorrect because the statute did not prohibit fighting words but instead prohibited words inciting violence. Fighting words are those that would cause a hearer to react violently against the speaker, while inciting words are those that cause a hearer to react violently against other than the speaker. Option C is incorrect because the state can restrict words inciting imminent violence even when uttered on public property. The location of the words is unimportant to the inciting-violence doctrine. Option D is incorrect because while laws classifying and burdening the rights of women and minorities receive heightened scrutiny, this law instead protects women and minorities, and heightened scrutiny would thus not be a basis on which to strike the statute.

399. **Evidence.** Option D is correct because a statement relating to a startling event or condition, made while the declarant was under the stress of excitement that the event or condition caused, is admissible under the excited-utterance exception to the hearsay rule. Option A is incorrect because the bystander's excited utterance is admissible under that exception to the hearsay rule. Option B is incorrect because the bystander's unavailability would not either bar or admit the testimony. The excited utterance is admissible whether the bystander is available or not. Option C is incorrect because the declarant's availability or unavailability is immaterial to an excited utterance's admissibility. Just because the bystander died does not mean that the statement is admissible. The statement is instead admissible as an excited utterance, even if the bystander had lived.

400. **Civil Procedure.** Option D is correct because although courts will not interfere with a verdict supported by evidence that reasonable jurors could accept, a trial judge and appellate court may reject a verdict against the great weight of the evidence, ordering retrial. Option A is incorrect because while errors in rulings, misconduct of counsel or witness, or other procedural defects may warrant new trial, so too may a verdict that is simply against the great weight of the evidence. The verdict alone may be the problem. Option B is incorrect because while jury-trial rights arise under state and federal constitutions, state and federal authority nonetheless exists for granting a new trial when a verdict is against the great weight of the evidence. Option C is incorrect because the question asks about a ruling on a motion for new trial. Judgment as a matter of law would not result in a new trial but in entry of a judgment in the insurer's favor.

Part V: Tables and Indices

This Part V has tables and indices for you to make the best use of the above multiple-choice questions, answers, and explanations. The above questions go from one subject to another subject, much as the Multistate Bar Examination questions would skip from subject to subject. To habituate yourself fully to the Multistate Bar Examination, you should at some point practice going from one subject to another, just as the above questions appear.

Yet you may also wish in your preparation for the exam to practice questions only in a certain subject. The following table is from the National Conference of Bar Examiners' website identifying the Multistate Bar Examination subjects, topics, and subtopics, in exactly the manner that the National Conference lists those subjects, topics, and subtopics (including the introductory text as to the allocation of questions within each subject). The superscript numbers are the multiple-choice questions. Use this table to test yourself on specific subjects, topics, and subtopics.

A. MBE Subjects Keyed to Multiple-Choice Questions

The following table shows you which of the foregoing multiple-choice questions address which of the seven Multistate Bar Examination-tested subjects civil procedure, constitutional law, contract law, criminal law and procedure, evidence, real property law, and tort law. Use this table to test yourself on the multiple-choice questions for any of those seven subjects.

Civil Procedure
1, 8, 15, 22, 29, 36, 43, 50, 57, 64, 71, 78, 85, 92, 99, 106, 113, 120, 127, 134, 141, 148, 155, 162, 169, 176, 183, 190, 197, 204, 211, 218, 225, 232, 239, 246, 253, 260, 267, 274, 281, 288, 295, 302, 309, 316, 323, 330, 337, 344, 351, 358, 365, 372, 379, 386, 393, 400

Contract Law
2, 9, 16, 23, 30, 37, 44, 51, 58, 65, 72, 79, 86, 93, 100, 107, 114, 121, 128, 135, 142, 149, 156, 163, 170, 177, 184, 191, 198, 205, 212, 219, 226, 233, 240, 247, 254, 261, 268, 275, 282, 289, 296, 303, 310, 317, 324, 331, 338, 345, 352, 359, 366, 373, 380, 387, 394

Criminal Law and Procedure
3, 10, 17, 24, 31, 38, 45, 52, 59, 66, 73, 80, 87, 94, 101, 108, 115, 122, 129, 136, 143, 150, 157, 164, 171, 178, 185, 192, 199, 206, 213, 220, 227, 234, 241, 248, 255, 262, 269, 276, 283, 290, 297, 304, 311, 318, 325, 332, 339, 346, 353, 360, 367, 374, 381, 388, 395

Real Property Law
4, 11, 18, 25, 32, 39, 46, 53, 60, 67, 74, 81, 88, 95, 102, 109, 116, 123, 130, 137, 144, 151, 158, 165, 172, 179, 186, 193, 200, 207, 214, 221, 228, 235, 242, 249, 256, 263, 270, 277, 284, 291, 298, 305, 312, 319, 326, 333, 340, 347, 354, 361, 368, 375, 382, 389, 396

Tort Law
5, 12, 19, 26, 33, 40, 47, 54, 61, 68, 75, 82, 89, 96, 103, 110, 117, 124, 131, 138, 145, 152, 159, 166, 173, 180, 187, 194, 201, 208, 215, 222, 229, 236, 243, 250, 257, 264, 271, 278, 285, 292, 299, 306, 313, 320, 327, 334, 341, 348, 355, 362, 369, 376, 383, 390, 397

Constitutional Law
6, 13, 20, 27, 34, 41, 48, 55, 62, 69, 76, 83, 90, 97, 104, 111, 118, 125, 132, 139, 146, 153, 160, 167, 174, 181, 188, 195, 202, 209, 216, 223, 230, 237, 244, 251, 258, 265, 272, 279, 286, 293, 300, 307, 314, 321, 328, 335, 342, 349, 356, 363, 370, 377, 384, 391, 398

Evidence
7, 14, 21, 28, 35, 42, 49, 56, 63, 70, 77, 84, 91, 98, 105, 112, 119, 126, 133, 140, 147, 154, 161, 168, 175, 182, 189, 196, 203, 210, 217, 224, 231, 238, 245, 252, 259, 266, 273, 280, 287, 294, 301, 308, 315, 322, 329, 336, 343, 350, 357, 364, 371, 378, 385, 392, 399

B. MBE Topics Table Keyed to Multiple-Choice Questions

The following table is from the National Conference of Bar Examiners' website identifying the Multistate Bar Examination subjects, topics, and subtopics. The superscript numbers are the multiple-choice questions. Use this table to test yourself on specific subjects, topics, and subtopics.

For example, if you want to practice specific property-law questions on only certain property-law topics or subtopics, then turn in this table to the Real Property subject to identify the topics and subtopics on which you want to work.

Civil Procedure
NOTE: ... Approximately two-thirds of the Civil Procedure questions on the MBE will be based on categories I, III, and V, and approximately one-third will be based on the remaining categories II, IV, VI, and VII.
  I. **Jurisdiction and venue**
      A. Federal subject matter jurisdiction (federal question,[344] diversity,[64] supplemental,[106] and removal[71])
      B. Personal jurisdiction[78,92,120]
      C. Service of process[57] and notice[351]
      D. Venue,[358] forum non conveniens,[372] and transfer[365]
  II. **Law applied by federal courts**
      A. State law in federal court[113]
      B. Federal common law[323]
  III. **Pretrial procedures**[183]
      A. Preliminary injunctions[141] and temporary restraining orders[148]

B. Pleadings[92] and amended[85] and supplemental[1] pleadings
C. Rule 11[99]
D. Joinder of parties and claims[127,134] (including class actions[8])
E. Discovery[155] (including e-discovery[162]), disclosure,[169] and sanctions[22]
F. Adjudication without a trial[29]
G. Pretrial conference[176] and order[15]

IV. **Jury trials**[190]
   A. Right to jury trial[36]
   B. Selection[197] and composition of juries[204]
   C. Requests for[211] and objections to[218] jury instructions

V. **Motions**[232]
   A. Pretrial motions, including motions addressed to face of pleadings,[386] motions to dismiss,[393] and summary judgment motions[225,379]
   B. Motions for judgments as a matter of law[239,246] (directed verdicts[239] and judgments notwithstanding the verdict[246])
   C. Post-trial motions,[253,260] including motions for relief from judgment[260] and for new trial[253]

VI. **Verdicts and judgments**[120]
   A. Defaults[323] and involuntary dismissals[337]
   B. Jury verdicts—types[267] and challenges[400]
   C. Judicial findings and conclusions[281]
   D. Effect; claim[50,134] and issue preclusion[288]

VII. **Appealability**[309] **and review**[316]
   A. Availability of interlocutory review[295]
   B. Final judgment rule[43]
   C. Scope of review for judge[302] and jury[274]

Constitutional Law

NOTE: The terms "Constitution," "constitutional," and "un-constitutional" refer to the federal Constitution unless indicated otherwise. Approximately half of the Constitutional Law questions on the MBE will be based on category IV, and approximately half will be based on the remaining categories—I, II, and III.

I. **The nature of judicial review**
   A. Organization and relationship of state and federal courts in a federal system[146]
   B. Jurisdiction[90,146,258]
      1. Congressional power to define and limit[90]
      2. The Eleventh Amendment[258] and state sovereign immunity[391]
   C. Judicial review in operation[125,174,202,258,265]
      1. The "case or controversy" requirement,[202] including the prohibition on advisory opinions,[258] standing,[125] ripeness,[174] and mootness[202]
      2. The "adequate and independent state ground"[48]
      3. Political questions and justiciability[265]

II. **The separation of powers**
   A. The powers of Congress[13,132,237,279]
      1. Commerce,[13] taxing,[132] and spending[279] powers
      2. War, defense,[300] and foreign affairs[76] powers

3. Power to enforce the 13th,[237] 14th,[13,41,97,139,146,195,237] and 15th[377] Amendments
4. Other powers[279]
B. The powers of the president[55,230]
1. As chief executive, including the "take care" clause[230]
2. As commander in chief[300]
3. Treaty and foreign affairs[76] powers
4. Appointment[55,307] and removal[307] of officials
C. Federal inter-branch relationships[76,286]
1. Congressional limits on the executive[76]
2. The presentment requirement[314] and the president's power to veto or to withhold action[370]
3. Non-delegation doctrine[76]
4. Executive, legislative, and judicial immunities[286]

III. **The relation of nation and states in a federal system**[111]
A. Intergovernmental immunities[209,223]
1. Federal immunity from state law[209]
2. State immunity from federal law, including the 10th Amendment[223]
B. Federalism-based limits on state authority[69,167]
1. Negative implications of the commerce clause[69]
2. Supremacy clause and preemption[321]
3. Authorization of otherwise invalid state action[328]

IV. **Individual rights**
A. State action[41]
B. Due process[216]
1. Substantive due process[6]
a. Fundamental rights[6,244]
b. Other rights and interests[335]
2. Procedural due process[195]
C. Equal protection[139,251]
1. Fundamental rights[293]
2. Classifications subject to heightened scrutiny[160]
3. Rational basis review[104,209]
D. Takings[118]
E. Other protections, including the privileges and immunities clauses,[139] the contracts clause,[237] unconstitutional conditions,[342] bills of attainder,[27] and ex post facto laws[20]
F. First Amendment freedoms[272]
1. Freedom of religion and separation of church and state[188]
a. Free exercise[153]
b. Establishment[181]
2. Freedom of expression[34,62,83,104]
a. Content-based regulation of protected expression[83]
b. Content-neutral regulation of protected expression[34]
c. Regulation of unprotected expression[349,398]
d. Regulation of commercial speech[62]

e. Regulation of, or impositions upon, public school students, public employment, licenses, or benefits based upon exercise of expressive or associational rights[342,384]
f. Regulation of expressive conduct[356]
g. Prior restraint, vagueness, and overbreadth[104]
3. Freedom of the press[349,363]
4. Freedom of association[97]

Contracts

NOTE: Examinees are to assume that Article 2 and Revised Article 1 of the Uniform Commercial Code have been adopted and are applicable when appropriate. Approximately half of the Contracts questions on the MBE will be based on categories I and IV, and approximately half will be based on the remaining categories—II, III, V, and VI. Approximately one-fourth of the Contracts questions on the MBE will be based on provisions of the Uniform Commercial Code, Article 2 and Revised Article 1.

I. **Formation of contracts**[86]
   A. Mutual assent[65]
      1. Offer[93,114] and acceptance[58,121]
      2. Indefiniteness or absence of terms[79]
      3. Implied-in-fact contract[128 & 135]
      4. "Pre-contract" obligations based on reliance[254]
   B. Consideration[51,116]
      1. Bargain[163] and exchange and substitutes for bargain: "moral obligation,"[107] reliance,[268] and statutory substitutes[170]
      2. Modification of contracts[72]: preexisting duties[226]
      3. Compromise[226] and settlement of claims[100]

II. **Defenses to enforceability**
   A. Incapacity to contract[296]
   B. Duress[338]
   C. Undue influence[205]
   D. Mistake,[37] misunderstanding[345]
   E. Fraud,[184] misrepresentation,[142] and nondisclosure[352]
   F. Illegality,[30] unconscionability,[44] and public policy[261]
   G. Statute of frauds[240]

III. **Parol evidence**[317] **and interpretation**[2]

IV. **Performance,**[247] **breach, and discharge**
   A. Conditions[109]
      1. Express[23]
      2. Constructive[212]
      3. Obligations of good faith and fair dealing in performance and enforcement of contracts[191]
      4. Suspension or excuse of conditions by waiver,[317] election,[331] or estoppel[268]
      5. Prospective inability to perform:[303] effect on other party[289]
   B. Impracticability[149] and frustration of purpose[359]
   C. Discharge of contractual duties[9]
   D. Express and implied warranties in sale-of-goods contracts[366]

Preparing for the Multistate Bar Examination

        E. Substantial and partial breach[16] and anticipatory repudiation[303]
V.   **Remedies**
        A. Measure of damages for breach;[310] protecting the expectation interest[233]
        B. Consequential damages: causation,[324] certainty, and foreseeability[156]
        C. Liquidated damages and penalties[373]
        D. Avoidable consequences and mitigation of damages[324]
        E. Rescission[352] and reformation[380]
        F. Specific performance; injunction against breach; declaratory judgment[387]
        G. Restitutionary[233] and reliance recoveries
        H. Remedial rights of breaching parties[387]
VI.   **Third-party rights**
        A. Third-party beneficiaries[177,275,282]
            1. Intended beneficiaries[275]
            2. Incidental beneficiaries[177]
            3. Impairment or extinguishment of third-party rights[394]
            4. Enforcement by the promisee[282]
        B. Assignment of rights[198] and delegation of duties[219]

Criminal Law and Procedure

NOTE: Approximately half of the Criminal Law and Procedure questions on the MBE will be based on category V, and approximately half will be based on the remaining categories—I, II, III, and IV.

I.   **Homicide**
        A. Intended killings[66,388]
            1. Premeditation,[171] deliberation[157]
            2. Provocation[157,388]
        B. Unintended killings[80,157,171]
            1. Intent to injure[157,206]
            2. Reckless and negligent killings[171,206]
            3. Felony murder[220,276]
            4. Misdemeanor manslaughter[185]
II.   **Other crimes**
        A. Theft[108,147,360,374,381] and receiving stolen goods[269]
        B. Robbery[73,115,178,374,381]
        C. Burglary[143,360,367,395]
        D. Assault[157,367,374] and battery[164,367]
        E. Rape[199]; statutory rape[192,199]
        F. Kidnapping[276]
        G. Arson[220,290]
        H. Possession offenses[297]
III. **Inchoate crimes; parties**[101]
        A. Inchoate offenses
            1. Attempts[94,199]
            2. Conspiracy[59,150]
            3. Solicitation[213]
        B. Parties to crime[87,101,150,213,353]

IV. **General principles**
    A. Acts and omissions[311,353]
    B. State of mind
        1. Required mental state[147,164,171,367]
        2. Strict liability[192]
        3. Mistake of fact[115,164,199] or law[192]
    C. Responsibility
        1. Mental disorder[164,206]
        2. Intoxication[164,206]
    D. Causation[157,171]
    E. Justification[164,192] and excuse[122,192,367]
    F. Jurisdiction[304]
V. **Constitutional protection of accused persons**
    A. Arrest,[136,234,241,339] search[24,52,129,241,255,325] and seizure[10]
    B. Confessions[31,241] and privilege against self-incrimination[3,38,45,332,346]
    C. Lineups[17] and other forms of identification[227]
    D. Right to counsel[255]
    E. Fair trial[248] and guilty pleas[262]
    F. Double jeopardy[234]
    G. Cruel and unusual punishment[283]
    H. Burdens of proof[150,178] and persuasion[178]
    I. Appeal[318] and error[248,318]

Evidence

NOTE: All Evidence questions should be answered according to the Federal Rules of Evidence, as restyled in 2011. Approximately one-third of the Evidence questions on the MBE will be based on category I, one-third on category V, and one-third on the remaining categories—II, III, and IV.

I. **Presentation of evidence**
    A. Introduction of evidence
        1. Requirement of personal knowledge[14,273]
        2. Refreshing recollection[147]
        3. Objections[322] and offers of proof[322]
        4. Lay opinions[7]
        5. Competency of witnesses[273]
        6. Judicial notice[217]
        7. Roles of judge and jury[329]
        8. Limited admissibility[49,119,287]
    B. Presumptions[70]
    C. Mode and order[343]
        1. Control by court[231,336]
        2. Scope of examination[231]
        3. Form of questions[231,336]
        4. Exclusion of witnesses[231]
    D. Impeachment, contradiction, and rehabilitation
        1. Inconsistent statements[161] and conduct[105]

2. Bias and interest[35]
3. Conviction of crime[280]
4. Specific instances of conduct[56,301]
5. Character for truthfulness[42]
6. Ability to observe, remember, or relate accurately[112]
7. Impeachment of hearsay declarants[161]
8. Rehabilitation of impeached witnesses[308]
9. Contradiction[161]

E. Proceedings to which evidence rules apply[238]

II. Relevancy and reasons for excluding relevant evidence
A. Probative value[133,273]
1. Relevancy[126]
2. Exclusion for unfair prejudice,[133] confusion,[336] or waste of time[343]

B. Authentication[14,217] and identification[238]

C. Character and related concepts
1. Admissibility of character[91]
2. Methods of proving character[189]
3. Habit and routine practice[245]
4. Other crimes,[280] acts,[189] transactions, and events[189]
5. Prior sexual misconduct of a defendant[259]

D. Expert testimony
1. Qualifications of witnesses[266]
2. Bases of testimony[266]
3. Ultimate issue rule[350]
4. Reliability and relevancy[266]
5. Proper subject matter for expert testimony[21,266,350]

E. Real, demonstrative, and experimental evidence[357]

III. Privileges and other policy exclusions
A. Spousal immunity[252] and marital communications[28]
B. Attorney-client[63,196] and work product[63]
C. Physician/psychotherapist-patient[364]
D. Other privileges[112]
E. Insurance coverage[84]
F. Remedial measures[49,287]
G. Compromise, payment of medical expenses, and plea negotiations[371]
H. Past sexual conduct of a victim[259]

IV. Writings, recordings,[175,238] and photographs[133]
A. Requirement of original[133,175,238]
B. Summaries[378]
C. Completeness rule[385]

V. Hearsay and circumstances of its admissibility[119]
A. Definition of hearsay[49,119,175,245]
1. What is hearsay[77,119,175,245]
2. Prior statements by witness[161]
3. Statements attributable to party-opponent[140,210]
4. Multiple hearsay[182,203,315]

B. Present sense impressions[7,161,315] and excited utterances[399]
C. Statements of mental, emotional, or physical condition[224,315]
D. Statements for purposes of medical diagnosis and treatment[315]
E. Past recollection recorded[77,294]
F. Business records[77,154,168,245,315]
G. Public records and reports[217,294]
H. Learned treatises[392]
I. Former testimony;[203] depositions[385]
J. Statements against interest[98]
K. Other exceptions to the hearsay rule[175,280]
L. Right to confront witnesses[168]

Real Property

NOTE: Approximately one-fifth of the Real Property questions on the MBE will be based on each of the categories I through V.

I. Ownership
   A. Present estates
      1. Fees simple[242]
      2. Defeasible fees simple[291]
      3. Life estates[60]
   B. Future interests
      1. Reversions[291]
      2. Remainders,[291,298] vested[298] and contingent[291]
      3. Executory interests[67,291]
      4. Possibilities of reverter,[291] powers of termination[298]
      5. Rules affecting these interests[291]
   C. Co-tenancy
      1. Types
         a. Tenancy in common[172,277]
         b. Joint tenancy[158]
      2. Severance[158]
      3. Partition[284]
      4. Relations among cotenants[172,277,284]
      5. Alienability,[277] descendibility,[277] devisability[158]
   D. The law of landlord and tenant
      1. Types of holdings[130]: creation[312] and termination[144]
         a. Terms for years[312]
         b. Tenancies at will[312]
         c. Holdovers[144] and other tenancies at sufferance[312]
         d. Periodic tenancies[312]
      2. Possession[144] and rent[312]
      3. Assignment[25] and subletting[25]
      4. Termination (surrender,[144,312] mitigation of damages,[319] and anticipatory breach[319])
      5. Habitability[319] and suitability[319]
   E. Special problems
      1. Rule Against Perpetuities[81,291]: common law[81] and as modified[291]

2. Alienability,[305] descendibility,[242] and devisability[242]
3. Fair housing/discrimination[326]

II. **Rights in land**[102]
A. Covenants at law[263] and in equity[186]
1. Nature[263] and type[186]
2. Creation[186]
3. Scope[46,263]
4. Termination[186]
B. Easements,[32,249] profits,[396] and licenses[18]
1. Nature and type
2. Methods of creation[137]
a. Express[53]
b. Implied[249,256]
i. Quasi-use[389]
ii. Necessity[249,389]
iii. Plat[256]
c. Prescription[32,53]
3. Scope[32]
4. Termination[18]
C. Fixtures[11] (including relevant application of Article 9, UCC[11])
D. Zoning (fundamentals other than regulatory taking)[4,256]

III. **Contracts**
A. Real estate brokerage[326]
B. Creation and construction
1. Statute of frauds[186,193] and exceptions[39]
2. Essential terms[193]
3. Time for performance[151,214]
4. Remedies for breach[151]
C. Marketability of title[95]
D. Equitable conversion (including risk of loss)[214]
E. Options[305] and rights of first refusal[305]
F. Fitness and suitability[319]
G. Merger[186]

IV. **Mortgages/security devices**
A. Types of security devices
1. Mortgages[74,165,382] (including deeds of trust[32])
a. In general[74,165,207]
b. Purchase-money mortgages[207,340]
c. Future-advance mortgages[74]
2. Land contracts[333]
3. Absolute deeds as security[333]
B. Some security relationships
1. Necessity[382] and nature of obligation[340]
2. Theories: title,[340] lien,[340] and intermediate[340]
3. Rights and duties prior to foreclosure[340]
4. Right to redeem[333,361] and clogging equity of redemption[333]

C. Transfers by mortgagor[165,347,382]
  1. Distinguishing "subject to"[347] and "assuming"[165,347]
  2. Rights and obligations of transferor[347,382]
  3. Application of subrogation[354] and suretyship principles[354]
  4. Due-on-sale clauses[347]
D. Transfers by mortgagee[347,361]
E. Payment,[354] discharges,[361,382] and defenses[361]
F. Foreclosure[165,207]
  1. Types[207]
  2. Rights of omitted parties[207]
  3. Deficiency[165] and surplus[207,333]
  4. Redemption after foreclosure[333,361]
  5. Deed in lieu of foreclosure[333]

V. **Titles**
A. Adverse possession[53,102,123,284]
B. Transfer by deed[88,186]
  1. Warranty[200] and non-warranty deeds (including covenants for title[200])
  2. Necessity for a grantee[179] and other deed requirements[186]
  3. Delivery[179] (including escrows[179])
C. Transfer by operation of law and by will[81,158,298]
  1. In general[179]
  2. Ademption[368]
  3. Exoneration[368,382]
  4. Lapse[368,375]
  5. Abatement[368]
D. Title assurance systems
  1. Recording acts[221,235] (race,[340] notice,[221,340] and race-notice[74])
    a. Indexes[270]
    b. Chain of title[221,270]
    c. Protected parties[221,235]
    d. Priorities[221,270]
    e. Notice[221,235,249,270]
  2. Title insurance[200]
E. Special problems
  1. After-acquired title[151,228] (including estoppel by deed[151,228])
  2. Forged instruments[235] and undelivered deeds[179]
  3. Purchase-money mortgages[207]
  4. Judgment and tax liens[158]

Torts

NOTE: The Torts questions should be answered according to principles of general applicability. Examinees are to assume that there is no applicable statute unless otherwise specified; however, survival actions and claims for wrongful death should be assumed to be available where applicable. Examinees should assume that joint and several liability, with pure comparative negligence, is the relevant rule unless otherwise indicated. Approximately half of the Torts questions on the MBE will be based on category II, and approximately half will be based on the remaining categories—I, III, and IV.

I. **Intentional torts**
   A. Harms to the person, such as assault,[145] battery,[68] false imprisonment,[75] and infliction of mental distress[82]; and harms to property interests, such as trespass to land[152] and chattels,[166] and conversion[61]
   B. Defenses to claims for physical harms
      1. Consent[89]
      2. Privileges and immunities: protection of self[173] and others; protection of property interests[180]; parental discipline; protection of public interests[187]; necessity[187]; incomplete privilege

II. **Negligence**[19]
   A. The duty question,[194] including failure to act,[229] unforeseeable plaintiffs, and obligations to control the conduct of third parties[201]
   B. The standard of care[208]
      1. The reasonably prudent person: including children,[96] physically and mentally impaired individuals,[215] professional people,[117] and other special classes
      2. Rules of conduct derived from statutes[264] and custom[103]
   C. Problems relating to proof of fault,[250] including res ipsa loquitur[257]
   D. Problems relating to causation[285]
      1. But for[271] and substantial causes[278]
      2. Harms traceable to multiple causes[292]
      3. Questions of apportionment of responsibility among multiple tortfeasors, including joint and several liability[26]
   E. Limitations on liability and special rules of liability[222]
      1. Problems relating to "remote" or "unforeseeable" causes,[306] "legal" or "proximate" cause,[299] and "superseding" causes[110]
      2. Claims against owners and occupiers of land[124]
      3. Claims for mental distress not arising from physical harm[243]; other intangible injuries
      4. Claims for pure economic loss[236]
   F. Liability for acts of others[313]
      1. Employees and other agents[320]
      2. Independent contractors and non-delegable duties[327]
   G. Defenses[397]
      1. Contributory fault, including common law contributory negligence[334] and last clear chance,[341] and the various forms of comparative negligence[131]
      2. Assumption of risk[348]

III. **Strict liability and products liability**[138]: **common law strict liability,**[390] **including claims arising from abnormally dangerous activities,**[355] **and defenses to such claims**[362]; **claims against manufacturers**[369] **and other defendants**[376] **arising out of the manufacture and distribution of products, and defenses to such claims**[383]

IV. **Other torts**[47]
   A. Claims based on nuisance,[159] and defenses
   B. Claims based on defamation[12] and invasion of privacy,[40] defenses, and constitutional limitations

C. Claims based on misrepresentations,[5] and defenses
D. Claims based on intentional interference with business relations,[33,54] and defenses

C. Answer Sheets

The following pages offer four sets of blank answer sheets to use as you test yourself on the questions. Each set of blank answer sheets is the same, giving you four opportunities to work through all questions. The fifth set of answer sheets has the answers to each question. You should be able to hold your completed answer sheet over the actual answers to easily mark your right and wrong answers.

Notice that the answer sheets have you answer in seven columns, one for each Multistate Bar Examination subject. By marking and scoring your answers in these columns, you can easily see how many right and wrong answers you have scored in each subject so that you can adjust your studies accordingly.

Questions 1-100

Civil Procedure	Contract Law	Criminal Law & Procedure	Real Property	Torts	Constitutional Law	Evidence
1	2	3	4	5	6	7
8	9	10	11	12	13	14
15	16	17	18	19	20	21
22	23	24	25	26	27	28
29	30	31	32	33	34	35
36	37	38	39	40	41	42
43	44	45	46	47	48	49
50	51	52	53	54	55	56
57	58	59	60	61	62	63
64	65	66	67	68	69	70
71	72	73	74	75	76	77
78	79	80	81	82	83	84
85	86	87	88	89	90	91
92	93	94	95	96	97	98
99	100					
/15	/15	/14	/14	/14	/14	/14
					Total:	/100

Questions 101-200

Civil Procedure	Contract Law	Criminal Law & Procedure	Real Property	Torts	Constitutional Law	Evidence
		101	102	103	104	105
106	107	108	109	110	111	112
113	114	115	116	117	118	119
120	121	122	123	124	125	126
127	128	129	130	131	132	133
134	135	136	137	138	139	140
141	142	143	144	145	146	147
148	149	150	151	152	153	154
155	156	157	158	159	160	161
162	163	164	165	166	167	168
169	170	171	172	173	174	175
176	177	178	179	180	181	182
183	184	185	186	187	188	189
190	191	192	193	194	195	196
197	198	199	200			
/14	/14	/15	/15	/14	/14	/14
					Total:	/100

Questions 201-300

Civil Procedure	Contract Law	Criminal Law & Procedure	Real Property	Torts	Constitutional Law	Evidence
				201	202	203
204	205	206	207	208	209	210
211	212	213	214	215	216	217
218	219	220	221	222	223	224
225	226	227	228	229	230	231
232	233	234	235	236	237	238
239	240	241	242	243	244	245
246	247	248	249	250	251	252
253	254	255	256	257	258	259
260	261	262	263	264	265	266
267	268	269	270	271	272	273
274	275	276	277	278	279	280
281	282	283	284	285	286	287
288	289	290	291	292	293	294
295	296	297	298	299	300	
/15	/15	/14	/14	/14	/14	/14
					Total:	/100

Questions 301-400

Civil Procedure	Contract Law	Criminal Law & Procedure	Real Property	Torts	Constitutional Law	Evidence
						301
302	303	304	305	306	307	308
309	310	311	312	313	314	315
316	317	318	319	320	321	322
323	324	325	326	327	328	329
330	331	332	333	334	335	336
337	338	339	340	341	342	343
344	345	346	347	348	349	350
351	352	353	354	355	356	357
358	359	360	361	362	363	364
365	366	367	368	369	370	371
372	373	374	375	376	377	378
379	380	381	382	383	384	385
386	387	388	389	390	391	392
393	394	395	396	397	398	399
400						
/15	14	/14	/14	/14	/14	/15
					Total:	/100

Questions 1-100

Civil Procedure	Contract Law	Criminal Law & Procedure	Real Property	Torts	Constitutional Law	Evidence
1	2	3	4	5	6	7
8	9	10	11	12	13	14
15	16	17	18	19	20	21
22	23	24	25	26	27	28
29	30	31	32	33	34	35
36	37	38	39	40	41	42
43	44	45	46	47	48	49
50	51	52	53	54	55	56
57	58	59	60	61	62	63
64	65	66	67	68	69	70
71	72	73	74	75	76	77
78	79	80	81	82	83	84
85	86	87	88	89	90	91
92	93	94	95	96	97	98
99	100					
/15	/15	/14	/14	/14	/14	/14
					Total:	/100

Questions 101-200

Civil Procedure	Contract Law	Criminal Law & Procedure	Real Property	Torts	Constitutional Law	Evidence
		101	102	103	104	105
106	107	108	109	110	111	112
113	114	115	116	117	118	119
120	121	122	123	124	125	126
127	128	129	130	131	132	133
134	135	136	137	138	139	140
141	142	143	144	145	146	147
148	149	150	151	152	153	154
155	156	157	158	159	160	161
162	163	164	165	166	167	168
169	170	171	172	173	174	175
176	177	178	179	180	181	182
183	184	185	186	187	188	189
190	191	192	193	194	195	196
197	198	199	200			
/14	/14	/15	/15	/14	/14	/14
					Total:	/100

Questions 201-300

Civil Procedure	Contract Law	Criminal Law & Procedure	Real Property	Torts	Constitutional Law	Evidence
				201	202	203
204	205	206	207	208	209	210
211	212	213	214	215	216	217
218	219	220	221	222	223	224
225	226	227	228	229	230	231
232	233	234	235	236	237	238
239	240	241	242	243	244	245
246	247	248	249	250	251	252
253	254	255	256	257	258	259
260	261	262	263	264	265	266
267	268	269	270	271	272	273
274	275	276	277	278	279	280
281	282	283	284	285	286	287
288	289	290	291	292	293	294
295	296	297	298	299	300	
/15	/15	/14	/14	/14	/14	/14
					Total:	/100

Questions 301-400

Civil Procedure	Contract Law	Criminal Law & Procedure	Real Property	Torts	Constitutional Law	Evidence
						301
302	303	304	305	306	307	308
309	310	311	312	313	314	315
316	317	318	319	320	321	322
323	324	325	326	327	328	329
330	331	332	333	334	335	336
337	338	339	340	341	342	343
344	345	346	347	348	349	350
351	352	353	354	355	356	357
358	359	360	361	362	363	364
365	366	367	368	369	370	371
372	373	374	375	376	377	378
379	380	381	382	383	384	385
386	387	388	389	390	391	392
393	394	395	396	397	398	399
400						
/15	/14	/14	/14	/14	/14	/15
					Total:	/100

Questions 1-100

Civil Procedure	Contract Law	Criminal Law & Procedure	Real Property	Torts	Constitutional Law	Evidence
1	2	3	4	5	6	7
8	9	10	11	12	13	14
15	16	17	18	19	20	21
22	23	24	25	26	27	28
29	30	31	32	33	34	35
36	37	38	39	40	41	42
43	44	45	46	47	48	49
50	51	52	53	54	55	56
57	58	59	60	61	62	63
64	65	66	67	68	69	70
71	72	73	74	75	76	77
78	79	80	81	82	83	84
85	86	87	88	89	90	91
92	93	94	95	96	97	98
99	100					
/15	/15	/14	/14	/14	/14	/14
					Total:	/100

Questions 101-200

Civil Procedure	Contract Law	Criminal Law & Procedure	Real Property	Torts	Constitutional Law	Evidence
		101	102	103	104	105
106	107	108	109	110	111	112
113	114	115	116	117	118	119
120	121	122	123	124	125	126
127	128	129	130	131	132	133
134	135	136	137	138	139	140
141	142	143	144	145	146	147
148	149	150	151	152	153	154
155	156	157	158	159	160	161
162	163	164	165	166	167	168
169	170	171	172	173	174	175
176	177	178	179	180	181	182
183	184	185	186	187	188	189
190	191	192	193	194	195	196
197	198	199	200			
/14	/14	/15	/15	/14	/14	/14
					Total:	/100

Questions 201-300

Civil Procedure	Contract Law	Criminal Law & Procedure	Real Property	Torts	Constitutional Law	Evidence
				201	202	203
204	205	206	207	208	209	210
211	212	213	214	215	216	217
218	219	220	221	222	223	224
225	226	227	228	229	230	231
232	233	234	235	236	237	238
239	240	241	242	243	244	245
246	247	248	249	250	251	252
253	254	255	256	257	258	259
260	261	262	263	264	265	266
267	268	269	270	271	272	273
274	275	276	277	278	279	280
281	282	283	284	285	286	287
288	289	290	291	292	293	294
295	296	297	298	299	300	
/15	/15	/14	/14	/14	/14	/14
					Total:	/100

Questions 301-400

Civil Procedure	Contract Law	Criminal Law & Procedure	Real Property	Torts	Constitutional Law	Evidence
						301
302	303	304	305	306	307	308
309	310	311	312	313	314	315
316	317	318	319	320	321	322
323	324	325	326	327	328	329
330	331	332	333	334	335	336
337	338	339	340	341	342	343
344	345	346	347	348	349	350
351	352	353	354	355	356	357
358	359	360	361	362	363	364
365	366	367	368	369	370	371
372	373	374	375	376	377	378
379	380	381	382	383	384	385
386	387	388	389	390	391	392
393	394	395	396	397	398	399
400						
/15	/14	/14	/14	/14	/14	/15
					Total:	/100

Questions 1-100

Civil Procedure	Contract Law	Criminal Law & Procedure	Real Property	Torts	Constitutional Law	Evidence
1	2	3	4	5	6	7
8	9	10	11	12	13	14
15	16	17	18	19	20	21
22	23	24	25	26	27	28
29	30	31	32	33	34	35
36	37	38	39	40	41	42
43	44	45	46	47	48	49
50	51	52	53	54	55	56
57	58	59	60	61	62	63
64	65	66	67	68	69	70
71	72	73	74	75	76	77
78	79	80	81	82	83	84
85	86	87	88	89	90	91
92	93	94	95	96	97	98
99	100					
/15	/15	/14	/14	/14	/14	/14
					Total:	/100

Questions 101-200

Civil Procedure	Contract Law	Criminal Law & Procedure	Real Property	Torts	Constitutional Law	Evidence
		101	102	103	104	105
106	107	108	109	110	111	112
113	114	115	116	117	118	119
120	121	122	123	124	125	126
127	128	129	130	131	132	133
134	135	136	137	138	139	140
141	142	143	144	145	146	147
148	149	150	151	152	153	154
155	156	157	158	159	160	161
162	163	164	165	166	167	168
169	170	171	172	173	174	175
176	177	178	179	180	181	182
183	184	185	186	187	188	189
190	191	192	193	194	195	196
197	198	199	200			
/14	/14	/15	/15	/14	/14	/14
					Total:	/100

Questions 201-300

Civil Procedure	Contract Law	Criminal Law & Procedure	Real Property	Torts	Constitutional Law	Evidence
				201	202	203
204	205	206	207	208	209	210
211	212	213	214	215	216	217
218	219	220	221	222	223	224
225	226	227	228	229	230	231
232	233	234	235	236	237	238
239	240	241	242	243	244	245
246	247	248	249	250	251	252
253	254	255	256	257	258	259
260	261	262	263	264	265	266
267	268	269	270	271	272	273
274	275	276	277	278	279	280
281	282	283	284	285	286	287
288	289	290	291	292	293	294
295	296	297	298	299	300	
/15	/15	/14	/14	/14	/14	/14
					Total:	/100

Questions 301-400

Civil Procedure	Contract Law	Criminal Law & Procedure	Real Property	Torts	Constitutional Law	Evidence
						301
302	303	304	305	306	307	308
309	310	311	312	313	314	315
316	317	318	319	320	321	322
323	324	325	326	327	328	329
330	331	332	333	334	335	336
337	338	339	340	341	342	343
344	345	346	347	348	349	350
351	352	353	354	355	356	357
358	359	360	361	362	363	364
365	366	367	368	369	370	371
372	373	374	375	376	377	378
379	380	381	382	383	384	385
386	387	388	389	390	391	392
393	394	395	396	397	398	399
400						
/15	/14	/14	/14	/14	/14	/15
					Total:	/100

Answers to Questions 1-100

Civil Procedure	Contract Law	Criminal Law & Procedure	Real Property	Torts	Constitutional Law	Evidence
1 B	2 C	3 C	4 D	5 D	6 A	7 C
8 B	9 A	10 A	11 A	12 D	13 C	14 A
15 D	16 D	17 C	18 B	19 C	20 D	21 C
22 A	23 D	24 B	25 C	26 B	27 A	28 A
29 B	30 B	31 B	32 B	33 B	34 D	35 B
36 D	37 C	38 C	39 B	40 C	41 B	42 C
43 A	44 A	45 A	46 A	47 C	48 A	49 D
50 D	51 D	52 D	53 C	54 D	55 A	56 D
57 C	58 B	59 A	60 B	61 C	62 C	63 D
64 D	65 D	66 D	67 A	68 B	69 B	70 B
71 C	72 B	73 D	74 C	75 D	76 D	77 B
78 A	79 D	80 C	81 D	82 D	83 D	84 B
85 B	86 A	87 C	88 D	89 D	90 A	91 A
92 D	93 B	94 D	95 D	96 C	97 D	98 A
99 D	100 A					
/15	/15	/14	/14	/14	/14	/14
					Total:	/100

Answers to Questions 101-200

Civil Procedure	Contract Law	Criminal Law & Procedure	Real Property	Torts	Constitutional Law	Evidence
		101 B	102 A	103 B	104 A	105 A
106 B	107 B	108 A	109 B	110 B	111 C	112 B
113 D	114 C	115 D	116 C	117 B	118 D	119 B
120 A	121 D	122 C	123 B	124 A	125 C	126 A
127 B	128 B	129 D	130 C	131 A	132 D	133 B
134 D	135 C	136 D	137 B	138 A	139 B	140 B
141 A	142 B	143 B	144 B	145 C	146 D	147 D
148 C	149 B	150 A	151 C	152 B	153 B	154 A
155 C	156 C	157 A	158 D	159 A	160 A	161 B
162 A	163 C	164 B	165 D	166 A	167 D	168 D
169 A	170 B	171 A	172 C	173 C	174 D	175 B
176 B	177 C	178 B	179 D	180 D	181 B	182 C
183 A	184 D	185 B	186 C	187 C	188 B	189 C
190 B	191 D	192 B	193 D	194 D	195 A	196 B
197 B	198 B	199 B	200 A			
/14	/14	/15	/15	/14	/14	/14
					Total:	/100

Answers to Questions 201-300

Civil Procedure	Contract Law	Criminal Law & Procedure	Real Property	Torts	Constitutional Law	Evidence
				201 B	202 C	203 A
204 C	205 D	206 C	207 C	208 A	209 C	210 B
211 A	212 A	213 B	214 B	215 B	216 D	217 D
218 C	219 D	220 C	221 B	222 D	223 A	224 A
225 C	226 C	227 B	228 A	229 C	230 B	231 A
232 D	233 B	234 B	235 A	236 B	237 C	238 D
239 D	240 D	241 B	242 A	243 A	244 C	245 C
246 B	247 C	248 D	249 A	250 A	251 A	252 A
253 C	254 B	255 D	256 C	257 C	258 D	259 B
260 C	261 D	262 B	263 A	264 D	265 C	266 B
267 D	268 B	269 D	270 C	271 D	272 B	273 C
274 A	275 A	276 A	277 D	278 D	279 D	280 A
281 D	282 C	283 C	284 B	285 A	286 B	287 C
288 B	289 B	290 D	291 B	292 A	293 B	294 D
295 A	296 C	297 A	298 D	299 C	300 B	
/15	/15	/14	/14	/14	/14	/14
					Total:	/100

Answers to Questions 301-400

Civil Procedure	Contract Law	Criminal Law & Procedure	Real Property	Torts	Constitutional Law	Evidence
						301 D
302 B	303 A	304 D	305 C	306 A	307 C	308 A
309 C	310 C	311 A	312 B	313 B	314 B	315 B
316 A	317 A	318 C	319 D	320 A	321 C	322 D
323 C	324 B	325 B	326 B	327 A	328 A	329 B
330 C	331 C	332 B	333 A	334 D	335 A	336 A
337 C	338 B	339 D	340 D	341 B	342 D	343 D
344 A	345 C	346 C	347 C	348 A	349 D	350 C
351 D	352 B	353 C	354 A	355 D	356 B	357 B
358 D	359 D	360 D	361 B	362 B	363 C	364 A
365 C	366 D	367 A	368 A	369 B	370 D	371 D
372 A	373 A	374 D	375 C	376 B	377 A	378 C
379 C	380 C	381 C	382 D	383 A	384 B	385 B
386 A	387 C	388 C	389 C	390 B	391 B	392 C
393 B	394 D	395 C	396 A	397 C	398 A	399 D
400 D						
/15	/14	/14	/14	/14	/14	/15
					Total:	/100

Conclusion

A. Perspective

What, really, is the bar exam? Lawyers, law students, law professors, and others actually give several different answers. Most practically, the bar exam is a licensing test. You take the bar exam to get a law license. In that sense, the bar exam is not one last awful punishment inflicted on law students before they hit easy street on their way to a rainbow's end pot of gold. The bar exam is simply something you must do first before you practice law. Keeping the bar exam in that perspective can help. The bar exam is certainly not anything even remotely close to facing combat, indeed not even close to fighting fires or patrolling dangerous streets. Not only is your physical safety never at risk, your preparation and the exam itself are both in relative comfort, with no extreme heat or cold like the millions who work outdoors daily face. You will be well fed at all times and have every other modern convenience throughout. In that sense, preparing for the bar exam and even *taking* the bar exam are both positions of rather extraordinary *privilege*. Treat the whole experience for what it truly is, which is a premier if not *the* premier professional-preparation experience, and you will have gained appropriate perspective.

B. Growth

The bar exam does more than qualify you for licensure for a highly desirable professional career. The bar exam is also probably the single greatest challenge that a person can choose today to promote one's own development of clear thought and sound reason in pursuit of social, economic, and other good. The bar exam itself may not be the greatest fun, but it can be an indispensable spur to profound development. After the bar exam, you will likely feel differently about yourself than you did when you began bar studies because indeed you *are* different after the exam. You will have studied, organized, digested, and integrated your law knowledge into a highly useful whole. You will have also learned new self-management skills and new skills at reading, summarizing, reviewing, recalling, writing, and analyzing. Your new capacities will serve you well not only in a law career but in life. Yet you will also have increased your appetite for personal and professional growth. Passing the bar exam is not all that you will accomplish. As you recover from the bar exam, you may for a while not think about anything big as your next career or life step. Yet soon enough, you will be looking for that next challenge, and then the one after it, and the next one, and beyond to ever greater pursuits. You will have developed such personal and professional capacities that you will soon yearn to entrust them to appropriate ambitions. After the bar exam, you should relax and celebrate but also know that you will have more to achieve and celebrate in the future.

C. Outcomes

The one thing that makes the bar exam so frightful for so many examinees is not arduous bar-exam preparation or the conditions of the test itself. You can study intensely for an extended period, and you can manage a two-day test. The experience is nothing even remotely as risky and arduous as military boot camp. No, the one thing that makes the bar exam so frightful for so many is *not passing*. Examinees have several common reasons for fearing not passing, most of them pretty sensible, like the additional wait and cost of taking it again, the examinee's disappointment and embarrassment, the potential loss of a job or job opportunity, delay in hiring, and the disappointment of family and friends. When one thinks about each of these things, though, one realizes that they are each entirely manageable. They are, if you will, *first-world* problems, not third-world problems. *If* they happen, and you have no reason to believe in advance of your earnest preparation that they probably will, you can and will survive them. The other remarkable thing about these concerns, in addition to each of them being not such great concerns in the grand scheme of things, is that with responsible commitment to earnest preparation they are not all that likely. Most examinees who take the bar exam pass the bar exam. Even for those who do not pass on their first try, many examinees who retake the bar exam pass the bar exam on their second or subsequent try.

D. Alternatives

Law practice is a dream career for many of us. Law students routinely get to taste that dream in the clinical part of their law school curriculum. You have heard how special law practice can be, and you have probably already experienced at least some of that allure. While the sound allure is in law practice's meaning, the benefits of practice are also material. Studies continue to show substantial average increases in earnings with licensure for law practice. Yet lawyers who pass the bar exam often move immediately or soon into other careers, for many different reasons. Law practice under licensure is just one of many careers pursued by those who earn a law degree. Many who earn a law degree never take a bar exam because they have no need for doing so. Your decision to take the bar exam is likely a good-to-great decision, the outcome of which you largely control. At least, you control many things influencing whether you will pass the bar exam. Other things you cannot control. Life goes on while you prepare for the bar exam, and life may keep you from preparing adequately or even from taking the bar exam at all. Even with your best effort, circumstances may conspire to lead you down a different path than the bar exam and licensure. Keep the perspective that while you value hugely the challenge of taking and passing the bar exam, you are doing more than taking a licensure exam. No matter the outcome, by giving bar preparation and the exam your best, you are proving once again your deepest commitment and faith. Those of us who have prepared for and taken the bar exam have something special to share, something more special than we would have had if we had *not* taken the bar. But for you, as for any examinee, only the future knows just what that special thing is. Keep the bar exam, and preparing for the bar exam, in perspective. For one last help, consider this concluding humorous but true story, contributed by a noble professional who after passing the bar went on to become both a distinguished judge and international mediator. If he passed the bar exam under the circumstances that he describes, then you too can pass.

Though he had solid plans for his law career, indeed employment already lined up, the young man had decided to return to his parents' house while studying for the bar exam, where he hoped that he would not only save room-and-board costs but also have the peace, comfort, and familiar social support of a warm and welcoming home. That his beloved younger sister would be at home from college was more consolation than distraction, especially when he was able to make the home's quiet basement his bar-exam command center. And indeed, everything went fine as the bar exam approached until a fire suddenly engulfed the first floor of the home. As the family stood safely outside counting their blessings but shocked at the sudden loss, the young man caught the attention of one of the firefighters. Could he possibly, the young man asked, rescue his precious bar-preparation notes and materials, so critical to his career, from the basement? In through the flames, smoke, and hosed water went the brave firefighter who moments later came back out proudly holding the sodden and blackened bar materials. The family took temporary residence crammed together in a single motel room where the only study solitude the young man could find was to hole up in the tiny bathroom. Uncomfortable sitting on the closed toilet lid to study, the young man instead slumped down in the bathtub for hours at a time poring over his charred, smoke-smelling bar materials, not the perfect way to prepare for the bar but yet, as it turned out, wholly sufficient. He passed, just as you will with due diligence.

Acknowledgments

The authors thank Western Michigan University Thomas M. Cooley Law School and its board of directors, President and Dean Don LeDuc, other leaders, and faculty and staff members. The school's practice-access mission serves the nation ably in increasing the law profession's diversity while ensuring public access to markets and public confidence in the quality of justice. The authors thank Auxiliary Dean Devin Schindler and Professors Paul Sorensen, Marjorie Gell, Chris Hastings, and Chris Trudeau for contributing questions or commenting on and correcting questions. The authors thank Auxiliary Dean David Tarrien for comments on design. The authors thank Head of Public Service Aletha Honsowitz for library support. Most of all, the authors thank the many students and graduates of the law school's Grand Rapids campus whose ambition, insight, and perseverance informed and inspired the authors in this work. We hope it serves future students and graduates well.

About the Authors

Nelson Miller is a professor and associate dean at Western Michigan University Thomas M. Cooley Law School. Before coming to the law school, Dean Miller practiced civil litigation for 16 years, representing individuals, corporations, agencies, and public and private universities. He has since published well over thirty books and dozens of book chapters and articles on law, law school, and law practice, and edited other books. The State Bar of Michigan recognized Dean Miller with the John W. Cummiskey Award for pro-bono service, while the law school recognized him with its Great Deeds award for similar service. He was among two dozen law professors recognized nationally in the Harvard University Press study *What the Best Law Teachers Do*. Dean Miller earned his law degree at the University of Michigan where he was on law review and graduated Order of the Coif, before joining the firm that later became Fajen and Miller, PLLC, his practice base before moving full-time into law teaching. At the law school, Dean Miller teaches Torts I, Torts II, Civil Procedure II, Personal & Professional Responsibility, Employment Law, Michigan No-Fault Insurance Law, and other courses, while administering the Grand Rapids campus and Western Michigan University affiliation.

Tonya Krause-Phelan is a professor and auxiliary dean at Western Michigan University Thomas M. Cooley Law School. Before coming to the law school, Dean Krause-Phelan practiced private criminal defense and was an Assistant Public Defender with the Kent County Office of the Defender in Grand Rapids, Michigan. While in private practice, Dean Krause-Phelan also served as adjunct professor for Ferris State University teaching Criminal Law and Procedure and lectured on a variety of criminal law topics. She also served on the faculty for the United States District Court for the Western District of Michigan's Hillman Trial Advocacy Program. Dean Krause-Phelan frequently appears as a commentator for radio, television, print, and internet media sources. She has also served as editor of *The Informant*, a publication of the former Kent County Criminal Defense Bar, and *Right to Counsel*, a publication of the Criminal Defense Attorneys of Michigan. At the law school, Dean Krause-Phelan teaches Criminal Law, Criminal Procedure, Defending Battered Women, Criminal Sentencing, and Ethics in Criminal Cases, while assisting with the West Michigan Defenders Clinic and coaching national mock-trial and moot-court teams.

CPSIA information can be obtained
at www.ICGtesting.com
Printed in the USA
BVHW01s1644020518
515050BV00013B/282/P